Managing Across Cultures: Issues and Perspectives

Edited by
Pat Joynt
Henley Management College and
Norwegian School of Management
and
Malcolm Warner
Judge Institute of Management Studies
University of Cambridge

INTERNATIONAL THOMSON BUSINESS PRESS
I ⓉP An International Thomson Publishing Company

London • Bonn • Boston • Johannesburg • Madrid • Melbourne • Mexico City • New York • Paris
Singapore • Tokyo • Toronto • Albany, NY • Belmont, CA • Cincinnati, OH • Detroit, MI

Managing Across Cultures: Issues and Perspectives

First published by International Thomson Business Press

I(T)P A division of International Thomson Publishing Inc.
       The ITP logo is a trademark under licence

British Library Cataloguing-in-Publication Data
A catalogue record for this book is available from the British Library

First edition 1996

Typeset in the UK by J&L Composition Ltd, Filey, North Yorkshire
Printed in the UK by Clays Ltd., St Ives plc

ISBN 0–415–13558–3

International Thomson Business Press   International Thomson Business Press
Berkshire House   20 Park Plaza
168–173 High Holborn   14th Floor
London WC1V 7AA   Boston MA 02116
UK   USA

http://www.thomson.com/itbp.html

Managing A
Issues and

4

72 74 80

173-75

Contents

Contributors

Carlos Alberto Arruda is a member of faculty at the Fundaceo Dom Cabral, Belo Horizonte, Brazil.

Nancy J. Adler is a Professor of Organizational Behaviour and Cross-Cultural Management at the Faculty of Management, McGill University, Montreal, Canada.

Jean-Louis Barsoux was recently a Research Fellow at Templeton College, Oxford, United Kingdom.

Susan Bartholomew is a University Lecturer in International Management at the Judge Institute of Management Studies, University of Cambridge, Cambridge, United Kingdom.

Pierre Berthon is a Tutor at Henley Management College, Henley-on-Thames, United Kingdom.

Tony Chapman is Managing Director and Vice President for Personnel Decisions International (PDI) Europe.

Hans-Dieter Ganter is Professor of Sociology at Fachhochschule Kehl, Germany.

Geraldine Darlington is a Director of Integra Research Group Ltd and currently a Research Associate at Henley Management College, Henley-on-Thames, United Kingdom.

Charles M. Hampden-Turner is a Permanent Visitor at the Judge Institute of Management Studies, University of Cambridge, and a Professor (on extended leave) from the Wright Institute, Berkeley, Cambridge, USA.

Dr Frank Heller, is Director of the Centre of Decision Making Studies, The Tavistock Institute, London, United Kingdom.

Ian Henry is an Associate Director at Planned Business Development (UK) Ltd.

David J. Hickson is Professor of International Management and Organisation at University of Bradford Management Centre, Bradford, United Kingdom.

Richard M. Hodgetts is a Professor of Business in the Department of Management and International Business at Florida International University, Florida, USA.

Geert Hofstede is currently Senior Research Associate at the Institute for Research on Intercultural Cooperation (IRIC), Maastricht and Tilburg, The Netherlands. He was formerly Emeritus Professor of Organisational Anthropology and International Management at the University of Limburg, Limburg, The Netherlands.

Yao-Su Hu is Vice President (Academic) Hong Kong Shue Yan College, Hong Kong, and a Visiting Professor both at SPRU (Sussex University) and at Henley Management College, Henley-on-Thames, United Kingdom.

Pat Joynt is PowerGen Professor of Management Development at Henley Management College, Henley-on-Thames, United Kingdom and on the faculty of the Norwegian School of Management, Norway.

Lars Kolvereid is Professor of Entrepreneurship at the Bodø Graduate School of Business, Bodø, Norway.

Alfred Kieser is Professor of Organizational Behaviour in the Faculty of Business Administration, University of Mannheim, Germany.

Christopher A. Leeds, is a Maitre des Conferences, University Nancy 2, Lorraine, France.

Fred Luthans is George Holmes Distinguished Professor of Management at the University of Nebraska-Lincoln, Nebraska, USA.

Iain McCormick PhD is a director in the strategic human resources consulting firm Renwick McCormick & Co Ltd, Hong Kong.

Arthur H. Money is a Professor of Management, Henley Management College, Henley-on-Thames, United Kingdom.

Krzysztof Obloj is Professor of Strategic Management and Director of the Executive MBA Program at the School of Management, University of Warsaw, Poland.

Karel Pavlica is a lecturer in Economics at the University of Economics, Prague, Czech Republic.

Leyland Pitt is Professor of Management Studies at Henley Management College, Henley-on-Thames, and Brunel University, United Kingdom.

Peter B. Smith is Professor of Social Psychology at the University of Sussex and Director of the Centre for Research into Cross-Cultural Organisation and Management (CRICCOM) which is jointly located at the University of Sussex and Roffey Park Management Institute, United Kingdom.

Rosemary Stewart is Director of the Oxford Health Care Management Institute at Templeton College, Oxford, United Kingdom.

Richard Thorpe is Professor in Management in the Department of Management at Manchester Metropolitan University, United Kingdom.

Ingrid Tollgerdt-Andersson is Assistant Professor at the Institute of Economic Research, Lund University, Sweden.

Anders Törnvall is Professor of Management at the Department of Management and Economics, Linköping University, Sweden.

Fons Trompenaars is Managing Director of the Centre for International Business Studies in the Netherlands.

Ian Turner is a Tutor at Henley Management College, Henley-on-Thames, United Kingdom.

Rosalie L. Tung is Professor of International Business in the Faculty of Business Administration, Simon Fraser University, Barnaby, British Columbia, Canada.

Peter Walgenbach is a Research Assistant in Organizational Behaviour in the Faculty of Business Administration, University of Mannheim, Germany.

Peter G.P. Walters is Professor of Business Studies and Head of the Department of Business Studies, The Hong Kong Polytechnic University, Kowloon, Hong Kong.

Malcolm Warner is Professor and Fellow, Wolfson College, Cambridge and a member of the faculty at the Judge Institute of Management Studies, University of Cambridge, United Kingdom.

Preface

This edited volume represents the work of an international network of management scholars in a wide range of countries (Brazil, Canada, Czech Republic, France, Hong Kong, Germany, Netherlands, Norway, Poland, Sweden, UK, USA) and even more universities and business schools. It also builds on a previous collaboration between the two editors, whose earlier volume *Managing in Different Cultures* (Oslo: Universitetsforlaget, 1986) appeared over a decade ago.

Most of the chapters in this present collection are original contributions to the field and were specially commissioned for the book. Some are revised versions of papers given as contributions to symposia held in 1994 and 1995 on cross-cultural management. These workshops were organized by the European Institute for the Advanced Study of Management, Brussels, and Henley Management College, Henley-on-Thames. Others are adapted from papers already published which have been updated and revised. We are grateful to the journals and publishers concerned for their permission to reproduce parts of such papers here or to cite from them.

We would also like to show our appreciation to both former editorial staff at Routledge and present editorial staff at International Thomson Business Press for all their help, particularly those who originally commissioned the volume, namely Ms Rosemary Nixon and Ms Frania Weaver, as well as to copy-editor Anne Simpson and all other colleagues concerned.

Finally, we would like to thank our secretaries, Ms April Burt and Ms Jo Grantham, for their administrative support in the putting together of the book.

Pat Joynt.
Malcolm Warner.
January, 1996.

Acknowledgements

We should like to thank the following journals and/or publishers for permission to reproduce parts of, or cite from, articles previously published by the authors.

For chapter 2, the *Journal of International Business Studies*.

For chapters 7 and 8, *The International Encyclopaedia of Business and Management*, (ed. M. Warner) Routledge, London, (1996) 6 volumes.

For chapter 16, the *University of Wales Business & Economic Review*.

For chapter 18, the *European Management Journal*.

For chapter 20, the *International Small Business Journal*.

For chapter 22, the *California Management Review* and the Regents of University of California.

Figures

Tables

Part I

General introduction

Chapter 1

Introduction: Cross-cultural perspectives

Pat Joynt and Malcolm Warner

INTRODUCTION

As more and more organizations cross national borders, people will need to broaden their views on competition and, more importantly, vis-a-vis other national behaviours (see Ohmae 1990). If the world is to survive and flourish, we all need to know more about the differences rather than concentrating on the similarities. Culture and subculture are probably the most important aspects in this change to global behaviours.

There are hundreds of cultures and subcultures of consequence that are relevant to the subject of cross-cultural management. The task of integrating all of these into an integrated whole is almost impossible. Not only may the domain vary from the small group, to a department, to an organization, but one must also consider the nation state, the region and possibly the globe. The cultural focus may also vary from those factors that are above the water in an 'iceberg' metaphor, such as behaviours and abilities, to those factors that are hidden, such as values, attitudes, beliefs and identity.

The key concept we focus on is culture, which we believe to deserve some attention as far as a definition is concerned. Culture has been adapted from the Latin *cultura* which is related to *cultus*, cult or worship. *Cult* in Latin means to inhabit, till or worship and *are* is defined as 'the result of'; thus in the broadest sense, one might define culture as 'the result of human action' (Berthon 1993). Earlier, the term was closely associated with socially elitist concepts like refinement of the mind, tastes and manners based on superior education and upbringing. It has also been identified with the intellectual side of civilization, particularly in its German spelling (Heller 1985). In Europe, before the Second World War, the term *Kultur* was used extensively to support arguments on the social and racial superiority of some groups over others. The definition that, perhaps, best fits the concept is that culture is a 'collective programming of the mind', 'collective soul' or some type of 'social glue' that holds people together. Hall (1959) suggests that culture is the pattern of taken-for-granted assumptions about how a given collection of people should think, act, and feel as they go about their daily affairs. Other definitions include:

- common values
- common beliefs
- common attitudes
- common behaviour
- common norms
- heroes
- morals
- symbols
- customs
- rituals
- ceremonies
- assumptions
- perceptions
- etiquette
- patterns of . . .

We often thought of culture in macro-terms such as an American culture, an English culture, a French culture, a German culture, a Scandinavian culture and so on. Today, however, we have expanded the concept to include the organizational or corporate level; thus one can talk of an IBM culture, a GM culture, a PowerGen culture, a Shell culture and so on (Deal and Kennedy 1982; Schein 1985). For our purposes here, we will think of culture in terms of the more macro-examples mentioned above.

There are currently two main approaches towards the application of culture and its consequences in a managerial and organizational setting. One approach, often labelled *divergency*, suggests that we should study culture because management is different in Scandinavia than it is in Germany, the UK, the US, and so on. Another label for this approach that is found in the organizational behaviour literature is *contingency* theory. Divergency theory assumes that elements such as differing values and behaviours, differing stages of economic development and unevenly distributed global resources will guarantee global diversity.

By contrast, *convergency* theory suggests that because of technology, structure and a global orientation by many firms, it is not necessary to practice cross-cultural management. Convergency theory involves pragmatic issues that can push one in the direction of adopting a 'one best way' approach to the management of organizations world-wide. The two approaches, divergence and convergence (*emic/etic*) represent two sides of the same coin as the debate concerning which approach is most relevant will continue to exist for many years to come. The pivotal question for managers and those studying management to ask is as follows: what is more important, the transfer of behaviours and techniques from country to country in a more uniform world, or the need for more knowledge on a richer variety of management practices and techniques? We hope to make a contribution to this debate in this edited collection.

PLAN OF THE BOOK

We now turn to the plan of the book. After the above introductory remarks of the editors, there follow five chapters dealing with general themes which arise from managing across cultures. Susan Bartholomew and Nancy Adler review the now burgeoning literature on cross-cultural management, discussing the dynamics of knowledge generation in a transnational world. After this, in Chapter 3, Gerry Darlington attempts to sum up the substantive theoretical contributions to the literature in the field. Next, Frank Heller discusses the role of social science in the study of economic and cultural transformations. Christopher Leeds then goes on to discuss pragmatic and wholist approaches to management in emerging and newly-emerging democracies. Last, Peter Smith takes 'another look' at national cultures and the values of employees in organizations.

The second part of the book presents area-studies each dealing with a single country or a set of them, or even a wider geographical area. We start the section with a chapter by Fred Luthans and Richard Hodgett on US management. They particularly focus on how American business is trying to recreate a competitive culture. Next, in Chapter 8, Leyland Pitt and colleagues try to analyse clusters of characteristics of countries in order to make cultural comparisons. Chapter 9 is a contribution by Geert Hofstede, 'On Images of Europe', perhaps the leading scholar in the field. In Chapter 10, Ingrid Tollgerd-Anderson attempts a comparative study of leadership characteristics across a number of countries in Europe. Next, Carlos Alberto Aruda and David Hickson look at managerial decision-making and societal culture in England and Brazil. In Chapter 12, Rosemary Stewart and colleagues also undertake a two-country comparative study of British and German managers. Following this, Richard Thorpe and Karel Pavlica match British and Czech managers, looking for comparisons and contrasts. A switch of focus to Asia introduces the next set of chapters. Rosalie Tung looks at 'Managing in Asia', taking a cross-cultural approach. Next, Anders Tornväll examines work and work motivation in Japan and Sweden. Following this, Warner focuses on culture, education and industry in Japan, especially on their management studies programmes. Last, in Chapter 17, Charles Hampden-Turner looks at what he calls 'A World Turned Upside Down' with special attention to doing business in Asia.

The third part of the book deals with a selection of cross-cultural issues. To start it, Ian Turner analyses the role of structural choice in international companies. Next, Iain McCormick and Tony Chapman focus on executive relocation in different parts of the world. Krzysztof Obloj and Lars

Kolvereid also cast their nets widely to look at entrepreneurs in different environments covering Britain, Norway and Poland. Peter Walters, in Chapter 21, links the influence of culture on consumer behaviour in the context of global market segmentation. Last, Yao-Su Hu and Malcolm Warner look at cross-cultural factors and comparative advantage.

CONCLUDING REMARKS

Culture can have a powerful impact on management and organization behaviour. The challenge for management scholars is to determine what practices will work where and how much cultural adaptation is necessary, if any. Frank Heller (1985) suggests, for instance, that culture should be approached in the same way one would approach an aggressive patient – without prejudice but with a resolute intention not to be bowled over or hoodwinked into prescribing either a placebo or the patient's own medicine. In the final analysis, awareness of culture helps us to understand each other better and understanding is often the essence of successful management. We hope this edited volume not only contributes to analysis and scholarship in the field, but also to more effective organizational analysis in cross-cultural settings.

REFERENCES

Berthon, P.R. (1993) Psychological type and corporate cultures: relationships and dynamics, *Omega*, **21**(3), pp. 329–44.

Deal, T.E. and Kennedy, A.A. (1982) *Corporate Cultures: The Rites and Rituals of Corporate Life*, Addison-Wesley, Reading, MA.

Heller, F. (1985) Some theoretical and practical problems in multinational and cross-cultural research on organisations in *Managing in Different Cultures* (eds P. Joynt and M. Warner) Universitetsforlaget, Oslo pp. 11–22.

Hall, E.T. (1959) *The Silent Language*, Doubleday, New York.

Ohmae, K. (1990) *The Borderless World*, McKinsey & Co Inc, New York.

Schein, E.H. (1985) *Organizational Culture and Leadership*, Jossey-Bass, San Francisco.

FURTHER READING

Hofstede, G. (1980) *Cultures Consequences: International Differences in Work-Related Values*, Sage, Beverly Hills, CA. and London.

Joynt, P.D. (1990) *Organizational Research involving Internal Networks and External Strategic Alliances: A Theoretical Review of Strategic Alliances*, Norwegian School of Management, Oslo.

Joynt, P.D. and Warner, M. (1985) (eds) *Managing in Different Cultures*, Universitetsforlaget, Oslo.

Warner, M. (1996) *Comparative Management: A Reader*, Routledge, London 4 volumes.

Chapter 2

Building networks and crossing borders: the dynamics of knowledge generation in a transnational world

Susan Bartholomew and Nancy J. Adler

INTRODUCTION

National boundaries are losing their meaning as economic frontiers (Kobrin 1995). As Ohmae (1990: 18) states: 'On a political map, the boundaries between countries are as clear as ever. But on a competitive map, a map showing the real flows of financial and industrial activity, those boundaries have largely disappeared.' The central determinant of global integration today is technology (Kobrin 1991). However, the rapid pace of technological change is not only increasing transnational economic integration; it is also changing the fundamental nature of the relations between nations and firms (Keohayne and Nye 1989; Kobrin 1995). The knowledge which drives innovation is increasingly generated through networks of firms (Shan, Walker and Kogut 1994) and through the social networks of individuals (Powell 1990). Technology both creates, and is created through, an inter-linked economy.

Today firms build competitive advantage through their position in, and through their managers' participation in, such global technological networks. Firms which lack the capability to develop, sustain and learn from these relationships will fall behind. These changes in the dynamics of economic competition are changing the nature of knowledge needed to inform global human resource management. Are management scholars publishing sufficient research to inform CEOs' choices among strategic approaches to managing people worldwide? Is organizational behaviour and human resource management research leading or lagging the needs of business?

This chapter first discusses these two key trends in global competition: the increasing technological intensity of industry and the emergence of the transnational firm. It then summarizes the publishing trends in research on international organizational behaviour and international human resource management and discusses their relevance to conducting transnational business in the technology-driven economy. In so doing, the chapter views the academic field of management from a professional

discipline perspective. That is, it assumes that one of the primary functions of an academic discipline in a professional school is to advance
knowledge while informing the practice of its relevant constituency. In
the case of academic management, that professional constituency is practising managers and executives worldwide.

TRENDS IN GLOBAL ECONOMIC COMPETITION

The present and future economic environment may be distinguished from
the past by two interrelated trends: the marked rise in the technological
intensity of many industries and the increasing transnational integration
of the economy. The growth of the technology-based economy is first
discussed. The implications of the intensification of technological competition are then related to the emergence of the transnational firm.

The escalation of technological intensity

Beck (1992) offers a useful typology for understanding the critical industries which drive economic growth during different eras. Since the industrial revolution, we have passed through three eras of economic growth –
from a commodity-driven economy to a mass-manufacturing economy
and then to a technology-driven economy. Every economic era may be
considered to have 'its *engines* – a handful of strategic industries that drive
the entire economy' (Beck 1992: 20; emphasis in original). In the 'commodity economy,' which encompassed the period from the industrial
revolution to circa 1918, industry was based primarily on trade in such
key products as cotton, iron, and steel:

> In the mid-nineteenth century, economic life revolved around commod-
> ities, shipped in massive quantities by the new steamship lines and
> railways to feed the hungry mills and belching smokestacks of
> Manchester, Birmingham and the other great centres of the new indus-
> trial age. By 1850, the new manufacturing processes had combined
> with free trade to usher in a period of unprecedented prosperity,
> with Britain at the top of the world
>
> (Beck 1992: 23)

In the early twentieth century, however, new technologies began to
change industrial processes. In the United States, the pioneering work
of Henry Ford in mass-manufacturing technology ushered in a new era of
economic competition:

> By the time Ford's vast Rogue River assembly plant west of Detroit had
> roared into life in 1918, his manufacturing genius had already carried
> capitalism onto a higher road . . . No one guessed that within a few

short years, Ford's idea of bringing affordable automotive technology to the masses would turn him into America's richest man, transform the very nature of the economy and ignite the greatest period of industrial expansion the world had ever seen

(*Beck 1992: 27*)

In the 'mass-manufacturing economy' (from approximately 1918 to approximately 1981) national economic strength was derived largely from the capacity of a nation's firms to harness mass-manufacturing technology, as typified in the automotive and machine tool industries.

Today, however, 'a new, technology-driven circle of growth has replaced the aging manufacturing ring'. The new economy, which this source considers to have begun circa 1981, is 'driven by technology, information and innovation' and will form the basis of industrial competition well into the next century. The driving engines of the technology economy are information technologies, computers and semiconductors, telecommunications, and health and medical care. Building on this current 'technology economy', the author posits that we are on our way to a 'fourth circle' of economic competition which will be dominated by the scientific advances of genetic engineering:

It's readily apparent that the new technologies will revolutionize a staggering number of today's industries . . . but compared with the changes being wrought by the wonders of biotechnology and genetic engineering, we haven't seen anything yet

(*Beck 1992: 165*)

In industries which draw on new advances in biotechnology, competitive success is built on the continuous generation of knowledge, which in turn obsolesces at a rapid rate. Firms are in a race against the clock and against each other to generate patents for new products and processes.

The escalation of the technological intensity of industry has been identified as the primary determinant of the global integration of firms (Kobrin 1991). However, rapid technological change has not only increased integration of firms across national borders, it has also generated a new set of motivations for firms to engage in international activity. As a result, the fundamental dynamics of relations between firms from different countries have changed. We now consider the nature of these changes, and their implications for managing people worldwide.

The emergence of the transnational firm

To understand how present and future cross-border relationships are different from the past, it is important to consider how the underlying motivation for international business activity has changed. Traditional motives for firms to internationalize may be essentially classified as resource-seeking and market-seeking (Bartlett and Ghoshal 1995). Resource-seeking behaviour is driven by the desire either to access key supplies, such as minerals, energy and scarce natural resources, or to lower costs in factors of production, such as labour. These motivations are dominant in firms in commodity-based industries in which competitive advantage is based on access to (or control of) key resources like coal or steel and also in mass-manufacturing industries in which competitive advantage is enhanced by driving down costs of a large pool of unskilled labour. Market-seeking behaviour is also characteristic of firms in mass-manufacturing industries, which seek to exploit economies of scale and scope in production in order to generate a source of competitive advantage over domestic rivals.

The manner in which these different motives generated an evolutionary internationalization process of firms has been elaborated in the well-known product cycle theory of Raymond Vernon (1966).[1] The underlying premise of this theory is that the internationalization process begins with an innovation that has been created in a firm's home country. In the early stages of the product's introduction, foreign markets are served through domestic production, thereby generating exports. At this stage, firms are often characterized as having what Bartlett and Ghoshal (1989; 1995) term an 'international strategic mentality' in which the foreign location is regarded as a distant outpost supplementing sales or supplying raw materials for the domestic operation. As international operations are considered essentially as appendages to the domestic operation, such firms may function effectively from within an ethnocentric, domestic perspective.

As the product matures and production processes become more standardized, the firm enters a new stage. To meet (and further stimulate) foreign demand, firms establish production facilities in markets previously served by exports. At this stage, firms are often characterized by a 'multinational strategic mentality', in which differences in national markets and operating environments are recognized and emphasized (Bartlett and Ghoshal 1989; 1995). Firms build multiple, locally responsive strategies to support the particular requirements of each foreign location and operate from a fundamentally polycentric perspective (Perlmutter and Heenan 1974). In other words, the foreign operation has substantial autonomy from headquarters and the organization culture of each foreign subsidiary comes to reflect the national culture of the host country.

In the third stage of the product cycle, the product becomes highly standardized and competition becomes dominated by cost considerations. In order to respond to cost competition, firms create products for the world market and manufacture on a global scale. At this stage, firms are often characterized as having a 'global strategic mentality' in which the emphasis is on standardization of global operations, and central co-ordination from headquarters (Bartlett and Ghoshal 1989; 1995). In order to co-ordinate geographically dispersed activities for maximum global efficiency, such firms aim to integrate these culturally diverse operations into a single, unified organizational culture. Locally responsive strategies are no longer viable within a centralized, standardized global operation; firms operating with this strategic approach aim to produce and sell 'the same thing, the same way, everywhere' (Levitt 1983).

The product cycle theory provides a constructive means to describe the evolutionary internationalization process of firms which was characteristic of the commodity and manufacturing driven eras. However, the increasing technological intensity of industry has given rise to a new set of dynamics. Firms in high-technology industries which draw heavily on basic science develop innovative capability by tapping into centres of excellence worldwide, regardless of the evolutionary stage of their production (Casson and Singh 1993). Instead of a single pre-eminent centre of innovation (in the home country) which is implied in the product cycle model, high-technology firms draw on multiple locations which form an interactive network for innovation (Cantwell 1995). The technological imperative has thus underpinned the emergence of a new strategic mind-set framing firms' international activity, which has been labelled a 'transnational strategic mentality' (Bartlett and Ghoshal 1989; 1995). Transnational firms require strategies which are *simultaneously* locally responsive and globally integrative. Operations are dispersed but specialized, building on location-specific advantages and innovations are developed and diffused worldwide:

> As major global competitors achieve parity in the scale of their operations and their international market positions, the ability to link and leverage knowledge is increasingly the factor that differentiates the winners from the losers and survivors
>
> (Bartlett and Ghoshal 1989: 12)

In summary, the dynamics of global competition have changed profoundly. Although some industries remain based on commodities or mass-manufacturing, the critical industries which will drive economic growth into the next century are those fuelled by technology, information and innovation. Building and sustaining competitive advantage in this environment requires firms to develop a transnational strategic mind-set and the capabilities to link and leverage knowledge worldwide. Building, sustaining and learning through transnational networks requires a new set of skills from managers and a new set of challenges for firms' human resource management strategies and systems (Adler and Bartholomew 1992b). Is the generation of academic research keeping pace with the changing demands on firms for managing people in the transnational, technology-driven economy? In order to answer this question, we now review the actual trends in academic research on international organizational behaviour and human resource management (OB/HRM). In the subsequent sections, we then discuss the relevance of these research trends to the changing dynamics of global competition.

TRENDS IN RESEARCH ON INTERNATIONAL OB/HRM

Adler (1983) reviewed publishing trends in cross-cultural management for the decade of the 1970s. From her survey of twenty-four leading management journals, she reported that only 4.2% of research articles focused on organizational behaviour issues from a cross-cultural or international perspective. Given the dramatic increase in transnational business activity over the last decade, one would expect to see a substantial increase in the proportion of international articles published. However, similar trends to those in the 1970s were documented for the 1980s (Godkin, Braye and Caunch 1989; Peng, Peterson and Shyi 1990; McEvoy 1991) none of which showed a significant increase.[2]

Adler and Bartholomew (1992a) examined the publishing trends in international OB/HRM for the period between 1985 and 1990 and analysed the shifts in content and perspective in the field since the 1970s. This analysis identified the leading indicators of new trends and new knowledge in the field. The methodology of this study and the three central trends in international OB/HRM research which the study identified are summarized below.

Methodology of analysing publishing trends

A data base search was conducted of 73 academic and professional management journals including 28,707 articles for the five-year period leading up to the decade of the 1990s (October 1985 to September 1990). Both articles and journals were then classified to determine the extent of internationalization.

Article Classification. Articles focusing on organizational behaviour and human resource management (OB/HRM) issues were identified as well as those taking an international or cross-cultural perspective. As summarized in Table 2.1, all identified international OB/HRM articles were then classified on three dimensions: the international scope of the article; the inclusion, or lack thereof, of culture in the analysis; and the researcher's assessment of the impact of culture. Identified articles were first classified according to their international scope, as either foreign national (single culture), comparative international, or international interaction:

1 *Foreign National* articles are those focusing on organizational behaviour or human resource management issues in one country other than the United States or Canada, such as an article documenting managerial styles in Thailand;
2 *Comparative International* articles are those focusing on the comparison of organizational behaviour or human resource management issues in two or more countries, such as a comparison of recruitment practices in France and Germany;
3 *International Interaction* articles are those focusing on the interaction among organization members from two or more countries, such as an analysis of the interaction among Japanese managers and Mexican employees in a Japanese owned plant in Mexico.

Second, all articles were further classified according to their inclusion of culture, as cultural or not cultural:

1 *Cultural* articles are those which address, implicitly or explicitly, the concept of culture.[3] An example of a cultural article would be an analysis of the relationship of Chinese social traditions to managerial style in the People's Republic of China.
2 *Not Cultural* articles are those which neither present culture as a variable nor as a construct. For example, a description of the human resource management practices in the head office of a multinational corporation would be classified as 'not cultural'.

Third, to assess the impact of culture on management practices, articles within the cultural category were sub-classified a third time according to the researcher's conclusion that either:

(a) *Culture makes a difference*; or,
(b) *Culture does not make a difference* to the phenomena addressed.

This third classification was necessary because the initial classification as cultural did not imply that culture was found to be a significant variable; it simply meant that culture, as a variable or construct, was not ignored.

Journal Classification. In addition to classifying articles, journals were classified as primarily facilitating academic, professional, or academic/professional discourse based on two criteria: audience and methodology. The classification of journals according to audience was derived from Barley, Meyer and Gash's 1988 study in *Administrative Science Quarterly* which identified two communities of discourse: 'one that can be said to encode the practitioner's view of an issue and another, the academic's perspective . . . ' (1988: 28):

> The universe of articles published in journals or books whose stated or reputed audience consists of consultants, managers or the general

Table 2.1 Classification of articles

Cultural dimensions:	International scope		
	Foreign national	*Comparative international*	*International interaction*
Inclusion of Culture			
Not Cultural Articles	125	20	47
Cultural Articles	163	127	179
Culture's Impact			
Culture Makes A Difference	(152)	(114)	(175)
Culture Does Not Make a Difference	(11)	(13)	(4)
Total Articles	288	147	226

n = 661 articles

public may be designated as the stream of practitioner-oriented discourse. Similarly, all papers published in outlets aimed at theorists and researchers can be said to constitute the corpus of academic thought on the matter

(Barley et al., 1988: 28)

The survey builds on Barley *et al.*'s framework by using both audience and methodology as criteria. As shown in Figure 2.1, those journals publishing articles using accepted research methodologies which are read primarily by academics were classified as 'academic'. Those journals using journalistic reporting along with some academic methodologies which are read primarily by managers were classified as 'professional'.

	AUDIENCE	
	Academics	Managers and Executives
Accepted Research Methodologies	Academic Discourse	Academic/Professional Discourse
METHODOLOGY		
Journalistic Reporting	N/A	Professional Discourse

Figure 2.1   Communities of discourse

Those journals using accepted academic research methodologies, yet whose primary audience is executives and managers, were classified as 'academic/professional'. Thus, the study expanded the prior framework to include a third category of journal which reflected the highest degree of discourse among the academic and professional communities.[4]

This framework was then used to establish relevant communities of discourse for international human resource management issues. As shown in Table 2.2, each of the 73 journals included in this study was classified into one of the three relevant communities of discourse for global human resource management issues.

Key trends in international OB/HRM research

Of the 28,707 articles surveyed, a quarter (25%) were organizational behaviour or human resource management (OB/HRM) and a third (33%) were international. The intersection of these two groups – referred to as 'international OB/HRM' – was the focal category for this study. Of all articles, 2.3% (661) were classified in the international OB/HRM category. This group of international OB/HRM articles represents 9.3% of all OB/HRM articles. As previously discussed (see Table 2.1) each of the 661 international OB/HRM articles was classified on three dimensions: international scope, inclusion of culture, and culture's impact.

From the analysis, three key trends emerged.[5] First, there has been an overall shift in the types of international OB/HRM articles published, from foreign national and comparative research to more research on international interaction. Second, the importance of considering culture and its significance in international OB/HRM research has become well-recognized. Third, whereas the overall publication of international OB/HRM articles has not increased over the past two decades, the community of discourse among academics and professionals is leading the other two communities in publishing international, interaction, and cultural OB/HRM articles. Each of these trends in international OB/HRM research is now discussed in terms of its relevance to transnational firms in a technology-driven economy.

THE IMPORTANCE OF CROSS-CULTURAL INTERACTION

The first key trend is the shift from single country studies and comparative articles to publications focusing on cross-cultural interaction. Compared with research in the 1970s, the proportion of total international OB/HRM articles focusing on interaction in the 1980s almost doubled (20% to 34%; see Table 2.3). Over the same two decade period (1970–1990), the proportion of comparative articles decreased significantly (34% to 22%), while the proportion of foreign national articles remained largely

Table 2.2 Journal categories

Academic

Academy of Management Journal
Academy of Management Review
Administrative Science Quarterly
Advanced Management Journal
Group and Organization Studies
Human Relations
International Studies of
    Management and Organization
Journal of Business Research
Journal of International Business
    Studies
Journal of Management
Journal of Applied Behavioral
    Science
Journal of Applied Psychology

Management International Review
Journal of Management Studies
Strategic Management Journal
Organization Studies
ASCI Journal of Management
Human Systems Management
International Journal of Industrial
    Organization
Journal of Organizational Behaviour
Journal of Business Ethics
Journal of Economic Behaviour and
    Organization
Journal of Managerial Psychology
Journal of Occupational
    Psychology

Academic/Professional

Harvard Business Review
Human Resource Management
Columbia Journal of World Business
California Management Review
Organization Dynamics
Academy of Management Executive
Sloan Management Review

Professional

New Management
Vital Speeches
Business Horizons
Business Month
Business Quarterly
Business Week
Across the Board
Forbes
Fortune
Management Japan
Journal of General Management
Asian Business
Far Eastern Economic Review
Personnel Management
Personnel Review
Women in Management Review
Business
Journal of Management
    Development
Tokyo Business Today
International Journal of Manpower
China Business Review
Business Japan

Journal of Management Consulting
Economist
Canadian Business
Canadian Manager
Executive Excellence
Nation's Business
Report on Business
Human Resource Planning
Management Review
Personnel Administrator
Training
Management Decision
Multinational Business
Futures
Management Today
Journal of General Management
Management Japan
International Journal of Manpower
    World
Journal of Business Communication
Management World
Personnel Journal
Training and Development Journal

n = 73 journals

unchanged (46% to 44%) (see Adler 1983 and Adler and Bartholomew, 1992a). We now consider the importance of understanding cross-cultural interaction to the process of technological innovation, and to the effectiveness of transnational firms.

Cross-cultural interaction and technological innovation

Technological innovation derives from the complex integration of advances in basic knowledge with a view of market opportunity (Nelson and Winter, 1982; Tapon, 1989). Firms in technology-driven industries thus have high requirements to access and diffuse the latest developments in basic research. Three different types of organizational arrangements may be defined for governing the exchange of scientific knowledge or technology: markets, hierarchies and networks. Transaction costs economics traditionally distinguished between only two arrangements: markets and hierarchies (Coase 1937; Williamson 1975). Market exchanges occur between legally distinct bodies, individuals or firms, such as in a technology licensing agreement or R & D contract. Exchanges within hierarchies are those organized by managerial authority within the firm, such as the exchange of information between scientists within the same firm, or the transfer of technology from headquarters to a wholly-owned subsidiary. Powell (1990) argues that networks are a separate form of organization. Exchanges through networks take place between distinct entities, as in market exchanges, but are not enforced by legal contracts or competitive pricing mechanisms. Rather, the exchanges within networks are predicated on trust.

Strategic networks of firms and the social networks of individual scientists are central to the innovative capability and performance of high-technology firms (Shan, Walker and Kogut 1994):

> Social networks have assumed such importance because conducting exchanges of scientific knowledge through social networks overcomes problems of uncertainty, appropriability and human capital immobility which cannot be effectively resolved by conducting such exchanges exclusively through either hierarchies or markets
>
> (*Powell 1990: 303*)

Understanding interaction is critical for technology-driven firms, since networks are inherently relational and entail reciprocal interaction (Kobrin 1995). As exchanges within networks are built on trust and shared norms, understanding the dynamics of cross-cultural interaction is particularly important since there appear to be different national norms in the socialization of scientists (Westney, 1993). Furthermore, innovation itself is enhanced through the diversity of perspectives brought to the R &

Table 2.3 Historical comparison: the 1970s with 1985–1990

	International OB/HRM articles as a percent of all OB/HRM articles %	Foreign national* %	Comparative* %	International Interaction* %
1970s	14	46	34	20
1980s				
Total	9	44	22	34
Academic	12	53	29	18
Professional	7	37	18	46
Academic/Professional	16	34	15	51

*as % of all international OB/HRM articles

D process by scientists from different cultural backgrounds – a process of cultural synergy (see Adler 1984).

Cross-cultural interaction and the transnational firm

Structural changes inherent in responding to a transnational environment also have implications for international interaction's increasing salience. For example, to achieve simultaneous global integration, local responsiveness and worldwide learning (Bartlett and Ghoshal, 1989) transnational firms increasingly form strategic alliances and partnerships (see Harrigan 1985; Perlmutter and Heenan, 1986; Pucik 1988, among others). Not only have such partnerships increased in number but, more importantly, they have also changed in nature; in particular:

> In contrast to traditional single market joint ventures between large multinational firms and much smaller local firms, the new alliances are often formed by partners of comparable strength . . .
>
> *(Pucik 1988: 78)*

Ghoshal and Bartlett (1990) suggest that the transnational firm should actually be seen as an interorganizational network, rather than a hierarchy. As discussed above, networks are inherently relational, and are built upon reciprocal interaction and interdependence. In this new, more egalitarian form of transnational business relationship, there is no longer one dominant national culture at headquarters along with multiple foreign operations dominated by each individual local culture (as in firms with polycentric, 'multinational strategies'). Similarly, there is no longer one dominant corporate culture into which foreign subsidiaries are assimilated (as in firms with 'global strategies'). Rather, in firms with transnational strategies, there is a network of 'alliances among equals.'

As summarized in Table 2.4, the global human resource management implications of these 'alliances among equals' require executives and management scholars to change the nature of both their research and their discourse. In transnational environments, proactively creating a transnational organization culture becomes more important than reactively assimilating into a dominant partner's national culture. To integrate worldwide employees into such a globally cohesive organization culture, while simultaneously enhancing local responsiveness, transnational managers must understand cross-cultural interaction. Well-managed cultural interaction helps transnational firms create a human network capable of leveraging knowledge around the world and thereby enables them to increase their capacity to develop and diffuse innovations worldwide. Transnational firms therefore benefit most from research on how people from different nations interact as well as from research on how to use that interaction for the benefit of the firm.[6] Single culture and comparative cultural studies documenting national differences, in and of themselves, are consequently less informative in addressing transnational dynamics than are studies focusing on interaction.

Trends in international OB/HRM research suggest that both the academic and professional communities have recognized the need for increased research on cross-cultural interaction. Qualitatively, this shift – to focusing on interaction – is a particularly important trend in the generation of relevant management knowledge given that within-culture management patterns, whether documented in a single country or compared across several countries, do not seem to accurately predict the behaviour of managers when interacting with foreign colleagues (see Adler and Graham 1989; Adler 1994).

THE PERSISTENCE OF CULTURAL DIFFERENCES

The second key trend identified in international OB/HRM research is that culture's impact on managerial behaviour has become well recognized. For years, scholars argued about the impact of culture on management. One group of scholars maintained that managers' behaviour worldwide was becoming more similar (convergence),[7] while other scholars concluded that it was maintaining its dissimilarity (divergence).[8] Trends in OB/HRM research suggest that the verdict now appears to be cast in favour of divergence: both academics and professionals see culture as important to consider and as making a difference. Seventy-one percent of international OB/HRM articles included the concept of culture and of these, almost all (94%) concluded that culture makes a difference to the organizational behaviour and human resource management issues being studied (see Table 2.5). The persistence of cultural differences is now discussed in relation to technological innovation and the dynamics of transnational firms.

Cultural differences and technological innovation

The importance of country-specific factors in shaping technological development is implicit in a number of recent streams of literature, including work labelled as technological accumulation theory (e.g. Cantwell 1989) the resource-based view of strategy (e.g. Porter 1990) work on country patterns of organization (Westney 1993) and studies of national innovation systems (e.g. Nelson 1993). From this perspective, technological development is considered a country-specific phenomenon, rooted in the skills, capabilities and knowledge which accumulate over time in distinct socio-institutional contexts. Although technological innovation may be increasingly generated through transnational networks, national differences in technological capabilities persist:

Table 2.4 Cultural dynamics and the evolution of strategy and structure

Strategic mindset*	International	Multinational	Global	Transnational
Strategy	None	Country specific: Locally responsive	Globally Integrated	Locally responsive, Globally integrated, & Worldwide learning
Structure	Centralized Hierarchy	Decentralized Hierarchy	Centralized Hierarchy	Network of equals Non-hierarchical
Cultural perspective	Parochial	Culturally relative	Headquarters' ethnocentric	Culturally synergistic
Cultural differences	Ignored	Recognized in foreign locations Adapted to in foreign locations	Recognized throughout organization Minimized by assimilating into dominant organizational culture	Recognized throughout organization Valued and used to the firm's advantage
Dynamics of Cultural Interaction	Cultural Dominance	Cultural Adaptation (to foreign markets & clients)	Cultural Accommodation (to dominant organizational culture)	Cultural Synergy, collaboration, and learning
Cultural Research of Greatest Value	None	Foreign national & Comparative research	Comparative research, and the subject of interaction research focusing on minimizing the impact of cultural diversity.	International interaction research, especially studies focusing on using cross-cultural interaction to the firm's benefit.

*The terminology used to classify the different strategic mindsets is based on Bartlett and Ghoshal, 1995.

The effects of techno-globalism on national technological specialisation does not seem . . . to be leading to any greater uniformity in patterns of strength and weaknesses. Nations are becoming *increasingly* different and the international operations of large firms are exploiting and developing this diversity

(*Archibugi and Michie 1995: 136*; emphasis in original)

Persistent national differences in technological capabilities are thus considered a driving force of the globalization of technology. International technological cooperation derives from the *complementarity* of knowledge and capabilities embedded in firms from different national contexts (Shan and Hamilton 1991). Dosi, Pavitt and Soete (1990: 269) argue that 'the significant growth of such international technology agreements is precisely the illustration of the crucial firm- and country-specific technological advantages rooted in skills and knowledge'. Studies of national technological advantage to date have been conducted from the perspective of economic theory and have largely ignored the role of culture; only recently has research begun to explicitly address how culture shapes specific patterns of national technological specialization (e.g. see Hampden-Turner and Trompenaars 1993; Hill 1995; Bartholomew 1995). With culture as one of its central concepts, research in international OB/HRM should continue to generate knowledge relevant to understanding the basis of country-specific innovative capabilities and the motivations of firms to tap into the technological advantages embedded in firms from other cultural contexts.

Cultural differences and the transnational firm

Culture was seen as making a difference slightly more frequently in research on international interaction than in similar comparative and single country studies. Given the shift to interaction (see the first trend), the role of culture in international OB/HRM research should continue to gain importance. While the importance of culture is increasing, perhaps more significantly, the nature of culture's role in international interaction is also changing. As suggested in the section on trends in global economic competition (above) international interaction from a multinational or global strategic mind-set takes place primarily within hierarchies: at the micro-level, between managers and subordinates from different countries and at the macro-level, between headquarters and subsidiaries in different countries. In both cases, for contextual and historical reasons, one party, and therefore one culture, traditionally dominates. As summarized in Table 2.4, the fundamental dynamics governing cross-cultural interaction in previous eras have therefore been ones of cultural influence by the dominant partner and cultural compromise and adaptation by the sub-

Table 2.5 International scope and cultural focus of international OB/HRM articles

ARTICLES	International scope			Cultural focus		Cultural impact	
	Foreign national* %	Comparative* %	International interaction %	Not cultural* %	Cultural* %	CMAD* %	NCMAD** %
Total academic	53	29	18	34	66	91	9
Total professional	37	18	46	28	72	96	4
Academic/ professional	34	15	51	16	84	96	4
Total	44	22	34	29	71	94	6

n = 661 international OB/HRM articles
CMAD = culture makes a difference
NCMAD = culture does not make a difference
* as a % of all international OB/HRM articles
** as a % of cultural articles

ordinate partner. Accordingly, most traditional international interaction research has studied the role of culture, implicitly or explicitly, in terms of such hierarchical dynamics.

By contrast, in today's transnational firms, individual and organizational relationships are defined increasingly by networks of equal status players, not by hierarchies of dominance and subordination. Unlike their predecessors, transnational firms no longer have a single national culture which inherently defines their organizational culture. For example, the senior executives in transnational firms are generally of numerous nationalities, not strictly from the headquarters' nationality. Similarly, transnational firms no longer have a single world headquarters, but rather multiple headquarters which they disperse worldwide. Likewise, in forming alliances among equal foreign partners, transnational firms create structures in which there is minimal national cultural dominance inherent in the relationships. These patterns are quite dissimilar to the dominance of a single nationality found in traditional international firms.

Evidently, in such an environment, the role of culture changes. The less hierarchical type of cross-cultural interaction taking place both within the organization and between the organization and its external environment has specific implications for culture's function and its salience. As highlighted in Table 2.4, rather than understanding cultural influence, compromise and adaptation within organizational hierarchies, executives in transnational firms need to know how managers from different cultures learn from each other as equals. Collaborative learning – rather than influence, compromise and adaptation – becomes paramount.

While enhancing such worldwide learning capability is a key reason for transnational firms to form joint ventures and strategic alliances (Kogut 1988: 23), the mere structural formation of such alliances does not, in and of itself, guarantee enhanced organizational learning:

> Whether collaboration leads to competitive surrender or revitalization depends foremost on what employees believe the purpose of the alliance to be. It is self-evident: to learn, one must *want* to learn
>
> (*Hamel et al. 1989: 138*)

From this perspective, American firms currently appear to be at a cultural disadvantage. According to Hamel, Doz and Prahalad (1989: 138), 'Western companies won't realize the full benefits of competitive collaboration until they overcome an arrogance borne of decades of leadership' – decades of hierarchical and cultural dominance. By contrast, Japanese firms, for example, have appeared to be more receptive to learning from joint ventures and strategic alliances: according to one Japanese senior executive, 'Our Western partners approach us with the attitude of teachers . . . We are quite happy with this, because we have the attitude of students' (Hamel *et al.*, 1989: 138). It would appear that the United States' previous position of hierarchical, cultural and economic dominance in most international partnerships has become a barrier to realizing the potential learning inherent in many of today's less hierarchical transnational alliances. If American firms are to be as successful in a transnational environment as they have been in the past, this barrier to cross-cultural learning must be overcome.

The second trend is highly significant in that it highlights managers' and researchers' recognition of the importance of culture in understanding and managing the human dynamics of global firms. In combination with the first trend (the shift to interaction), the second trend is particularly important for transnational firms in technology-based industries because continuous learning through global R & D networks can only take place through continuous international interaction. As the nature of interaction within and between firms shifts from hierarchies of dominance to networks of equals, the need for knowledge about how people from different cultures collaborate and learn together is increasing. Transnational firms recognize that while cultural influence, adaptation, and compromise remain necessary approaches, they are no longer sufficient. The initial stages of the same recognition among the academic and professional publishing communities are implicit in the second trend.

INTEGRATION OF ACADEMIA AND INDUSTRY: LEADING THE WAY IN GENERATING KNOWLEDGE

The third major trend reveals that the community of discourse among academics and professionals, rather than either the academic or the professional communities taken separately, is leading in publishing OB/ HRM articles relevant to transnational firms in the technology-driven economy. As indicated in Table 2.5, a clear pattern of leadership has emerged from this third category of journals (those documenting discourse among academics and professionals) which publishes:

1 more international OB/HRM articles as a proportion of all OB/HRM articles than do either the academic or the professional journals;
2 more international OB/HRM articles as a proportion of all OB/HRM articles today than was reported in the 1970s (and is the only category of the three to do so);
3 more research on international interaction than either the academic or professional communities alone;
4 more international OB/HRM articles that include culture as a construct than do either the academic or professional communities alone;
5 more articles finding culture to be relevant than either of the other two communities.

Contrary to prior supposition, both rigour and relevance are possible. These results reveal that the methodological requirements of rigorous research do not pose an insurmountable barrier to the advancement of relevant knowledge in international OB/HRM and certainly do not excuse the publication of irrelevant studies, especially by academics. Clearly the reward structures of academic institutions still encourage research that is of questionable relevance (see what we call *The Parochial Dinosaur: The Organizational Sciences in a Global Context*, Boyacigiller and Adler 1991). However, whereas international research is clearly more difficult, time consuming and expensive to conduct than domestic research (as extensively documented by Boyacigiller and Adler 1991 and 1995; Adler 1984; Graham and Gronhaug 1989, among others) relevant international research is not more challenging than irrelevant international research.

Also contrary to prior supposition, the results of this survey reveal that it is not primarily the professional community which stimulates such relevant research, but rather the interaction between the academic and professional communities. To date, the academic community, by itself, has remained primarily dedicated to single culture and comparative research which, while still necessary, is no longer sufficient – and therefore no longer as relevant – for the competitive environment of today's transnational firm. Structurally, the academic community works on 'slow cycle time'; significant time-lags occur between changes in firms' competitive environment and changes in scholars' conceptualizations. Even longer time-lags occur between research design and ultimate research publication. While the corporate community has been rapidly decreasing its response time in order to increase relevance and competitiveness, the academic community has not as yet invented processes for just-in-time research. On the other hand, the professional community by itself, while more cognizant than the academic community of the changing competitive environment, continues to lack the rigorous conceptual and analytical frameworks needed to understand the impact of such changes on organizational behaviour. The professional community has remained much more focused on the creation of transnational business strategies than on their implementation through human systems. It appears that both academics and professionals, when operating solely from within their own community's perspective, continue to be subject to historical limitations which reduce their ability to see beyond past patterns and trends. These limitations are particularly restricting during a period, such as the current one, in which the nature of international management behaviour is undergoing such a profound shift.

Interaction between the academic and professional communities appears to create a synergy of discourse which transcends some of the fundamental limitations restricting each community's individual contribution. This interaction among the two communities creates a larger body of rigorous and relevant knowledge about international OB/HRM in general and about international interaction in particular, than does either individual community. Recognition of this third trend is fundamentally important in identifying, creating, and encouraging sources of future knowledge within the field.

CONCLUSION

Global competition requires firms and their members to continually work with and learn from people worldwide. As more firms become transnational, business relationships will take place increasingly within networks of equals rather than within hierarchies of dominance and subordination. Discourse on transnational OB/HRM in the technology-driven economy therefore requires a conceptual shift: from a hierarchical perspective of cultural influence, compromise and adaptation, to one of collaborative cross-cultural learning. At present, the community of discourse uniting academics and professionals is leading in publishing rigorous OB/HRM research that is relevant to this changing competitive environment. Interestingly, this synergy in scholarship reflects the new dynamics of innovation in technology-driven industries. High-technology firms are highly dependent on advances in basic science which are often generated in universities and public research laboratories. The integration of basic research and market-driven R & D, which underpins industrial innovation, thus increasingly depends upon the integration of the academic and industrial communities. As the generation of technology requires greater collaboration between universities and firms, so too does the generation of relevant knowledge on managing transnational networks depend on further collaboration between the academic and professional communities of discourse.

ACKNOWLEDGEMENTS

Portions of this chapter are adapted from Nancy J. Adler and Susan Bartholomew's article 'Academic and Professional Communities of Discourse: Generating Knowledge on Transnational Human Resource Management,' in *Journal of International Business Studies*, 23(3), 1992: 551–569, with permission.

The financial support of the Social Science and Humanities Research Council (SSHRC) of Canada is gratefully acknowledged.

ENDNOTES

1 A frequently used model describing the post-World War II evolution of firms
   postulates three phases. While the three-phase model was originally espoused

by Vernon in 1966, he further elaborated it (see 1971 and 1981) as did many other commentators, (see, for example, Ghadar 1986). A cultural component and the human resource management implications were added in 1989 (see Adler and Ghadar 1990a and b).

2 Graham and Gronhaug (1989) documented a corresponding paucity of cross-cultural and multinational research in leading marketing journals.

3 This category is not limited to a particular theory of culture. Therefore it includes such diverse conceptualizations as: culture as a mind-state, a social enactment, or an ecological variable.

4 The fourth category (journalistic articles written for academics), while conceptually defined, is, in reality, a nonexistent category. Although academics read journalistic articles, they do so in professional and popular journals. There are no journalistic articles written primarily for academics within the 73 journals surveyed (nor any at all that we know of).

5 For a detailed report of the results, see Adler and Bartholomew 1992a.

6 See Adler 1984, on cultural synergy.

7 'Adherents of the convergence (or universalistic) perspective argue that organizational characteristics across nations are mostly free of the particularities of specific cultures (e.g. Cole 1973; Form 1979; Hickson, Hinnings, McMillan and Schwitter 1974; Kerr, Dunlop, Harbison and Myers 1952; Negandhi 1979, 1985)' (Adler, Doktor and Redding 1986: 300). Also note Chapter 1.

8 'Adherents of divergence argue that organizations are culture-bound, rather than culturally free, and are remaining so (e.g. Hofstede 1980; Laurent 1983; Lincoln, Hanada and Olson 1981; Meyer and Rowan 1977)' (Adler, Doktor and Redding 1986: 301).

REFERENCES

Adler, N.J. (1994) Competitive frontiers: women managing across borders, in *Competitive Frontiers: Women Managers in a Global Economy*, (eds N.J. Adler and D.N. Izraeli) Blackwell Publishing: Cambridge MA, pp. 22–40.

Adler, N.J. (1983) Cross-cultural management research: the ostrich and the trend. *Academy of Management Review*, 8, pp. 226–32.

Adler, N.J. (1984) Understanding the ways of understanding: cross-cultural management methodology reviewed, in *Advances in International Comparative Management* (Vol. 1). (ed R.N. Farmer) JAI Press, Greenwich, CT, pp. 31–67.

Adler, N.J. and Bartholomew, S. (1992a) Academic and professional communities of discourse: generating knowledge on transnational human resource management. *Journal of International Business Studies*, 23, pp. 551–69.

Adler, N.J. and Bartholomew, S. (1992b) Managing globally competent people. *Academy of Management Executive*, 6, pp. 52–65.

Adler, N.J. and Ghadar, F. (1990a) International strategy from the perspective of people and culture: the North American context, in *Research in Global Strategic Management: International Business Research for the*

Twenty-First Century; Canada's New Research Agenda, Volume 1, (ed A.M. Rugman) JAI Press, Greenwich, Conn., pp. 179–205.

Adler, N.J. and Ghadar, F. (1990b) Strategic human resource management: a global perspective, in *Human Resource Management in International Comparison* (ed R. Pieper) de Gruyter, Berlin/New York, pp. 235–60.

Adler, N.J. & Graham, J.L. (1989) Cross-cultural interaction: the international comparison fallacy. *Journal of International Business Studies,* **20,** pp. 515–37.

Adler, N.J., Doktor, R., and Redding, S.G. (1986) From the Atlantic to the Pacific century: cross-cultural management reviewed. *Journal of Management,* **12,** pp. 295–318.

Archibugi, D. and Michie, J. (1995) The globalisation of technology: a new taxonomy. *Cambridge Journal of Economics,* **19,** pp. 121–40.

Bartlett, C.A. and Ghoshal, S. (1989) *Managing Across Borders: The Transnational Solution,* Harvard Business School Press, Boston.

Bartlett, C.A. and Ghoshal, S. (1995) *Transnational Management,* 2nd edn, Irwin, Chicago.

Beck, N. (1992) *Shifting Gears,* Harper Collins, Toronto.

Boyacigiller, N. and Adler, N.J. (1995) Insiders and outsiders: bridging the worlds of organizational behavior and international management, in *International Business Inquiry: An Emerging Vision* (eds B. Toyne and D. Nigh) The University of South Carolina Press, Columbia, South Carolina, pp. 22–102.

Boyacigiller, N. and Adler, N.J. (1991) The parochial dinosaur: the organizational sciences in a global context. *Academy of Management Review,* **16,** pp. 262–90.

Cantwell, J. (1995) The globalisation of technology: what remains of the product cycle model? *Cambridge Journal of Economics,* **19,** pp. 155–74.

Cantwell, J. (1989) *Technological Innovation and Multinational Corporations,* Basil Blackwell, Oxford.

Casson, M. and Singh, S. (1993) Corporate research and development strategies: the influence of firm, industry and country factors on the decentralization of R & D, *R & D Management,* **23,** pp. 91–107.

Coase, R.E. (1937) The nature of the firm. *Economica,* November, pp. 386–405.

Cole, R.E. (1973) Functional alternatives and economic development: an empirical example of permanent employment in Japan. *American Sociological Review,* **38,** pp. 424–38.

Dosi, G., Pavitt, K., and Soete, L. (1990) *The Economics of Technical Change and International Trade,* New York University Press, Washington Square, New York.

Form, W. (1979) Comparative industrial sociology and the convergence hypothesis. *Annual Review of Sociology,* **5,** pp. 1–25.

Ghadar, F. (1986) Strategic considerations in the financing of international investment, in *The Multinational Enterprise in Transition* (eds P. Grub, F. Ghadar and D. Khambata), The Darwin Press, Princeton, N.J.

Godkin, L., Braye, C.E., and Caunch, C.L. (1989) U.S. based cross-cultural management research in the eighties. *Journal of Business and Economic Perspectives*, **15**, pp. 37–45.

Graham, J.L. and Gronhaug, K. (1989) Ned Hall didn't get a haircut; or why we haven't learned much about international marketing in the last twenty five years. *Journal of Higher Education*, **60**, pp. 152–57.

Hamel, G., Doz, Y., and Prahalad, C.K. (1989) Collaborate with your competitors – and win. *Harvard Business Review*, **67**, pp. 133–39.

Hampden-Turner, C. and Trompenaars, F. (1993) *The Seven Cultures of Capitalism*, Doubleday, New York.

Harrigan, K.R. (1985) *Strategies for Joint Ventures*, Lexington Books, Lexington, MA.

Hickson, D.J., Hinnings, C.R., McMillan, C.J.M., and Schwitter, J.P. (1974) The culture-free context of organization structure: a tri-national comparison. *Sociology*, **8**, pp. 59–80.

Hill, C. (1995) National institutional structures, transaction cost economizing and competitive advantage, *Organization Science*, **6**, pp. 119–31.

Hofstede, G. (1980) *Culture's Consequences: International Differences in Work-Related Values*, Sage, Beverly Hills, CA.

Keohayne, R.O. and Nye, Jr., J.F. (1989) *Power and Independence*, 2nd edn, Scott, Foresman and Company, Glenview, Ill.

Kerr, C.J., Dunlop, J.T., Harbison, F.H., and Myers, C.A. (1952) *Industrialism and Industrial Man*, Harvard University Press, Cambridge, MA.

Kobrin, S.J. (1991) An empirical analysis of the determinants of global integration, *Strategic Management Journal*, **12**, pp. 17–32.

Kobrin, S.J. (1995) Transnational integration, national markets and nation-states, in *International Business Inquiry: An Emerging Vision*, University of South Carolina Press, Columbia, South Carolina (in press).

Kogut, B. (1988) Joint ventures: theoretical and empirical perspectives. *Strategic Management Journal*, **9**, pp. 319–32.

Laurent, A. (1983) The cultural diversity of Western management conceptions. *International Studies of Management and Organization*, **8**, pp. 75–96.

Levitt, T. (1983) The globalization of markets. *Harvard Business Review*, May–June, pp. 93–102.

Lincoln, J.R., Hanada, M., and Olson, J. (1981) Cultural orientations and individual reactions to organizations: a study of employees of Japanese-owned firms. *Administrative Science Quarterly*, **26**, pp. 93–115.

McEvoy, G.M. (1991) *Publication Trends in International Human Resource Management: The Decade of the 1980s*. Working paper, Utah State University, pp. 1–21.

Meyer, J.W. and Rowan, B. (1977) Institutional organizations: formal structures as myth and ceremony. *American Journal of Sociology,* **83**, pp. 340–53.

Negandhi, A.R. (1979) Convergence in organizational practices: an empirical study of industrial enterprise in developing countries, in *Organizations Alike and Unlike,* (eds C.J. Lammers and D.J. Hickson) Routledge & Kegan Paul, London, pp. 323–45.

Nelson, R.R. (ed) (1993) *National Innovation Systems: A Comparative Analysis.* Oxford University Press, New York.

Ohmae, K. (1990) *The Borderless World,* Harper Business, New York.

Peng, T.K., Peterson, M.F., and Shyi, Y-P. (1990) Quantitative methods in cross-national management research: trends and equivalence issues. *Journal of Organizational Behaviour,* **12**, pp, 87–107.

Perlmutter, H.V. and Heenan, D.A. (1986) Cooperate to compete globally. *Harvard Business Review,* **64**, pp. 136–52.

Perlmutter, H.V. and Heenan, D.A. (1974) How multinational should your top managers be? *Harvard Business Review,* **52**, pp. 121–32.

Porter, M. (1990) *The Competitive Advantage of Nations,* The Free Press, New York.

Powell, W.W. (1990) Neither market nor hierarchy: network forms of organization. *Research in Organizational Behavior,* **12**, pp. 295–36.

Pucik, V. (1988) Strategic alliances, organizational learning, and competitive advantage: the HRM agenda. *Human Resource Management,* **27**, pp. 77–93.

Root, F. (1988) Some Taxonomies of International Cooperative Agreements, in *Cooperative Strategies in International Business* (eds F. Contractor and P. Lorange) Lexington Books, Lexington, MA.

Shan, W. and Hamilton, W. (1991) Country-specific advantage and international cooperation. *Strategic Management Journal,* **12**, pp. 419–32.

Shan, W., Walker, G., and Kogut, B. (1994) Interfirm cooperation and startup innovation in the biotechnology industry. *Strategic Management Journal,* **15**, pp. 387–94.

Vernon, R. (1981) Sovereignty at bay ten years after. *International Organization,* **35**, pp. 517–29.

Vernon, R. (1971) *Sovereignty at Bay: The Multinational Spread of U.S. Enterprises,* Basic Books, New York.

Vernon, R. (1966) International investment and international trade in the product cycle. *Quarterly Journal of Economics,* **80**, pp. 129–44.

Westney, D.E. (1993) Country patterns in R & D organization: the United States and Japan, in *Country Competitiveness: Technology and the Organizing of Work* (ed Bruce Kogut) Oxford University Press, New York.

Williamson, O.E. (1975) *Markets and Hierarchies: Analysis and Antitrust Implications,* Free Press, New York.

FURTHER READING

Bartholomew, S. (1995) The globalisation of technology: a socio-cultural perspective, in *Technology, Innovation and Competitiveness*, (eds J. Howells and J. Michie) Edward Elgar, Cheltenham (in press).

Barley, S.R., Meyer, G.W., and Gash, D.C. (1988) Cultures of culture: academics, practitioners and the pragmatics of normative control. *Administrative Science Quarterly*, **33**, pp. 24–60.

Contractor, F. & Lorange, P. (1988) Why should firms cooperate? The strategy and economics basis for cooperative ventures in *Cooperative Strategies in International Business* (eds F. Contractor and P. Lorange) Lexington Books, Lexington, MA.

Doz, Y. and Prahalad, C.K. (1986) Controlled variety: a challenge for human resource management in the MNC. *Human Resource Management*, **25**, pp. 55–71.

Galbraith, J.R. and Kazanjian, R.K. (1986) Organizing to implement strategies of diversity and globalization: the role of matrix designs. *Human Resource Management*, **25**, pp. 37–54.

Ghoshal, S. and Bartlett, C.A. (1990) The multinational corporation as an interorganizational network, *Academy of Management Journal*, **15**, pp. 603–25.

Hambrick, D.C., Korn, L.B., Frederickson, J.W., and Ferry, R.M. (1989) *21st Century Report: Reinventing the CEO*. Korn Ferry and Colombia University's Graduate School of Business, New York, pp. 1–94.

Heenan, D.A. and Perlmutter, H.V. (1979) *Multinational Organization Development: A Social Architectural Perspective*, Addison Wesley, Reading, MA.

Lyles, M. (1990) A research agenda for strategic management in the 1990s. *Journal of Management Studies*, **27**, pp. 363–75.

Nelson, R.R. and Winter, S.G. (1982) *An Evolutionary Theory of Economic Change*. Harvard University Press, Cambridge, MA.

Pucik, V. and Katz, J.H. (1986) Information, control and human resource management in multinational firms. *Human Resource Management*, **25**, pp. 121–32.

Tapon, F. (1989) A transactions cost analysis of innovations in the organization of pharmaceutical R & D. *Journal of Economic Behaviour and Organization*, **12**, pp. 197–213.

Chapter 3

Culture: a theoretical review

Gerry Darlington

INTRODUCTION

This chapter reviews some of the current approaches to understanding national culture and suggests the kind of material that could be included in cross-cultural awareness programmes. As Maruyama (1980, 1982 and 1984) shows, Western thought is characterized by categories, distinctions and separateness, whereas Eastern thought is concerned with continuity and connectedness.

Let us consider whether multi-cultural teams, or businesses, perform differently to mono-cultural ones. Culture, as the 'shared understanding of meaning' is the core of stability in societal organizations. In this vein, Moss Kanter and Corn (1994) argue that 'cultural factors [either] fan the flames of intergroup conflict or encourage the acceptance of differences'. Their work shows that sensitivity to cultural differences minimized organizational tension, particularly in situations of acquisition or merger.

There are over 160 definitions of 'culture' alone, as documented by Kroeber *et al.* (1985) and a great deal of new material has been published recently. Mead's (1951) widely accepted anthropological definition of culture is, 'a body of learned behaviour, a collection of beliefs, habits and traditions, shared by a group of people and successively learned by people who enter the society'.

Society in this context can apply to any level of culture, e.g. nation, organization or profession. While in most instances a person's nationality is a sufficient indicator of their culture (where culture is the norm of that nationality), many societies now contain a variety of ethnic groups and individuals may easily be influenced by cultures other than their apparent nationality. Since, for example, developing a team requires the successful integration of individuals, an *individual's* cultural orientations may need to be determined. To apply national norms to a specific group of individuals would be to perpetrate the 'reserve ecological fallacy' described by Hofstede (1991).

Much of the prior work surveyed suggests a need to develop better ways of communicating and cooperating within and between organizations. Cross-cultural understanding should help us to achieve this, as evidenced by the work of Maznevski (1994). Her work indicates that cross-cultural awareness training significantly increases the ability of a multi-cultural team to perform a set task successfully.

In the global communication age, employees at all levels in organizations communicate with customers and colleagues in different countries. International business is increasingly important to the long term success of many companies (Hambrick *et al.*, 1989) and it is crucial, therefore, to establish and manage good relationships across different cultures. As Adler and Bartholomew (1992) indicate, there is a need for 'a conceptual shift: from a hierarchical perspective of cultural influence, compromise and adaptation, to one of collaborative cross-cultural learning' (see also Chapter 2 in this volume). Earley and Singh (1995) emphasize the need to gain a deeper understanding of the relationship of management to cultural and national characteristics, instead of just focusing on convergence, divergence and differential competition.

PATTERNS AND DIFFERENCES

It is clear that the existence of ethnic groups within nation states requires cultural understanding to enable successful integration. Integration means being able to participate in the society of the nation state without sacrificing one's own culture and without becoming socially isolated. Tayeb's (1988) work is particularly significant in this area. To understand some of the patterns and differences inherent in national culture, several different approaches to understanding the topic are considered, as shown in Table 3.1.

A great deal of emphasis has been placed by researchers on Value Orientation studies, including developments of the original Kluckhohm and Strodtbeck (1960) instruments and validations of Hofstede's (1982) dimensions – see Chapters 6 and 9 in this volume, for example. A summary of the different orientations or dimensions used by researchers over time is shown in Table 3.2.

Leeds (1994) shows how Trompenaar's, Hofstede's and Lessem and Neubauer's work relates to pragmatic and wholistic approaches to management in emerging and newly emerging democracies, concluding that, 'managers worldwide are gradually learning to reconcile contradictions or apparent opposites'.

Geert Hofstede (1991: 5) describes culture as, 'the collective programming of the mind which distinguishes the members of one group or category of people from another'. Hofstede, like Mead (1951), goes on to suggest that culture is learned, not inherited. If this is true, then it follows that it is possible to learn new cultural traits and to unlearn old ones. This means that it may be possible to integrate cultural differences when generating strategic options.

Cultural programming involves a diffuse range of elements (based on Czinkota and Ronkainen (1993), Hofstede (1991) and Trompenaars (1993)):

- Language – both verbal and nonverbal
- Economics
- Religion
- Politics
- Social institutions, social strata or classes and family structure
- Values
- Attitudes
- Manners
- Customs
- Material items
- Aesthetics
- Education

Berthon's (1993) in turn sees culture as the results of human actions and shows the clear link between the idea of 'mental programming' and the consequences of behaviour derived from this. Kanungo and Medonca (1994) suggest that HRM policies and practices, which are used to control and direct behaviour and performance, are largely the result of managerial beliefs.

Potter (1994) has developed a model of self-concept, based on Dilts' unified field model of NLP (O'Connor and Seymour 1990), which helps to explain the deep-rooted nature of cultural elements. The extent to which people share meaning and can thus develop synergistic integration with those from other cultures, will depend on their awareness of their own deeply held values and beliefs and their awareness of others' values and beliefs. Once this awareness has been raised, they can choose to make behavioural adjustments to enhance their capability to work successfully with people from other cultures.

Hofstede's work deals primarily with *differences* between national cultures. He and his co-workers show that national cultures differ along five dimensions. (His earlier work indicated only four, but incorporating work that attempts to remove Western bias suggests a possible fifth dimension. Based on 'Confucian Work Dynamism', Hofstede called this dimension Long-term Orientation). He further asserts and illustrates, by means of selected historical examples, that these dimensions do not change greatly over time. This implies that attempts to fundamentally change another culture by means of money, propaganda or arms are likely to be unsuccessful.

Various writers have re-assessed Hofstede's work and found it to be largely validated. Smith (1994) summarizes the findings of a meta-analy-

Table 3.1 Comparison of national culture studies

Researchers	Perspective	Methodology	Implications
Hofstede (1982, 1991, 1991a)	Differences in behaviour	Work related value survey	Distinct national cultures
Trompenaars (1984) Hampden-Turner and Trompenaars (1993)	Differences in behaviour	Value Orientations Dilemmatics	Distinct national cultures e.g. Seven Cultures of Capitalism – different sustainability
Lessem and Neubauer (1994)	Multiple levels of difference based on philosophies	Comparative surveys of art, religion, literature, philosophy and societal constructs	Four diverse management systems form a basis for European unity
Bonthous (1994)	Types of intelligence system	Comparative analysis of preferred styles	Need to develop a balance of all styles to avoid an organizational learning disability
Said (1991, 1994)	National literature	Comparative analysis of textual style and content	Appreciate the differences and recognize we make culture as part of self-organization process
Tayeb (1988, 1994)	National and Corporate	Literature, cultural and work attitude surveys	Proposed causal model of culture

Maznevski (1994)	Differences in Value Orientation	Value Orientations Training Intervention with Performance Assessment	Proposed Model of Synergistic Integration
Di Stefano (1992)	Differences in Value Orientation	Case Studies Literature review	Profile of effective global executives
Adler (1991)	Trends in OB/HRM publishing	Literature Review	Shift to Cross-Cultural interaction; Recognition of Culture's importance; Leadership of Academic/ Professional Community of Discourse
Heller and Wilpert (1981)	Participation in Decision Making	IPC Questionnaire	Five methods of Decision Making and Power Displacement Effect
Laurent (1983)	Managers' implicit theories on management	Questionnaire survey	Country clusters of implicit theory, e.g. organizations as authority systems.

Table 3.2 Comparison of cultural dimensions

	Kluckhohn and Strodtbeck (1961)	Hall (1960, 66, 73) Hall & Hall (1987)	Hofstede (1984 ... 1991)	Trompenaars (1984 ... 1993)	Trompenaars and Hampden-Turner (1994)	Maznevski (1994)
Human Nature	Good, Evil, Neutral, Mixed: Changeable, unchangeable	Agreements	Uncertainty Avoidance index	Universalism: Particularism	Universalism: Particularism	Good/evil: Changeable
Relation to Nature	Subjugation Harmony Mastery		Uncertainty Avoidance index	Internal: External Orientation	Inner: Outer Directed	Subjugation Mastery Harmony
Activity Orientation	Doing, Being, Being-in-becoming	Monochronic, Polychronic (interacts with individualism)	Masculinity index	Achievement: Ascription	Achievement: Ascription, Analysing: Integrating	Doing, Being, Containing and Controlling (Thinking)
Human Relationships	Individual, Collective, Hierarchical	Amount of space, Possessions, Friendship, Communication	Power Distance index, Individualism index	Equality: Hierarchy. Individualism: Collectivism. Affective: Neutral	Equality: Hierarchy. Individualism: Communitarianism.	Individual, Collective, Hierarchical
Relation to Time	Past, Present, Future	Past, Future	Long-term Orientation	Sequential: Synchronic Past, Present, Future	Sequential: Synchronic	
Space Orientation	Public, Private, Mixed	Public, Private,				

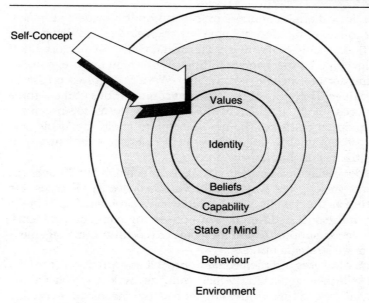

Figure 3.1 Model of self-concept
Source: Potter (1994)

sis by saying that cultural diversity is not disappearing and that two of the Hofstede dimensions (Power Distance Index and Individualism Index) find parallels in all of the more recent large scale surveys. These two dimensions are reliably linked to day-to-day behaviour, difficulties in cross-cultural negotiation, joint venture management and team work in multi-nationals. However, care should be taken when interpreting Hofstede's scores. For example, the relatively strong collectivist score for Iran might lead one to suppose that, in general, Iranians would cooperate well in a team. Tayeb (1979) notes, however, that there is little in the background of most Iranians to push them to co-operate with interpersonally constituted teams or work groups. Kiani and Latifi (1995) suggest that Iran is best viewed as an individualistic culture.

Hofstede's work is based primarily on surveys carried out among matched samples of IBM personnel while he was employed as the manager of the Personnel Research Department of IBM Europe. This has attracted criticism from some people, but it is generally accepted that Hoppe's (1990) large scale work validates the generalizability of the Hofstede survey outside IBM.

For each of his dimensions, some key differences occurring at the extremes of each scale are shown in Hofstede's *Culture Consequences* (1991a) and *Cultures and Organisations* (1991). Hofstede compares the relative scores for different countries on several multidimensional maps, in an attempt to show the kind of behaviour expected as the norm for a particular nation. Using Hofstede's basic framework, Kiani and Latifi (1995) have developed a mechanism to interpret Iranian culture, demonstrating the impact of Ancient, Islamic and Western cultures on Iran's work related values. They show how different combinations of these three main sub-cultures result in different observable patterns for organizational and individual cultures. The model helps to avoid the 'ecological fallacy' and assists in interpreting the results of Hofstede's IBM survey in the context of the rest of Iranian culture.

Like Hofstede (1982) and Laurent (1983), Trompenaars (1993) believes there is no one prescriptive way to achieve excellence in all cases. He describes culture as the 'way in which people solve problems' and shows that different cultures have different ways of solving common problems. This approach lends support to the idea that cross-cultural management can generate more strategic options.

Trompenaars also uses a dimensional approach and proposes a model for corporate cultures, suggesting which countries reflect which model. Trompenaars' advice is practical and shows, by means of everyday dilemmas, better ways to deal with other cultures and a more likely prediction of response to given situations.

A recent work by Trompenaars and Hampden-Turner (1993) has built on the cross-cultural survey work started by Trompenaars in his original thesis (1984) and continued to the present day – see chapter 17 in this volume – by surveying attendees of his cross-cultural management seminars throughout the world. This work does not detail the methodology, which is amply covered in preceding texts and articles (1993). It is clearly aimed at practising managers and international workers. The authors focus on seven valuing processes and frame these as dilemmas that force the respondents to 'take sides'. They then generate models of seven different modes of capitalism, present in each country of the title.

The authors say that people from the same country will try to resolve dilemmas in the same way, as cultural cohesion is a prerequisite for stability in a society. They go on to say that the two horns of these dilemmas form a virtuous circle, which appears to make conflict resolution easier. However, they feel that this may merely allow 'cultural ships to pass in the night'. As members of different cultures may reach the same point on the virtuous circle simultaneously, it may be thought that consensus or mutual understanding has been reached. However, if there is no real understanding of how the different parties reached the same point a lasting sense of cohesion, co-operation and appreciation of differences may not be attained. This concept implies that shared meaning and cultural cohesion are also important prerequisites for multi-cultural teams. Cross-cultural awareness training should help to generate real

Table 3.3 Seven countries' normative responses to dilemmas (adapted from Trompenaars and Hampden-Turner 1993)

Universalism USA, Britain, Germany, Sweden	**Particularism** France, Japan
Analysis USA, Britain, Netherlands, Sweden	**Integration** France, Germany, Japan
Individualism USA, Britain, Netherlands, Sweden	**Communitarianism** France, Germany, Japan
Inner-direction USA, Britain, Germany	**Outer-direction** Sweden, Netherlands, France, Japan
Status by Achievement USA, Britain, Sweden, Germany, Netherlands, Japan	**Status by Ascription** France
Equality USA, Germany, Britain, Netherlands, Sweden	**Hierarchy** France, Japan
Time as sequence USA, Sweden, Netherlands, Britain, Germany	**Synchronized view of time** France, Japan

understanding. The book attempts to explain differences between cultures but is not prescriptive in nature. It does try to show, however, which forms of capitalism may be more sustainable than others. In common with other authors, such as Kohn (1992), Trompenaars and Hampden-Turner feel that co-operation is more likely to lead to long term success than competition.

Table 3.3 summarizes each country's different position within the dilemmas, based on the norms found in the authors' surveys.

Trompenaars' latest samples are ones of convenience, collected over a period of years, at a variety of venues.

The authors accept that they must be biased by their own culture. Their dream is 'a world culture in which all paths lead to a shareable integrity'. If this is possible, the implications for economic, spiritual and intellectual growth and harmony are profound. As Trompenaars later indicated in an interview with Bruce Lloyd (1993) of the Strategic Planning Society this does not mean one uniform culture, but a world where differences are accepted and valued.

COMPARISONS OF SETS OF DIMENSIONS

A comparison of the different sets of dimensions used by different leading authors in this field is shown in Table 3.4. Given that repeat studies by

Table 3.4 Comparison of dimensions used in three texts on culture

Hofstede (1991) *Culture's Consequences*	Trompenaars (1993) *Riding the Waves of Culture*	Trompenaars and Hampden-Turner (1993) *The Seven Cultures of Capitalism*
Power Distance Index		Equality/Hierarchy
Individualism Index	Individualism/ Collectivism	Individualism/ Communitarianism
Masculinity Index		
Uncertainty Avoidance Index		
Long-term Orientation	Time as Sequential/ Synchronic Past, Present, Future	Time as Sequential/ Synchronic
	Universalism/ Particularism	Universalism/ Particularism
	Achievement/Ascription	Achievement/Ascription
	Internal/External Orientation	Inner/Outer Directed
	Affective/Neutral	
	Specific/Diffuse	
		Analysing/Integrating

these authors generates different sets of dimensions, it may be appropriate to question the reliability of the instruments used.

Trompenaars has developed his dimensional theory further, indicating preferred styles of organization for different national cultures. His model shows that differences can be observed in relationships between employees, attitudes to authority, ways of thinking and learning, attitudes to people, ways of changing, ways of motivating and rewarding, criticism and conflict resolution. Trompenaars suggests that the implication for strategy is that managing across different cultures gives more ways to achieve goals. He further suggests that the only system that will genuinely enable management across cultures is that of Strategic Control as described by Goold and Campbell (1990). They and Goold and Quinn (1990) do not themselves highlight cross-cultural management as an advantage of strategic control. In their early work, Goold and Campbell suggest that Strategic Planning, Strategic Control and Financial Control 'appear to be the most viable options for managing a large diversified company'. Their later work suggests that Strategic Control is often the best option for ensuring long-term performance. It is not explicitly stated by them that this approach generates more options, but they do refer to the importance of shared meaning.

UNDERSTANDING EUROPEAN CULTURES

Lessem and Neubauer (1994) take a different analytical approach, focusing on understanding European cultures and attempting to synthesize their findings into a European management model. They believe that as the knowledge-based economy becomes more prevalent, then it is those ideas and concepts underpinning knowledge that are truly important, i.e. the *philosophies* that pervade a culture. They define the four most significant of these as *pragmatism, rationalism, wholism* and *humanism*. Their concept of intercultural management is shown diagrammatically in Figure 3.2.

After examining the philosophies and management systems of the different countries within Europe, Lessem and Neubauer synthesize their findings into a table of European Management Characteristics. They believe this can form the basis of a consolidated European management system. A European management system is, according to them, a management framework that could be used by all types of organization throughout Europe. Finally, they make the case for an integrated way of learning and raising European management consciousness to achieve the target of a fully functioning European economy. As Leeds (1994) suggests, business

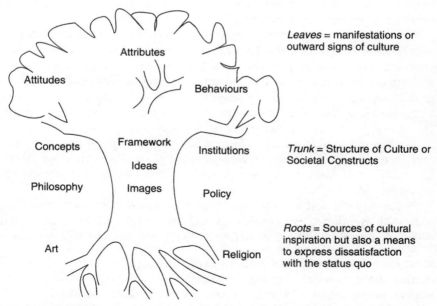

Figure 3.2 Concept of intercultural management, adapted from Lessem and Neubauer (1994)

people are concerned with understanding how those four ideas can be reconciled or integrated. Lessem and Neubauer's European Management Characteristics are summarized in Table 3.5.

The main difference between this and the work described on dimensions is that Lessem and Neubauer differentiate four management styles to represent European diversity. They argue that *excessive* differentiation weakens individual cultures. Once again though, it is apparent that cultural differences generate options, the integration of which may enhance performance.

ENVIRONMENTS AND CULTURES

Jean-Marie Bonthous (1994) suggests the primary reasons for business failure are inadequate information regarding the business environment and lack of understanding of foreign cultures. He proposes that wholistic business intelligence consists of all the elements shown in Figure 3.3.

Bonthous proposes a useful model for a 'balanced integration of intelligence' and demonstrates, in Figures 3.4 and 3.5, how five different countries appear to behave along the four polar coordinates of his model.

Bonthous argues that all four dimensions of the model shown are equally critical for an organization or nation to provide creative intelligence responses. A failure to understand other cultures and organizations in these terms is likely to reduce the chance of business success with those other cultures and organizations.

Bonthous maintains that Dimension 1 of his model is essential for effectiveness and forms the foundation of intelligence systems. Dimension 2 allows growth and the breaking of new ground. Dimension 3 structures this growth, while Dimension 4 sequences and orders the growth. A lack of ability in any one dimension is effectively an organizational learning disability. Once again, the understanding of difference and the development of a broader range of styles appears to be the key to business success. According to Figure 3.5, Bonthous contends that Japan and Sweden are more likely to be successful than other countries shown. Germany and America appear to suffer from the most pronounced potential 'learning disability'.

Heller and Wilpert's (1981) study of participation in decision-making indicated significant differences in the behaviour of managers from different countries with regard to five methods of decision-making, namely:

- manager's own decision without explanation;
- manager's own decision with explanation;
- prior consultation with subordinates before making decision;
- joint decision-making with employees; and
- delegating responsibility for making the decision to employees.

Table 3.5 European management characteristics (after Lessem and Neubauer 1994)

Dimension	Characteristic Western	Northern	Eastern	Southern
Corporate	**Commercial**	**Administrative**	**Industrial**	**Familial**
Managerial Attributes				
Behaviour	Experiential	Professional	Developmental	Convivial
Attitude	Sensation	Thought	Intuition	Feeling
Institutional Models				
Function	Salesmanship	Control	Production	Personnel
Structure	Transaction	Hierarchy	System	Network
Societal Ideas				
Economics	Free Market	Dirigiste	Social Market	Communal
Philosophy	Pragmatic	National	Wholistic	Humanistic
Cultural Images				
Art	Theatre	Architecture	Music	Dance
Culture	Anglo-Saxon	Gallic	Germanic	Latin

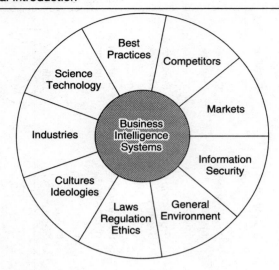

Figure 3.3 Bonthous' (1994) Model for business intelligence systems

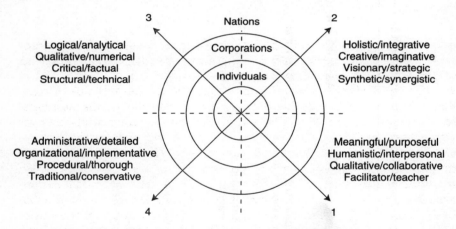

Figure 3.4 Bonthous' (1994) four dimensions of an intelligent culture

They also showed that subordinates often indicate that their manager uses a more participative style than reported by that manager. They termed this the 'power displacement effect'.

A main concern with the research on national culture to date is that it has been primarily carried out with what are now recognized as Western biases and Western methodologies. A more Oriental approach is given by the writings of Said (1991; 1994) who, by comparing seminal literature for a variety of countries, gives a wholistic and deep insight into cultures. The

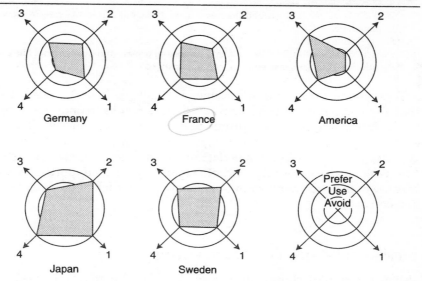

Figure 3.5 Preferred intelligence styles for five countries

models given by other researchers may in some ways reinforce stereotypes, in that they are still classifying groups of people, who are made up
of different individuals, into categories.

Said's (1994) view of culture lends support to the use of value orientations for the individual, rather than the use of collective norms, as a basis
for successful teambuilding. The notion of culture as an artificial construct
was echoed by Lessem and Neubauer's work and also by the Futures
Group of the Strategic Planning Society, which referred in discussions to
the relatively recent emergence of the nation state, the speed with which
fundamentalism re-emerged in Iran and the likely return to 'small nationalism' in Europe. The artificiality of culture was further highlighted on an
Open University programme that described the investiture of the Prince
of Wales as an 'invented tradition' – made real by using archaic sounding
language and ritual imagery. This lends support to the argument that
culture is learned and we can choose to learn or unlearn cultural traits.
The key points to emerge from Said's work are that differences should be
valued constructively, rather than in a separatist way, and that society is a
self-organizing system which generates its own culture.

Tayeb (1988) carried out a literature survey, a national culture survey
and a work attitudes survey which led her to propose the following causal
model:

CONTINGENCY VARIABLES→Conditions for organizations→Formalization, centralization, communication

POLITICAL-ECONOMIC→Conditioning of markets, labour→Control strategies, rewards and punishments
⌐Social Characteristics⌐
CULTURAL VARIABLES→Work related attitudes→Formalization, power and autonomy, delegation of authority, consultation, communications

Tayeb defined the relevant variables as shown in Table 3.6. She believes that application of this model reveals a more wholistic understanding of the differences in national cultures than 'residual' approaches, like Hofstede's (Tayeb 1994). Her model suggests that cultural variables arise as a result of political and economic factors via changes in social characteristics. Potter's model of self-concept (Figure 3.1) also supports this view, because of the two-way flow of influence between each of the circles of the archetype.

DIFFERENCES AND INTERPRETATIONS

Using the model shown in Figure 3.6, the differences between the approaches described so far can be highlighted. Hofstede, Trompenaars and Hampden-Turner effectively concentrate on the 'evidence' of national culture. By measuring such features as value orientations, they rationalize societal constructs and suggest degrees of viability of cultural types. Their vision is 'shareable integrity'. Lessem and Neubauer attempt to survey all aspects of the model, accepting rather than rationalizing societal constructs. They propose differentiation into four types of European management, followed by integration into unity. Their vision appears to be the same as the evidential school, except that it implies that fewer degrees of freedom (cultural styles) are more likely to generate success than the multiplicity of styles possible with the dimensional models. Tayeb attempts a causal integration of all elements of the model to enhance understanding. Bonthous is effectively focusing on the behavioural aspects of the evidence of national cultures, by comparing intelligence methods in different countries. No causal explanation is given, but an increased repertoire of intelligence behaviours is recommended to enhance learning. Said apparently focuses on the arts component of inputs to culture. However, it could be argued that a broad selection of literature contains all the other elements of the model. Said's vision is one of anti-separatism and mutual respect among cultures.

Maznevski (1994) argues that individual cultural awareness is best raised by examining Value Orientations and has used a modified version of Kluckhohn and Strodtbeck's (1961) Value Orientations Instrument to establish cultural position at the beginning of her training sessions. Maznevski's work indicates that raising cultural awareness can lead to improved performance in culturally diverse teams. DiStefano and Lane

Table 3.6 Variables associated with Tayeb's causal model

Organizational Variables	Contingency Factors	Political Economic Factors	Cultural Factors
Centralization	Industry	Economic system (e.g. Capitalist)	Society family, religion, education, class structure, mass media, labour movement, political regime
Perceived autonomy	Product	Trade Union status	
Specialization	Technology	Industrialization	
Formalization	Market Share		National Cultures honesty, trust, independence, group attitudes, tolerance, resourcefulness, attitudes to seniors, acceptance of responsibility, coping with uncertainty, friendliness, fatalism
Span of Control	Size		
Communication Pattern	Age		
Control Systems	Ownership		
Reward Systems	Control		Work Attitudes to power and authority, tolerance of ambiguity, commitment, trust, individualism, job expectations, attitude to control systems, information sharing, participation

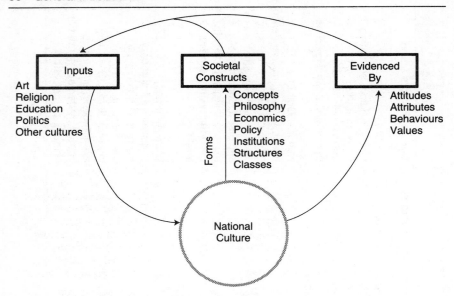

Figure 3.6 A summary model of approaches to national culture

(1992) conclude from a literature review that effective global executives are those with the ability to:

– develop and use global strategic skills
– manage change and transition
– manage cultural diversity
– design and function in flexible organization structures
– work with others and in teams
– communicate
– learn and transfer knowledge in an organization.

They point out that developing these skills is a lifelong activity and it is unlikely that one person can encompass all of the abilities.

The idea that cultural diversity can be managed is echoed in Adler's (1991) work. Adler (1991) found that culturally diverse groups were either very effective or very ineffective, while mono-cultural teams were closely centred around average effectiveness. She concluded that cultural diversity can lead to superior performance when it is well-managed. It is clear from this and from recent work on international manager competences by Gay (1994) that more attention needs to be given to understanding the mechanisms involved in multi-cultural team cooperation and performance.

Given the different researchers' contributions to a wholistic understanding of national culture, combining the findings for different countries

Table 3.7 Combined approaches for France and Germany

	Germany	France
Hofstede, Trompenaars, Hampden-Turner	Universalist Integrative Communitarian Inner-directed Status by achievement Egalitarian Time as sequence	Particularist Integrative Communitarian Outer directed Status by ascription Hierarchical Time as synchronicity
Lessem and Neubauer	Industrial corporation Developmental behaviour Intuitive attitude Production function Systemic structure Social market economy Wholistic philosophy Musical art forms	Administrative corporation Professional behaviour Thinking attitude Control function Hierarchical structure Dirigiste economy National philosophy Architectural art forms
Bonthous	Avoid 'administrative/ detailed' dimension Use the remaining dimensions but show no strong preference for any	Use 'meaningful/ purposeful' dimension more than the other three, but show no marked preference for any

should further enhance understanding. In developing a cross-cultural awareness course, elements of each of the key approaches should perhaps be incorporated into the learning material. Taking Germany and France as examples (because they have been addressed by three of the approaches discussed), the combined findings observed are shown in Table 3.7.

Table 3.7 demonstrates that the different approaches are mutually supportive and, when taken together, provide more information about each culture. The table also highlights how differences can potentially offer more options. The similarities between cultures can be used as the basis for stability, co-operation and mutual respect of differences.

Although there has been an increasing interest in cross-cultural studies in recent years, there is still a great deal of scope for further research. In reviewing international OB/HRM research publications, Adler and Bartholomew (1992) conclude that rigorous academic research needs to catch up with the requirements of industry and that this will, perhaps, require further collaboration between academic and professional communities.

Given the recent changes in Eastern Europe and the opening of China to trade, it would be interesting to carry out more cultural dimensions surveys in these geographical territories. The information gathered may provide useful insights to facilitate cooperation and trade with these areas. There is scope to replicate Bonthous' work in other countries and synthesize the results. This could help companies to set up more appropriate intelligence systems for those countries and could also suggest which nationalities should co-operate to enhance their learning abilities.

The cultural dimensions surveys have not always replicated well. Also, as more studies are carried out, more dimensions seem to emerge. The work done so far warrants further investigation to see if problems arise from instrument reliability and validity or whether Hofstede's assumption that cultures do not change significantly over time is invalid.

Some work has already been done in this field that appears to suggest that Hofstede's work has some validity for the countries he studied, but breaks down when applied to communist regimes (Hoppe, 1990). Smith's (1994) work shows that at least two of Hofstede's dimensions are replicable, namely the Power Distance Index and the Individualism Index. It could be that the dimensional studies are not always replicable because some cultural elements are stable while others are not. Linked with this, it might be possible to identify those factors that facilitate cultural change. Examples of 'invented culture' could be examined to see which ones are enduring and what factors cause this. Given the increased exposure to other cultures, it could be helpful in trying to predict and manage cultural change to understand whether cultures become more homogeneous or entrenched when exposed to influences from external cultures.

It could be argued that Said's work is based on self-selection of key texts and is thus biased – even though he is using methods of analysis that are well accepted in the field of literature critique. A similar argument might be used to question Lessem and Neubauer's work. If these two groups of researcher theories are sound, then another worker, using his or her own self-selected sample ought to reach similar conclusions with a similar analysis. Lessem and Neubauer's work appears to be validated to an extent by the findings of Bonthous and Trompenaars and Hampden-Turner. Combining further the ideas of key researchers could help to generate a causal model for national culture that would provide better understanding of the issues involved in intercultural co-operation. Taking this approach could act as a validation (or otherwise) of Tayeb's work.

Testing Trompenaars' hypothesis that Campbell and Goold's method of strategic control enables cross-cultural management better than other modes of strategic management might have very useful implications for managers. In particular, it would be interesting to determine whether such a system of management really does generate more strategic options.

CONCLUDING REMARKS

The literature review indicates that raising cross-cultural awareness may lead to better communication, shared learning, the generation of more options and potentially better outcomes from the interactions between individuals in a multi-cultural group or organization. Each of the studies discussed reveals different facets of culture which, when taken in combination, could prove to be extremely effective in helping to promote cross-cultural awareness, learning and co-operation, which will in turn lead to more effective intercultural interaction.

REFERENCES

Adler, N.J. (1991) *International Dimensions of Organisational Behaviour*, 2nd edn, PWS-Kent Publishing Company, Boston.

Adler, N.J. and Bartholomew, S. (1992) Academic and professional communities of discourse: generating knowledge on transnational human resource management. *Journal of International Business*, **23**, pp. 551–69.

Berthon, P.R. (1993) Psychological Type and Corporate Culture: Relationship and Dynamics. *Omega*, Vol. 21, pp. 329–44.

Bonthous, J.M. (1994) Culture – the missing intelligence variable. *The Strategic Planning Society News*, March.

Czinkota, A. and Ronkainen, I.A. (1993) *International Marketing*, 3rd edn, The Dryden Press, Orlando.

DiStefano, J.J. and Lane, H.W. (1992) *International Management Behaviour*, 2nd edn, PWS Kent, Boston.

Earley, P.C. and Singh, H. (1995) International and intercultural management research: what's next? *Academy of Management Journal*, **38**, pp. 327–40.

Gay, K. (1994) *Assessing the Importance of Cultural Empathy within a Framework of International Management Competence*. EIASM Workshop, Cross-cultural Perspectives: Comparative Management and Organization, Henley Management College, UK.

Goold, M. and Campbell, A. (1990) *Strategies and Styles: The Role of the Centre in Managing Diversified Corporations*, Blackwell, Oxford.

Goold, M. and Quinn, J.J. (1990) *Strategic Control: Milestones for Long Term Performance*, The Economist Books, London.

Hall, E.T. (1973) *The Silent Language*, Anchor Press, Garden City, N.Y.

Hall, E.T. (1966) *The Hidden Dimension*, Doubleday, Garden City, N.Y.

Hall, E.T. (1960) The silent language in overseas business. *Harvard Business Review*, May–June.

Hall, E.T. and Hall, M.R. (1987) *Hidden Differences: Doing Business with the Japanese*, Anchor Press/Doubleday, Garden City, N.Y.

Hambrick, D.C., Korn, B.L., Frederickson, J.W. and Ferry, R.M. (1989) *21st*

Century Report: Reinventing the CEO, Korn Ferry, New York and Colombia University's Graduate School of Business, pp. 1–94.

Hampden-Turner, C. and Trompenaars, F. (1993) *The Seven Cultures of Capitalism: Value Systems for Creating Wealth in the United States, Britain, Japan, Germany, France, Sweden and the Netherlands*, Doubleday, New York.

Heller, F.A. and Wilpert, B. (1979) Managerial decision-making: an international comparison in *Organisational Functioning in a Cross-Cultural Perspective* (eds England, Neghandi and Wilpert) Kent State, Kent.

Heller, F.A. and Wilpert, B. (1981) *Competence and Power in Managerial Decision-Making*, Wiley, Chichester.

Hofstede, G. (1982) Intercultural Cooperation in Organisations. *Management Decision*, **20**, pp. 53–67.

Hofstede, G. (1991) *Cultures and Organisations, Software of the Mind, Intercultural Cooperation and its Importance for Survival*, McGraw-Hill Book Company, London.

Hofstede, G. (1991a) *Culture's Consequences: Software of the Mind*, McGraw-Hill Book Company, London.

Hofstede, G. (1984) *Culture's Consequences: International Differences in Work-Related Values*, Sage, Beverly Hills.

Hoppe, M.H. (1990) *A comparative study of country elites: International differences in work-related values and learning and their implications for management training and development*, Unpublished PhD thesis, University of North Carolina at Chapel Hill.

Kanungo, R.N. and Medonca, M. (1994) Culture and performance improvement, *Productivity*, **35**, pp. 447–53.

Kiani, R. and Latifi, F. (1995) *The Impact of Ancient, Islamic and Western Culture in Iran's work-related values*. EIASM Workshop: Cross-cultural Perspectives: Comparative Management and Organisation, Henley Management College, UK.

Kluckhohn, F. and Strodtbeck, F.L. (1961) *Variations in Value Orientations*, Greenwood Press, Connecticut.

Kohn, A. (1992) *No Contest – The Case Against Competition*, Houghton Mifflin Company, New York.

Kroeber, A. and Kluckhohn, C. (1985) *Culture: A Critical Review of Concepts and Definitions*, Random House, New York.

Laurent, A. (1983) The cultural diversity of western management conceptions, *International Studies of Management and Organisation*, **8**, pp. 75–6.

Leeds, C. (1994) *Pragmatic and Wholistic Approaches to Management in Newly Emerging Countries*. EIASM Workshop: Cross-cultural Perspectives: Comparative Management and Organisation, Henley Management College, UK.

Lessem, R. and Neubauer, F. (1994) *European Management Systems: Towards Unity out of Cultural Diversity*, McGraw-Hill, London.

Lloyd, B. and Trompenaars, F. (1993) Culture and change: conflict or consensus? *Leadership and Organisational Development Journal*, **14**, pp. 17–23.

Maruyama, M. (1980) Mindscapes and science theories. *Current Anthropology*, **21**, pp. 389–600.

Maruyama, M. (1982) New mindscapes for future business policy and management, *Technology Forecasting and Social Change*, **21**, pp. 53–76.

Maruyama, M. (1984) Alternative concepts of management: insights from Asia and Africa, *Asia Pacific Journal of Management*, **1**, pp. 100–11.

Maznevski, M. (1994) *Synergy and Performance in Multi-cultural Teams*, PhD thesis University of Western Ontario.

Mead, M. (ed) (1951) *Cultural Patterns and Technical Change*, UNESCO, Paris.

Moss Kanter, R. and Corn, R.I. (1994) Do cultural differences make a business difference? Contextual factors affecting cross-cultural relationship success. *Journal of Management Development*, **13**, pp. 5–23.

O'Connor, J. and Seymour, J. (1990) *Introducing Neuro-linguistic Programming: The New Psychology of Personal Excellence*, Mandala, London.

Potter, J.R. (1994) Unpublished seminar material.

Said, E.W. (1991) *Orientalism*, Penguin, London.

Said, E.W. (1994) *Culture and Imperialism*, Vintage, London.

Smith, P. (1994) *National Cultures and the Values of Organisational Employees: Time for Another Look*. EIASM Workshop on Cross-Cultural Perspectives: Comparative Management and Organisation, Henley Management College, UK.

Tayeb, M. (1979) Cultural Determinants of Organisational Response to Environmental Demands. M. Litt. Thesis, University of Oxford.

Tayeb, M. (1988) *Organisations and National Culture*, Sage, London.

Tayeb, M. (1994) Organisations and national culture: methodology considered. *Organisation Studies*, **15**, pp. 429–46.

Trompenaars, F. (1984) *The Organisation of Meaning and the Meaning of Organisation – a comparative study on the conceptions and organisational structure in different cultures*, PhD thesis, University of Pennsylvania.

Trompenaars, F. (1993) *Riding the Waves of Culture: Understanding Cultural Diversity in Business*, The Economist Books, London.

Chapter 4

The role of social science in the study of economic and cultural transformation

Frank Heller

INTRODUCTION

In many countries in different parts of the world – particularly in Central and Eastern Europe – economic and cultural transformation has become a major area of study. What kind of information could be helpful for countries undergoing transformation? Are cultural-historical differences between countries a hindrance to the transfer of ideas or practices or are they successful recipes capable of being adapted in certain circumstances? If adaptation is possible, what are the conditions that facilitate or obstruct the process of transition or change in organizations?

Practice has leapt ahead of theory and evidence, so after 1945 Western Europe was impressed by the obviously successful American organizational practices and set about learning from their experience. Thirty years later, Japan was the model that led America and Western Europe to copy some of their practices – not always successfully. More recently, South Korea, Taiwan and Singapore have been studied by organizational analysts to discover what other countries can learn from the South East Asian tigers.

Countries of Central and Eastern Europe – for instance Poland, the Czech Republic, Hungary and Russia – have particularly acute problems in adjusting their over-centralized economic structures and organizational practices to the prevailing market-oriented western models – see Chapters 13 and 20 in this volume for example. Which examples and experiences are relevant for them?

Several social science disciplines, economics, sociology, psychology and anthropology, have carried out extensive studies on transformation practices and some of their findings are beginning to provide useful guidelines to policy makers. In this paper I will confine myself to discussing five topics related to transformation on which reasonably reliable evidence is available. The topics are: the importance of understanding equilibrium needs when planning for change; the necessity of developing institutional structures before the introduction of market mechanisms; the advantages for motivation and efficiency of some measure of influence-sharing within hierarchical organizations; the relevance of the work ethic; and the need to use a longitudinal analysis in which provision is made for different conditions to apply to different phases of the transformation process.

It is not claimed that these five topics are more important than any others, or that they will satisfactorily answer the questions I have asked, but I believe that organizations subjected to economic and cultural transformation will find that useful guidelines for change can be derived from the social science evidence presented on the five topics.

EQUILIBRIUM NEEDS

A much neglected but almost universal factor in the life of organizations is the need for continuity and equilibrium equivalent to the biological need for homeostasis. (Schön, 1971). This is the basis of resistance to change which students of organization observe everywhere. It operates at the level of individuals as well as organizations and has been neglected because in the second half of the twentieth century the opposite trend, namely turbulence, unpredictability and the need to adjust to competition and new technology, has been much in evidence.

The synchronic need for equilibrium and the diachronic need for change can and do coexist in an uneasy and potentially conflictual relationship which has to be understood and managed. However, a considerable volume of recent literature has supported the desirability for rapid change and pretended that it can be achieved easily and with low cost (Dawson 1994; McCalman and Paton 1992). At the organizational level a front runner is re-engineering, advocated by Hammer and Champy (1994) and in economics a strong supporter is Harvard's Jeremy Sachs, one of the early consultants to President Yeltsin's advisers in Russia. These approaches have run into many difficulties.

The case for rapid and painless change is often based on the writings of consultants who take a broad universalistic, rather than a contingency, approach to change. A contingency approach would carefully distinguish between situations where incremental or rapid change is more appropriate and successful. Two very experienced organizational analysts have come to the conclusion that claims of having achieved lasting and successful reforms are greatly exaggerated (Brunsson and Olson 1993).

In the last four decades China has gone through several very radical political upheavals but at the level of organization, in spite of extensive management development plans and new legislation, progress has been very slow (Whitley, 1992; Child, 1994; Warner, 1995a) but has nevertheless achieved a very high rate of growth.

Compared with China, Japan has had an uneventful, relatively tranquil four decades and with one or two exceptions, organizational life has retained its basic characteristics, most of which have deep historic roots

– see Chapter 14 in this volume, for example. One exception is in its treatment of quality, which was notoriously poor in the 1950s but within a decade and a half had established an enviable reputation for reliability which western countries are even now trying to emulate. This remarkable turn around was achieved through a combination of adopting an American statistical quality control programme (Deming 1982), building quality into its traditional group collaboration culture and adapting the ideas derived from British and Norwegian research on semi-autonomous work groups plus the rapid establishment of a government quality control agency. In this remarkable transformation, the important culturally sanctioned role of the government agency is sometimes under-estimated.

INSTITUTIONAL INFRASTRUCTURE

The strong corporatist influence exerted directly and indirectly by the Japanese government on industry is often cited as one of the reasons for the remarkable Japanese economic success. In 1960, the International Labour Office sent a French expert to Japan and a British expert to Argentina to help with their respective economic development. Both countries were then classified as under-developed. The two ILO experts contributed to one of the first cross-national comparative studies on managerial attitudes and values (Haire *et al.*, 1966). The results of this study show that Japan occupied an attitudinal value position significantly different from Europe, Argentina and Chile. By the 1970s, Argentina and Chile were still classified as under-developed, while Japan was beginning to attract the attention of American business school academics who wanted to discover the secret of their rapid progress.

The different rates of economic development would be explained by the new school of institutional economics in terms of what North (1990) calls the 'rules of the game'; that is to say, the institutional constraints or facilitators that provide a structure to everyday life and, in particular, to economic activity. North makes the important point that neo-classical economics cannot explain why poor or under-developed countries should not easily catch up simply by emulating the economic policies of the more successful economies. To explain why this catching up does not occur and why the differences are frequently perpetuated over long periods, one has to look at the institutional infrastructures, one of which is the educational system. Furthermore, one of the missing links in traditional economic theory is 'an understanding of the nature of human co-ordination and co-operation' (p. 11) and he mentions uniformities that are transmitted from one generation to the next and can be called 'culture' (pp. 36–7). He gives examples of informal conventions in modern society that solve co-ordination problems. An example is the punctuality habit, which is more highly developed in economically successful than unsuccessful societies. Economists see the outcome of informal conventions and habits, for instance the acceptance of 'my word is my bond' in terms of low transaction costs. Conventions acquire a moral force that has economic benefits.

If one looks at the different values between Argentina and Chile on the one hand and Japan on the other, as shown in the Haire *et al.* study (1966) and adds the institutional conditions listed by North, the differential rate of economic development of these two parts of the world is unsurprising.

Then there are formal institutional arrangements, like rules of contract, patent law, and clearly formulated property laws, monopoly rules, stock exchange regulation and surveillance and so on. These rules have to be accepted and enforced. At this point it is worth remembering that North is not only an economist but a recent Nobel laureate who goes on to disagree with most of his neo-classical colleagues by supporting a clear and important role for the state and an acceptance that voluntarism does not often work, so that formal social rules have to be coercively enforced (p. 58). He keeps his analysis largely in terms of transaction costs, saying that the successful enforcement of a purely voluntary system is prohibitively costly. He gives the example of countries that spend large amounts of scarce financial resources on higher education when investment in elementary education has a much higher social rate of return in Third World countries. In such cases, he argues, governments should have stepped in when the market did not allocate resources appropriately (p. 80).

The same theoretical approach would also explain the coexistence of rapid privatization and ferocious criminal activity in the former Soviet Union, where no attempt was made to impose the kind of legal-structural control mechanisms which are taken for granted in countries practising a competitive market economy. North is not afraid to make simple, almost banal points, like drawing attention to the cost of useless inspection or multiple form-filling which one finds very much in evidence in China and South America. Central and East European countries often use bureaucratic procedures to create employment as well as to control dishonesty; they were more successful in the former than in the latter intention. These procedures continue when they have outlived their original function. For instance in 1994, trying to buy a ticket for an international train at Budapest's main station was an obstacle course. However, it was quite easy to pay on the train, where the conductor would pretend that he had temporarily run out of tickets so that he could keep the cash.

Japan, on the other hand, uses bureaucratic procedures intelligently and is prepared to incur transaction costs for elaborate inspection procedures, form-filling and delaying tactics to slow down or restrict the importation of foreign products.

Two other points from Douglass North's institutional economics are important for understanding issues of transformation. One is his emphasis on skills and competence to produce *adaptive efficiency* which is concerned with developing the rules and structures that support a growing economy through time and are quite different from the traditional emphasis on *allocative efficiency*. Adaptive efficiency emphasizes the acquisition of knowledge and supports risk and innovation leading to the second point, which shows that societal and economic changes are marginal adjustments in an incremental process based on routines, customs, traditions and conventions supported by formal rules and informal conventions. Adaptation and change are slow processes.

Most of the new angles in North's economics, in particular his stress on the role of formal and informal institutions, have extensive antecedents in other social science disciplines since the writings of Herbert Spencer (*First Principles*, 1862). However, this analysis has now become more important by being linked with transaction costs and economics, which is a discipline that has easy access to policy makers. Policy makers in transforming economics have been heavily preoccupied by the important role of the market as the centrepiece of a system which, according to Hayek (1945) will fairly automatically regulate prices and other factors to return to equilibrium. Institutional economics pays much more attention to actors inside organizations, their motivation and effectiveness (Williamson 1985). Another important theoretical approach which substantially reduces the role of the market is put forward by Herbert Simon (1991) who bases his arguments on empirical socio-psychologically oriented research. He strongly supports the need for transforming economies to pay attention to intra-organizational mechanisms like co-ordination, incentives, power, authority, quality and employee satisfaction. Simon concludes that the economies of modern industrialized society can more appropriately be called organizational economies than market economies (Simon 1991: 42).

DISTRIBUTION OF ORGANIZATIONAL POWER

The industrial organizational models we admire change over time. In the nineteenth century the preferred role models came from Britain; in the early part of the twentieth century, under the influence of Frederick Winslow Taylor, they came from the United States. After the Second World War, there were three models in rapid succession: first, the United States, sheltered from the immediate ravages of the war, then Scandinavia, and third, Japan from about 1975. Who next?

In the 1960s a number of influential publications explored the reason why American business earned a higher return on invested capital than European business (OECD 1968; Diebolt 1968; Caves 1968). Was the efficiency gap due to technology, inventiveness, capital investment, or the quality of management? A considerable body of informed opinion came to the conclusion that the gap was managerial (Granick 1962; PEP 1965; Smith 1968; Haenni 1969). Servan Schreiber, in his influential *The American Challenge* (1967) looked at the various alternative explanations and came to the conclusion that American organizations were more democratically run than European organizations. To check this view, an eight-country cross-national research project was designed to explore the possibility that American business executives shared influence more extensively than their European counterparts (Heller and Wilpert 1981). While very significant country differences were found, the USA-Europe gap in democratic decision making was only partly confirmed. Swedish top and second level managers practised more participation than USA managers, but top level American managers behaved more democratically than their counterparts in the Netherlands, Germany, the UK, and Spain. More important than participation differences among countries was the finding that democratic decision making practices, wherever they occur, liberate competence.

Since then, this topic (under a variety of names) has become an important focus of analysis in comparative studies of managerial efficiency between countries. The terms used include: leadership styles, participation, involvement, semi-autonomous groups, team working, empowerment, co-operation, consensus management, and organizational democracy.

The extraordinarily rapid and successful economic growth of Japan has led to attempts all over the world to copy quality circles and other participative practices. At least one well known American consultant and academic has gone on record with the view that if American industry wants to compete in the world, it has to adopt Japanese-style democratic decision making practices (Lawler 1986). Presumably such a recommendation would apply to any country or organization eager to compete in the world.

However, the transfer of allegedly successful practices from one country to another has not always been easy, smooth or effective. There are several reasons: one is the ubiquitous resistance to change analysed earlier, another is a misunderstanding of the essential ingredients of the practice or the attempt to cut corners and, of course, there is always the possibility that certain practices have, as Douglass North has argued, long incrementally developed gestation periods which cannot be instantly adopted in a different socio-economic setting. The failure of quality circles in other countries has been well documented. (Drago 1988; Lawler *et al.* 1992).

Doubts have been raised about the uniqueness of the Japanese system or understanding it correctly in the popular literature [Abegglen 1958; Dale 1986; Ouchi 1981). Some comparative studies have found surprisingly little difference between the Japanese leadership style and that used in other countries (Misumi 1984). Xu (1989), for instance, compared large samples of Chinese managers with Misumi's findings on Japanese managers and found almost no difference.[1] A replication study in China of managerial decision styles in Britain (Heller *et al.*, 1979) also found only small differences (Ma and Heller 1991).[2] The stereotyped view that all important decisions in Japanese companies are taken by the bottom up *ringi seido* method is a gross over-simplification (Heller and Misumi 1987). It has even been alleged that a substantial element in the Japanese organizational culture can be traced back to the fairly pervasive impact of Taylorism on Japanese companies, starting with the introduction of motion studies into Nippon Electric in 1908 and the translation of Taylor's *Scientific Management* into Japanese in 1912 (Warner 1994).

Similarly, it is not possible to understand the Chinese management system today without an understanding of the heavy and perseverating influence of the 'legacy of High Stalinism' which became deeply entrenched in all large-scale Chinese enterprises during the 1950s (Kaple 1994). Even so, a knowledge of historic-cultural differences does not substantially help policy-makers who want to speed up the process of transformation. For instance, there is little doubt that the distribution of power in organizations plays an important part in understanding the process of economic development looked at in a historic perspective. Given our present knowledge about the positive effect influence-sharing practices have on liberating hidden resources of skill and innovation and how much they contribute to flexible group-determined work practices, it is tempting to advise countries in transition from statism to a market system to adopt such practices, often abbreviated into the acronym HRM (Human Resource Management). Such advice could be counter-productive.

In the case of China, two experienced analysts (Child 1994 and Warner 1995a) agree 'that HRM is too culturally infused with Western values to be as yet on the Chinese menu' (Warner 1995b). We must also remember that several of the East Asian 'Little Dragon' countries have used very controversial autocratic hierarchical structures with no power distribution and such autocracy is often credited with being functional in early stages of development (McRae 1994).

In the case of some Central and East European countries one could expect that their historic cultural alignment with Western Europe would soon lead enterprises to use HRM practices, but this is not yet in evidence. In this connection the role of joint ventures may be very important in Central and Eastern European countries as they have been in China. For instance, a joint Hungarian-British food processing company has developed a high profile in HRM practices, almost certainly influenced by the fact that the British partner in the joint venture has for many years had an excellent reputation for participative, joint consultative management (Markóczy 1993). For an American example, see Balaton (1994).

WORK RELATED VALUES

The relation of work values to economic development has become an important issue since the well-known work of Max Weber (1930) and Richard Tawney (1926). Both, in different ways, came to the conclusion that the rise and growth of capitalism in Western Europe was significantly influenced by Protestantism; hence the term 'the Protestant Work Ethic'. While this historic relationship was well documented, its post-modern validity was worth examining.[3] A multi-national team from Germany, Belgium, Israel, the United States, Japan, the Netherlands, Yugoslavia and Britain conducted extensive research and came to the somewhat unexpected conclusion that the work ethic was alive and well in Japan, Israel and Yugoslavia – countries in which Protestantism was conspicuously absent. At the same time, the Work Ethic, or more precisely the values which gave centrality to working in people's lives compared with other activities, came low in Britain, Germany and the Netherlands (MOW 1987).

One interpretation of this finding is to associate high work centrality scores with people who were ambitious to achieve high real standards of life[4] and who lived in countries that had become industrialized later than the countries that scored low on work centrality (Heller, 1987). In this interpretation, one would expect the Little Dragon as well as Central and Eastern European countries to have high work centrality, but one would also expect work centrality to diminish as the real standard of life increases and offers people a choice of other activities. In this interpretation there need be no connection between the work ethic and productivity.

A closer look at the work ethic statistics produces a useful policy-oriented finding that brings us back to the discussion on the distribution of organizational power. If we take the total seven-country sample of over 14,000 individuals and divide them by the nature of their work, we find that irrespective of country, work centrality is consistently higher in jobs that enjoy a measure of autonomy and self-direction (MOW, 1987: 261–263).[5] In policy terms this means that if countries in transition from centralized to decentralized economies want to benefit from a population that identifies with a high work centrality, then it would be worth persuading companies to redesign as many jobs as possible to give them a higher degree of influence or even to legislate for a measure of organizational democracy, as Germany did after the Second World War (IDE, 1981b). In other words, decentralizing a command economy at the macro level or organizational ownership could be paralleled by a decentralization of the intra-organizational command structure.

HISTORY, LONGITUDE AND PHASES

In a way, everything I have said so far shows that the analysis of transition issues requires a historic-longitudinal design or interpretation. I want to underscore this now with a few examples from each of the sections covered so far.

I have started by showing that equilibrium rather than change is the natural and preferred condition for individuals as well as society. This does not preclude development and adjustment in conformity with changing circumstances. It does call into question the functionality of a deliberate imposition of rapid alien conditions.

Institutional economics, looking at the historic development and evolution of organizational life comes to similar conclusions by showing that the growth of formal and informal rules of the game is an incremental process, although there is no reason why this should take as long as it does in many of the under-developed countries.

Institutional theories have looked at the transformation processes in Eastern Europe and have concluded that 'the reforms have been based on the unrealistic assumption that the spontaneous market mechanism does exist' whereas they would argue that 'markets cannot be established overnight and, moreover, they require conscious and deliberate action by the state; consequently, the argument goes, it was a mistake to attempt to stabilize the post-socialist economies with purely market-oriented macro economic measures which may be effective only under properly functioning market mechanisms, implying rational behaviour at the micro level' (Rosati 1994: 429). These arguments are not against the use of markets but in support of a carefully phased and planned introduction.

Most of the arguments and nearly all the research on the distribution of organizational power neglect the developmental aspect and I have given a number of examples. In addition, it can be shown that differences in influence distribution occur at different phases of the decision process and can be justified functionally. The first systematic cross-national investigation of power in the longitudinal decision process was reported by Heller, Drenth, Koopman and Rus (1988). It took place in the Netherlands, Yugoslavia and Britain. Some years later this research design was replicated on a sample of Chinese and British companies (Ma and Heller 1991). The decision process was divided into four phases: start up, development, finalization and implementation. In strategic decision, the cycle could take over a year. The amount of influence (participation) exercised by employees differed significantly over the four phases. Lower level employees had almost no influence in the first three phases, but were able to participate to some extent in the implementation phase. Foremen had some influence in the start up phase and more in implementation. At these two levels the Chinese results were very similar to Britain's. At the Representative Body level there were important differences. In the Chinese companies, the Representative Body had much less influence in all phases, but least in the final phase. British Representative Bodies exercised on average more influence than workers and foremen and were particularly influential during the implementation of the decision. The policy implication of this finding is that democratization is not an all or nothing process; by having influence distributed by phases, it is possible to take account of skill differences in the process of transformation and, nevertheless, to achieve some of the beneficial motivating and competence utilization outcomes which modern research has demonstrated.

SUMMARY AND CONCLUDING REMARKS

Comparative studies of the process of transforming economies from one system to another are sometimes geared towards issues that have little policy relevance. In this chapter we have dealt with five topics derived from social science research that have potentially practical implications for organizational policy makers.

We started by asking a few questions. Given that we recognize important historic, legal, structural and socio-cultural differences between countries, what scope is there for learning from each other? Are the differences so profound that each country has to find its own unique transformation path? Alternatively, is the economic success of one politico-economic system so overwhelmingly obvious that the best option for developing or transforming countries is to adopt all the main characteristics of the successful model?

These questions and possible alternatives between positions will be debated for a long time and require a very extensive review of evidence and choices between different theories. There is a tendency for these debates to be strictly discipline-oriented so that theories derive, *inter alia*, from economics, or from sociology or social psychology, but I believe that ultimately, solutions require a problem-oriented systems perspective in which disciplinary knowledge will be used sparingly (Bertalanffy 1993).

In the meantime, the present chapter tries to make a limited contribution to the problems faced by economies in transformation by analysing a number of policy-relevant topics which straddle the major disciplines.

In the first place, I argue that change, particularly radical change, is not a natural process for either individuals or organizations. While change is with us all the time and has become more ubiquitous and fast moving in recent decades, it is usually resisted and often sabotaged. Successful reform or transformation has to be carefully planned for timing, phasing, appropriate speed, and socio-cultural considerations.

Secondly, a relatively new school of economics which would support the psycho-social evidence on the problematics associated with rapid change, also stresses the need for a careful build up of formal and informal structures to facilitate the transformation process. While structural economics accepts the market as a mechanism, it gives more important emphasis to an analysis of processes and transactions between and within organizations and their costs. The transactions are facilitated or obstructed by structures and control mechanisms, many of which are most appropriately carried out or monitored by the state. Attempts to move quickly from a centralized to a market system without the necessary structural, social, legal and political institutions firmly in place, is likely to be disastrous.

Then there is the question of the distribution of power from the state to organizations, between organizations (monopoly or competition) and within organizations (organizational democracy). The location of power at these levels varies extensively between highly and less highly developed economies. Economic success seems to be positive with different models of power concentration (Far East versus Western economies) but it seems that in a longitudinal analysis, power concentration is more usual in early phases of development, while decentralization occurs in later phases.

The longitudinal-phase approach in relation to the problems of transition and power needs to be developed much further and should be conceptualized in a system perspective from macro, via meso, to micro levels of change. The important role of the work ethic in stimulating economic development for instance can, it seems, be traced back to the difference between centralized (hierarchical) versus decentralized (semi-autonomous) job design, irrespective of country. This means that under the hierarchical Tayloristic organizational designs practised in the countries under Soviet influence, the work ethic would be low. As these countries try to adjust to a more decentralized market-oriented behaviour, they could also attempt to design work to give individuals and groups more influence over their work cycle. The research findings suggest that democratizing organizational decision making could significantly increase the work ethic, thus facilitating economic transformation. This could explain why Japan, Israel and Yugoslavia scored high on the work ethic. Many years later, when economies are highly developed and produce a satisfactory standard of life, other life interests will take precedence and the work ethic can then afford to take up a lower priority. This could explain the relatively low work centrality scores of Germany, Netherlands and the UK (MOW 1986: 88).[6] This example further supports the need for treating economic and cultural transformation within a longitudinal phase model so as to obtain more accurate policy-relevant guidelines.

ENDNOTES

1 The comparison was based on an extensively validated scale called PM developed by Misumi and derived from the well-known Ohio Leadership study distinction between concern for people compared with concern for productivity.
2 The scale used in this research was based on the Influence-Power-Continuum (IPC) extensively used in previous research, for instance Heller 1971; IDE, 1981.
3 Following Toynbee, I use the term 'post-modern' to describe the period between the two world wars and beyond (Docherty 1993: 2).
4 I endorse Erikson's (1993) assessment that 'by the 1950s, it had already become clear that, in spite of its widespread use, per capita GNP is an insufficient measure of the well-being of citizens. A real standard of life includes living space, opportunities to travel and choose to practice a variety of sports and leisure activities.'
5 This comes out particularly clearly in a sub-sample of 6,000 who were chosen to represent certain 'target groups', some of which were skilled and others not.
6 In this schema, a low work ethic score can characterize countries or organizations at an early as well as a late stage of economic development. It applies to an early stage if work structures are hierarchical and non-participatory but also to a late stage when standards of living have risen to a point where people choose to reduce the centrality of work in order to give more time and weight to leisure, family, or social pursuits.

REFERENCES

Abegglen, J.C. (1958) *The Japanese Factory: Aspects of its social organisation*, The Free Press, Glencoe, Ill.

Balaton, K. (1994) Implementing corporate management system abroad: General Motors in Hungary, in *Convergence versus Divergence: The Case of the Corporate Culture* (eds C. Makó and P. Novoszáth) Institute for Social Conflict Research, Hungarian Academy of Sciences, pp. 123–50.

von Bertalanffy, L. (1993) *General System Theory: Foundation, Development, Applications*, rev. edn, 11th printing. George Braziller, New York.

Brunsson, N. and Olsen, J. (1993) *The Reforming Organization*, Routledge, New York and London.

Caves, R.E. and Associates (1968) *Britain's Economic Prospects*, Allen & Unwin, London.

Child, J. (1994) *Management in China During the Age of Reforms*, Cambridge University Press, Cambridge.

Dale, P. (1986) *The Myth of Japanese Uniqueness*, Croom Helm, London.

Dawson, P. (1994) *Organizational Change: A Processual Approach*, Paul Chapman, London.

Deming, W.E. (1982) *Quality, productivity and competitive position*, MIT Centre for Advanced Engineers Studies, Boston, MA.

Diebolt, J. (1968) Is the gap technological? *Foreign Affairs*, **46**, pp. 276–91.

Docherty, T. (ed) (1993) *Postmodernism: A Reader*, Harvester Wheatsheaf, London.

Drago, R. (1988) Quality circle survival: an exploratory analysis. *Industrial Relations*, **27**, pp. 336–51.

Erikson, R. (1993) Descriptions of inequality: The Swedish approach to welfare research, in *The Quality of Life* (eds M. Nussbaum and A. Sen) Clarendon Press, Oxford, pp. 67–83.

Granick, D. (1962) *The European Executive*, Weidenfeld and Nicolson, London.

Haenni, P. (1969) Management gap in a world context: a spectral analysis. *Progress, Unilever Quarterly*, **2**, 1969, pp. 106–14.

Haire, M., Ghiselli, E.E. and Porter, L.W. (1966) *Managerial Thinking: An International Study*, John Wiley & Sons, New York.

Hammer, M. and Champy, J. (1994) *Reengineering the Corporation: A Manifesto for Business Revolution*. Brealey, London.

Hayek, F. (1945) The use of knowledge in society. *American Economic Review*, **35**, pp. 519–30.

Heller, F.A. (1971) *Managerial Decision-Making: A Study of Leadership And Power Sharing Among Senior Managers*, Tavistock Publications, London.

Heller, F.A. (1987) The disappearing work ethic. *Business and Economics Review*, **3**, Cardiff Business School, UWIST.

Heller, F.A. and Wilpert, B. (1981) *Competence And Power In Managerial Decision Making: A Study Of Senior Levels Of Organization In Eight Countries*, John Wiley & Sons, Chichester.

Heller, F.A. and Misumi, J. (1987) Decision making, in *Organizational Psychology: An International Review* (eds B. Bass, P. Drenth and P. Weissenberg) Sage Publications, Beverly Hills, pp. 207–19.

Heller, F.A., Drenth, P., Koopman, P. and Rus, V. (1988) *Decisions In Organizations: A Longitudinal Study Of Routine, Tactical And Strategic Decisions*, Sage Publications, London and Beverly Hills.

IDE (Industrial Democracy in Europe Research Group (1981a) *European Industrial Relations*, Oxford University Press.

IDE (Industrial Democracy in Europe Research Group) (1981b) *Industrial Democracy In Europe*, Oxford University Press.

Kaple, D. (1994) *Dream of a Red factory: The Legacy of High Stalinism in China*, Oxford University Press, Oxford.

Lawler, E. (1986) *High Involvement Management: Participative Strategies For Improving Organizational Performance*, Jossey-Bass, San Francisco.

Lawler, E., Ledford, G. and Mohrman, S. (1992) *Employee Involvement and Total Quality*, Jossey-Bass, San Francisco.

Ma, Jian Hong and Heller, F.A. (1991) A phase-related analysis of influence distribution within organizations: A China-Britain comparison. *Tavistock Institute paper*.

Markóczy, L. (1993) Managerial and organizational learning in Hungarian-Western mixed management organizations. *The International Journal of Human Resources Management,* **4**, pp. 273–304.

McCalman, J. and Paton, R. (1992) *Change Management: A Guide to Effective Implementation,* Paul Chapman, London.

McRae, H. (1994) *The World in 2020,* Harper Collins, London.

Misumi, Jyuji (1984) Decision making in Japanese groups and organizations, in *International Yearbook Of Organizational Democracy,* Volume II (eds B. Wilpert and A. Sorge) John Wiley & Sons, Chichester, pp. 525–39.

MOW (Meaning of Working) (1987) *The Meaning of Working,* Academic Press, London.

North, D.C. (1990) *Institutions, Institutional Change and Economic Performance,* Cambridge University Press, Cambridge.

OECD (1968) *The Technological Gap: General Report,* Paris.

Ouchi, W.G. (1981) *Theory Z – How American Business Can Meet the Japanese Challenge,* Addison-Wesley, Reading, MA.

PEP Report (1965) *Thrusters and Sleepers,* Allen and Unwin, London.

Rosati, D.K. (1994) Output decline during transition from plan to market: a reconsideration. *The Economics of Transition,* **2**, pp. 419–41.

Schön, D.A. (1971) *Beyond the Stable State.* The 1970 Reith Lectures, Maurice Temple-Smith, London.

Servan Schreiber, J. (1967) *The American Challenge,* Hamish Hamilton, London.

Simon, H.A. (1991) Organizations and markets. *Journal of Economic Perspectives 1991,* **5**, pp. 25–44.

Smith, D. (1968) The 'gap' that is a chasm. *International Management,* May.

Spencer, H. (1862) *First Principles.*

Tawney, R.H. (1926) *Religion and the Rise of Capitalism: A historical study.* Holland Memorial Lectures 1922, John Murray, London.

Warner, M. (1994) Japanese culture, western management: Taylorism and human resources in Japan. *Organization Studies,* **15**, pp. 509–33.

Warner, M. (1995a) *The Management of Human Resources in China,* Macmillan, Basingstoke.

Warner, M. (1995b) Managing human resources in East Asia. *The International Journal of Human Resource Management,* **6**, pp. 177–80.

Weber, M. (1930) *The Protestant Ethic and the Spirit of Capitalism,* George Allen & Unwin, London.

Whitley, R.D. (1992) *Business systems in East Asia: Firms, Markets and Societies,* Sage, London.

Williamson, O.E. (1985) *The Economic Institutions of Capitalism,* The Free Press, New York.

Xu, Lian-cang (1989) Comparative study of leadership between Chinese and Japanese Managers based upon PM theory in *Advances in Industrial Organizational Psychology* (eds B.J. Fallon, H.P. Pfister and J. Brebner) Elsevier Science Publishers BV, North Holland, pp. 253–59.

Chapter 5

Pragmatic and wholist approaches to management in emerging and newly emergent democracies

Christopher Leeds

INTRODUCTION

Research on democracies in the recent past reveals a range of opinions as to the precise number of countries which meet democratic standards (Almond 1993: 124, 126; Birch 1993: 46; Sorensen 1993: 18–20). Those outside Northern America and Western Europe with a relatively older, stronger democratic tradition include Japan, India, Uruguay, Chile, Botswana and Costa Rica. Emerging, or emergent, democracies since the early 1980s include Hungary, Poland, the Czech Republic, Bulgaria and Slovakia in Central Europe; South Korea, Singapore and Malaysia in Asia; Argentine, Brazil and Nicaragua in Central and South America; The Gambia and Morocco in Africa; Sri Lanka, Papua New Guinea and The Lebanon. Areas particularly notable in terms of economic progress and industrial modernization since 1980 are Latin America, South East Asia and Central Europe. Most of the mature democracies are part of the Western world.

Insights into how people think and communicate across cultures can be gained from research in disciplines such as philosophy, psychology, neurosciences, sociology, anthropology and human resources management. From the earliest times, people have reflected on the meaning of existence and how they personally related to the wider cosmos. The concepts of pragmatism and wholism are pertinent to problems of establishing harmonious parts-whole relationships, whether in the broad fields of knowledge, religion or politics, or in specific areas such as business management.

William James (1842–1910), psychologist and philosopher, argued that people are a mixture of opposite ingredients. In philosophy the relevant terms, he suggests, for how people interpret the universe are the rationalist (who appreciates abstract eternal principles) and the empiricist (who stresses facts). As people need both facts and principles, the difference is one of emphasis (James, 1907: 19–20).

A later work, which includes a synopsis of the philosophy of James, stresses empiricism/pragmatism as contrasting with monism (original synonym for wholism) rather than with rationalism (Perry 1919: 242). Ideas are generally only valued if shown to have rapid aplicability in reality, or if they can be verified by perception, proven consistency or general utility (Perry 1919: 199, 205). Lessem and Neubauer (1994) point out in a recent work, discussed in section 1, that rationalism philosophically stands in an intermediate position between pragmatism and wholism and that these three philosophies or ideas, together with humanism, are not only the core values respectively of different parts of Europe but are found world-wide. Rationalism shares with pragmatism an analytical approach and with wholism an intellectual synthesizing one. Pragmatism shares a practical orientation with humanism.

The newer democracies are undergoing rapid political, social and economic changes. Studies by Hofstede (1991), Trompenaars (1993), Lessem and Neubauer (1994) and others point to the extremely diverse nature of Western Europe culturally, with significant areas sharing features found in management and business practices elsewhere. Consequently, this chapter outlines two broad categories of both pragmatism and wholism. The first, covering most of the West, shares common elements including rationalism and universalism (section 1). This form is compared with the second which reflects important areas of the non-Western values or traits shared, including humanism and particularism (section 2). Owner-entrepreneurs or managers generally who deal with, or work within, the newer democracies will no doubt appreciate from this study that many specific problems they face in achieving whole-parts harmonies, as in the case of relations between head office and subsidiaries, are echoed in other aspects of life.

1 UNIVERSALISM, PRAGMATISM AND WHOLISM

In the early 1970s Hofstede (1991) developed four dimensions based on tests of work values among IBM managers in over 50 countries – see Chapter 9 in this book. European countries in the survey included Austria, Switzerland, Greece and the former Yugoslavia. European countries are situated near, if not at the end of these four dimensions – low/high Power Distance, Individualism-Collectivism, Masculinity-Femininity, weak/strong uncertainty avoidance. Later, after a further study by Michael Hoppe in the early 1980s validated his research, Hofstede found that in relation to his four dimensions, Europe was not particularly unique culturally compared with the rest of the world (Hofstede 1993: 9,10). More recent research came to a similar conclusion (Lessem and Neubauer 1994: 28,35).

Hofstede found that Northern Europe and Northern American societies are characterized by high individualism and that individualism is much lower elsewhere, including parts of Southern Europe such as Greece and Portugal. Universalism implies that certain beliefs or practices apply globally and that rules or laws ought to be enforced equitably and uniformly. In business, the general maxim is that sound practices and procedures involve treating everyone the same (Hofstede 1991: 66; Triandis 1990: 83).

Hofstede places universalism and particularism as sub-categories of individualism and collectivism respectively. In contrast, Trompenaars develops universalism-particularism as a special dimension distinct from individualism-collectivism. His findings, however, tend to confirm the belief that universalism and individualism are closely correlated. Like Hofstede, he carried out a survey in over 50 countries, but this time among Shell managers.

One of the questions asked by Trompenaars in his world-wide survey tested adherence to traffic laws (universalism) as against loyalty to a particular friend, possibly in serious trouble because he had hit a pedestrian while exceeding the speed limit. The most universalistic responses ('telling the truth') came from Northern American and Northern European participants – see Chapter 17 in this book.

The lower end of the scale included managers from quite a number of newly emergent democracies. Below are some examples.

Explanations for the particularistic responses are provided in section 2.

Carl Jung (1875–1961), Swiss psychiatrist and psychologist, describes the four functions of consciousness as: thinking, sensation, intuition and feeling. Two writers, basing their findings relating to the brain primarily on the work of Carl Jung and the Myers Briggs duo (mother and daughter) provide philosophical and psychological evidence for four basic Western European management styles based on four core values respectively (Lessem and Neubauer 1994: 20–4). *Pragmatism* describes the Anglo-Saxons (including the United States and Canada), seen as primarily sense-based, supported by thinking. *Rationalism* characterizes the Franco-Nordic group (thinking supported by intuition) and *Wholism* the Germanic cluster (largely intuition and feeling) associated with Japanese values. *Humanism* is applied to the Italian/Latin group (feeling supported by intuition).

Lessem and Neubauer regard Britain as the country most representative of pragmatic behaviour, although pragmatism also extends further afield, including Scandinavia and the United States. They consider Scotland to be the part of Britain most affected by rationalism. Surprisingly, these researchers only refer to Holland and Sweden as having elements of a wholistic approach in addition to Germany, the country most representative of this value. The results of various surveys, as summarized by Ronen (1986) and discussed below, place Austria, Switzerland and Germany in the same cultural cluster.

Much of the world, based on the findings of various researchers, has

Table 5.1 % of universalitic responses

Order	22	23	24	25	30	26	27	28
Country	France	Japan	Singapore	Spain	Greece	Uruguay	Thailand	Mexico
% Universalistic	68	67	67	65	58	65	63	61

Order	31	32	33	35	36	37	38	
Country	Bulgaria	H.K.	Malaysia	Indonesia	Russia	Venezuela	S. Korea	
% Universalistic	56	56	55	47	42	34	28	

(Adapted from Trompenaars 1993: 35)

been divided into broad regions sharing common core values, management styles and work values. One such classification by Ronen and Shenkar (Ronen 1986: 262) splits Western Europe into five categories, which in some cases overlap with non-European countries. These are Near Eastern, (Greece, Yugoslavia, Turkey, Iran); Anglo (Britain, Ireland, United States, Canada, Australia, South Africa); Latin European (Italy, Spain, Portugal, France, Belgium); Nordic (Finland, Norway, Denmark, Sweden); and Germanic (Germany, Austria, Switzerland).

Ronen (1986) stresses that such a categorization is not definitive and that a number of these countries may also fit into other combinations. France and Belgium, for example, are alternatively placed in a category of their own, as is Greece within the Latin European group. The overall categories are useful, however, in distinguishing between countries largely influenced respectively by pragmatic traditions (the Anglo group) and wholism (the Germanic group) within the Western world.

Hofstede (1991) places over fifty countries in four categories, based on two of his four original cultural dimensions, namely uncertainty avoidance and power distance. Category 1 (likened to a village market) covers eleven countries characterized by small power distance (flat hierarchies in business) and weak uncertainty avoidance. These are basically the 'pragmatic' countries (including Canada, United States, Australia, New Zealand, Ireland, Britain, Sweden, Norway and Denmark), the most individualist and universalistic which rely often on ad hoc solutions to problems.

Category 2 (well-oiled machine) characterized by low power distances and strong uncertainty avoidance, covers the Germanic areas (West Germany, Austria, Finland and a large part of Switzerland) and three other established democracies – Costa Rica, Israel and Finland. Features include following well-defined and thought-out principles and procedures within an egalitarian ethos. Categories 3 and 4 (the latter including Southern Europe and a large number of newly emergent democracies) are discussed in section 2.

The older democracies and most prominent market economies are in categories 1 and 2, except for France, Italy and Japan. Holland has been said, in terms of management style, to be mid-way between Britain (in the same category 1) and Germany, (category 4) combining informal, pragmatic and consensual, fairly structured, approaches (Simonet 1992: 92, 96). This indicates the possibility of harmonizing pragmatic and wholistic styles of management.

Rationalism is a core Western universal value associated with a structured, ordered world and different aspects of this concept link with pragmatism and wholism respectively. Until the seventeenth century, the teachings of churchmen and scholars tended to be accepted, based on classical Greek thinking, as 'how things were'. The Greeks believed that all knowledge and truth originated in ideas discovered through rational thought processes, independent of the real world. René Déscartes, French philosopher, argued in *Discourse on Method* (1637), following Plato, that scientific conclusions can be formed by purely logical deduction from self-evident premises. However, he differed from the Greeks in stressing that each individual person could do this by analysis through deconstructing wholes into various constituent parts, rather than merely relying on the received wisdom of others. Rationalism pervades business organizations today to the extent that they conform to Weberian bureaucratic, formalized and structured forms.

Humanism in the Renaissance period highlighted not only the civilizing influence of classical studies of ancient Greece and Rome but, in a more general sense, emphasized the human or personal dimension in life as opposed to rationalism ideas, deterministic dogmas, ideologies and utilitarian science. Humanism is discussed in more detail in section 2. Early pragmatic thinkers include Elizabethan statesman Francis Bacon and the philosophers John Locke and David Hume. Pragmatism challenged the belief, held by many philosophers from Plato up to and including Déscartes, that much useful knowledge results from a priori thinking or innate ideas. In contrast the pragmatists argued, as Locke did in *Essay Concerning Human Understanding* (1690), that knowledge came from experience, or the association of ideas occurring close in space or time. Pragmatism also developed as a revolt against doctrinaire, 'wholistic' thought patterns associated with idealist or metaphysical German thinkers such as Spinoza, Kant and Hegel.

Pragmatism implies adapting to a situation as it evolves, being flexible, practical and realistic. Pragmatists dislike making detailed plans or extensive commitments in advance which may require fundamental alterations. Pragmatists, relying on sense experience, examine an event or process in its various components. They value finite knowledge, envisaging parts of reality which are self-sufficient though possibly related, without necessarily being aware of the whole. They think inductively, focusing on fragmented pieces of information, specific details and immediate problems, moving rapidly from one urgent matter to another. Their qualities have been associated with the early entrepreneurial stages of a business. Considered to be improvisers, they often thrive in unfamiliar, uncertain conditions. Effective implementation of projects may be delayed by cautious incrementalism and short-termism, or determination to act without sufficient background preparation.

British pragmatism is reflected generally in those aspects of the legal system which are based on precedents and case law and in politics by the uncodified and partially unwritten constitution characterized by conventions or accepted practices. British management has been associated historically with pragmatism or practical experience rather than with professionalism or theory. Managers are expected to be dynamic, quick-witted, decisive and opportunistic – qualities valued more than specific qualifications (Handy 1987: 10). Planning in respect to forecasting long-term changes or identifying market opportunities has been considered rudimentary in most British companies, outside the largest and most sophisticated (Mole 1990: 103).

In Britain and the United States 'laissez-faire' economic theory, expounded by Adam Smith in the *Wealth of Nations* (1776), advocated a minimalist state role in which the parts (businesses and other private organizations) are prioritized at the expense of the whole. Since then the industrial culture in both these countries tends to encourage a conception of the firm as a private autonomous entity capable of surviving with minimum government intervention and help (Barnett 1986: 269; Borden 1991: 95). This approach, more important at certain periods such as that prevailing in Britain since 1979, allows businesses to operate independently and pragmatically and to thrive in unfamiliar situations. Anglo-American free market ('Darwinian') capitalism favours a stock-holder model of a company, whereby satisfying one part of the whole, the investor or shareholder, has been, historically, the primary business goal.

Idealistic wholism, in contrast to pragmatic realism, involves integrating parts into a whole, thereby creating unity, harmony and interrelatedness (Lessem and Neubauer 1994: 224). Notable 'wholist' thinkers include Johann Goethe and Rudolph Steiner, the latter associated with the educational philosophy and range of schools for educating the whole child. Romanticism, mysticism and especially intuition plays an important role in German thinking. Kant argued that innate ideas or *Anschauung* were the determining factor in mental life, a way of understanding the nature of something outside ourselves.

Wholistic thinkers give precedence to the whole rather than the parts and the totality is often considered more unified or greater than the parts. Sometimes metaphysically-oriented thinkers took their ideas to extravagant lengths. For Hegel, the State personified the whole, individual ideas of freedom having to reflect the interests of the State. 'In civilized nations true bravery consists in the readiness to give oneself wholly to the service of the State so that the individual counts but as one amongst many' (quoted in Peters 1969: 135).

Numerous practical examples can be found outside philosophy whereby integrated wholes have characteristics not capable of being reduced to autonomous parts. The concept applies, for example, to a mechanical system such as a computer or car, which only functions correctly if all parts are working together, or to the human body which adapts organically, with moderate repair strategies for coping with damage. A practical business example is the hope that when two businesses merge the new whole will achieve greater success than each did separately. Wholists or intuitives, deductive thinkers, tend to look for the meaning or wider context behind an event and endeavour to integrate differentiated parts together, removing artificial man-made boundaries and focusing on co-operation. In business, an overall comprehensive view is taken of problems. Thinking, planning and decisions are conceived within a long-term perspective, qualities valued for consolidating estabished firms.

The German social market form of capitalism reflects wholistic thinking. The State plays an important continuing steering role in the life of its citizens, reflected in the early development of social welfare legislation, and the later creation of a two-tier system in industry. The latter encourages manager-employee co-operation involving supervisory boards as well as boards of management. German capitalism, practised also in parts of Northern and Central Europe, focuses on long-term planning and co-operation between the various partners within a stakeholder model, including managers and workers in a company and others.

At the macro level, integration is an important characteristic of German business to the extent that firms frequently form clusters or networks, a meta-enterprise, which co-operate for certain purposes while competing in others (Lessem and Neubauer 1994: 244–5). Such businesses have a primarily reciprocal relationship with other business partners, possibly suppliers, distributors, sub-contractors, bankers or unions. Alternatively, a business may co-operate with similar businesses through exchanging information to save costs and duplication. Sometimes, one firm is the predominant unit in the constellation, known in Japan as a nebula or *kereitsu*, where the individual parts operate in an interdependent manner, complementing the work of the others. This structural form, common in Germany, Japan and Italy (for example, among smaller firms in Emilia Romagna) is rapidly expanding elsewhere, discussed further in section 3.

Integration is also often interpreted in terms of co-ordinating the technical skills and activities of various experts within a business. The latter, no matter what their grade or rank, may meet regularly to resolve production and administrative problems based on long-term perspectives and consensual decision-making. Any possible gaps, errors or problems are usually envisaged in advance so that projects, production plans etc., can proceed smoothly. Invariably, it takes a long time to make a decision, but is normally implemented quite rapidly.

Michael Albert (1991: 119,133) shares the opinion of Lessem and Neubauer that the Germanic form of social market capitalism and management style is the closest of all Western countries to the Japanese equivalent. In terms of attributes such as the quality and efficiency of production, marketing and customer service, industrial relations, worker motivation and identification with the company, evidence from the 1980s pointed to the leaders being certain Asian countries, such as Japan, Taiwan and South Korea and countries such as Germany, Switzerland, Denmark and Sweden (Hampden-Turner 1994: 37,39,62). Whereas in the Lessem and Neubauer model the Anglo and Germanic styles are linked to the United States and Japan respectively, Henzler distances Eurocapitalism from these other countries. He stresses the combination of social individualism and efficient collectivism within the three forms of Eurocapitalism, the Germanic, Mediterranean (including France) and the British (closest to the American model) (Henzler 1994: 29).

A whole range of communication and behavioural patterns are associated with low context, monochronic, largely Western societies and high context, polychronic, mainly non-Western societies and Southern Europeans. Edward T. Hall, the creator of this broad cultural dimension, contrasts the deductive wholistic thinking cultures of the indigenous peoples of North America, such as the Navajo, with the more fragmented low context inductive thinking of Euro-Americans who focus on parts or 'bits' (Hall 1976: 84). Germany and Switzerland are close to the United States at the low context end of the dimension, prizing direct explicit communication patterns (Hofstede 1991: 60). In this respect, Germanic 'wholism' differs considerably from the non-Western, especially Asian and Japanese forms, associated with high context behavioural patterns reflected in indirect communication.

Galtung's four-part typology specifies particular regions of the world. He differentiates between Nippon (circular, holistic) Teuton (intellectual and logical) Latin (rhetoric, dialectic, stylistic) and Saxon (experiential) (Galtun 1981: 827–8, 833). This suggests that the Latin mode of communication and thinking (often indirect) has, in many respects, greater affinity than the Germanic with the Japanese mode.

A French group of researchers differentiate in business between a functionalist model (Anglo-Saxon, notably American) and a personalist (Southern Europe, especially French) model. In the Anglo-American organizational type, the manager submits himself to the order and rationality of the organization rather than to his superior. The relationship between staff is based on the function they do, or envisaged as doing, on a professional or contractual basis. The aim is to isolate problems which are then analysed and handled separately in a time-efficient manner. Structure is conceived as a mere tool which can be adopted so as to best achieve the tasks at hand (Amado, Faucheux and Laurent 1990: 650–651) (Laurent 1986: 95) implying, in effect, flexible, pragmatic work practices.

In the past, neurologists believed in the one brain theory, the brain functioning largely in a rational manner.

Robert Ornstein, noted for his work on the two hemispheres of the brain in the early 1970s, suggests that during early development nerve cells compete with one another to survive. Subject to a certain kind of stimulation, cells connect to others forming neural groups. Because of experiences early in infancy, the nervous system of a person becomes wired up in a particular way. As a result 'individuals have different brains because of their early experiences' (Ornstein 1991: 126). Neuroscientists today generally accept that the brain can be split into two parts, but with the qualification that the qualities possessed by each overlap. There is no rigid compartmentalization of function.

Characteristics of low and high context societies respectively bear affinities with features originally associated exclusively with the two hemispheres of the brain. In general Western, especially Anglo-American, societies tend to favour scientific, analytical, rational and logical thinking processes, associated formerly with left brain. In contrast, the more collectivist non-Western world leans towards synthetic, wholistic, emotional and intuitive thinking processes, considered earlier right brain attributes (Mintzberg 1989: 55) (Trompenaars 1985: 37). For example, African societies value qualities such as a person's spontaneity, unpredictability, unique movements and uninhabited self expression (Triandis 1989: 82). In Western civilization a 'rational' ethic influences the conduct of daily life (Weber 1961: 233). Procedures adopted in many disciplines originating in the West – such as economics, psychology and management sciences – reflect rationalism. Leibniz, Déscartes and Plato were mathematicians, while Kant evinced a concern for mathematical exactitude.

A further point, however, is that the German affinity for flux implied no rigid rational mould restraining their restless inner emotions. The Germans, as shown in Hegelian philosophy, tend to focus on metamorphosis or change as a constant in their history. Frequently, Germans emphasize 'becoming' rather than 'being' reflected in the greater use of *'werden'* than *'sein'*. The German fondness for flow or movement, epitomized by the water symbol, is shared with the Japanese (Lessem and Neubauer 1994: 148).

Jung argues that the reaction in the West against the intellect in favour of feeling or intuition is a mark of cultural advance. He deplores the one-sided development of a person's potential, abstract reasoning being valued higher than humanist, moral or aesthetic considerations (Jung 1962: 85,138).

2 PARTICULARISM, PRAGMATISM AND WHOLISM

Lessem and Neubauer (1994) stress the similarities between the German approach to business and management and the Japanese equivalents. Statistics also show on a number of accounts that during the eighties the most dynamic businesses appear to have been those linked to wholist traditions in the West and Asia, discussed in section 1 (Hampden-Turner 1994). However, a case can be argued that on various grounds Mediterranean capitalism is closest in Europe to non-European forms, including the dynamic Asian economies. Certainly, with the notable exception of many middle- and small-sized businesses in Italy, the economies in Southern Europe and the majority of businesses are much weaker in terms of competitivity than their Asian counterparts. However, other factors also need to be considered.

Hofstede's survey reveals France and Italy to be highly individualist, his results being based on the IBM locations in the northern parts of these countries, with Germany moderately individualist. In contrast, other studies find Germany and France to be collectivist (see Table 5.2). Greece and Portugal were found in the Hofstede survey of managers to be collectivist, and more so than Japan (Hofstede: 1991). Collectivism or communitarianism in Northern Europe and Japan tends to be associated with groups above the level of the family and kin, in contrast to, say, parts of Southern Europe and China.

An additional model of pragmatism and wholism (to that discussed in section 1) can be constructed, encompassing most of Southern Europe and much of the non-Western world. Features include particularism, humanism, personalism, collectivism, organic structures and medium to high context behavioural patterns in business. Pascal Fleury's map suggests that the North-South European divide corresponds to a line cutting across France, Italy and former Yugoslavia (Fleury 1990: 128). In Western Europe it may coincide with Protestant-Catholic allegiances. Consequently Southern Europe might start, culturally if not geographically, somewhere between Holland and Belgium (Trompenaars 1993).

Hofstede's first two categories, relating to power distance and uncertainty avoidance scales, have already been discussed (section 1) and contrast with the last two. The third category 'family' or 'personal bureaucracy' (large power distance and weak uncertainty avoidance) characterizes East and West Africa, South Africa, India, Jamaica, Malaysia, Indonesia, the Philippines, Hong Kong and Singapore. Employees rely on a strong 'Father Figure' but little codification (Hofstede 1991: 140–146). Loyalty and a sense of duty are integrating factors above discipline and formal structure. The largest category (category 4- 'pyramid of people') covers virtually all Latin America, Southern Europe, France and Belgium, Pakistan, Thailand, Iran, Taiwan, South Korea and Japan. Organizations are characterized by large power distance and strong uncertainty avoidance, implying the need for many rules and dislike of unfamiliar risks. Employees tend to rely heavily on hierarchy and clear orders from a superior.

For Asians, an organization is not a soulless machine but an entity created in the image of a family, or what the Japanese call *sempai-gohai*, in which top people are conceived of as parents (Hampden-Turner 1994: 73). Evidence suggests that similar conceptions exist in Southern Europe. In category 4 the boss may be seen as a paternal autocrat who, with his managers collectively, are respected as experts or wise elders. They are expected to be understanding and nurturing, who can inspire dedication from employees whom they may regard as children. All four Mediterranean countries in Hofstede's category 4 – Spain, Portugal, Italy and Greece – are noted for small to medium size family-oriented businesses and so have some affinity with category 3 – 'family'.

Laurent (1983: 79) has contrasted Latin (including Belgium, France and Italy) and Northern European and North American management style. Despite the noted bureaucratic traditions of the French, Laurent's observations that French and Italian managers report a hazy notion of organizational structure coincide with the findings of Phillipe d'Iribarne in the case of the French. Danish and British managements report a clearer notion of organizational structure.

Latin European management tends to personalize authority, power flowing directly from a person exercising it rather than being derived from his official role or defined function (Amado, Faucheux and Laurent 1990: 650–1). Frequently, Mediterranean businesses develop organically according to the needs of management. Italian and Greek managers, for example, may develop plans opportunistically rather than adhere rigidly to procedures or principles (Mole 1990: 55,188). Organic structures and personalism allow scope for pragmatic thinking in terms of creativity and innovation, and for particularistic practices such as modifying or bending rules, known in France as System D (Amado, Faucheux and Laurent 1990: 657). Laurent's survey in twelve countries discovered that managers were more generally conceived of as experts by employees in the following: Belgium (49%), France and Italy (59%), Indonesia (67%) and Japan (77%) (Laurent 1986: 94).

A study by Hampden-Turner and Trompenaars of seven countries involved seven cultural dimensions. Summary results (see Table 5.2) reveal that Britain, the United States and the Netherlands remain completely on one side (A column), while France is the only country to remain exclusively on the other (B column).

Dimensions 2–3 indicate wholistic tendencies, shared by France and Germany, but Germany also supports many values in common with the more individualist areas of Northern Europe and North America. France is revealed as the country most strongly associated with traditional or non-Western values.

Trompenaars' survey of Shell managers in over fifty countries included research among a narrower band of countries (Trompenaars 1985). His findings later formed the basis of Hampden-Turner's observations regarding the ordering of twelve countries. These related to six questions which tested primarily the same key cultural dimensions as just enumerated above in the seven country study. If points 1 to 12 are allocated to each country, depending on the exact position of each in relation to Column A end of the dimension in regard to these questions, the results are as shown

Table 5.2 Seven cultural dimensions: Results of a 7 country survey

A	B
1. Universalism	Particularism
2. Analysing	Integrating
3. Individualism	Communitarianism
4. Inner-directed	Outer-directed
5. Time as sequence	Time as Synchronization
6. Achieved Status	Ascribed Status
7. Equality	Hierarchy

A	B
USA 1–7	France 1–7
UK 1–7	Japan 1–4, 6–7
Netherlands 1–7	Germany 2–3
Sweden 1–3, 5–7	Sweden 4
Germany 1, 4–7	
Japan 5	

in Table 5.3. They reveal the positioning of West Germany within the Northern European, North American group, and the closer proximity of Latin countries to non-Western countries.

In contrast to the form of pragmatism typical in many individualistic Western, especially Anglo-American societies, pragmatism in less individualistic societies is characterized notably by particularistic practices. Particularism denotes first the tendency of flexibly interpreting laws and rules depending on the context. A Turkish visitor to the United States records that an American, in an isolated region, who could see that no traffic was in the vicinity, stopped at a stop sign. The Turk observed that in Turkey everyone would interpret the law in context, in the sense of only applying it when believed prudent and practical to do so (Victor 1992: 149). In universalistic societies, people temper pragmatic behaviour to the prior requirement of generally adhering to established procedures, rules or laws.

De Bono (1991) associates Western thinking with hard, inflexible, rock-like logic, associated with binary knife-edge distinctions ('is' or 'is not', A or not A). This tendency he traces back to Aristotelian logic, undoubtedly a cause among many of the tendency towards universalistic thinking in the West today. Edward de Bono recommends 'water logic' associated with movement 'to' rather than the static 'is'. 'Water flows according to the gradient (context) and shapes or forms according to its external confines (circumstances)' (de Bono 1991: 8). Pragmatism, as envisaged by de Bono and Bergquist, approximates that typifying many non-Western, especially Asian, cultures. Bergquist refers to creative multiplistic thinking, multiple truths and realities. 'Truth must always be viewed

Table 5.3 Responses in relation to left-brain end of dimension

Position	Country	Points	Position	Country	Points
1	US	(7)	7	Greece	(42)
2	Britain	(26)	8	Italy	(46)
	Holland	(26)	9	France	(49)
	W. Germany	(26)	10	Japan	(50)
5	Sweden	(33)	11	Venezuela	(58)
6	Spain	(40)	12	Singapore	(65)

(Adapted from findings cited in Hampden-Turner 1994: 49)

within its particular context and with regard to its purpose and use' (Bergquist 1993: 226–7). Water, a symbol of pragmatic adaptability for de Bono, is perhaps the most important of the Lao Tzu symbols, the originator of Taoism (Tzu 1963: 113).

Most Asian societies, including overseas Chinese communities, in countries such as South Korea, Taiwan and Malaysia, are strongly influenced by Confucianism. Despite the strong ethical basis, Confucianism does not imply belief in an ultimate authority such as an all-seeing God. In general, humanism pervades Confucian ethical philosophy (Smith 1973: 80). Norms on how to behave tend to be based on 'family piety', on relationships with specific people in close proximity (Redding 1993: 62). Confucius (551–479 BC) exalted virtue and righteousness as the foundation of government, but did not establish fixed principles as to what people should or should not do. His position on morals represented a basically pragmatic position. People would discover how to behave righteously in concrete situations. Appropriate conduct in one context might not be so in another (Smith 1973: 68).

In 1916 Henry Fayol, guru of French management stated that principles are flexible and capable of adaptation to every need, which he called the 'law of the situation' (Fayol 1949: 26). Such an approach to pragmatism suits Mediterranean Europeans, including the French. Although many businesses may be conceived on a rational or structured basis theoretically, managers and supervisors usually resent being closely monitored and like discretion in how orders are executed (Leeds 1994: 16–17).

3 ACCOMMODATING CONTRASTING SYSTEMS AND PRACTICES

Max Weber (1961) originally equated bureaucracy with efficiency and fairness, everyone being served impartially according to rational objective criteria. Ideally, organizations would operate as envisaged in Hofstede's 'well-oiled machine' model. In practice, organizations tend, whether in the public or private sector, to be influenced by the values of their own national cultures. They may be inefficient or counter-productive (Hall 1976: 219). Bureaucrats, the administrators, especially in the public sector, are frequently viewed negatively, associated with red tape and delays, avoiding risks and evading responsibility by 'passing the buck'.

Enterprising managers in newly emergent democracies seek ways of modernizing outdated techno-bureaucratic management styles subject in the past to political influences. In many of these newer democracies the State presence is still significant in terms of intervention in, and regulation of, the economy and society. Many of the former State-controlled organizations of industrial-economic significance in East-Central Europe have been privatized. The most important of the emergent democracies in this region are the Visegrad Four – the Czech Republic, Poland, Hungary, Slovakia – and possibly Slovenia and Bulgaria.

According to reports, many of the owner-entrepreneurs in privatized or newly created businesses in Eastern-Central Europe want the benefits of capitalism, such as regular high profits, without experiencing the drawbacks of risks and losses (Drucker 1992: 121). The new entrepreneurs, according to a study in Hungary, Poland and the former Czechoslovakia, include older members of the *nomenklatura* and a category known as *les combinards* (schemers or fiddlers). These two groups want power and quick profits, often from activities neither strictly entrepreneurial nor honest (Frybes 1992: 36–7).

Central European Management has been described as collective with a continuing, if lessening progressively, bureaucratic approach. Work values prized include equity; group unity for motivation; avoidance of personal conflicts; repetitive behaviour; the dislike of taking risks and the prime goal of benefits going to the managers ahead of employees, shareholders and customers (Prokopenko 1994: 155,159). Prokopenko urges the acceleration of movement towards the Western entrepreneurial management culture associated with individualism, prizing of wealth as a goal, informality, innovative behaviour, seizing opportunities, and prioritizing customer orientation. Certainly this vision fits in with pragmatic values. These include flexibility, realistic focus on practicalities such as productivity and profitability and the valuing of autonomy which encourages risk-taking, including anticipating proactively future developments. Prokopenko criticizes continuing bureaucratic mentalities in East-Central Europe. However, bureaucratic traditions exist in business elsewhere. Hofstede's cluster four includes Southern European countries reputed for State involvement in industry, the management often being closely connected with politics (Henzler 1994: 27). Moreover, as discussed in section 2, bureaucratic constraints are moderated by pragmatic and particularistic practices.

The collectivist work place practices in former Communist societies (Turner 1994: 9) and elsewhere, have strengths frequently overlooked by reformers. North American and Western European companies are developing increasingly integrative practices including team-work and consensual decision-making. Bureaucratic traditions in Asian countries, such as Hong Kong, Singapore and Japan, have not prevented these collectivist countries making rapid economic progress. The leader provides a clear broad wholistic vision. Individuals, noted for deference and discipline, participate actively in implementing the shared vision, providing the parts, feeding in information on a 'bottom-up' basis (Hampden-Turner 1994: 59). Group activity can lead to greater insights than might be attained individually. The organization structure tends to be organic or fluid, with senior management not passing down detailed instructions, but rather allowing subordinates discretion in the implementation on a pragmatic basis of the shared vision and general policies.

Often entrepreneurial qualities in Western businesses are associated with newer and medium- to small-sized businesses, usually family controlled, bureaucratic tendencies developing as a business becomes much larger. Schein argues that this applies to the United States. The owner-entrepreneur is able to combine wholism, pragmatism and the humanistic 'personal touch', thinking intuitively, taking risks and treating individuals as distinct persons. The professional manager in contrast is bureaucratic and impersonal, laboriously analysing details, acting cautiously and treating individuals as members of categories such as employees or suppliers (Schein 1983: 26). Trompenaars points out that larger companies are likely to resemble his Eiffel Tower 'bureaucratic' model while smaller ones will resemble the family model or the 'incubator' (composed of gifted, individual-minded, creative specialists) (Trompenaars 1993: 161).

Modernizing or restructuring programmes designed to increase business efficiency are frequently based on Western cultural values. Concepts such as empowerment, de-layering and autonomy are associated with lower power distance, weak uncertainty avoidance and high individualism. When applied to businesses in collectivist societies where individuals are not accustomed to stand out from the group, difficulties may occur. Efforts to remodel or modify behavioural patterns threaten the collectivist values of societies accustomed to dependency, paternalism and harmony and attitudes of self-effacement rather than assertiveness (Harris and Moran 1987: 410). In addition, efforts to encourage greater self-autonomy and individualism among employees can weaken the influence of kin-groups. If an African worker needs motivating, for example, a manager might discuss the matter with the employee's family or ethnic group since group values play a crucial role in influencing individual behaviour (Kamden 1990: 235-8).

Managers in Africa face the challenge of adapting their sense of 'communal belonging' to modern conditions (Koopman 1991: 53). Koopman, a South African entrepreneur, helped his employees overcome their dependency mentalities – influenced by traditional ascriptive communities – by transforming his autocratically-run hierarchical business into an integrative system. He enabled his workforce to develop a sense of individual personal worth. They became involved in determining the rules and practices of the reorganized company and in its running on a democratic basis (Koopman 1991: 55–56).

An on-going issue in a large, international company is finding better ways of co-ordinating the 'whole-parts' or head office-subsidiaries relationship more effectively. Tension can naturally arise if headquarters reflect Western values and the subsidiaries reflect non-Western values, with the former trying to standardize or globalize to an excessive degree. Subsidiaries in more particularistic cultures may pretend to comply with central directives, especially when under scrutiny, but otherwise function in the manner they feel suits them best (Trompenaars 1993: 41–42). A solution for the Western-based head office is to globalize in those areas where it is both necessary and possible, but to allow discretion locally in other areas as to how certain instructions or objectives should be implemented.

Certain current developments in international business could help managers overcome bureaucratic or dependency mentalities and achieve an equilibrium between the parts and the whole at the level of a company, especially within an ethnically-mixed workforce and at the wider level of a firm's external interactions. Over the last ten years two contrasting tendencies have become noticeable in domestic and international business – integrative universalism taking place side by side with fragmented regionalism or cultural relativism. This has led to the recognition of the merits of both aspects, reflected in the notion of 'glocalism' (being big and uniform in some aspects, small, local and diverse in others). Certain organizations, especially those employing a high proportion of experts, are increasingly approaching confederal structures, with rigid reporting structures giving way to all-directional, web-like communication links (Peters 1993: 181,188). Such cross-functioning allows freer exchange of knowledge and experience compared to previous rigid hierarchies, flatter structures as a result of the elimination of middle management, and a close relationship between leaders and others akin to the orchestral 'conductor-players' model.

A synthesizing perspective marks the current move towards balancing adversarial traditions with co-operative approaches, the latter commonly associated with practices found in many areas of the more collectivist non-Western world. An illustration is the German notion of 'competitive co-operation' or the Japanese 'kyo-sie' – denoting global symbiotic co-operation (discussed in section 1). A loose network structure between interdependent entities helps to prevent businesses becoming larger.

Managers increasingly envisage simultaneously the big picture and also how the parts interact (the 'forest-trees' metaphor). Excessive macro thinking results in vital details being ignored, while too much micro thinking leads to a failure to grasp how the parts fit into the whole. Pragmatic or empirical skills help managers handle perpetual changes, including volatility of markets. Increasingly, they become adept at mastering paradox or reconciling the values of systematic/structured/bureaucratic practices with the opposing values of particularism, organic practices or contingency thinking (Peters 1989; 1993: 185, 213). The merits involved in disentangling or deconstructing need to be balanced against the advantages of integrative skills. The leader or manager interprets his role increasingly not as controlling, but of interacting with people inside and outside the business, of smoothing out the 'rough edges' to create a harmonious whole (Graham 1991: 64–5, 70–1).

In a 1925 lecture, Mary Follett emphasized the 'Law of the Situation' as a general principle for businesses run on integrative or co-operative principles (Follett 1973: 112). Follett had a similar interpretation to that of Fayol. For Fayol the 'Law of the Situation' indicated flexible common sense rule interpretation, but for Follett it meant that both managers and employees executed their functions in the manner considered most appropriate at the time without need for constant instructions or supervision. This implied flexible work practices. The situation had its own logic, authority and order, to which both managers and subordinates were bound. Subordinates could voice their own ideas, and interpret instructions as they felt best (Follett 1973: 19, 30). Expanding Asian economies in the eighties showed how businesses could combine respect for traditional values such as hierarchy and status with pragmatic flexibility in decision-making.

CONCLUSIONS

James suggests that few of us are inevitably either tough-minded, fact-bound, pragmatists or pluralists on the one hand or tender-minded, principle-bound, rationalists or monists. The world is inevitably one from one viewpoint, or many from another. It is both one and many, 'a sort of pluralistic monism' (James 1907: 23). Basically, the point made by James reinforces the main theme of this chapter, that pragmatism and wholism are fundamental universal concepts symbolizing inductive or deductive thinking and parts-whole dichotomy or relationships, however the parts-whole relationship is conceived.

Although pragmatism and wholism tend traditionally to be seen as opposed ideas, collectivist cultures are used to forming synergies. Managers worldwide are gradually learning to reconcile contradictions or apparent opposites. Polarites include individualism and collectivism, autonomy and control, loose (organic) and tight (systemic), top-down structures of imposed values and bottom-up structures (open to new ideas), instrumentalism and personalism, globalism and localism.

Innovative firms will increasingly be those able to motivate employees to think of their organization as a whole rather than in terms of parts – specific roles. The greater prevalence of autonomous teams working on special projects represents a reconciliation of individualism and collectivism, by which individual autonomy and initiative combine with group activity and consensual decision-making.

Unidimensional culture continuums may not necessarily express all the various complex patterns in interpersonal relations. Though Trompenaars investigated achievement-ascription as one of his seven dimensions, he admitted that all countries ascribe and achieve in certain ways (Trompenaars 1993: 105). Further, all countries combine both individualist and collectivist tendencies, and variations exist within societies. Any convergence that might occur in the future is likely to result from changes in both Western or non-Western patterns.

A number of important studies continue to explore modes of thinking and personality types based on cultural influences, often identified with parts of the brain, despite the discrediting of the theory relating to the two hemispheres.

Lessen and Neubauer argue that pragmatism, wholism, rationalism and humanism are core philosophical values not only valid worldwide but as applying separately to different parts of Europe. Herrman (1996: 30) makes explicit the four-way division of the brain implicitly understood in Lessen and Neubauer's research. His four thinking styles represent the two halves of the cerebral cortex and the two halves of the limbic system (Herrmann 1996: 15). Herrmann's division of the brain into upper left, upper right, lower left and lower right resembles, in the traits associated with each of these quadrants A, D, B and C, those commonly attributed to pragmatism, wholism, rationalism and humanism. Appropriate training, Herrmann suggests will help people analyse, strategize, organize or personalize, as the occasion demands, and to develop whole brain thinking skills. Miller (1991: 147) favours a two dimensional model contrasting analytic-holistic and objective-subjective continuums. The latter corresponds closely with the systematic–organic and the functional–personalist distinctions noted earlier. Miller associates objective with rationalism and impersonalism, and subjective with, in effect, humanist values and personalism.

In summary, the more impersonal and low context form of analytic pragmatism and integral rational objectivity, particularly marked in Northern Europe, contrast with the personalized high context form of humanist subjectivity and wholism prevalent elsewhere. In practice no irrevocable barriers exist, and businessmen will increasingly adapt their communicating styles across the world as they confront individual and group cultures which differ from their own personal and group traditions.

REFERENCES

Albert, M. (1991) *Capitalisme contre Capitalisme*, Seuil, Paris.

Almond, G.A., Bingham Powell Jr., G. and Mundt, R.J. (1993) *Comparative Politics – A Theoretical Framework*, Harper Collins, New York.

Amado, G., Faucheux, C. and Laurent, A. (1990) Changement Organisationnel et Realites Culturelles – Contrastes Franco-Americains (Organizational Changes and Cultural Changes) in *L'Individual Dans L'Organisation* (The Individual in the Organisation) (ed J-F. Chanlat) Eska/University of Laval Press, Québec pp. 629–61.

Barnett, C. (1986) *The Audit of War*, Macmillan, London.

Barsoux, J-L. and Lawrence, P. (eds) (1990) *Management in France*, Cassell, London.

Bergquist, W. (1993) *The Post Modern Organization – Mastering the Art of Irreversible Change*, Jossey-Bass, San Francisco.

Birch, A.H. (1993) *The Concepts and Theories of Modern Democracy*, Routledge, London.

de Bono, E. (1991) *I am Right, You are Wrong*, Penguin, London.

de Bono, E. (1994) *Parallel Thinking – From Socrates to de Bono Thinking*, Viking, London.

Borden, G.A. (1991) *Cultural Orientation – An approach to Understanding Intercultural Communication*, Prentice Hall, Englewood Cliffs, NJ.

Drucker, P.F. (1992) *Managing for the Future*, Butterworth/Heinemann, Oxford.

Fayol, H. (1949) *General and Industrial Management*, Pitman, London.

Fleury, P. (1990) Au-dela des Particularismes, quels fonds commun universel? (Beyond the particular, what is the commonly accepted universal core?). *Intercultures*, **8**, pp. 119–30.

Follett, M.P. (1973) in *Dynamic Administration: the Collected Papers of Mary Follett* (eds E.M. Fox and L. Urwick) Pitman, London.

Frybes, M. (1992) Les nouveaux entrepreneurs d'Europe de l'Est, in *L'Autre Europe* (eds G. Mink and J.C. Szurels), Presses de CNRS, Paris, pp. 25–38.

Galtung, J. (1981) Structure, culture and intellectual styles: An essay comparing Saxonic, Teutonic, Gallic and Nipponic approaches. *Social Science Information* **20**, pp. 817–56.

Graham, P. (1991) *Integrative Management*, Blackwell, Oxford.

Hall, E.T. (1976) *Beyond Culture*, Doubleday, New York.

Hampden-Turner, C. and Trompenaars, F. (1994) *The Seven Cultures of Capitalism*, Doubleday, New York.

Hampden-Turner, C. (1994) *Corporate Culture: From Vicious to Virtuous Circles*, Piatkus, London.

Handy, C., Gow, I., Gordon, C., Randlesome, C. and Moloney, M. (1987) *The Making of Managers: A report on management education, training and development in the USA, West Germany, France, Japan and the UK.* National Economic Development Council, London. pp. 103.

Handy, C. (1993) *The Empty Raincoat*, Hutchinson, London.

Harris, P.R. and Moran, R.T. (1987) *Managing Cultural Differences*, Gulf, Houston.

Henzler, H.A. (1994) *Europreneurs*, Bantam, London.

Herrmann, N. (1996) *The Whole Brain Business Book*, McGraw-Hill, New York.

Hofstede, G. (1991) *Culture and Organisations*, McGraw-Hill, Maidenhead.

Hofstede, G. (1993) *Images of Europe*. Valedictory Address, University of Limburg at Maastricht, 1 October. Department of Economics and Business Administration, pp. 21.

d'Iribarne, P. (1989) *La Logique de l'Honneur* (The Logic of Principle), Seuil, Paris.

James, W. (1907) *Pragmatism*, Meridian Books, New York.

Jung, C.G. (1962) *The Secret of the Golden Flower*, Routledge and Kegan Paul, London, Foreword and Commentary.

Kamden, E. (1990) 'Temps et Travail en Afrique', in *L'Individu dans L'Organisation – Les Dimensions Oubliées* (ed J.F. Chanlat) Eska/Laval University Press, Quebec, pp. 231–54.

Koopman, A. (1991) *Transcultural Management*, Blackwell, Oxford.

Laurent, A. (1983) The cultural diversity of western conceptions of management. *International Studies of Management and Organisation*, **12**, pp. 75–96.

Laurent, A. (1986) The cross-cultural puzzle of international HRM. *Human Resource Management*, **25**, pp. 91–102.

Leeds, C. (1994) France, in *Global Perspectives on Organisational Conflict*, (eds M. Afzalur Rahim and A. Blum) Praeger, Westport, Connecticut, pp. 11–32.

Lessem, R. and Neubauer, F. (1994) *European Management Systems*, McGraw-Hill, Maidenhead.

Miller, A. (1991) *Personality Types – A Modern Synthesis*, University of Calgary, Calgary.

Mintzberg, H. (1989) *Mintzberg on Management: Inside our Strange World of Organizations*, The Free Press, New York.

Mole, J. (1990) *Mind your Manners – Managing Culture Clash in the Single European Market*, The Industrial Society, London.

Ornstein, R. (1991) *Evolution of Consciousness – The Origins of the Way We Think*, Simon and Schuster, New York.

Perry, R.B. (1919) *Present Philosophical Tendencies*, Longmans, Green and Co.

Peters, R.S. (1969) Hegel and the Nation-State in *Political Ideas*, (ed D. Thomson) Penguin, Harmondsworth, pp. 130–42.

Peters, T. (1989) *Thriving on Chaos*, Pan Books, London.

Peters, T. (1993) *Liberation Management*, Pan Books, London.

Prokopenko, J. (1994) The transition to a market economy and its implications for HRM in Eastern Europe in *Human Resource Management in Europe* (ed P.S. Kirkbride) Routledge, London, pp. 147–63.

Redding, S.G. (1993) *The Spirit of Chinese Capitalism*, Walter de Gruyter, Berlin.

Ronen, S. (1986) *Comparative and Multinational Management*, John Wiley, New York.

Schein, E. (1983) The Role of the Founder in Creating Organizational Culture. *Organizational Dynamics*, **12** pp. 13–28.

Simonet, J. (1992) *Pratiques du Management en Europe*, Les Editions D'Organisation, Paris.

Smith, D.H. (1973) *Confucius*, Temple, London.

Sørensen, G. (1993) *Democracy and Democratization*, Westview, Boulder, CO.

Triandis, H.C. (1989) Cross-cultural Studies of Individualism and Collectivism, in *Nebraska Symposium*, University of Nebraska Press, Lincoln, Nebraska, pp. 41–130.

Trompenaars, F. (1985) *Organization of meaning and the meaning of organization in a comparative study on the conception of organizational structure in different cultures*. Unpublished Ph.D. Thesis, University of Pennsylvania.

Trompenaars, F. (1993) *Riding the Waves of Culture*, Nicholas Brealey, London.

Turner, L. (1994) *From 'Old Red Socks' to Modern Human Resource Managers?* Working Paper 94–28. Centre for Advanced Human Resource Studies, Cornell University. pp. 74.

Tzu, Lao (1963) *The Way of Lao Tzu (Tao-te Ching)* Translated with an introduction by Wing-Tsit Chan, Bobbs-Merrill Company, Indianapolis.

Victor, D.A. (1992) *International Business Communication*, Harper Collins, New York.

Weber, M. (1961) *General Economic History*, Collier, New York (Trans. F.H. Knight).

Chapter 6

National cultures and the values of organizational employees: time for another look

Peter B. Smith

NATIONAL CULTURES AND THE VALUES OF ORGANIZATIONAL EMPLOYEES: TIME FOR ANOTHER LOOK

For the past two decades, discussions of world-wide differences in the values of organizational employees have been focused around the pioneering study of Geert Hofstede (1980). His extensive analysis of questionnaire responses of IBM employees suggested that differences in national cultures can be thought of as varying along just four dimensions – see chapter 9 in this book – which Hofstede identified as Individualism-Collectivism, Power Distance, Uncertainty Avoidance and Masculinity-Femininity. Scores on these dimensions were initially assigned to 40 nations on the basis of the averages of scores for individual respondents from each nation, which were then subjected to further statistical analysis. Further research permitted the numbers of nations represented to be later increased to 53. Scores on the first two of these dimensions proved to be strongly negatively correlated to one another, so that with few exceptions the countries rated high on Individualism were also rated low on Power Distance.

This exemplary study has substantial continuing strengths, not least the extensiveness of its samples and the precision with which samples from different countries were equated. However, the passage of time increases the need to set this study within the context of more recent work (see also Chapters 3 and 9 in this volume). In this way we may be able to essay some answers to a series of questions which remain unresolved following Hofstede's work.

First, we need to know the degree to which Hofstede's results are generalizable to employees working in organizations other than IBM. It has been widely assumed that IBM has, or at least used to have, a highly distinctive organizational culture. Did this in any way affect the findings he obtained? Furthermore, for his main analysis Hofstede selected from his overall sample only those respondents who worked in marketing and servicing. What types of results are obtained when other samples are selected?

Second, the four dimensions which were identified by Hofstede emerged from analysis of questionnaires which were originally designed by IBM staff for quite other purposes. As Hofstede himself acknowledges, the formulation of these questions might have left undetected other important dimensions of cultural variation. Are these four dimensions the main ones or indeed the only ones upon which we should be focusing?

Third, the IBM data were collected in the late sixties and early seventies. Since that time a great deal of social change has occurred in many, if not all, parts of the world. Has increasing modernity reduced or changed the types of cultural difference which were apparent at that time? Furthermore, many businesses have become much more internationalized in their operations. Even if the dimensions along which cultures are differentiated remain relatively similar, might it not be the case that some organizations have made substantial progress toward the creation of a transnational culture?

Fourth, we need to investigate more fully the consequences of different patterns of values for the operation of one or another organization. Hofstede very properly pointed out that his characterizations concerned whole cultures and that one could not necessarily predict the behaviour of an individual or of an organization within that culture simply on the basis of the score for the culture as a whole. If characterizations of national culture provide only weak guidance as to the behaviour of those within organizations within a culture, would we not do better to analyse the cultures of organizations rather than of nations, as exemplified by some of the more recent work of Hofstede himself (Hofstede *et al.*, 1990)?

Finally, the current internationalization of business increases interest in an issue which Hofstede's original work did not address at all, namely, what can be said about interactions between organization members who come from differing cultural backgrounds? Are there distinctive ways in which specific partners in joint ventures, in multi-cultural teams or in cross-national negotiations may be expected to misunderstand one another?

Each of these questions will be addressed in turn within this discussion. We should note in passing, however, that the problems of doing valid cross-cultural research are legion. The most obvious of these are that familiarity with different types of research measure and willingness to impart valid information to strangers themselves vary with culture. Furthermore, precisely equivalent translations of questionnaires or interview schedules are frequently impossible and exact matching of samples on, for instance, age or gender is vitiated by the fact that age and gender also have different significances in different cultures. Expectations of a female manager in Oslo are not the same as those of a female manager in Riyadh. The significance of a manager being aged, say, 30 in Hong Kong is different to its significance in London.

Given these difficulties, rather than searching for the definitive and most valid study, the best strategy is probably to survey a wider range of studies. Where studies with different kinds of weakness yield findings which support one another, the chances are increased that their findings are not caused by the weaknesses of their methods, but rather by having measured some aspect of underlying differences between the cultures sampled. Let me now address the five questions posed above in turn.

THE UNIQUENESS OF THE IBM SAMPLE

This issue may be fairly quickly resolved. Hoppe (1990) surveyed 1544 very senior administrators from business, government, academia and non-profit organizations, who had attended a series of seminars in Salzburg, Austria. The data were collected in 1984. He used the same questionnaire items as those upon which Hofstede had based his dimensions. Responses were obtained from participants in 17 West European nations, Turkey and the USA. The country rankings obtained by Hoppe showed close similarity with Hofstede's rankings of the same countries upon three of Hofstede's four dimensions, namely Individualism-Collectivism, Power Distance and Uncertainty Avoidance. On the Masculinity-Femininity scale there was a less close match, which may have been due to unusual attributes of Hoppe's Swedish sample. Although this study does not encompass a world-wide sample, it provides strong evidence that within a sample that differed substantially from the original IBM sample in terms of age, gender, seniority and type of work, nations were nonetheless rank ordered along the Hofstede dimensions in rather similar ways. We can discount the possibility that there is something very distinctive about IBM employees.

KEY DIMENSIONS OF CULTURAL VARIATION

The IBM questionnaire upon which Hofstede's conclusions were based was designed by a predominantly North American/West European group. Hofstede (1980) himself includes at the end of his book a description of his own values, as encouragement to others to examine whether these values or those implicit in the questionnaire might have in some way influenced the results of his analyses. This challenge was picked up by a group of researchers based in Hong Kong and referring to themselves as the Chinese Culture Connection (1987). They designed a questionnaire based upon traditional Chinese sayings, which was then translated into a variety of languages and administered to students in 22 countries. The dimensions of variation which emerged from responses to this were then correlated with the Hofstede scores for the relevant countries. This study revealed dimensions similar to Individualism-Collectivism, Power

Distance and Masculinity-Femininity but not Uncertainty Avoidance. Furthermore, an additional dimension named as Confucian Work Dynamism based upon traditional Chinese values such as deference, thrift, loyalty and long-term commitment was identified. Hofstede (1991) concludes that this fifth dimension should be added to his earlier four, though he prefers to call it Long-Term Time Perspective.

A further set of surveys which permits comparison is that assembled by Trompenaars (1993) – see Chapter 17 in this book. This comprises responses from diverse samples of more than 10,000 organizational employees in 46 countries to a questionnaire which proposes altogether seven dimensions of cultural variation. Not all of these will be considered here. The databank differs from that used by Hofstede, in that it is drawn from diverse convenience samples of organizational employees in each country, with little control over the composition of the sample. A recent analysis of scores for 43 countries from this databank by Smith, Dugan and Trompenaars (1994), using the multidimensional scaling technique, identified two principal dimensions of variation. One dimension, termed Utilitarian Involvement-Loyal Involvement separates the scores of countries on the basis of items defining the firmness and continuity of their group memberships. The other is named as Egalitarian Commitment versus Conservatism. Egalitarian Commitment countries are those (mostly Western) countries in which respondents endorse items which favour adherence to generalized rules and laws as to what is just and right. Trompenaars (1993) describes these countries as high on Universalism and on Achievement. In contrast, countries high on Conservatism are those where respondents endorse items defining their first obligations as being not to abstract laws or concepts of justice, but to those who are close to them. These obligations include not just peer to peer obligations, but also, for instance, the mutual obligations of superiors and subordinates to one another. East European countries scored particularly highly upon Conservatism thus defined. Trompenaars describes these countries as high on Particularism and on Ascription.

The two dimensions emerging from this analysis of the Trompenaars databank are both somewhat correlated with the two Hofstede dimensions of Individualism-Collectivism and Power Distance, as represented in Figure 6.1.

However, there is an apparently crucial difference between the Hofstede sample and the Trompenaars sample. The Trompenaars samples include data from 10 ex-Communist states, mostly in Eastern Europe, whereas the IBM study necessarily excluded such countries. If the Trompenaars databank is re-analysed, excluding the ex-Communist states, then the resulting dimensions which emerge are much closer to those of Hofstede. Thus, despite the precision of the Hofstede country samples and the lack of control over the Trompenaars country samples, two rather

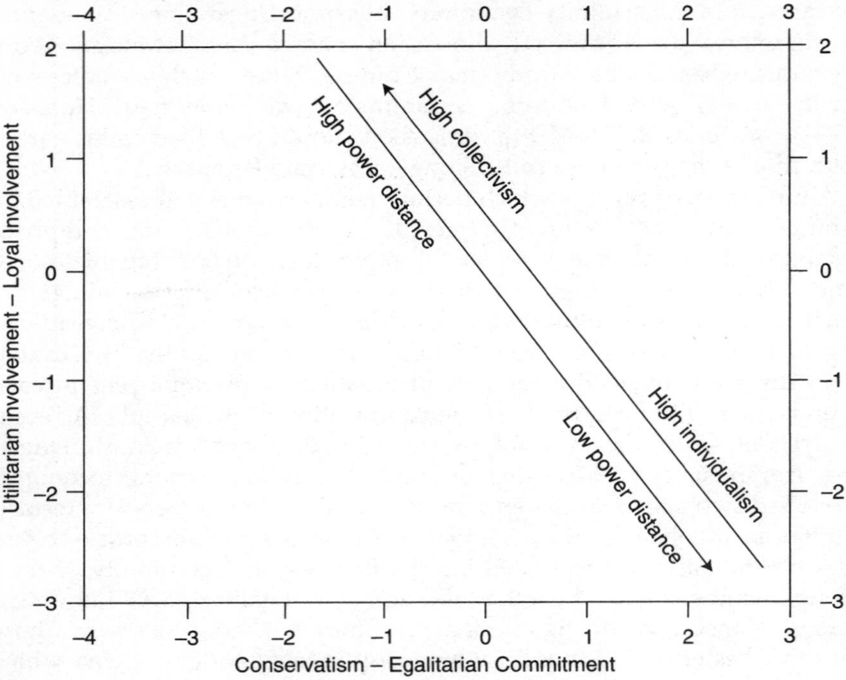

Figure 6.1 Comparison of Hofstede and Trompenaars' dimensions for 33 countries

similar dimensions of variation emerge from each when the nations compared are equated. The implications of this are that the Hofstede dimensions of Individualism-Collectivism and Power Distance continue to summarize well the variations to be found between the nations included in his original survey, but that there is a distinctive pattern of values to be found principally among East European nations which must be added in order to gain a more complete picture. Respondents in this area espouse values which are utilitarian, but which are 'conservative' in that they favour commitment to one's own immediate circle, rather than endorsing more abstract values of what is just or fair.

The Trompenaars survey includes few questions relevant to the remaining Hofstede dimensions, so it need be no surprise that dimensions related to Uncertainty Avoidance or Masculinity-Femininity did not appear. Trompenaars does have measures related to time perspective, but it is not yet clear that valid ways of measuring this complex dimension have been identified.

If we consider the three post-Hofstede surveys so far reviewed, it is apparent that dimensions similar to Individualism-Collectivism and

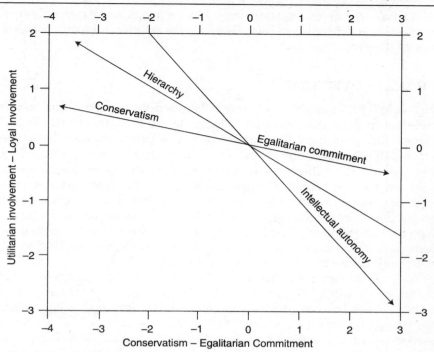

Figure 6.2 Comparison of Schwartz and Trompenaars' dimensions for 26 countries

Power Distance have emerged from all of them, whereas the appearance of the other dimensions has been less reliable. One further large-scale series of surveys is relevant, though its subjects were students and teachers, rather than business employees. Schwartz (1994) has surveyed values espoused in almost 50 countries, and identified seven 'domains' of values. Schwartz avoids the use of the terms Individualism and Collectivism, as he has criticisms of the way in which these terms have been defined (Schwartz, 1990). However, five of his domains are significantly related to the dimensions consistently emerging from the other surveys. These are named as Hierarchy, Affective Autonomy, Intellectual Autonomy, Conservatism and Egalitarian Commitment. The correlation of these domains with the dimensions emerging from the Trompenaars databank are shown in Figure 6.2. For clarity of presentation, Affective Autonomy has been omitted, but its correct positioning is close to that of Egalitarian Commitment. Although the Schwartz data used to construct this figure were derived from school teachers rather than business employees, there is an evident convergence, particularly between his domains of Egalitarian Commitment and Conservatism and the Trompenaars dimension which has been given the same name. Once again, a study using different methods and different samples yields results which are broadly supportive of the earlier results.

CHANGES OVER TIME

Hofstede (1980) examined differences between the section of his sample collected in the sixties and that collected in the early seventies. He concluded that there was some evidence that all cultures were becoming more individualistic, but no evidence for change along his other three dimensions. The differences in questionnaires and other measurement instruments used within different studies here considered make it well-nigh impossible to measure with any precision whether such uniform global effects are occurring. What is rather easier is to compare whether national cultures are still rank ordered in similar ways as in the past along comparable dimensions. For instance, Hofstede identified the USA as the most individualistic culture within his sample.

Yang (1988) has provided a wealth of evidence that modernization leads to increasing individualism, in a wide variety of nations. More recently there has been widespread concern, for instance in Japan, that the younger generation no longer feel bound by traditional values. Some studies have found Japanese students to endorse values just as individualistic as those espoused by American students. Nonetheless, if we examine the multi-nation studies outlined above, we find that they all still agree with Hofstede's finding that Western European and Anglo countries are more individualistic than those in Asia, Africa and Latin America.

If we try for more precise specification of which values predominate where, then the problem of differing definitions of dimensions comes to the fore. For instance, the data from Trompenaars suggest that East Europeans are more individualistic than West Europeans or North Americans.

Another recent multi-nation survey suggests that North European managers are more individualistic than North Americans. Smith and Peterson (1994) asked samples of managers in 25 countries how they handled a series of eight routine work events, such as the hiring of a new subordinate. The project was based on a model of leadership as a process of 'event management' which had been advanced earlier (Smith and Peterson, 1988). Their questionnaire included eight different ways in which managers might handle events and different frequencies in the use of these was noted for each country. It was found that reported reliance on one's own experience and training was strongly correlated with Hofstede scores for individualism. In countries that score higher on collectivism and power distance, reliance was stronger upon one's boss and upon formal rules and procedures. In China, India and Iran there was greater reliance on 'widespread beliefs in my country as to what is right'. For purposes of the present discussion, the crucial point is that in this survey reliance on one's own experience and training was higher in the Netherlands, UK, Germany and Finland than it was in USA.

A further problem in determining whether change has occurred over time is the increasingly multicultural composition of many nations. The more diverse a nation, the more sampling differences may lead researchers to contradictory conclusions. Thus, ethnic diversity underlines the hazards of characterizing nations by a single series of scores upon a series of dimensions. Seen in this light, the debate as to whether the most valid set of dimensions of cultural variability have been identified is best redefined as a debate as to whether these dimensions can tap variations within, as well as between, nations. This leads to consideration of the fourth question posed above.

NATIONAL CULTURES VERSUS SUBCULTURES

A great deal has been written in recent years concerning the application of the concept of culture to organizations and this is not the place to explore that literature in any detail. Culture has been defined in a multitude of different ways and when suitably formulated can assist in the analysis not just of nations or organizations but also of work teams. Depending upon one's perspective, one can see either nations or organizations or work teams as homogeneous and sharing crucial properties, or as heterogeneous and disparate. The choice of level of analysis must depend upon what question one wishes to answer.

Hofstede's definition of culture as the 'collective programming of the mind' (1991: 5) implies the existence of rather basic and deep-seated differences in national cultures. If particular work organizations were able to select or socialize their members in ways which created equally profound 'programming', then we should expect that the rise of multinational organizations should be accompanied by the weakening of national differences. This should be particularly apparent within studies which used measures that ask in detail about specific work behaviours, rather than in those which detect differences in more abstractly formulated values.

The Smith and Peterson (1994) study described earlier has a bearing on this issue. In this study managers were not only asked to describe how they handled work events, but also to evaluate how well these events had been handled. This provides access not just to the manager's description of what usually happens, but also some expression of sentiment as to what courses of action are actually preferred. It was found that in all countries except China, managers evaluated reliance upon one's own experience and training significantly positively. Furthermore, in all countries, managers evaluated negatively events which had been handled in conjunction with their boss. Thus the study provides some evidence for a universal – or at least very widespread – pattern of endorsement of individualistic ways of handling organizational events.

However, this does not give the full picture. Some other ways of handling events were seen as significantly positive in some nations and significantly negative in others. For instance, relying upon 'unwritten rules as to how things are usually done around here' was seen negatively in ten countries, but positively in Brazil and Portugal. Involving one's subordinates was evaluated positively in Germany, UK, India, France, Finland, Mexico and Australia, but negatively in Korea, Nigeria, Brazil, Iran and the Philippines. Thus there are also continuing substantial differences in the way in which actions are evaluated in organizations in different parts of the world. Whether it is the uniformities or the continuing diversity which is more important is best considered in the context of intercultural interactions.

INTERCULTURAL INTERACTIONS

Among the dimensions of cultural variation under discussion, it is undoubtedly the case that Individualism-Collectivism has attracted most attention in recent years. Numerous studies have been completed comparing the behaviour of those who endorse individualistic and collectivist values. Comparisons include preferences for different leader styles, negotiation behaviours, conflict resolution procedures, communication styles, allocation of resources, group conformity, competitive behaviours and so forth (Smith and Bond 1993).

While many of these studies have found marked differences, one needs to attend carefully to the detail of the studies. For instance, researchers rather often have characterized the samples they have studied as individualist or collectivist simply on the basis of the scores Hofstede and others have assigned to a given pair of nations. Only in a minority of cases have researchers actually measured the values endorsed by the people whose behaviour they were studying. Many studies therefore fall victim to the 'ecological fallacy' against which Hofstede and others have cautioned. Just because the Hofstede score for, say, Korea shows high collectivism, it does not follow that any particular Korean, or any small sample of Koreans are necessarily collectivists. To do fully valid research one needs to determine the actual values of those whom one is studying. However, as larger numbers of studies accumulate and the consistency of their findings can be evaluated, we can have greater confidence in the differences reported. It is clear that the day-to-day behaviours of organization members in individualist/low power distance cultures do differ substantially from those of organization members in collectivist/high power distance cultures.

This is nowhere more apparent than in joint ventures and mergers. Child *et al.* (1990) for instance, have identified the different types of human resource management problems encountered by American, European, Japanese and Hong Kong partners within joint ventures in China. It is apparent that many of the specific difficulties concerning selection, training, pay and promotion experienced by US and to a lesser extent European partners in Chinese enterprises are explicable in terms of the different conception of the individual held by Western managers to those obtaining in China.

Even within Western organizations, it was noted some time ago that managers working in multinational organizations expressed values closer to those typical of their national culture than did managers who were not working in multinationals (Laurent 1983). Recent examples abound of organizations which have entered into mergers on the basis of economic considerations and then found their performance impeded by divergences in culturally-rooted assumptions as to how to do business.

CONCLUSIONS

This brief exploration of the legacy of Hofstede's pioneering study points toward three conclusions. First, there are no indications that the cultural diversity mapped by Hofstede is in process of disappearing. Recent studies show just as much diversity as do those done earlier. Second, two at least of the dimensions identified by Hofstede find parallels in all of the more recent large-scale surveys. There is room for debate as to how precisely these dimensions may best be defined, but little doubt that they encompass important aspects of the cultural variations to be found around the world. Third, there is substantial evidence, too substantial to consider in any detail here, that these two dimensions do not simply identify values endorsed by managers. They are reliably linked to the ways in which managers describe their day-to-day behaviour and to the types of difficulties which arise in cross-cultural negotiation, joint venture management and team-work within multinationals.

REFERENCES

Child, J., Boisot, M., Ireland, J., Li, Z. and Watts, J. (1990) *The Management of Equity Joint Ventures in China*, China-EC Management Institute, Beijing.

Chinese Culture Connection (1987) Chinese values and the search for culture-free dimensions of culture. *Journal of Cross-Cultural Psychology*, **18**, pp. 143–64.

Hofstede, G. (1980) *Culture's Consequences: International Differences in Work-Related Values*, Sage, Beverly Hills, CA.

Hofstede, G. (1991) *Cultures and Organizations: Software of the Mind*, McGraw Hill, London.

Hofstede, G., Neuijen, B., Ohayv, D.D. and Sanders, G. (1990) Measuring organizational cultures: A qualitative and quantitative study across twenty cases. *Administrative Science Quarterly*, **35**, pp. 286–315.

Hoppe, M.H. (1990) A comparative study of country elites: International differences in work-related values and learning and their implications for management training and development. University of North Carolina at Chapel Hill. Dissertation.

Laurent, A. (1983) The cultural diversity of Western conceptions of management. *International Studies of Management and Organization*, **13**, pp. 75–96.

Schwartz, S.H. (1990) Individualism-collectivism: critique and proposed refinements. *Journal of Cross-Cultural Psychology*, **21**, pp. 139–57.

Schwartz, S.H. (1994) Cultural dimensions of values: Towards an understanding of national differences, in *Individualism and Collectivism: Theory, Method and Applications*, (eds U. Kim, H.C. Triandis, C. Kagitcibasi, S.C. Choi and G. Yoon) Sage, Thousand Oaks, CA.

Smith, P.B. and Bond, M.H. (1993) *Social Psychology across Cultures: Analysis and Perspectives*, Harvester-Wheatsheaf, Hemel Hempstead.

Smith, P.B., Dugan, S. and Trompenaars, F. (1994) National culture and managerial values: A dimensional analysis across 43 nations, *Journal of Cross-Cultural Psychology*.

Smith, P.B. and Peterson, M.F. (1988) *Leadership, Organization and Culture: An Event Management Model*, Sage, London.

Smith, P.B. and Peterson, M.F. (1994) *Leadership as event management: A cross-cultural survey based upon middle managers from 25 nations*. Paper presented as part of a symposium at the International Congress of Applied Psychology, Madrid.

Trompenaars, F. (1993) *Riding the Waves of Culture*, Brealey, London.

Yang, K.S. (1988) Will societal modernisation eventually eliminate cross-cultural psychological differences? in *The Cross-Cultural Challenge to Social Psychology* (ed M.H. Bond), Sage, Newbury Park, CA.

Part II
Area-studies

Chapter 7

Managing in America: recreating a competitive culture

Fred Luthans and Richard M. Hodgetts

INTRODUCTION

After suffering some setbacks in the 1980s and the early 1990s, American management has staged a comeback of its competitiveness. After trailing the Japanese for a number of years, the Geneva, Switzerland based World Economic Forum in 1995 named the USA as the world's most competitive nation for the second year in a row (the Japanese have slipped to 4th). US firms have found that they are once again able to compete with anybody, anywhere, anytime, and anyway (the '4 Anys' competitive environment). The resurgence of American management can be explained in many ways, but probably result from a combination of factors (Hodgetts 1993). Most informed observers of the excellence of today's American management would include a foundation of select classical management concepts, new organizational structure developments, a quality emphasis and the very recent emergence of both learning and world-class organizations. What-ever the exact reasons, the fact is that an increasing number of American companies are now able to compete effectively against both domestic competitors and outside multinational corporations (MNCs) doing business in the US and the global market-place.

Instead of just adapting and reacting to changes in the now extremely competitive international environment, American management is trying to proactively anticipate change. For example, an old line company such as Chrysler has been extremely successful in the minivan business and with their new compact the Neon, because Chrysler management now realizes that strategies based only on market research-based information may not be most effective. Customers often do not know what they want and companies need to take a risk, innovate and offer products that delight customers and exceed their expectations. Despite these recent developments, it must be realized that much of the 'new' American management is really not new at all. There is still a grounding in classic management thought. However, traditional management now only serves as a point of departure, a historical context. There is a new paradigm, not just incremental change driving today's American management. Examples of this new paradigm include empowerment, customer- and quality-driven output and generative learning. Such new paradigm approaches are giving American firms the edge in the competitive battles. The following sections first start with classical American management concepts, but the chapter is then devoted to the new American management involving organization developments, total quality, learning and world class organizations.

CLASSICAL AMERICAN MANAGEMENT

While there have been dramatic changes in American management (see Hodgetts 1993), an understanding of classic concepts is still necessary, not only to provide a historical context for today's approaches, but also because many managers in the US still greatly depend on them. The classical concepts are still widely used in both the structure and functioning of American business. The classical organizational design concepts relate to the formal techniques used in determining authority-responsibility relationships and job assignments. The classical management process involves the functions of decision making, communication, and control.

Classical organizational design

The classic organization design in America has its roots in the bureaucratic model of pioneering German sociologist Max Weber. The ideal characteristics of this bureaucratic form include:

1 clear-cut division of labour
2 a hierarchy of positions, with each lower one being controlled and supervised by the one immediately above
3 a consistent system of abstract rules and standards which help ensure uniformity in the performance of duties and co-ordination of tasks
4 a spirit of formal impersonality in which duties are carried out
5 employment which is based on technical qualifications and protected from arbitrary dismissal.

Major American organizations such as AT&T, General Motors and General Electric have depended upon this form of organization structure until very recently. At the heart of this classical approach were four basic structural factors: job definitions, departmentalization, span of control and decentralization and delegation of authority.

A job definition is a summary of the tasks to be carried out by an individual performing a particular job. The use of such definitions has been pivotal to classical organizational design and has been greatly expanded through research in the organizational behaviour field through job design. For example, job enlargement has been widely used on tasks where a large percentage of time is needed to pass material from one worker to the next. As a result, in companies such as Compaq, there are now teams of three individuals who collectively assemble each computer. This approach not only helps increase productivity and quality, but also leads to reductions in absenteeism and turnover.

Departmentalization is the process of combining jobs into groups on the basis of common characteristics. The most popular arrangement in traditional American firms has been functional departmentalization, in which work activities are grouped on the basis of the job being done. For example, manufacturing firms are typically departmentalized into three major functional departments: production, marketing and finance. Another common arrangement is product departmentation or divisions, which groups together the activities associated with a particular product line. The product department most often operates as a profit centre. American auto firms have long used this type of arrangement by creating divisions that focus on a specific product lne, i.e. GM Cadillac, Chrysler vans and Ford Taurus. A third common arrangement is customer departmentation, which is designed to meet the needs of specific customer groups. For example, retail stores will have major departments for men's clothing, women's apparel and children's wear.

Span of control is another classical concept and refers to the number of individuals a manager directly supervises. There are a number of factors that influence the span, including the amount of time that must be spent with each subordinate, the competence and experience of the personnel and the ability of these individuals to work on their own. While some enterprises seek to keep the span of control within a specified range such as 3 to 8, most organizations allow contingency variables such as difficulty of the task and personal characteristics of the manager and subordinates to dictate the ideal span. In recent years, there has been a movement to widen the span, thus flattening the structure. These flat, horizontal structures are discussed in the next major section.

Decentralization, perhaps the most far thinking of the classical concepts (it is very close to today's empowerment), relates to the number and importance of decisions pushed down the organization hierarchy to the lowest levels. The further down the management decisions are made, the greater the degree of decentralization. Closely related is the classical concept of delegation, which is where the manager gives authority to subordinates to make decisions affecting their area of responsibility. Both of these concepts, decentralization and delegation, have been successfully used by American management through the years. The traditional guideline for effective American management has been: Push authority as far down the structure as possible. Much of General Motors' success in the twenty-five years following World War II was attributed to their decentralized structure and management delegating to their subordinates. Now, General Motors and other American firms are finding that such classical principles do not go far enough and radically different organizational structures are now required.

Classical management functions

Classical American management focuses on the functions managers perform in the organization structure to accomplish goals and objectives. Going back to the early part of this century, American management borrowed from the French management pioneer Henri Fayol the functions of plan, organize, command, co-ordinate and control. These functions evolved over the years into the three most closely associated with classical American management: decision making, communication and control.

Decision making as used in classical American management simply refers to the process of choosing between alternatives. The goal for this decision process is to make rational choices by carefully analysing situations, determining alternative courses of action, weighing the benefits and drawbacks associated with each and choosing the one that offers the best solution. Mathematical modelling and computer analysis have been employed in this classic decision process by large American firms. Examples of the use of decision modelling include economic forecasting, comparison of alternative investments, decision tree analysis, linear programming techniques and, most recently, economic value analysis (EVA).

The decision making process also is associated with the behavioural side of American management. In particular, when decisions require creativity or innovation, quantitative modelling is replaced by subjective techniques such as brainstorming, synectics, or nominal grouping. Some organizations have gone so far as to test their managers to identify those that are heavily right brain (creative, spontaneous, intuitive) and those that are left brain (logical, sequential, rational). Teams are then formed that can draw on the analytical strengths of both types of thinkers. The effectiveness of this approach is controversial, but is nevertheless still used in advertising, research or new product development teams.

Communication in classical management involves the process of conveying meanings. As a function of management, communication is used to carry information throughout the organization. Typical examples include: downward communication in the form of memos and reports; upward communication in the form of suggestion programmes and open door policies that provide feedback on problem areas; and horizontal communication in the form of interdepartmental meetings and reports which are used to co-ordinate activities. In addition, recognition is given to informal or 'grapevine' communications in classical American organizations. There are a variety of ways that information can be informally passed. The most informal common communication channel is through a selective process in which some people are deliberately included on the grapevine and others are deliberately excluded.

Controlling is the classical management process of evaluating performance according to the plans or objectives and then taking any action that is deemed necessary. This process is closely tied to the other management functions and helps create a closed loop between decision making, communication and control. Like decision making, the control process has been greatly quantified through the use of mathematical models and techniques that provide numerical feedback. However, also like decision making, there is a great deal of non-quantitative control traditionally used by American managers. For example, most managers through the years have relied heavily on anecdotal feedback from their customers regarding the quality of service and how it can be improved. Additionally, there has been continual change in performance measures as managers have reassessed their evaluation procedures. For example, many firms have traditionally determined their cost of capital and used it as a factor in evaluating performance. However, recently there has been a growing trend towards including equity capital in this calculation. This newer form of control requires managers to generate a profit that pays for the cost of borrowed funds as well as providing a return on invested capital.

The classic organizational design and management functions briefly discussed here have played a major role in the history of American management. However, since the 1980s a number of significant developments have occurred which are bringing about major changes in the American approach to management. The rest of this chapter describes this new approach to American management.

NEW ORGANIZATIONAL DEVELOPMENTS

There are a host of organizational developments that have dramatically changed American management. Some of the most significant include downsizing, reengineering and information technology.

Downsizing

In the 1980s American firms began facing growing competitive pressures in both domestic and international markets from overseas multinationals (see Hamel and Prahalad 1994). In an effort to reduce costs and increase profitability, an increasing number of companies began to downsize by not filling the positions of those who quit or retired, eliminating jobs at middle levels of management and delegating or empowering those in the lower levels of the structure. The overall effect was a flattened hierarchy that allowed being closer to customers and being able to respond to local differences in international operations. Along with this flattened structure went increased training so that the remaining personnel could handle greater work responsibility. In particular, cross-training became popular so that employees in the new structure could be assigned to a variety of tasks and perform each well. Also, work teams were created to replace individualism that previously dominated the American work environment. The new approach encouraged working in teams and by using their cross-training they were able to collectively increase productivity. Well-known American firms such as AT&T, Ford Motor and General Electric all reported significant increases in productivity and profit because of such restructuring.

Reengineering

Although American organizations went through massive downsized restructuring in recent years, at a more micro process level, reengineering also has become common. Popularized in a best selling book by Hammer and Champy (1993), *reengineering* can best be defined as 'the fundamental rethinking and radical redesign of business processes to achieve dramatic improvements in critical, contemporary measures of performance, such as cost, quality, service, and speed' (p. 32). This reengineering process typically involves a total redesign of operations, but because of its radical nature, some American managers have been slow to accept the idea. However, an increasing number of managers, especially from large corporations, are now conceding that their operations cannot be made more effective unless they are willing to radically reengineer their operations. Unfortunately, this has often resulted in 'headcount' reductions of personnel and resulting loss of commitment for those remaining. Although reengineering should not be equated with downsizing, this has often been the case and the fallout has not been good for American management.

Despite the potential problems, there have been a number of successful reengineering efforts in American firms. An example is IBM Credit, which used to approve customers for credit by using a five step process that took from six days to two weeks. After carefully studying the credit process, IBM management reengineered credit approvals by putting one person in charge of handling each request and giving that individual the authority to make the requisite decisions. As a result, IBM Credit was able to process 100 times as many requests as previously. There are many such success stories attributed to reengineering.

Information technology

Information technology, in the form of computers and related transmission, retrieval, storage and telecommunication technology, has greatly changed American management. Most US firms have now complemented or replaced their large, mainframe computer systems with microcomputers, some of which are linked to central computer facilities and others which function as stand-alone units. Other practical dimensions of information technology used by American managers include fax machines, electronic organizers, and lightweight, portable computers and telephones.

Implementing information technology has made American managers more efective. One way has been by reducing the time needed to send and retrieve information through the use of electronic mail. A second way has been through time savings in getting information. For example, Connecticut Mutual Life Insurance customer representatives now sit at IBM PCs, where they are able to call up the necessary forms and correspondence needed to answer customer questions. As a result, average responses to inquiries has declined from five days to two hours, 20% fewer people are needed for handling customer questions and productivity has risen by over 35% (Symonds 1992). Another way information technology has helped American managers is through the use of electronic data interchange or EDI. This approach allows customers, companies and suppliers to exchange information directly, computer to computer. For example, General Electric handles over 80% of its business transactions this way, eliminating more than 4 million business forms annually. Information technology is also effectively used through computer monitoring for collecting, examining and feeding back information about work results for the purpose of improving performance and developing employees. For example, computer monitoring is used at Hughes Aircraft Company to facilitate integrated production and quality control strategies and to help increase productivity (Griffith 1993).

TOTAL QUALITY EMPHASIS

Besides the organizational developments discussed so far, today's American management is committed to total quality. Although Total Quality Management or TQM is somewhat now passé, the recognition of total quality as a competitive advantage is alive and well in the US (see Hodgetts 1996a). The following sections describe some of the major characteristics of the total quality movement in the US.

Total quality core values

The philosophy of total quality is grounded in several core values. These values serve as the basis for the US government's national quality award, the Baldrige, as well as for state awards such as New York's Excelsior

Award and Florida's Sterling Award. The major core values can be briefly summarized as follows:

1 **Customer-driven focus**. All methods, processes and procedures are focused on meeting or exceeding the expectations of both internal and external customers.
2 **Leadership**. Management directs the overall total quality effort by first learning what total quality is all about and then giving full support.
3 **Full participation**. All personnel in the organization are provided with quality training and then become actively involved in implementing what they have learned.
4 **Reward system**. A reward system is developed that is capable of motivating the personnel and ensuring continual support for the overall effort.
5 **Reduced cycle time**. Strong attention is given to reducing the amount of time needed to complete tasks by continually analysing work procedures and work flows and then streamlining the process and eliminating unnecessary, redundant nonvalue-adding steps.
6 **Prevention not detection**. The focus of all quality efforts is on identifying and preventing mistakes and errors from occurring rather than detecting and correcting them at a later date.
7 **Management by fact**. Feedback on total quality efforts are data-based and, where possible, quantitative, while lesser attention is given to qualitative forms of feedback such as anecdotal accounts, intuition, and gut feel.
8 **Long-range outlook**. Major consideration is given to identifying future levels of quality products and services, thus ensuring that the organization is able to at least meet, if not surpass, customer expectations.
9 **Partnership development**. An emphasis on total quality creates a co-operative relationship between the firm and both their customers and suppliers, thus allowing them to identify the goods and services that are demanded and develop a system for obtaining quality, reliable supplies at reasonable prices from outside sources.
10 **Public responsibility**. By sharing quality-related information with other organizations and creating jobs by increasing market share and growing, total quality organizations foster corporate citizenship and responsibility.

Formulation and implementation of strategies

In formulating and implementing a total quality strategy, American organizations typically follow four steps:

1 formulate a vision or mission statement
2 get top management actively involved

3 plan and organize the effort
4 implement and control the entire process.

Vision formulation and hammering out a mission statement involves a careful definition of where the company wants to go with quality. Four examples drawn from state quality award winners include:

Group Technologies: Never lose a customer.

Zytec: Provide unsurpassed quality, service and value.

Folger Coffee: Improve consumer and customer satisfaction.

AIL Systems Inc. AIL Systems Inc. is a leading systems integrator and producer of high technology electronic products for defense and commerical applications. Our mission is to meet or exceed the requirements and expectations of our customers with affordable products and services which are distinguished by their quality and innovation. The sustaining philosophy of our company is to continuously strive for higher levels of excellence in every aspect of individual and corporate performance (Hodgetts 1996a: 30).

Top management support for the quality strategy typically begins with the senior-level staff attending quality seminars and learning how the total quality process works. For example, at Globe Metallurgical, a steel firm with facilities in Ohio and Alabama and winner of a Baldrige award, top management received TQM training and was able to use these ideas to completely revamp the firm, streamline operations and sharply increase return on investment. The same is true for an increasing number of American firms, including well-known companies such as AT&T, Motorola and Xerox.

Planning and organizing the quality effort includes setting specific objectives, determining action plans for each unit and deciding how all of these activities will be effectively co-ordinated. At large firms such as Motorola, not only is there the famous six sigma goal, but also it has more specific quality objectives such as increasing quality by 100 times over a four-year period and having all efforts focused on one fundamental objective: total customer satisfaction. In pursuing such objectives, American companies typically designate a senior-level manager as the quality officer and charge this manager with helping create the necessary supporting infrastructure and overseeing the entire quality programme.

In implementing and controlling the total quality process, major attention is given to feedback systems. For example, at Federal Express there are 12 service quality indicators (SQIs) that provide specific feedback for control. Each Fed Ex SQI item is weighted on a scale of 1–10 and each of the dozen items is tracked and reported on a daily basis (Blueprints: 60–3). At Wainwright Industries, a Baldrige winner which builds a wide variety of precision parts and assembled systems from computer disk drive covers to housings for electric motor applications, the company measures feedback on delivery, quality, service and communication with every customer and grades its performance in each area (Hodgetts 1996a: 130–3).

The use of statistical process control techniques

Once the total quality values and strategies are formulated, then specific techniques are used in actual practice. These techniques range from simple data collection charts to statistical analyses of samples for the purpose of determining when to take corrective action. Several of the most common tools used in quality management in the US include:

1 **Flow charts** which provide a pictorial representation of the steps in a work process and allow employees to identify those which are critical to the work being performed and those which can be eliminated because they provide no value.
2 **Check sheets** which are used to quickly and accurately collect information regarding the number of times particular events occur, such as customer complaints regarding defective products or failure to deliver merchandise at the agreed upon time.
3 **Pareto charts** which allow personnel to identify the few causes that account for the majority of outcomes, such as two reasons that help explain 80% of all customer complaints.
4 **Cause-and-effect diagrams** (sometimes called fishbone analyses) which help identify the major reasons accounting for the problem under review and help cluster these problems into a handful of areas which can then be pinpointed for resolution.
5 **Scatter diagrams** which help graphically describe the relationship between two variables, such as the effect of increasing training on sales.
6 **Frequency histograms** which display the distribution of data using bar graphs and allow the observer to quickly and easily read the information and make a decision regarding whether or not the results are within acceptable levels of performance.
7 **Control charts** that use a running plot of collected data and compare these results to upper control and lower control limits in order to determine whether to leave things alone or to take corrective action.

The choice of statistical process control tools is based on the specific problem and many firms train their employees to be able to select the best one or two tools to use in solving specific problems. For example, when seeking to identify those problems that account for most of the outcomes, employees are taught to use Pareto analysis. When seeking to determine cause-effect relationships, scatter plots are the primary choice. This approach is sometimes referred to as the 'tool box,' because the employee chooses only the one or two best tools for conducting the analysis and bypasses the rest.

Empowerment

The concept of empowerment has become a cornerstone in the quality movement in American firms. An extension of the classical principle of delegation, empowered employees are given the information and resources as well as the authority to make decisions and to use resources in implementing them. The objective of empowerment is to encourage employees to become more personally involved in where the action is in improving the quality of products or service to customers. For instance, at American manufacturing firms such as Solectron (a national quality award winner), empowerment includes the authority of individual workers to stop the entire production line when a quality problem is uncovered. In firms where front-line employees deal directly with customers, empowerment allows them to exchange or replace products, provide additional or alternative services and authorize cash refunds, all without getting approval from their boss. For instance, at the Ritz-Carlton hotel chain, employees are authorized to spend up to $2000 to handle specific real problems such as mailing a suit to a customer who checked out and left it in his room; sending a pot of herbal tea and aspirin to a guest who had just checked in and had a cold; or renting a monitor and VCR because all of the hotel's units were in use and a client needed this equipment for a meeting scheduled to start immediately. At Motorola some mid-level managers are empowered to spend up to $5000 to assist customers or solve a quality problem, which is put back into their account at the beginning of the next day – so theoretically they are empowered to spend over $1 million annually (Hodgetts 1993).

Continuous improvement

Of the 'excellent' firms identified by Peters and Waterman in their best selling book (1982), many today would no longer be labelled as such. These firms rested on their achievements. Now, American management is committed to never being satisfied. They realize that total quality means always getting better. Known as continuous improvement (CI) in total quality, this is a process of continually making changes that increase the efficiency and effectiveness of a company's goods and services. CI relies on two major guidelines: constant incremental gains and an occasional breakthrough innovation. While breakthrough innovation is needed, the total quality approach gives it relatively less emphasis because it is unpredictable and non-incremental. Instead, American firms focus on CI, characterized by continual small gains.

In recent years, many quality-driven organizations have implemented a team approach as the best way to carry out this CI process. For example, at Baptist Hospital in Miami, CI teams have used techniques such as Pareto analysis, cause-and-effect diagrams and brainstorming to achieve a number of quality improvements including reducing the time that patients spend in the emergency department (ED), cutting inventory and reducing the time needed to admit and discharge patients. CI teams have also been instrumental in revising the ED patient survey so as to better identify trends, increase the number of phone lines in the treatment room and re-evaluate staffing requirements.

Another common approach used in continuous improvement is benchmarking, a process of comparing a company's current performance with that of organizations judged to be 'best in class'. Benchmarking commonly involves three steps:

1 An analysis of the best processes and procedures used throughout the organization (internal benchmarking), in order to determine if similar approaches can be used by other departments or units.
2 A study of the processes and practices used by rival firms (competitive benchmarking), in order to identify, set goals and copy, if relevant, the best practices in the industry.
3 An examination of organizations outside the industry (generic benchmarking) for the purpose of identifying, setting goals and copying or modifying closely related processes and practices that can be useful in helping the firm increase its own efficiency.

A good example is IBM Rochester, a Baldrige winner which designed and built the AS/400 minicomputer. In building the minicomputer, management learned about the benchmarking process in general from Xerox; the essence of six sigma quality standards from Motorola; resource manufacturing planning from the 3M Company; world-class defect prevention processes from IBM Raleigh; and the effective use of service representatives from Hewlett-Packard. As a result of these internal, competitive and generic benchmarking efforts, IBM Rochester developed and produced a minicomputer which proved to be the most successful product launch in the history of the company.

A 'must' for an effective CI process is the reward system. Quality improvements occur only if they are rewarded. In the US, such reward systems are obviously done with pay for quality performance, but also in innovative ways. For example, at the Ritz-Carlton hotels any employee can send a 'First Class' card – a 3" x 5" card designed with the company logo – to express his or her appreciation to anyone else in the organization for a job well done. The company also uses 'Lightning Srikes' – monetary rewards granted by a member of the Executive Committee to any employee for outstanding service. At Zytec the company uses a suggestion system as the basis of a seven-step process for rewarding CI:

1 For each idea employees submit, they receive a $1 token cash award plus a lottery ticket, which is presented at their work station.
2 The work group with the highest percentage of employee participation gets to display a trophy for a month, after which it is presented to another group.
3 Each month the lottery tickets are put in a hat and one is drawn for a day off with pay.
4 The winner of the day off with pay chooses a support or staff person to take over his or her job.
5 Each month the programme administrator asks for a volunteer from each work group to serve on the review board. This board reviews all ideas submitted that month and chooses the top three. The employees who submitted the top three ideas are given $100, $75 and $50, respectively.
6 Each month the programme administrator takes pictures of the three winners and places them on the bulletin boards.
7 A copy of the review board's minutes is published in the company newsletter each month (see Hodgetts 1993: 96).

Such innovative techniques are one reason why many American organizations are making total quality a reality in competitive world markets.

AMERICAN ORGANIZATIONS IN THE 21ST CENTURY

Many American managers believe that total quality has become just the cost of entry in today's global economy. Total quality is necessary but not sufficient. Radically different, new paradigm organizations that go beyond total quality are beginning to emerge. These new organizations can be called learning and world-class organizations (Luthans, Hodgetts, and Lee 1994). Although many of the characteristics of these emerging organizations are the same as those associated with total quality, in an additive sense they go beyond quality and provide more focus on world competitiveness and future success.

Learning organizations

Learning organizations are most widely recognized as having double loop (Argyris and Schon 1978) or generative (Senge 1990; 1991) learning in which change and/or problems are anticipated and either prevented or creatively solved the first time they appear. Unlike single loop or adaptive organizations that merely react to change and continually face and resolve recurring problems, learning organizations proactively anticipate change, analyse the root causes of problems, prevent their recurrence and, essentially, have learned how to learn.

Major characteristics of learning organizations

A major characteristic of learning organizations is the continuous scanning of the external environment. This monitoring allows learning organizations to remain alert to new technological and other environmental developments and incorporate them into all relevant aspects of the operation. For example, Packard Bell has been able to continually bring down its prices and maintain a growing market share in the highly competitive personal computer industry because of its ability to carry out effective external environmental scanning.

Another characteristic is the use of shared vision. Shared vision is used to create a personal commitment from all participants. Learning organizations accomplish this commitment by clearly spelling out their basic mission and overriding objectives. An example is Wild Oats, a successful health food chain based in Colorado, which does this through this basic statement of purpose:

> We are here to provide our customers with the best selection of whole foods and health-care products with an attitude of friendliness, eagerness to serve and readiness to educate. We are committed to making our store a pleasant place to shop and work and to be an active, responsible contributor to the lives of our staff, customers and community.

Traditional resource-based vs. knowledge-based learning organizations

Besides scanning the environment and shared vision, another characteristic of learning organizations is management's willingness and ability to generate and transfer new knowledge and technology throughout the enterprise. In this way, the learning organization develops a knowledge-based approach in which the information and knowledge of employees serve to create a distinctive core competency for the business. This is in sharp contrast with American organizations of the 1970s and 1980s which relied heavily on resources (money, materials, machinery) to provide them with a distinctive competitive edge.

Senge (1993) has recently contrasted the differences between these knowledge-based learning organizations and the more traditional resource-based organizations. For example, knowledge-based learning organizations differ from more traditional resource-based organizations by the way in which they create their vision. In the knowledge-based organization, vision can emerge from any level, although the senior-level management remains responsible for both refining and promoting this vision through the effective use of organizational processes. Other differences between resource-based and knowledge-based organizations include the ways in which ideas are formulated and implemented, the nature of organizational thinking, conflict resolution, leadership and motivation.

In knowledge-based organizations the formulation and implementation of strategies takes place at all levels. This is in sharp contrast to resource-based organizations where this activity begins at the top level and uses a cascading effect to work its way down to the lower levels. One of the major reasons that knowledge-based firms are able to carry out strategy formulation and implementation at any and all levels is that the employees are empowered with both the necessary authority and financial resources to take the necessary action. A good example is Zytec, where employees have $1000 each to spend in any way that will help improve internal and external customer service.

Another difference between traditional resource-based and knowledge-based learning organizations is seen in the nature of the thinking of managers and workers. In resouce-based organizations, personnel understand their jobs but there is little attention given to how these tasks interrelate or influence those of others. The flow of authority and the focus of attention tends to be hierarchical and vertical in nature. In contrast, learning organizations teach the personnel how their jobs and actions influence those of others in the enterprise and vice versa. An example is provided by Hanover Insurance. During the 1980s the firm steadily increased local control of regional operations, promoting a greater sense of ownership among the employees. Hanover also developed a claims management learning laboratory so that local managers could better understand how their decisions had an impact on others. As a result, these local managers soon discovered that some well-accepted practices used in the industry were contributing to problems such as escalating costs and premiums. By systematically rethinking the ways in which settlement costs were handled, Hanover was able to significantly reduce payouts.

Also, the difference between the two types of organizations is the way in which conflict resolution is handled. In the traditional system, disputes are mediated along political lines. Those with the most power or persuasive arguments carry the day. In contrast, learning organizations operate under the premise that conflicts often cannot be solved through the mere use of power or formal authority. Rather, effective solutions often require input from a wide array of personnel located throughout the organization, at all levels and functions. In turn, this results in the organization relying heavily on collaborative learning and the integration of diverse viewpoints. A good example is provided by General Electric, which is currently replacing hierarchical control with internal personnel co-operation and effective customer and supplier linkages.

Another major difference between resource-based and knowledge-based organizations is the way in which leaders both direct and motivate human resources. Leaders in resource-based enterprises rely heavily on rewards and punishment to ensure employee compliance. Leaders in knowledge-based enterprises inspire commitment and rely heavily on charismatic appeal to motivate human resources to ever-higher standards of performance.

World-class organizations

Some American firms are now going beyond learning organizations and creating what are becoming known as 'world-class organizations' or WCOs (Luthans, Hodgetts and Lee 1994). WCOs are recongized as leaders in their field because of their ability not just to dominate their respective markets, but to become the best in the world at what they do and create new demand for their present and future products and services. In large measure, WCOs have been able to change the paradigms of their industry by developing competencies that allow them to offer state-of-the-art products or services that not merely meet customer expectations but exceed them and add value for their customers. For example, Hewlett-Packard's insights into opportunities such as work stations, reduced instruction set architecture and the market for small printers and other peripherals helped propel the firm from an instruments company to a world-class information technology enterprise. Merck's insight into the changing environment of the pharmaceutical industry led it to purchase Medco, a large mail order pharmaceutical distribution company and sharply change the way all firms in the industry competed. CNN introduced round the clock news and proved that there was a world-wide demand for this service. Wal-Mart offered friendly service at rock-bottom prices and showed that there was a market in both rural and urban America. These American firms (and many others) have changed the paradigms of their industry by reinventing the way things are done (Hamel and Prahalad 1994).

The major pillars of world class organizations

WCOs in America have gone beyond total quality and even learning organizations in an additive, cumulative sense. We have recently identified six major pillars that seem to best characterize WCOs (Luthans, Hodgetts and Lee 1994).

The first critical pillar of the WCO is a customer focus. The customer is the centre of the organization's strategy. All systems and personnel are organized to serve the customer, whether internal or external. One of the most common ways of doing this is by flattening the structure discussed earlier. The flat structure allows personnel to be closer to the customer. Being close to the customer enhances the ability to gather information about the customer's current and future needs. By being customer focused, WCOs are able not only to meet customer needs but also create new demand for their goods and services. Hewlett-Packard made major gains in the printer market because it learned from customers how to redesign and simplify product offerings. This has led to products that are more reliable and less expensive and has helped generate increased demand.

A second pillar of WCOs is continuous improvement borrowed from the total quality movement. Through CI, WCOs learn to be faster and more effective than competitors. For example, after carefully studying its inventory control needs, Wal-Mart realized that Proctor & Gamble (P&G), one of its largest suppliers, was best qualified to determine when and how much inventory was needed in order to ensure that the stores did not run out of P&G merchandise. Wal-Mart turned over the restocking function to P&G, allowed P&G to decide what to ship and when and found that this arrangement reduced inventory and carrying costs and made it more price competitive than ever.

A third pillar of WCOs is the use of flexible organizational arrangements that allow them to respond quickly, decisively and correctly to competitive challenges. This flexibility has led WCOs to become 'virtual corporations', a term used to describe companies that on the surface appear to be huge, but underneath consist of only core competencies (Davidow and Malone 1992). A good example is Chrysler, which relies more heavily on outsourcing than many of the other auto firms. The outsourcing partners make Chrysler appear on the surface to be a much larger organization than it really is. The outsourcing has helped Chrysler drive down costs, increase efficiency, and raise profits. Besides outsourcing, some other examples of the flexibility of WCOs include: the use of modular or matrix organizations; the use of multifunctional and empowered teams; the simultaneous processing of ideas; cross-trained, multiple skilled workers; and innovative approaches to cycle time reduction.

A fourth pillar of WCOs is the use of creative human resource management (HRM) programmes that are designed to tap the full potential of the personnel. These HRM programmes might include the sharing of ownership of the problems and solutions under study; the communication of consistent organization goals and objectives to all levels; and the effective use of recognition and rewarding the team or a group through a gainsharing plan. An example of such creative HRM is AT&T Universal Card Services (UCS) which empowers its employees to take steps to reduce costs and improve customer service by creating teams that plan strategies for reducing problems on its 'Ten Most Wanted' list. As a problem is resolved, it is removed from the list and another 'Top 10' is put in its place. Thus the team face a never-ending list of issues and problems and they are encouraged to take responsibility for formulating solutions. This strategy has helped UCS maintain its reputation as one of the best customer-service-driven firms in the country. WCOs also provide a variety of reward systems, both non-financial and monetary. For example, Marlow Industries maintains a hall of fame and also uses service awards, perfect attendance awards, good housekeeping awards, team recognition awards, individual team bonuses, and profit sharing.

A fifth pillar of WCOs is an egalitarian climate in which everyone learns to value and respect one another, including customers, owners, employees, suppliers and the community. At Wal-Mart, for example, employees are called associates and all store managers have weekly meetings during which they hold open discussions with the associates for the purpose of reviewing operations and openly discussing new ideas for improving customer service. Some of the most important features of this egalitarian pillar include: open communication between all parties; a friendly environment; a mentoring, coaching, buddy system; active employee involvement and participation in all phases of operations; and sponsored community, wellness and family programmes.

The sixth and final pillar supporting WCOs is technological support. Many of the creative, innovative, or productive approaches of WCOs are made possible because of advances in technologies such as computer-aided design, computer-aided manufacturing, telecommunications, expert systems, distributed database systems, interorganizational information systems, multimedia systems and management information systems. Such technological support helps the enterprise use speed, information and differentiation to gain competitive advantages. For example, Wal-Mart's computer system allows it to track sales store by store, identify those items which are selling best and use this information to analyse customer demand and take appropriate follow up action. Another example is American Express's company AmeriTax, which provides electronic tax filing by creating an electronic linkage between the US Internal Revenue Service (IRS) and tax preparation firms. Through this interorganizational information system, AmeriTax offers tax return preparation service to its customers, while also developing a conduit for a larger set of financial products and services. Some of the key elements of the technological support pillar include: technology-human interface; modern information and telecommunication systems; distributed information/database systems; shared ownership of information; decentralization of decision making to the lowest level possible; and continuous technical training.

CONCLUSIONS

American management has definitely bounced back in recent years to become the most competitive in the world. More and more firms throughout the United States and the world are beginning to pay increasing attention to how American WCOs are managed. At present, American management continues to introduce new, innovative ideas that are helping to drive down costs, increase quality and gain market share. In particular, greater focus is being placed on customer service, total quality, speed, information technology, continuous improvement, outsourcing, and creative human resources management.

Obviously, not all American companies are WCOs and they can learn a lot from management in other countries. However, the ideas and characteristics of total quality, learning and world-class organizations are now being identified and implemented by an increasing number of American firms and others around the world. The best of the group are serving as benchmarks for the rest. However, despite these world-class standards, American management still understands that local differentiation and recognition of cultural differences when doing business around the world remains important to the success of organizations going into the 21st Century.

ACKNOWLEDGEMENT

This chapter draws in part on material published in the author's contribution to *The International Encyclopaedia of Business Management* (1996), (ed M. Warner) 6 volumes, Routledge, London, with permission.

REFERENCES

Argyris, C., and Schon, D. (1978) *Organizational Learning*, Addison-Wesley, Reading, MA.

Blueprints for Service Quality (1991) *The Federal Express Approach* American Management Association, New York.

Davidow, W.H. and Malone, M.S. (1992) *The Virtual Corporation*, Harper Collins, New York.

Griffith, T.L. (1993) Teaching big brother to be a team player: computer monitoring and quality. *Academy of Management Review*, 7: pp. 73–80.

Hamel,. G. and Prahalad, C.K. (1994) *Competing for the Future*, Harvard Business School Press, Boston.

Hammer, M. and Champy, J. (1993) *Reengineering the Corporation*, Harper Business, New York.

Hodgetts, R.M. (1993) *Blueprints for Continuous Improvement: Lessons from the Baldrige Winners*, American Management Association, New York.

Hodgetts, R.M. (1996a) *Implementing TQM in Small and Medium-Sized Organizations*, American Management Association, New York.

Hodgetts, R.M. (1996b) *Modern Human Relations at Work*, 6th edition, Dryden Press, Chicago.

Luthans, F., Hodgetts, R.M. and Lee, S.M. (1994) New paradigm organizations: from total quality to learning to world class. *Organizational Dynamics*, Winter, pp. 5–19.

Peters, T. and Waterman, R.H. (1982) *In Search of Excellence* Harper Row, New York.

Senge, P.M. (1993) Transforming the Practice of Management. *Human Resource Development Quarterly*, **4**: pp. 5–32.

Symonds, W.C. (1992) Getting Rid of Paper is Just the Beginning. *Business Week*, **32**: pp. 88–9.

Chapter 8

As the world spins: short-term changes in international clusters

Leyland Pitt, Pierre Berthon, Pat Joynt and Arthur Money

INTRODUCTION

There are two broad approaches to the study of international management. The traditional economic approach dates back to Adam Smith and focuses on the extension of macroeconomic theory to include an international or comparative perspective. The second approach, which is much younger in its origin, may be labelled the behavioural approach and usually takes a micro comparative perspective. The contents of this book are very much divided between the two perspectives, indeed one would expect this in an international world where both micro and macro perspectives are necessary to understand comparative behaviours.

Firms considering international strategies are faced by a bewildering array of potential foreign activities – continents, regions, countries and, of course, sub-activities within countries. The choice between them is key. Managers within the organization have to go through the act of dividing a heterogeneous population – in this case perhaps the whole world – into more distinct groups. Companies identify different ways to divide activities and to develop policies for local and international segments. As their activities are divided using various inputs, the company, hopefully, achieves fine precision.

Whilst the study of dividing the activities of a firm between the home country and the various international regions is interesting in terms of research and development, manufacturing, logistics, human resources management, finance, service and marketing, our focus in this chapter will be primarily on the first activity used in international expansion by the firm, namely marketing or more specifically export behaviour.

The assessment of international business opportunities usually begins with a screening process that involves gathering relevant information on each country and filtering out the less desirable countries. Walvoord (1980) has proposed a model for selecting foreign markets which includes a sequence of four filters to screen out countries. He breaks the process down into a series of steps, due to the large number of market opportunities that may be available. While a firm would not want to miss a potential opportunity, it is almost without exception not possible to conduct extensive market research studies in every one of the more than 150 countries in the world. (World Bank Atlas (1990) includes 185 countries and territories.) The screening process identifies good prospects and attempts to overcome two common errors of country screening (Root 1987). These are: first, ignoring countries that offer good potential for the company's products and services; and second, spending too much time investigating countries that are poor prospects for the company's products and services. The process thus allows the international marketer to quickly focus efforts on a few of the most promising market opportunities by using published secondary sources available in most business libraries and, nowadays, in electronic data-bases.

The first stage of the process uses macro, often economic, variables to discriminate between countries that represent basic opportunities and countries with little or no opportunity, or with excessive risk. Typical macro variables used to describe the market are those in terms of read-ily-available economic, social, geographic and political risk information. These statistics will indicate frequently, for example, that the country's population is too small, or that the personal disposable household income may be too low to provide a realistic market for the firm's products or services.

More recently other writers (Helsen, Jedidi and DeSarbo 1993; McLauchlin 1993; Ryans and Rau 1990) have considered the clustering of markets within the international sphere. Helsen *et al.* (1993) consider the use of country classification schemes in gaining an understanding about multinational diffusion patterns. Ryans and Rau (1990) clustered Europe on the basis of EC regions. Rather than considering the European Community as one homogeneous mass market, or a collection of small specialized markets, they predict that new Euroconsumer clusters will emerge. These clusters include customers who are close to each other geographically but not necessarily living in the same country. They suggest that a marketer, just by scanning the clusters, can see that there are significant differences between various European regions. For exam-ple, the average income in cluster 6 of their analysis (US$19,420) is three times that of their cluster 3 (US$6,530). Marketing such a non-essential item as entertainment, for example, would likely be far more successful in cluster 6. Cluster 6 consists of Denmark, Northern Germany, the Nether-lands and Northern Belgium and the authors suggest that Switzerland, Iceland, Sweden, Finland and Norway would be part of this cluster should they join the European Union. The cluster is also characterized by a high proportion of middle-aged people and is multi-lingual. While the dominant languages are French and German, consumers within this cluster also speak French and Italian and generally have a good command of English as well. Language also differentiates significantly between clusters identified by Ryans and Rau (1990). A marketer could only reach half of these clusters with any one particular language, such as German, French or Italian. In addition, age differences among the clusters would have their effect on the choice of products sold within each cluster. The cluster 3 already referred to (Spain and Portugal) is situated, obviously, in South Western Europe and is characterized by a young population with a lower than average income, many of whom only have command of one language, namely Spanish or Portuguese.

That global change is turbulent and dynamic goes without saying. However, the changes in the international environment in the period 1990–1994 were so dramatic as to be almost unique in modern history. Command economies fell like skittles and the Soviet Union dissolved; Germany was reunified; there was a major war in the Persian Gulf; major recession descended on most advanced economies in 1991 and 1992; apartheid gave way to democracy in South Africa, while paradoxically much of that continent fell into disarray. These were just some of the dramatic metamorphoses which the world underwent in the ebbing years of the era. In this chapter we describe a basic level of market segmentation for all the countries of the world, using a clustering procedure on a commercially available data base. More specifically, we show just how impermanent country clusters are, by means of a follow-up analysis of previous work (Pitt, Joynt and Money 1993; Pitt, Money and Berthon 1994). We suggest the approach as a useful addition to the first step in the procedure first described by Walvoord (1980).

GROUPING THE GLOBE – A K-MEANS CLUSTERING PROCEDURE

Recent advances in information technology have meant that a vast amount of business and marketing data is commercially available to managers, on relatively inexpensive media such as CD-ROM disks. One of these data bases is the Wayzata World Fact Book (1991; 1993). The World Fact Book is produced annually by the Central Intelligence Agency for the use of United States Government officials and the style, format, coverage and content are designed to meet their specific requirements. The data base contains pertinent economic, geographic, political, communications and demographic data for all of the world's countries, regions and territories. The user is able to address a numerical data base section by means of data base software, or simply by commonly used spread sheets such as Lotus 123® or Excel®.

Cluster analysis has the usual objective of separating objects into groups, such that each object is more like other objects in its group than like those. As a process that is concerned ultimately with classification and with techniques part of the field of numerical taxonomy (Sokal and Sneath 1963), cluster analysis has been used very productively in a number of marketing and marketing research applications. It can be applied to the investigation of useful conceptual schemes for grouping entities, hypothesis generation through data exploration and hypothesis testing, or for attempting to determine if types defined through other procedures are present in a data set (Aldenderfer and Blashfield 1984). Put simply, cluster analysis is a set of techniques designed to identify objects, people, or variables that are similar with regard to some criteria or characteristics. It is ideally suited to market segmentation because it aids in the orderly classification of the myriad data that typically confront the marketing researcher. Regardless of the clustering procedure used, however, the analyst still faces the task of describing them. One measure frequently used is the centroid – the average value of the objects contained in the cluster on each of the variables making up each object's profile. If the data are interval scaled and clustering is performed in original variable space, this measure appears quite natural as a summary description. To repeat, however, it is still up to the analyst to name clusters.

Clusters of countries

Using data on twenty-eight variables from the Wayzata (1991 and 1993) data bases, 168 countries and territories of the world were separated into five different clusters for 1991 and this process was repeated in 1993. Two important points should be made here. First, the world in 1991 (only a few years ago) was very different from what it was in 1993. The USSR still existed and the map of Eastern Europe was very different from what it is today. The conflict in regions such as the then Yugoslavia had not yet erupted. So the results from a similar procedure conducted on 1993 data might be quite different. The data base is updated annually however, so this is not a serious drawback. Second, the extraction of five clusters might also be seen as somewhat arbitrary – in a sense it is. Our not very strong argument is that the world consists of five inhabited continents or regions, so geographic proximity would be the most basic type of clustering there is. It will immediately be obvious however, that the analyst can choose however many clusters he or she wishes to and also that clusters can be sub-clustered further to provide deeper insights. Some degree of external validity is also given to the procedure by a replication.

In the case of some of the variables, data were used in unchanged form. These variables were:-

– Birth rate
– Death rate

- Fertility rate
- Economic growth rate
- industrial growth rate
- Infant mortality rate
- Inflation rate
- Labour force as % of population
- Life expectancy[1]: females
- Life expectancy: males
- Literacy: female
- Literacy: male
- Literacy: total[2]
- Net migration
- Population growth rate
- Unemployment as % of total workforce

In other instances, the variable was transformed to a per capita figure, in order to make comparisons more realistic – for example, it is not realistic or particularly insightful to compare two countries such as China (with more than a billion inhabitants) and Australia (with less than 17 million), on the basis of population, even though they are roughly the same size geographically. Neither is it realistic to compare the absolute defence spending[3] of the USA with that of Israel. However, when this is done on a per capita basis, the picture is quite meaningful. The per capita variables thus created and used were:

- Airports per capita
- Budgeted expenditure per capita
- Budgeted revenue per capita
- Defence expenditure per capita
- Exports per capita
- External debt per capita
- GDP per capita
- Highway km per capita
- Imports per capita
- Population density[4]
- Railways km per capita
- Inland waterways km per capita

The data were subjected to the *K*-Means clustering procedure under SPSS. The five clusters extracted for both periods are described broadly in Table 8.1. The distances between the final cluster centres are also reported in Table 8.1.

The clusters are named, and described, in terms of the distinctions between them on the 28 variables – the final cluster centres – in Table

Table 8.1 A broad description of the clusters

Number of Cases in each Cluster

Cluster	Number of Cases in Cluster 1991	Number of Cases in Cluster 1993
1	10	8
2	25	24
3	24	22
4	5	10
5	104	128
Total	**168**	**192**

Distances between Final Cluster Centres - 1991.

Cluster	1	2	3	4	5
1	.0000				
2	12679.8513	.0000			
3	6113.3783	6566.5275	.0000		
4	20253.1940	10950.7581	15176.2279	.0000	
5	17964.5752	5285.0379	11851.3116	9670.6663	.0000

Distances between final Cluster Centres - 1993.

Cluster	5	2	3	4	1
5	.0000				
2	4895.0231	.0000			
3	19929.3909	15034.6455	.0000		
4	9332.6728	4437.8066	10596.8950	.0000	
1	14463.4747	9568.6825	5465.9821	5130.9205	.0000

8.2. The clusters are discussed in more detail in Tables 8.3a to 8.3e. The five clusters and their names are shown graphically in Figure 8.1.

The countries in Cluster 1, 'The Truly Wealthy' are shown in Table 8.3a. These countries may be described as truly wealthy, as evidenced by the highest Gross Domestic Product per capita. These countries also export and import more per capita than the rest, have the greatest proportion of the population as part of the labour force, and the lowest levels of unemployment. Not surprisingly, the inhabitants of these countries enjoy the lowest infant mortality rates, the longest life expectancies and also the greatest levels of literacy, while experiencing the lowest levels of fertility and, hence, of population growth. In comparing the 1991 and 1993 clusters, it will be observed that three countries (Sweden, Iceland and Norway) dropped out of the cluster in 1993, to become members of

Table 8.2 The final cluster centres.

Cluster	1 (The Truly Wealthy)	2 (The In-betweens)	3 (The First World Countries 1991)	4 (The Economic Disasters) 1991 and In need of a Name 1993	5 (The Third World Countries) 1991
Airports per Capita 1991	0.0001	0	0	0	0
Airports per Capita 1993	0.0001	0	0	0	0
Birth Rate 1991	13.5	19.76	15.7083	26.2	37.1923
Birth Rate 1993	12.7500	20.8333	15.5455	19.3000	34.7500
Budget Expenditure per Capita	0.006	0.0019	0.005	0.0006	0.0003
Budget Expenditure per Capita	0059.	0018	0059	.0042	.0677
Budgeted Revenue per Capita 1991	0.006	0.0017	0.0052	0.0005	0.0002
Budgeted Revenue per Capita 1993	.0054	.0015	.0054	.0034	00198
Death Rate 1991	8.5	7.48	7.375	6.6	10.8558
Death Rate 1993	6.3750	7.71	7.64	7.3000	10.2422
Defence Expenditure per Capita 1991	0.0004	0.0005	0.0004	0.0001	0
Not available 1993					
Exports per Capita 1991	0.0098	0.0053	0.0024	0.0002	0.0002
Export per Capita 1993	.0119	.0058	.0018	.0049	.0003
External Debt per Capita 1991	0.0029	0.0011	0.0035	0.0008	0.0007
External Debt per Capita 1993	.0063	.0029	.0067	.0070	.0004
Fertility Rate 1991	1.73	2.636	2.1	3.1	5.0673

Table 8.2 Continued

Cluster	1 (The Truly Wealthy)	2 (The In-betweens)	3 (The First World Countries 1991)	4 (The Economic Disasters) 1991 and In need of a Name 1993	5 (The Third World Countries) 1991
Fertility Rate 1993	1.6500	2.841	2.057	2.4800	4.7172
GDP per Capita 1991	18970	6290.2	12856.6667	1201.6	1005.7885
GDP per Capita 1993	21056.8750	6022.2917	15590.9091	10460.0000	1127.7891
Economic Growth Rate 1991	2	2.2478	3.6957	−1.475	2.217
Economic Growth Rate 1993	1.6250	.8167	1.9636	2.7600	1.9578
Highway Km's per Capita 1991	0.0175	0.0056	0.0103	0.0037	0.0042
Highway Km's per Capita 1993	0.0136	0.0122	0.0091	0.0046	0.0046
Imports per Capita 1991	0.0061	0.0039	0.0054	0.0003	0.0003
Imports per Capita 1993	.0014	.0013	.0036	.0022	.0006
Industrial Growth Rate 1991	0.6	1.375	2.365	−8.3333	3.3582
Industrial Growth Rate 1993	.7875	1.3750	1.3114	3.7600	2.7531
Infant Mortality Rate 1991	7	19.32	9.4583	43.6	76.3365
Infant Mortality Rate 1993	7.6250	20.8750	9.0000	17.1000	66.5703
Inflation Rate 1991	5.37	28.4333	5.187	9725	56.4225
Inflation Rate 1993	4.4750	35.3042	6.0409	8.0300	63.6688
Labour Force as % of Population 1991	0.4972	0.3722	0.3778	0.3635	0.2662

Table 8.2 Continued

Cluster	1 (The Truly Wealthy)	2 (The In-betweens)	3 (The First World Countries 1991)	4 (The Economic Disasters) 1991 and In need of a Name 1993	5 (The Third World Countries) 1991
Labour Force as % of Population 1993	.5126	3352	.3845	.3956	.2789
Life Expectancy: Females 1991	80.6	75.68	79.25	72.2	61.9808
Life Expectancy: Females 1993	80.3750	75.5000	79.5000	77.4000	64.1172
Life Expectancy: Males 1991	73.9	69.64	73.0833	66.6	58.0385
Life Expectancy: Males 1993	74.0000	69.3750	73.3636	72.0000	59.6250
Literacy: Female 1991	99	83	82.1667	60.5	53.8586
Literacy: Female 1993	99.1250	83.2917	90.9091	88.2000	58.2969
Literacy: Male	98.75	88.7	89.25	81	69.4141
Literacy: Male 1993	98.8750	88.0833	93.1364	92.7000	71.0703
Literacy: Total 1991	99	87.0435	91.9091	77	62.1942
Literacy: Total 1993	99.0000	85.8333	92.1364	90.4000	64.8047
Net Migration 1991	3	−1.12	6.7917	−0.4	−1.2885
Net Migration 1993	2.8750	−.7083	4.9545	2.2000	1.5656
Population Density 1991	0.0908	0.0344	0.0343	0.0227	0.066
Population Density 1993	.0543	.0320	.0571	.0161	.0600
Population Growth Rate 1991	0.8	1.132	1.5083	1.9	2.5067
Population Growth Rate 1993	.7750	1.2371	1.2773	1.1500	2.4680

Table 8.2 Continued

Cluster	1 (The Truly Wealthy)	2 (The In-betweens)	3 (The First World Countries 1991)	4 (The Economic Disasters) 1991 and In need of a Name 1993	5 (The Third World Countries) 1991
Railways Km per Capita 1991	0.0009	0.0002	0.0004	0.0004	0.0002
Railways Km per Capita 1993	.0009	.0005	.0004	.0001	.0002
Unemployement as % of Total Workforce 1991	2.9111	7.0091	12.4333	27.5	16.8912
Unemployment as % of Total Workforce 1993	*3.8625*	*7.1682*	*12.6292*	*8.4900*	*18.5648*
Inland Waterways Km per Capita 1991	0.0001	0	0.0002	0.0002	0.0002
Inland Waterways Km per Capita 1993	*0.0003*	*0*	*0.0001*	*0.0001*	*0.0002*

Cluster 3 (the 'First World Countries'), while one country (Austria) joined the cluster.

Cluster 2, shown in Table 8.3b, is a cluster where a great deal of change has occurred. In 1991, we named this cluster 'The In-betweens' (Pitt, Joynt and Money 1993), as they were really in a First World – Third World dichotomy. They were generally much better off than the countries in Cluster 5, but hadn't yet reached the levels of economic performance of those in Clusters 1 and 3. The main distinguishing features of these countries was the highest defence spending per capita, and an employment situation very similar to the First World countries – on all other variables, they are fairly and squarely between First – and Third world. We stated at the time (Pitt, Joynt and Money 1993) that 'it is tempting to speculate that the move, when made, to either First or Third World cluster, will be dependent on the ability of many of these countries to overcome political turmoil'. Cluster 2 and, as will be seen later, Cluster 4, proved to be the two most dynamic clusters of the five. There has been much movement from and into Cluster 2. It will also be observed that the break-up of Eastern Europe has had an impact on Cluster 2 and that the exclusion of defence spending per capita as a clustering variable in the 1993 study has had a very marked effect.

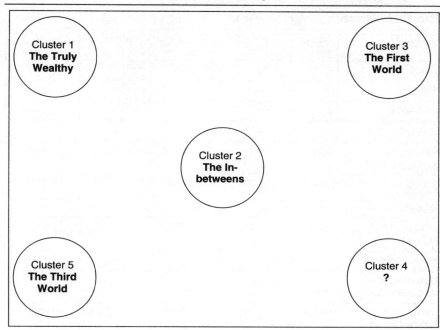

Figure 8.1 The five clusters and their names

Table 8.3a Cluster 1: 'The truly wealthy'

COUNTRY	Cluster 1991	In Cluster 1993?	If not, where moved to/where from?
Bermuda	1	Yes	
Canada	1	Yes	
Iceland	1	No	Moved to Cluster 3
Japan	1	Yes	
Liechtenstein	1	Yes	
Luxembourg	1	Yes	
Norway	1	No	Moved to Cluster 3
Sweden	1	No	Moved to Cluster 3
Switzerland	1	Yes	
United States	1	Yes	
Austria	3 ('First World')	Yes	Moved from Cluster 3

Table 8.3b Cluster 2: 'The in-betweens'

COUNTRY	Cluster 1991	In Cluster 1993?	If not, where moved to/where from?
Antigua	2	Yes	
Bahrain	2	Yes	
Barbados	2	Yes	
Bulgaria	2	Yes	
Cyprus	2	No	Moved to Cluster 4
Czechoslovakia	2	Yes	
Greece	2	Yes	
Guam	2	No	Moved to Cluster 3 ('First World')
Hungary	2	Yes	
Korea, South	2	Yes	
Libya	2	Yes	
Macau	2	Yes	
Malta	2	Yes	
Martinique	2	Yes	
Oman	2	Yes	
Poland	2	Yes	
Portugal	2	No	Cluster 4
Puerto Rico	2	Yes	
Reunion	2	Yes	
Saudi Arabia	2	Yes	
Seychelles	2	Yes	
Soviet Union	2	No	Country 'broken up' into Commonwealth of Independent States: most are now in Cluster 5: 'Third World Countries'
Yugoslavia	2	No	Country 'broken up'; insufficient data available on some 'new' states
Taiwan	New	Yes	
Croatia	New	Yes	Formerly part of Yugoslavia
Kuwait	3	Yes	Cluster 3 ('First World')
Moldova	New	Yes	Formerly part of CIS
Serbia and Montenegro	New	Yes	Formerly part of Yugoslavia
Trinidad and Tobago	5	Yes	Moved from 'Third World'

The countries in Cluster 3 have been named 'The First World Countries'. These are shown in Table 8.3c. While these countries have not attained the levels of economic development and welfare as The Truly Wealthies, they are nonetheless characterized by high wealth per capita and the highest average level of economic and industrial growth. Infant mortality is low, while life expectancy and literacy are high. Not surprisingly, inhabitants of Clusters 2, 4 and 5 wish to migrate to Cluster 3 – it has a high net migration rate. There have been some shifts into and out of the cluster, some countries moving 'down' to it, one moving 'up' from it, and some moving 'down' out of it, to Cluster 4.

In 1991, the five countries in Cluster 4 were named 'The Economic Disasters' by us (Pitt, Joynt and Money 1993), for obvious reasons. We wrote, 'In some ways these five countries are not dissimilar to the In-betweens, and inhabitants are generally better off than those in the Third World group. What distinguishes this small group of countries is their abysmal economic performance – a negative economic and industrial growth rate, massive inflation (Nicaragua had 12,000% in 1991!) and very high unemployment as a proportion of the total work-force. It is also interesting to note that it is in this cluster that there is the greatest discrepancy between male and female literacy.' These are shown in Table 8.3d. However, it would not be unfair to say that this cluster proved to be the most impermanent of these identified in 1991. None of the original five members are part of the cluster now (they have all moved to Cluster 5). We have called the 1993 Cluster 4 group 'In need of a name' – these countries are not quite First World, yet slightly better off than 'In-betweens'. It might be disconcerting for some nations to see that they have indeed moved from the 'First World' group 3 cluster.

By far the largest cluster of countries is that shown in Table 8.3e. There were 104 'Third World Countries' in 1991 and 128 in 1993, characterized generally by low to very low personal wealth, dismal economic performance, and little infrastructure. The break-up of Eastern Europe has also seen the ranks of this group swell. It is striking to see that while only one nation moved out of this group, a number moved into it and that this was not solely caused by political fragmentation. Economic mismanagement and decline played a considerable role. The death rate is the highest of all five clusters, infant mortality is considerably higher than that of the Truly Wealthies and life expectancies are markedly lower than all the other clusters. Literacy is low and approximately only one in four members of the population of these countries is employed. The fertility rate is more than twice that of Cluster 1, 2 and 3 as the populations of these countries grow at a rate more than three times that of the Truly Wealthies.

A graphical summary of the movements between the five clusters over the period 1991 to 1993 is shown in Figure 8.2.

Table 8.3c Cluster 3: 'The First World countries'

COUNTRY	Cluster 1991?	In Cluster 1993?	If not, where moved to/where from?
Australia	3	Yes	
Austria	3	No	Cluster 1 (The Truly Wealthy)
The Bahamas	3	No	Cluster 4
Belgium	3	Yes	
Brunei	3	No	Cluster 4
Cayman Islands	3	Yes	
Denmark	3	Yes	
Faroe Islands	3	Yes	
Finalnd	3	Yes	
France	3	Yes	
Germany	3	Yes	
Hong Kong	3	Yes	
Ireland	3	No	Cluster 4
Israel	3	No	Cluster 4
Italy	3	Yes	
Kuwait	3	No	Cluster 2
Monaco	3	No	Not included in 1993 study
Netherlands	3	Yes	
New Zealand	3	Yes	
Qatar	3	Yes	
Singapore	3	Yes	
Spain	3	No	Cluster 4
United Arab Emirates	3	Yes	
United Kingdom	3	Yes	
Andorra	New	Yes	
Aruba	New	Yes	
Iceland	1	Yes	Moved from Cluster 1 (The Truly Wealthy)
Norway	1	Yes	Moved from Cluster 1 (The Truly Wealthy)
Sweden	1	Yes	Moved from Cluster 1 (The Truly Wealthy)

Table 8.3d Cluster 4: 'The Economic Disasters' in 1991 and 'In need of a name' in 1993

COUNTRY	In Cluster 1991?	In Cluster 1993?	If not, where moved to/where from?
Albania	4	No	Cluster 5 (The Third World)
Cuba	4	No	Cluster 5 (The Third World)
Korea, North	4	No	Cluster 5 (The Third World)
Nicaragua	4	No	Cluster 5 (The Third World)
Peru	4	No	Cluster 5 (The Third World)
The Bahamas	No	Yes	Cluster 3 (First World)
British Vir	No	Yes	New in 1993
Brunei	No	Yes	Cluster 3 (First World)
Cyprus	No	Yes	Cluster 2
Ireland	No	Yes	Cluster 3 (First World)
Israel	No	Yes	Cluster 3 (First World)
Portugal	No	Yes	Cluster 3 (First World)
Slovenia	No	Yes	Part of former Yugoslavia
Spain	No	Yes	Cluster 3 (First World)
Virgin Islands	No	Yes	New in 1993

DISCUSSION

In this short chapter we have briefly described simple, longitudinal groupings of the countries of the globe. Using an inexpensive commercial database, five clusters were derived over two periods, by means of a K-means clustering procedure on a standard computerized statistical package. The operation is a relatively easy one. What do our groups mean and what can they be used for?

Earlier, we identified that our bias was international marketing/export. However, with small refinements the analysis could be used for other firm activities such as research and development, production logistics, human resource management, service, finance etc. The groups are, in themselves, market segments, which would have relevance to some marketer, somewhere, depending on his or her product or service. The Truly Wealthies would obviously be the first port of call for a marketer of high ticket items, and offerings to the elderly. Having saturated these markets, this marketer could then move on to the First World Countries, which would also be attractive to marketers of certain financial services, where high economic

Table 8.3e Cluster 5: 'The Third World Countries'

COUNTRY	In Cluster 5 1991?	In Cluster 5 1993?	If not, where moved to/ where from?
Afghanistan	5	Yes	
Algeria	5	Yes	
Angola	5	Yes	
Argentina	5	Yes	
Bangladesh	5	Yes	
Belize	5	Yes	
Benin	5	Yes	
Bolivia	5	Yes	
Botswana	5	Yes	
Brazil	5	Yes	
Burkina Faso	5	Yes	
Burma	5	Yes	
Burundi	5	Yes	
Cambodia	5	Yes	
Cameroon	5	Yes	
Cape Verde Islands	5	Yes	
Central African Republic	5	Yes	
Chad	5	Yes	
Chile	5	Yes	
China	5	Yes	
Colombia	5	Yes	
Comoros	5	Yes	
Congo	5	Yes	
Costa Rica	5	Yes	
Djibouti	5	Yes	
Dominican Republic	5	Yes	
Ecuador	5	Yes	
Egypt	5	Yes	
El Salvador	5	Yes	
Equatorial Guinea	5	Yes	
Ethiopia	5	Yes	

Table 8.3e Continued

COUNTRY	In Cluster 5 1991?	In Cluster 5 1993?	If not, where moved to/ where from?
Fiji	5	Yes	
Gabon	5	Yes	
The Gambia	5	Yes	
Ghana	5	Yes	
Grenada	5	Yes	
Guadeloupe	5	Yes	
Guatamala	5	Yes	
Guinea	5	Yes	
Guinea-Bissau	5	Yes	
Guyana	5	Yes	
Haiti	5	Yes	
Honduras	5	Yes	
India	5	Yes	
Indonesia	5	Yes	
Iran	5	Yes	
Iraq	5	Yes	
Ivory Coast	5	Yes	
Jamaica	5	Yes	
Jordan	5	Yes	
Kenya	5	Yes	
Laos	5	Yes	
Lebanon	5	Yes	
Lesotho	5	Yes	
Liberia	5	Yes	
Madagascar	5	Yes	
Malawi	5	Yes	
Malaysia	5	Yes	
Maldives	5	Yes	
Mali	5	Yes	
Mauritania	5	Yes	
Mauritius	5	Yes	

Table 8.3e Continued

COUNTRY	In Cluster 5 1991?	In Cluster 5 1993?	If not, where moved to/ where from?
Mexico	5	Yes	
Mongolia	5	Yes	
Morocco	5	Yes	
Mozambique	5	Yes	
Namibia	5	Yes	
Nepal	5	Yes	
Niger	5	Yes	
Nigeria	5	Yes	
Pakistan	5	Yes	
Panama	5	Yes	
Papua New Guinea	5	Yes	
Paraguay	5	Yes	
Philippines	5	Yes	
Romania	5	Yes	
Rwanda	5	Yes	
Sao Tome and Principe	5	Yes	
Senegal	5	Yes	
Sierra Leone	5	Yes	
Solomon Islands	5	Yes	
Somalia	5	Yes	
South Africa	5	Yes	
Sri Lanka	5	Yes	
Sudan	5	Yes	
Suriname	5	Yes	
Swaziland	5	Yes	
Syria	5	Yes	
Tanzania	5	Yes	
Thailand	5	Yes	
Togo	5	Yes	
Tonga	5	Yes	
Trinidad and Tobago	5	No	Moved to Cluster 2

Table 8.3e Continued

COUNTRY	In Cluster 5 1991?	In Cluster 5 1993?	If not, where moved to/ where from?
Tunisia	5	Yes	
Turkey	5	Yes	
Uganda	5	Yes	
Uruguay	5	Yes	
Venezuela	5	Yes	
Vietnam	5	Yes	
Western Samoa	5	Yes	
Yemen	5	Yes	
Zaire	5	Yes	
Zambia	5	Yes	
Zimbabwe	5	Yes	
Albania	No	Yes	Moved from Cluster 4
American Samoa	No	Yes	New in 1993
Armenia	No	Yes	New in 1993
Azerbaijan	No	Yes	New in 1993
Belarus	No	Yes	New in 1993
Bosnia and Herzegovna	No	Yes	New in 1993
Cuba	No	Yes	Moved from Cluster 4
Estonia	No	Yes	New in 1993
Georgia	No	Yes	New in 1993
Kazakhstan	No	Yes	New in 1993
North Korea	No	Yes	Moved from Cluster 4
Krgyzstan	No	Yes	New in 1993
Latvia	No	Yes	New in 1993
Lithuania	No	Yes	Moved from Cluster 4
Peru	No	Yes	Moved from Cluster 4
Russia	No	Yes	New in 1993
Tajikistan	No	Yes	New in 1993
Turkmenistand	No	Yes	New in 1993
Ukraine	No	Yes	New in 1993
Uzbekistan	No	Yes	New in 1993

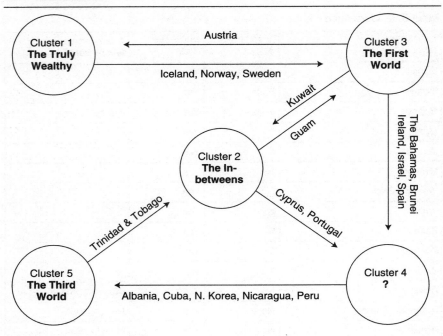

Figure 8.2 Movements between the clusters – 1991 to 1995

growth rate would be a critical factor. Marketers willing to accept higher risks, but looking for opportunities in countries where competition might be less aggressive, might profitably explore the In-betweens.

The impermanence of clusters and market segments is also illustrated. Depending on the viewpoints, world economic agencies and economic consultants at least, would probably have found a high demand for their services in the Economic Disasters in 1991, only to see this disappear (pessimistically), or bloom into the Third World! The Third World Countries would also be growth markets for infant care products, primary medical care and infrastructural development. They would of course also be prime targets for development and aid agencies. Obviously a practical criticism of this cluster might be that it is too large (and, unfortunately, growing), to be meaningful. Quite possibly it would make sense to break it down by a further process of clustering. Obviously, it is not the intention here to identify each and every product and service that would be well suited to each cluster, but simply to indicate broadly the relevance of the procedure, which brings us to the second point: What could they be used for? We suggest that the clusters might provide a useful tool to decision makers going through the filters in Walvoord's foreign markets selection model – the pharmaceuticals manager could eliminate all Cluster 1 and 3 countries as already having overcome a particular paediatric problem; the marketer of holiday homes on golf courses might eliminate all but three or four Cluster 1 countries (and numbers here also seem to be shrinking).

Also in 1991 (Pitt, Joynt and Money 1993), we pointed out that the astute observer would immediately recognize the impermanence of the clusters – that in all likelihood, a similar procedure conducted on the next year's database would result in different clusters. As can be seen from the longitudinal extension of the clustering, this has indeed happened, as Clusters 2 and 4 emerge as quite different from what they were. Cluster 4, certainly, emanates as a group of countries worth further consideration – not only do we need to describe them, we even need to name them! The famous curse from the largest country on the database still seems to be directed at the international manager: May you live in interesting international times!

CONCLUSIONS

This type of analysis, we can conclude, may prove to be more realistic than separating the world into geographic regions (Europe, America, Asia) or using a basic variable such as language or GNP to divide the world for purposes of international marketing.

ACKNOWLEDGEMENTS:

This chapter is partly based on a contribution by the authors to *International Encyclopaedia of Business and Management*, (1996) (ed M. Warner), Routledge, London, 6 volumes, with permission of the publishers.

ENDNOTES

1 Life expectancy of males and females differs substantially in some countries.
2 Literacy of males and females differs substantially in some countries.
3 For some reason the 1993 data base does not provide defence spending, so this variable was not used in the 1993 analysis.
4 Km^2 of total land area divided by total population.

REFERENCES

Aldenderfer, M.S., and Blashfield, R.K. (1984) *Cluster Analysis*, Sage, Beverly Hills, CA.
Helsen, K., Jedidi, K., and DeSarbo, W.S. (1993) A new approach to

country segmentation utilizing multinational diffusion patterns. *Journal of Marketing*, **57**, October, pp. 60–71.

McLauchlin, J.E. (1993) Communicating to a Diverse Europe. *Business Horizons*, January–February, pp. 54–6.

Pitt, L.F., Money, A.H., and Berthon, P. (1994) *Partitioning the Pacific: A Simple, Cluster Based Segmentation of the Nations Bordering the Pacific Ocean*. Proceedings of the Second Annual Conference on Global Business Environment and Strategy, Sun Valley, Idaho, August 1994, Pocatello, ID: Idaho State University, pp. 346–59.

Pitt, L.F., Joynt, P.C., and Money, A.H. (1993) *A Clustering of Countries: Using an International Database to Segment International Markets*. Workshop on European Co-operation to Honour Geert Hofstede, University of Limburg, Maastricht, The Netherlands, September, 1993.

Root, F.R. (1987) *Entry Strategies for International Markets*, Lexington Books, Lexington, MA.

Ryans, J.K., and Rau, P.A. (1990) *Marketing Strategies for the New Europe: A North American Perspective on 1992*, American Marketing Association, Chicago.

Sokal, R.R., and Sneath, P.H.A. (1963) *Principles of Numerical Taxonomy*, W.H. Freeman, San Francisco, CA.

Walvoord, R.W. (1980) Export Market Research, *Global Trade Magazine*, May, pp. 81–5.

WAYZATA World Factbook (CD-ROM Edition) (1991 and 1993) Wayzata Technology, Ic, Grand Rapids, MN.

World Bank (1990) *The World Bank Atlas*, The World Bank, Washington DC.

World Bank (1990) *The World Bank Atlas*, The World Bank, Washington DC.

FURTHER READING

England, G.W., *et al.* (1979) *Functioning Organization in a Cross-Cultural Perspective*, Kent State University Press, Kent, Ohio.

Granick, D. (1972) *Managerial Comparisons of Four Developed Countries: France, Britain, United States and Russia*, MIT Press, Cambridge, MA.

Hofstede, G. (1980) *Cultures Consequences: International Differences in Work-Related Values*, Sage, Beverly Hills, CA.

Laurent, A. (1985) The Cultural Diversity of Western Conceptions of Management, in *Managing in Different Cultures*, (eds P. Joynt and M. Warner) University Press, Oslo.

Chapter 9

Images of Europe: past, present and future

Geert Hofstede

INTRODUCTION

Once upon a time, not so long ago, in a pub at the Vrijthof in Maastricht, three women and four men were discussing Europe. The women were an historian, a lawyer and a medical doctor. The first three men were a geographer, a politician and an economist. The fourth man was the owner of the pub.

'Europe', said the geographer, 'is a peninsula of the Asian continent. It would objectively merit the name 'West Asia' as much as we talk about 'East Asia' for China, Japan and Korea. The population of West Asia is less than that of East or South Asia, but for the time being it is still the wealthiest of the three, although it will probably soon be passed in wealth by East Asia. The land borders between Asia and its Western peninsula are arbitrary; the Urals are not much of a mountain range; if one takes the train from here to China one doesn't meet any real obstacles until near the Mongolian border.'

'That is why Central Asian invaders had such an easy passage in past ages', said the historian. 'But the distinction between Europe, Asia and Africa existed already at the time of Herodotus, that is the fifth century BC.'

'Does the word "Europe" mean anything?' asked the pub-owner.

'The name' said the historian 'is supposed to have been derived from a Phoenician word *ereb* meaning 'darkness' or 'sunset'[1] (Herodotus, 1972 edition). The Phoenicians were the great sailors of the millennium before Christ and they came from the present Lebanon, so for them Europe was in the West, where the sun goes down. Herodotus, by the way, also wondered why three different names were used for Asia, Africa and Europe which were really one continent.'[2]

'Nice to know that Herodotus agreed with me', muttered the geographer. 'I would accept Africa as a separate continent, but the distinction between Europe and Asia is irrelevant, geographically and politically. The major border states, Russia and Turkey, cover both continents. I believe the reason why our ancestors treated the West-Asian peninsula as a separate continent and called it 'Europe' was that it allowed them to move the centre of the world this way: it inflated their self-image. The Chinese do the same. They do not refer to their part of the world as East Something: they call their country 'the Middle Empire', the centre of the world. We made Europe the centre; when the American continents were discovered, they were marginalized by calling them 'the New World' allowing us to be the old world. Nonsense of course, all continents are equally old.'

'The Old World included Asia and Africa.' corrected the historian. 'Anyway, Asia had the oldest civilizations. It seems that civilizations have followed the introduction of agriculture with a delay of some millennia. Agriculture has been introduced in Europe by gradual migration from South-West to North-East, starting in Anatolia, that is Asia[3] (Cavalli-Sforza 1993). European civilizations have moved the same way, starting with the Greeks, followed by the Romans. After the Romans Europe had little civilization at all for about a thousand years: it really deserved to be called the land of darkness, compared to other parts of the world like the Muslim countries and China.'

'But then the Europeans went out to discover the world.' interrupted the geographer.

'Civilizations have often expanded by travelling', said the historian. 'The new voyages of discovery started in the fifteenth century and soon developed into a competition among several European nations, first the Portuguese and later the Spaniards, the Dutch, the English and the French. Then they gradually developed what you called their inflated self-image of Europe as the centre of world civilization and progress. It reached its apex in the nineteenth century when they tried to divide the whole world into European colonies.'

'And in the meantime the Europeans fought each other.' said the politician, entering the discussion. 'Europe has been a very murderous place during these centuries, which doesn't make its claim at civilization too credible. I wonder whether Europe would still hold its leading position in the world if its countries had co-operated more? Now it lost out to North American in the twentieth century and more recently it is losing out to East Asia.'

'I don't like this talking about leading positions and losing out', said the geographer. 'The world is round and no part of it is more leading than another. Europe's inflated self-image should be over; Europe is just one part of the world and not its centre. To people living in or around the Pacific Basin – like in Hawaii or Samoa – Europe is not a very relevant place at all.'

'Present-day Europe', said the politician, 'nevertheless has got something that no other part of the world has got. I mean the European

Community, an attempt at voluntary economic and political integration of a number of nation states without the dominant power of a leading country. As I said these nation states have all fought each other, some quite recently. Shouldn't we be proud of the EC, certainly in this town of Maastricht where the 1991 Treaty was concluded?'

'I don't know whether there is much to be proud of' – this was the economist. 'The European integration hasn't been making much headway since Maastricht. It is moving from one disaster into the other. Also don't forget that the EC only covers half of Europe – 350 million people with some 400 million Europeans still standing by the side.'

'It is never easy to make fundamental changes,' protested the politician. 'It is pilgrim's progress: two steps ahead and one step back. When the step back is taken, people forget the two steps ahead. It is very unlikely that EC countries will evermore go to war against each other. Shouldn't we see the European Community as a laboratory for the world? If one realizes the size of the problems mankind has to cope with: overpopulation, exhaustion of resources, a wise use of nuclear and genetic engineering, national and religious fanaticisms, incurable diseases, there is no other way to survival than international co-operation. If only for that reason, the EC merits our commitment and our pride.'

'At one time', said the lawyer, clearing her throat, 'I believed the EC meant that Europe would grow to a common legal and judidical system. But what we have learned since is that a written law does not necessarily mean the same thing in different countries. Take the problems in implementing the 1985 Schengen Agreement about the opening of the internal borders and the control of the external borders. Like the new French government not wanting to move ahead with Schengen because of the Dutch way of handling drug addiction. It makes you realize that besides the written laws there are unwritten "living laws" in the minds of the people that differ from country to country and that you cannot harmonize by formal agreement. Besides, the institutions that have to implement them differ; the German police, for example, do not report to the civil authorities, the burgomasters, like in our country. And even more fundamentally, the mutual roles of the citizens and the authorities differ. There is more mutual trust between police and citizens in the Netherlands than in Belgium. Therefore in our country the police can rely more upon the help of the citizens in a crisis situation and the citizens upon the police, than in Belgium.'

'The mutual roles of patients and doctors are also different from country to country,' said the doctor. 'A dissertation at the University of Limburg in 1990 studied sickness absences from work in Belgium, Germany and the Netherlands. Controlling for all kinds of compounding factors, time lost from work in Belgium was three percent, in Germany five percent, and in the Netherlands eight percent (Prins 1990) two and a half times as much as in Belgium. I think the decisive cause is the attitude of the medical officers who have to certify these absences. We Dutch doctors are treating our patients more kindly and give more weight to their opinions. There is no evidence of real differences in health between the countries. Life expectancy at birth is about the same all over the EC, between 74 and 77 years[4] (World Development Report 1992). We see the same patient-oriented attitude in the Dutch position towards euthanasia and in our treatment of hard drug addicts to which you already referred.'

'You are really suggesting that our medical and our legal differences have common roots', said the lawyer.

'And very old roots at that', resumed the historian. 'Countries have remained separate precisely because there existed fundamental differences in thinking and feeling between them. Why do you think the Belgians revolted against the Dutch in 1830? The border between Belgium and the Netherlands revives the border between the Roman Empire and the barbaric Germanic tribes, which has been fixed in its present position in about the fourth century AD. The other national border close by here, the border between Germany and the Netherlands, follows the division of Charlemagne's empire among his three sons at his death in AD814. Since, the Netherlands have turned towards the sea and the German states have turned inland, which has resulted in quite different mentalities.'

'There seem to be as many mentalities as there are countries', reflected the doctor. 'Take the attribution of the causes of sickness. If they don't feel well, Germans – doctors and patients alike – tend to blame their hearts, French their liver and Brits their lack of self-control (Payer 1989). No wonder they cannot agree on the EC either.'

'Which is a great pity', said the economist with a sigh, 'For Europe is an enormous market. It potentially represents a tremendous economic power. Why does economic co-ordination meet such irrational barriers? With the present recession even the EC can hardly withhold governments from attempting the old pernicious national protectionism again, which can only make the recession worse as everybody should know. And why do the British resist a common Social Charter? And why are the Danes so difficult? And the problems are not only at the government level. Cross-border mergers of private firms and other forms of inter-business co-operation often run into trouble. Germany is the biggest trade partner of the Netherlands and yet several mergers between firms from the two countries have been dramatic failures. And this is only the EC. Include Eastern Europe and the irrationality becomes complete. Apart from being barbaric, the wars in the former Yugoslavia are ruining the economies of those countries for the next half century or more. Why would anybody want to do that?'

'Yes, it is horrible', said the politician uneasily, 'It is going back to the

Middle Ages but with modern weapons. But still I think that without the European Community things would be even worse, much worse. And to what extent are we responsible for Eastern Europe? Shouldn't they resolve their own problems first, like we should resolve ours? Some countries like Czechia and Hungary are already setting the example. In a decade or so, they may be ready to join the EC. Maybe the other former communist countries should first bundle their forces in a new common market of their own. Something like a neo-Comecon. That would be in a much better negotiating position than all those unstable old and new countries.'

'If I hear you all speak about Europe', said the historian, 'you confirm a truth that has existed for twenty-five centuries: Europe is a social construction'[5] (Bergen and Luckman 1966; Morgan 1986).

'That may be so', said the pub owner. 'But to me Europe has become a reality because I am from here. It was real luck that we got the EC Ministers' conference here in December 1991. I don't know what will happen to the Treaty, but everybody in Europe knows the name Maastricht now. Europe may be a social construction, but I feel no longer only a Mestreechter, a Limburger and a Dutch citizen, but also a European.'

MENTAL PROGRAMMING IN FIVE DIMENSIONS

The consensus of the discussion was that the way people think, feel and act in many different kinds of situation is somehow affected by the country they are from rather than by their being European. The country is of course not the only factor: in the discussion it was evident, for example, that among the seven participants the profession of the speaker affected his or her viewpoint and feelings. On top of that people's social class, education, generation, gender, working place and other collective characteristics also influence their thinking, feeling and acting. I have called these influences metaphorically 'collective mental programming'. Maybe 'pre-programming' is an even better term, because the programming is only partial: it is up to the individual what he or she does with it. The seven people in the pub called it 'different mentalities'. A fashionable term in sociology is 'habitus', a word introduced by the Frenchman Pierre Bourdieu (1980)[6].

For an explanation of the country influence on people's habitus we have to turn to social anthropology: the science of the functioning of human societies. Anthropology teaches us that all human societies, both traditional and modern ones, face some of the same basic problems; but the answers differ from one society to the next. What these problems are is a matter of empirical research. It has been one of the main purposes of my own research efforts over the past thirty years (Hofstede 1980; 1991). Many of you will know that I found four, and later five, universal problems to which people from different countries tend to give different answers. These explain differences in collective behaviour in many different spheres of life: in the family, at school, at work, in politics, and in the cherishing of ideas.

The first question deals with the inequality between people in any society. I expressed this in the term 'Power Distance'. The answers to the inequality questions stretch from: 'inequality is a normal and desirable thing', which means large Power Distance, to 'inequality should be avoided as much as possible', which means small Power Distance.

The second question deals with the relationship between individuals within a society. The answers to this question go from 'everybody for him or herself', which is called Individualism, to 'people should remain attached to tight groups throughout life', which is called Collectivism.

The third question deals with the social roles in a society related to being born as a boy or as a girl. The answers to this question range from 'social gender roles should be maximally different', which is called Masculinity, to 'social gender roles should be maximally overlapping', which is called Femininity. A large difference between gender roles leads to a 'tough' society; a large overlap to a 'tender' society.

The fourth question deals with the level of anxiety in a society when it is confronted with the Unknown. I expressed this in the term 'Uncertainty Avoidance'. The answers to this question range from fear, which means strong Uncertainty Avoidance, to curiosity, which means weak Uncertainty Avoidance.

The fifth question deals with the time perspective in a society for the gratification of people's needs. This runs from long, like a lifetime, to short, focusing on gratifying needs 'here and now'. I have labelled the range of answers to this question: Long-term versus Short-term Orientation. Long-Term Orientation implies a stress on virtuous living in this world, with Thrift and Persistence as key virtues. Short-Term Orientation goes together with a stress on finding the Truth with a capital T: Truth rather than Virtue assures salvation.

In my research, I have considered these five questions as dimensions of national mental programmes. For each dimension I have developed a yardstick to quantify, that is express in a number, the position of a country on that dimension relative to other countries. Quantification is a common way of simplifying complex information. Professors do it when they allocate grades to students on the basis of their answers on tests. Consumer organizations do it when they compare the performance of different products. In the case of dominant national mental programming I constructed the numbers for more than fifty countries on the basis of the answers to survey questions by large samples of similar employees from the multinational corporation IBM in 1970.

A key question for any type of quantitative scores is their reliability, that is, the extent to which different observers arrive at the same results. The reliability of research results can be determined by independent replications of the research. In social science independent replications are essential to make research respectable.

The most extensive replication of my research has so far been done by Michael Hoppe (1990) from North Carolina. His data were collected from alumni of the Salzburg Seminar in Salzburg, Austria. Salzburg Seminar participants are elites, 'current and future leaders in their respective countries. They include, among others, Chief Executive Officers of prestigious national and international companies, top-level administrators of national and international governments, diplomats, chancellors and deans of universities or colleges, supreme court justices, and artists (1990: 23)'. Hoppe obtained survey results from more than 1500 Salzburg alumni from nineteen, mainly European, countries in 1984, some fourteen years after my research data were collected. His research is therefore really independent from mine.

The differences in mental programmes he found between these elites were quite similar to what I had measured before and, allowing a margin of measurement error in both mine and his data, supported my quantifications. Limitations to the Salzburg sample are its smaller size (1500 versus over 100,000 for the IBM data) and the fact that the selection process of Salzburg participants is not necessarily matched from one country to the next. The respondent groups differ in composition across professions and political affiliations and for some countries this reduces the comparability of the answers to other countries.

Assuming that many of you have seen enough of my scores, in the remainder of this chapter I will mainly use Hoppe's country scores for differences between national mental programmes. I have to limit myself to the first four dimensions, because for the fifth dimension, Long-term Orientation, we have data for five European countries only.[7]

While I was working on this presentation Europe was very much in the news – mostly bad news, like the failure of the European Monetary System and the inability to take effective joint action in the former Yugoslavia. At times I regretted the choice of my topic. It is not easy to be reflective while the house is on fire. On the other hand it may be needed more than ever.

ARE EUROPEANS SPECIAL?

A first issue is whether Europeans are collectively different from other world citizens. Do they give similar answers to the problems of inequality, individualism, gender roles, and uncertainty?

Figure 9.1 is based on data from sixteen European countries: Austria, Belgium, Britain, Denmark, Finland, France, Germany, Greece, Ireland, Italy, the Netherlands, Norway, Portugal, Spain, Sweden and Switzerland;

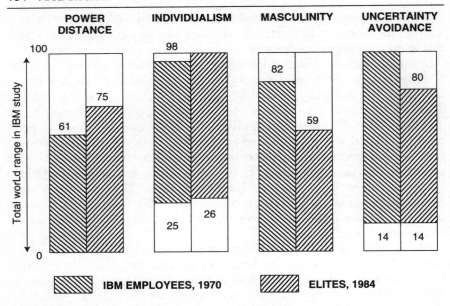

Figure 9.1 Range of scores for 16 European countries

no East-European countries were included. It shows the difference between the highest and the lowest scores on each dimension among the sixteen countries, compared to the maximum difference found in the entire world. The entire world means more than fifty countries.

The diagram shows that, for example, on Power Distance the scores for these European countries in the 1970 IBM study fell in the lower 61% of the world range and in the 1984 elites study they fell in the lower 75% of the world range. For Individualism the scores fell in the upper 75% etc. So, in both studies European countries varied strongly in the answers their citizens gave to questions related to the same basic problems of human societies. The extremes not found among these sixteen European countries are very large Power Distances, very low Individualism; that is, strong Collectivism and very strong Masculinity. But the differences are still large enough to consider Europe a small-scale model of the world in terms of variety in mental programming.

LATIN VERSUS GERMANIC MINDS

In the discussion the historian said that the border between Belgium and the Netherlands near Maastricht revives the border between the Roman empire and the barbaric Germanic tribes. In fact, the inheritance of the Roman empire cuts through the middle of the European Community. On

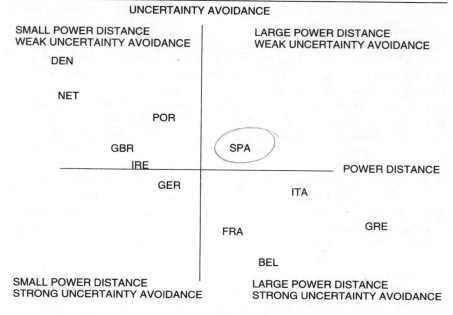

UNCERTAINTY AVOIDANCE

SMALL POWER DISTANCE
WEAK UNCERTAINTY AVOIDANCE

LARGE POWER DISTANCE
WEAK UNCERTAINTY AVOIDANCE

DEN

NET

POR

GBR   SPA

IRE   POWER DISTANCE

GER   ITA

FRA   GRE

BEL

SMALL POWER DISTANCE
STRONG UNCERTAINTY AVOIDANCE

LARGE POWER DISTANCE
STRONG UNCERTAINTY AVOIDANCE

Figure 9.2 Power distance versus uncertainty avoidance scores for 11 EC countries (Hoppe 1990)

the Latin side we find Belgium, France, Italy, Portugal and Spain, all countries speaking a Romance language, plus Greece; on the Germanic side Britain, Denmark, Germany, Ireland, Luxemburg and the Netherlands, all countries speaking a Germanic language. Although parts of some of the Germanic countries have also been under Rome for some time – like Southern Germany and Britain – the Roman civilization has not settled there. Flanders is the only Germanic-speaking region that acquired a Latin mentality, because it was dominated by French-speaking overlords.

The Roman empire – the first large empire in the heart of Europe – was characterized by a single power centre (implying large power distances) and a uniform system of laws (implying strong avoidance of uncertainty). In Figure 9.2 I have plotted the scores on Power Distance and Uncertainty Avoidance for eleven countries from the EC (all except Luxemburg for which I have no data).

The diagram is based on Hoppe's Salzburg study of elites in 1984. Power Distance scores are plotted horizontally from left to right. Uncertainty Avoidance scores vertically from top to bottom. In comparison to the 1970 IBM study, the 1984 Salzburg study scores are most different for Portugal and Spain: the elites indicate much smaller Power Distances and weaker Uncertainty Avoidance. Spain and Portugal both went from dictatorships to democracies in this period. The Salzburg Seminar is likely to have selected the elites who stood for democracy, not the ones who stood for dictatorship. The IBM data have not selected respondents on this criterium so they were probably more representative of the thinking of the total population.

The points representing the eleven countries are all close to the top left to bottom right diagonal of the diagram. This means that for EC countries, Power Distance and Uncertainty Avoidance vary together. This is a peculiarity of this group of countries which not necessarily applies to other countries.

The Latin countries present medium to large Power Distances and medium to strong Uncertainty Avoidance, the Germanic countries smaller Power Distances and weak to medium Uncertainty Avoidance. In fact the diagram looks somewhat like the map of Europe, with Greece in the South-East and Denmark and the Netherlands in the North-West, but the plot was not based on geographical data but on mental programmes. The inheritance of the Roman empire survives in the minds of the populations of the Latin countries. The long shadow of Emperor Augustus shows in this diagram. The Germanic countries never knew the same centralization of power, nor a universal system of laws, implying greater equality and tolerance for uncertainty.

On the Germanic side the extreme country is Denmark; this was also the case in the 1970 IBM study. The Danes are characterized by very small Power Distances and very weak Uncertainty Avoidance. This fact explains the hesitation of the Danish voters in ratifying the Maastricht Treaty. The small population of Denmark – 5 million out of 350 million for the whole EC – has a strong sense of equality; thus a referendum on the Treaty was inescapable. The Danish voters are critical about transferring part of their government power to Brussels, which will increase its distance. They are also critical about receiving more EC directives for which they may feel no need.

Surprisingly, Denmark among the twelve EC countries has the best record of application of EC directives in its national legislation. Belgium, on the opposite side of the Power Distance and Uncertainty Avoidance scales, has the worst record. The need for, or the rejection of, rules as a function of Uncertainty Avoidance is emotional, not instrumental; so if there is a strong need for rules, this does not mean that the rules established will also be followed. In Denmark the feeling is that rules should only be established when really needed, but then they should also be followed.

In both the IBM and the Salzburg study, Germany occupies a middle position in the diagram with small Power Distance but medium Uncertainty Avoidance. Britain and Ireland are close to Germany in this diagram, but they produced lower scores on both dimensions in the IBM study: they were in between Denmark and the Netherlands. German Uncertainty Avoidance stands for clear rules; because Power Distances are small, indicating a sense of equality, these rules apply irrespective of persons. To Dutch observers in the different cross-border studies I have been involved in, German mental programming is legalistic.

René Olie from our department, jointly with Petra Aler from the Rheinisch-Westfälische Technische Hochschule Aachen, has over the past years studied why German–Dutch mergers of business companies have such a poor success record. In one case of a failed merger the new international corporation, on the advice of a famous consultancy firm, introduced a product-based divisional structure. This new structure cut right across the legal structure of the corporation, which still followed national lines. It turned out that the Dutch were able to work within this set-up; the Germans were not (Olie 1994).

IRIC, the Institute for Research on Intercultural Co-operation of which I have been the founding director, studied cross-border co-operation between the police forces of Belgium, Germany and the Netherlands; for this project IRIC collaborated with METRO, the research institute of the Law department of this university. One difference between Germany on the one side and the Benelux countries on the other is the amount of discretion left to a police officer to report or not to report infringements of the law. Both in the Netherlands and in Belgium the 'principle of expediency' applies, which means that the police officer may decide whether or not to report a law infringement. In Germany the 'principle of legality' applies, which means that every law infringement should be reported. The police officer has no discretion in this respect. In practice, reporting every infringement is not always possible, but this is something German police officers don't like to talk about: to them it would mean confessing that they have acted illegally.

In my 1980 book, I have showed that Uncertainty Avoidance is negatively associated with 'citizen competence', that is the extent to which citizens believe they can effectively participate in local political decisions; whether they feel they can get the local political system to move on issues important to them, or whether they feel helpless in front of that system (like the personalities in Kafka's novels) (Hofstede, 198;: 173,178). The rank order of the three border countries on Uncertainty Avoidance, both in the 1970 IBM study and inthe 1984 Salzburg alumni study, is: Belgium very high, Germany medium, Netherlands lowest. The same order is reflected in the two areas mentioned in the pub discussion: sickness absence and relationship between police and citizens. In both cases Belgium and the Netherlands are far apart, in spite of having been neighbours forever and shaped by the same historical events, sharing a common language, collaborating in the Benelux Union since 1960 and being indistinguishable to travellers from overseas. I found no other case in the world of two neighbouring countries having so much in common and still showing such differences in their mental programming.

LONE VERSUS TOGETHER AND TENDER VERSUS TOUGH MINDS

In the next figure I have plotted the scores for the same eleven countries on the two remaining dimensions: Individualism and Masculinity. The figure is again based on Hoppe's Salzburg study of elites. Individualism scores are plotted vertically from top to bottom, Masculinity scores horizontally from left to right. Again, the Salzburg study scores are most different from the IBM scores for Portugal and Spain: the elites from Portugal score more masculine, and those from Spain more individualist and more feminine.

On Individualism the extreme countries are Britain, which scores very individualist in both studies, and Greece, which scores collectivist. The problems of the ratification of the Maastricht Treaty by Britain are well known. The Brits – like the Danes – have acquired several exception clauses. The most sensitive issue for Britain is the Social Chapter. This sets minimum standards for working conditions in the member

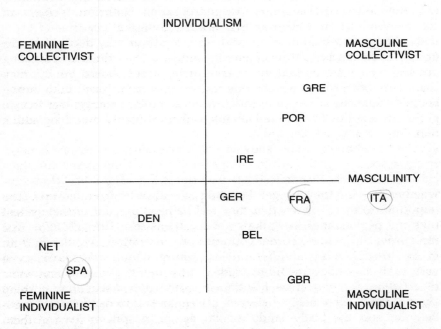

Figure 9.3 Masculinity versus Individualism scores for 11 EC countries (Hoppe 1990)

states. British individualism implies a strong belief in the market and in Britain this includes the labour market. Working conditions are supposed to be a topic for negotiation between employers and labour unions. Governments should not interfere in this process. The argument that labour, as the weaker party, should be protected by laws does not appeal to the fairly masculine British mentality which leaves little sympathy for anything weak. The twelve year regime of Prime Minister Margaret Thatcher has strongly manifested both individualism and masculinity. It has stressed those individualist values on which Britain differs most from other EC members.

In the case of Greece, the EC has hurt itself against Greek nationalism in the recognition of the former Yugoslav state of Macedonia as an independent country. Greece combines strong Uncertainty Avoidance (as we saw in the previous figure) with Collectivism. Uncertainty Avoidance stands for intolerance of what is different, Collectivism for loyalty to one's own group and hostility to other groups. Collectivism is at the root of ethnic conflicts anywhere in the world. The Greeks have argued that allowing a country to call itself Macedonia represents a threat to Greek sovereignty because Northern Greece is also called Macedonia. Imagine the Dutch refusing Belgium the right to call its North-Eastern province Limburg, because this means a threat to the Dutch province of Limburg which they will probably want to annex. In individualist Netherlands such an argument would be ridiculous, in collectivist Greece it is not.

The Netherlands, both in the Salzburg study and in the IBM study, figures as the most feminine of the EC countries. The Dutch have a strong sympathy for the underdog and the anti-hero which, within the EC, they share only with the Danes. In this respect they differ from both neighbours Germany and Belgium; the difference shows, among other things, in the tender approach of the Dutch to sickness absence and drug addiction.

EASTERN EUROPE

The last part of this chapter will be devoted to Eastern Europe. The classification of countries into East- and West-European was imposed by the former Iron Curtain, but it is historically unfounded. Now that the Curtain has been lifted we can start to look behind it. We find an extremely diverse collection of nations, some with homogenous and some with heterogeneous populations, some industrially developed and some agrarian, some relatively rich and some extremely poor. The only thing these nations share is the experience of communist rule but this experience has been relatively short, historically speaking – for most of them some forty-five years only.

Communism was an attempt to stop history and to make it obey new rules; to clean people's minds of their historically developed programmes and to re-program them. This was an arrogant claim; an attempt by political leaders to play God. It has bitterly failed. History resumes according to the old rules where it was interrrruped.

Now, however, a similar arrogance can be noticed in the claims of those Western economists and politicians who believe that after the failure of communism they can turn the people of the East-European nations into free market capitalists. They don't know history, and they seem to ignore that there is such a thing as collective mental programming.

Communism was closer to the mental programmes of many East-European peoples than is free market capitalism. In the eyes of many people in Eastern Europe, the communist period was not all that bad. To quite a few it was better than anything they had known before. The French anthropologist Emmanuel Todd (1983) has argued that the ideology of communism fits the traditional family structures in those countries. I think he oversimplified; he overlooked other influences, and he did not take account of the fact that only in Russia communism was a native development; in the other East-European countries it was imposed by military force. But at least Todd pointed to a source of metal programmes that politicians cannot change. In my research it shows up as Collectivism. Americans sometimes use the word 'collectivism' for 'state collectivism', as a synonym for 'communism'. This is not what I mean; I use the word in the sense of group collectivism; but the group collectivist mind is also more prone to accept state collectivism.

Free market capitalism presumes an individualist mentality, which is exactly the opposite. Everyone for him or herself and the invisible hand of enlightened self-interest will lead us all to the common good. This ideology stems from Adam Smith who was a Scot; it is most actively practised and preached in the UK and the USA. No country of continental Western Europe has ever fully embraced it. In my research, I have shown a statistical relationship between the degree of Individualism of countries and their national wealth. However, the arrow of causality is not from individualism to wealth, but from wealth to individualism (Hofstede, 1991: 75–6). A country becomes more individualistic after it has increased in wealth, but not necessarily wealthier after it has become more individualistic. This means that free market capitalism is more suitable for wealthy countries than for poor ones and unlikely to make poor countries wealthy as quite a few economists seem to believe.

Relatively well-to-do Eastern European countries are Czechia, Poland, Hungary, Slovenia and Estonia. In these a certain measure of capitalism has the best chances, but it should still be capitalism European style, say, German style not American or British style.

In the poorer East-European countries, the demise of communism has not eased the way for capitalism. The only visible alternative to communism in these countries is militant nationalism; we can find daily testimonies of it in our newspapers. Like communism, nationalism is based on group collectivism: 'It is them or us'. Collectivism combined with strong Uncertainty Avoidance produces an explosive mixture: strong Uncertainty Avoidance stands for intolerance of others, of 'What is different, is dangerous'. This mixture exists in the case of Greece, but mitigated by the fact that Greece is a relatively prosperous country which therefore undergoes individualist influences.

The Hungarian political philosopher István Bibó has written about the 'national materialism' of the East-European countries, a state of mind which the Western Europeans cannot understand. It has grown out of the daily fight for mere survival. 'One of the most characteristic features of the soul that has been tortured by fear and feelings of insecurity and major historical traumata and injuries is, that it does not want to make a living out of its own existence but it takes the position that it has a lot to demand from life, from history and from the others. In this state of mind the individual loses his sense of moral obligations and responsibilities towards the community. He uses every moral rule to prove his own demands . . .' (Bibo 1986: 238; Varga 1993).

This, I am afraid, brings us to what is happening in Yugoslavia, where people have reached a state of mind that Western Europeans cannot

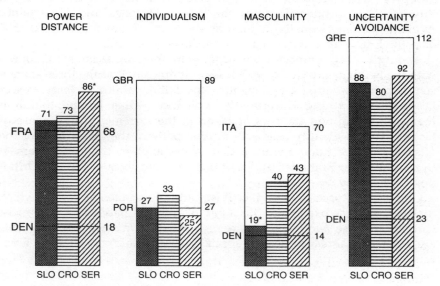

* significantly different from other 2 republics at .05 level
DEN = Denmark, FRA = France, GBR = Great Britain, GRE = Greece, ITA = Italy,
Por = Portugal; SLO = Slovenia, CRO = Croatia, Ser = Serbia

Figure 9.4 Scores for Yugoslav republics vs. EC countries

understand at all and where the endless so-called peace conferences only seem to be a forum to repeat each party's demands on history. The IBM study contains data from a Yugoslav agent of IBM. This spring I went back to the data, which were collected in 1971, and split them into Slovenia, Croatia and Serbia; the company did not have sufficient employees in the other republics. The results are shown in Figure 9.4, together with the scores for the highest and lowest EC country on each dimension.

What strikes us first is the similarity among the three Yugoslav republics. In all three republics of the former Yugoslavia the 1971 scores showed large Power Distances, Collectivism and strong Uncertainty Avoidance. Slovenia scored Feminine, the other two republics medium on Masculinity. Serbia manifested a significantly larger Power Distance than the two other republics; it was also slightly more Uncertainty Avoiding and Collectivist. Twenty years before Serbians started the Yugoslav civil war their compatriots within the IBM agency gave evidence of the state of mind conducive to explosive nationalism; and their two sister republics produced only slightly different answers.

The Serbian data from 1971 show a combination of large Power Distance plus strong Uncertainty Avoidance unequalled anywhere in my research in Europe. In 1988, before the breakdown of communism, my French co-author Daniel Bollinger administered the IBM questions to a group of engineers, more or less matched with the IBM employees, in Russia.[8] They produced scores for Power Distance and Uncertainty Avoidance almost equally as high as the Serbs. From the original IBM data the European country that comes closest is Greece.

About the only countries at present where the population sympathizes with the Serbians are Greece and Russia. It appears that the three share a common mental programming: it is the Latin pattern of large Power Distance plus strong Uncertainty Avoidance – like Hoppe found in France, Belgium and Italy – but taken to the extreme. With a sense of history we can identify it as a Byzantine pattern, the inheritance of the offspring of the Roman empire that lasted another thousand years in Byzantium after Rome fell and that presently survives in Eastern Orthodox Christianity.

Greece and Russia score Collectivist, but not as much as Serbia, which makes them less explosive. But signs of militant nationalist and racist currents in these two countries are regularly in our news. Such currents are a potential threat to peace, especially if economic conditions deteriorate.

CONCLUDING REMARKS

Regardless whether one considers free market capitalism desirable for Eastern Europe, one should face the fact that in most countries concerned the population's mental programming does not allow it. For the same reasons the poorer East-European countries will also have to do without democracy, at least for the foreseeable future, – let us say the next fifty years or so. Democracy presumes at least a minimum level of individualism: 'one man one vote' is an individualist principle. We also saw that individualism presupposes a minimum amount of wealth. Therefore democracy is for the wealthy or moderately wealthy countries only.[9] This is unfair, but I can't change it. It is as unfair as the law of Jesus Christ according to St Matthew: 'He who has, to him shall more be given.'[10]

You may consider me a pessimist, or taking a static view of societies. I only try to be realistic. Mental programmes do change, but slowly and not according to anyone's master plan. Changes take decades, if not centuries. If the inheritance of the Roman Empire still separates Belgium from the Netherlands, two countries in intimate contact over two thousand years, one should not believe one can change the minds of Serbs, Russians or Albanians within a few years. In planning, we better take mental programmes as given facts.

ACKNOWLEDGMENTS

This chapter is taken from a valedictory address to the Department of Economics and Business Administration, University of Maastricht, October 1993.

The author thanks Maaike, Rokus and Bart Hofstede for comments on draft versions of this address; Johannes Putsch and Lilian ter Horst for their drawings; Philip Lincoln and Piet-Hein Veldman for making the diagrams, and Frank van Heusden for the references to Herodotus.

ENDNOTES

1 The Phoenician word *ereb* has the same root as the Arab word *Maghreb* which also means 'The West'. The similarity of the name to Europa, the beautiful princess abducted by god Zeus (who for the occasion had disguised himself as a bull) is therefore accidental, except that in the legend Europa was a Phoenician princess. Herodotus (1972 edition: 285) wrote: 'As for Europe, nobody knows if it is surrounded by sea, or where it got its name from, or who gave it, unless we are to say that it came from Europa, the Tyrian woman, and before that was nameless like the rest. This, however, is unlikely; for Europa was an Asiatic and never visited the country which we now call Europe, but only sailed from Phoenicia to Crete and from Crete to Lycia.' Herodotus evidently didn't know Phoenician.

2 Herodotus commented: 'Another thing that puzzles me is why three distinct women's names should have been given to what is really a single land-mass . . .' (The Histories, Book Four, p. 285).

3 This is reflected in the results of recent research into the frequency distribution of human genes in Europe.
4 World Development Report, 1992, Table 1. The figures are 77 years for the Netherlands versus 76 for Belgium and Germany.
5 This, of course, has been inspired by a wonderful little book: Peter Berger and Thomas Luckman, The Social Construction of Reality. The title of this chapter 'Images of Europe' was inspired by Gareth Morgan, Images of Organization.
6 Bourdieu's definition of habitus can be translated as 'a system of permanent and transferable dispositions'; it 'functions as the basis for practices and images . . . which can be collectively orchestrated without an actual conductor'; see Pierre Bourdieu, Le sens pratique pp. 88–9.
7 Britain, Germany, the Netherlands, Poland and Sweden.
8 This study was part of a consulting project of CEGOS–Cooperation, Paris, France. The number of responses was 55, but not all were ethnic Russians; the group contained some Baltic and some Armenian members. The scores were Power Distance 93, Individualism 47, Masculinity −1, Uncertainty Avoidance 75.
9 The reverse is not true: wealth is possible without democracy, as Singapore and Hong Kong show.
10 From the New Testament, Matthew 13:12.

REFERENCES

Berger, P. and Luckmann, T. (1966) *The Social Construction of Reality*, Penguin Books.
Bibó, I. (1986) The misery of the Eastern European small states, in *Selected Studies, Vol II*, Magvetô Publishing House, p. 238.
Bourdieu, P. (1980) *Le Sens Pratique*, Editions de Minuit, Paris.
Cavalli-Sforza, L.L. and Piazza, A. 'Human genomic diversity in Europe: A summary of recent research and prospects for the future. *European Journal of Human Genetics*, 1993, 1, pp. 3–18.
Herodotus, *The Histories*, translated by Aubrey de Sélincourt and revised by A.R. Burn, Penguin Classics, 1972, Book Four.
Hofstede, G. (1980) *Culture's Consequences: International Differences in Work-Related Values*, Sage, Beverly Hills, CA.
Hofstede, G. (1991) *Cultures and Organizations: Software of the Mind*, McGraw Hill, London.
Hoppe, M.H. (1990) A comparative study of country elites: international differences in work-related values and learning and their implications for management training and development. University of North Carolina at Chapel Hill. Dissertation.
Morgan, G. (1986) *Images of Organization*, Sage, Newbury Park, CA.
Olie, R.L. (1994) European transnational mergers. University of Limburg. PhD thesis.
Payer, L. (1989) *Medicine and Culture: Notions of Health and Sickness in Britain, the US, France and West Germany*, Victor Gollancz, London.

Prins, R. (1990) Sickness absence in Belgium, Germany (FR) and the Netherlands: a comparative study. University of Limburg, PhD Dissertation.

Todd, E. (1985) *The Explanation of Ideology: Family Structures and Social Systems*, Basil Blackwell, Oxford.

Chapter 10

Attitudes, values and demands on leadership – a cultural comparison among some European countries

Ingrid Tollgerdt-Andersson

INTRODUCTION

During the last decade, leadership research has been the target of much interest. A dominating aim has been, and still is, how to predict who will be a successful leader. It is not only in scientific research that there has been a noticeable interest in leadership. The private and public sectors have also turned their attention to the importance of the leader. There are naturally many different reasons for this current interest. Continually increasing competition and the pronounced trend towards internationalization, together with a marked complexity in company structure, have resulted in a clear need for more and better leaders. Widespread, rapid changes are often a source of unrest and an efficient way of handling structural changes is to have a competent leader (Kotter 1988). It is always difficult to forecast future scenarios, but it seems probable that the change processes which have characterized the 1980s and even the early 1990s will continue. A brief mention will be made here of the processes that may be expected to have far-reaching consequences for economic activity and, thus, for leadership:

The process of internationalization exerts an important influence on industry and commerce. New markets, increased competition and multi-national companies are only a few examples of the consequences of internationalization. The growth of the European Community, the development of the Eastern European States and the competition from other continents are some aspects which will lead to an even more pronounced internationalization. It has been suggested that new regions such as the Baltic, Mid-European and Mediterranean regions will emerge. Here several decisions of industrial, administrative, economic and cultural character may be made. The implication is that the individual nations will gradually decline in importance and that Europe, or rather the European Community, will play an increasingly central role.

Regarding Europe today, the importance of mapping out and developing **European management** as a competitive parameter in relation to

American and Japanese management is discussed more often. Among other things the EC aims at strengthening European industry and commerce and closer co-operation can be expected in the future. The attempt to create a single European market can be seen as a reaction to and a part of the process of internationalization. Economic co-operation is one way of matching interational competition. This situation presents a challenge to management (Lorbiecki 1993: 2–4). Managers in international organizations will need to understand foreign cultures and to adapt decision making accordingly. Otherwise it will be extremely difficult to co-operate in a productive and developing manner. Management today is perceived as an activity which cannot be separated from its cultural context (Lorbiecki 1993: 2–4). If Europe, and naturally the individual countries in the Economic Community, is to hold a strong position in face of constantly increasing international competition, it is important to analyse attitudes, values and demands regarding leadership. Analysing attitudes and values is one way to understand the cultural differences. Do the European countries have anything in common regarding their views on management? Can national differences be co-ordinated in order to ensure creative and competitive co-operation across national boundaries?

Another influential change process is that due to *technological development.* Society has undergone an enormous transformation, especially as regards computerization and this development is likely to continue. It has resulted in a rapid increase in information flow and has decreased distances in the world considerably as far as communication is concerned. It is no longer necessary for a company to conduct all of its business activities in the same place, the same country or even the same continent.

The economic structure is constantly subject to change. A noticeable one is seen in the traditional manufacturing and processing industry, which provides employment for a decreasing proportion of the working population, whereas the service branch involves an increasing number of employees. The changeover from a traditional industrial society to a *service society,* to some extent entails new evaluations and leaders are faced with the necessity for new and different leadership abilities. It is often said that Western Europe is entering a post-industrial phase with partially new attitudes and values. The individual plays a more central role in this post-modern society. Rapid changes necessitate competence and flexibility and the need for a leader who is able to motivate personnel is becoming increasingly obvious.

Unemployment is a common problem for the EC and can be expected to persist for some time to come. In spite of this we can expect a shortage of skilled and well educated labour-power around the turn of the century. Both private and public sectors need competent leaders at different levels within the organization and it is therefore imperative to try and solve this potential problem before it is too late.

If change processes and their consequences are to be dealt with successfully, it will involve greater demands on efficient leadership at different levels within an organization and this means that the leadership factor will become increasingly important (Kotter 1988; House, Spangler and Woycke 1991: 364–96).

LEADERSHIP

During the latter years the leader has been assumed to have a crucial effect on the success of the company, both from a psycho-social and an economic point of view. Scientific research shows that a leader influences not only such important aspects within an organization as job satisfaction and commitment, but also effectiveness and economic success (Finkelstein and Hambrick 1990: 484–503; Hambrick and Mason 1984: 193–208; Kotter 1982, 1988; Meindel, Ehrlich and Dukerich 1985: 78–102; Smith, Carson and Alexander 1984: 165–76; Tollgerdt-Andersson 1989, 1990; Heller, 1992). In my own research on attitudes, values and demands of executives, i.e. their spontaneous leadership theories, I have found an extremely clear relationship between spontaneous leadership theories and the economic results of the company (Tollgerdt-Andersson, 1989; 1990). This method of studying ideas and values is in line with recent international research results on leadership (Lord, DeVader and Allinger 1986: 402–9; Finkelstein and Hambrick 1990: 484–503; Hollander and Offerman 1990: 179–89; Jacob and Jaques 1987: 7–65; Kouzes and Posner 1987). A leader's values and expectations are important not only in order to understand the present situation, but also to understand future developments within industry and commerce. An executive's view of reality is of great importance for the success of the company (Hambrick and Mason 1984: 193–208), a fact confirmed by recent research (Finkelstein and Hambrick 1990: 484–503; Niehoff, Enz and Grover 1990: 337–52). Pearce and Zahra (1991: 135–53) found that a strong, active management appeared to increase the financial success of a company. In view of the increasing internationalization, it is interesting to see if there are any differences between countries and cultures regarding their attitudes, values and demands on leadership. This knowledge can be important when companies from different countries are acquired by each other or establish co-operation. The knowledge can also be of value when transferring or appointing executives.

AN INTERNATIONAL COMPARATIVE STUDY OF ADVERTISEMENTS FOR EXECUTIVES

Introduction

Research has shown that there seem to be clear cut cultural differences between the extension of and focus on leadership in companies in different countries (Ayal 1988) as well as differences in values and attitudes towards leadership (Nunez 1990: 25–9; Tollgerdt-Andersson 1989; 1992). Hofstede's (1980) well-known study found marked cultural differences regarding power distance, uncertainty avoidance and individualism. An American study (Skapinker 1989) supported the view that there are substantial cultural variations in attitudes to leadership. Skapinker studied 1500 executives' expectations and requirements of management in the 21st century. He found that executives in the USA, Western Europe, Japan and Latin America had clearly different opinions. Cultural differences have also been found in the choice of methods used in the recruitment of executives. A study by Shackelton and Newell (1991: 23–36) showed that there were considerable differences between French and British companies when it came to selecting executives. Employment interviews were common in both countries. When it came to other selection methods, French companies tended to rely largely on graphology, whereas in Great Britain more importance was placed on references. In Great Britain, psychological tests and 'assessment centres' were also used more often than in France. Similar cultural differences were also found in an experiment (Hofstede 1980) where French, British and German students were given a case study to solve. When presented with a problem of an organizational nature (a conflict between a sales section and a product-development section), they interpreted the cause of the problem in completely different ways. The French saw the managing director as the cause of the problem, the Germans considered it due to the lack of a written policy and the British attributed it to a lack of interpersonal communication.

Research (Cherns 1982; Payer 1989) also pointed to cultural differences regarding continental Europe versus the rest of the English-speaking world, a fact which is mirrored in views on leadership and selection methods. Naulleau and Harper (1993) analysed the profound differences between France and Great Britain concerning the hierarchy of managerial functions, leadership and the patterns of authority (to be compared with Hofstede's power distance), access to top management, education and training of managers and communication patterns and styles. The journal *International Management* (1990) expressed the idea that one of the most important obstacles in the way of the EC is the existence of profound cultural differences. At the same time, these are considered to be founded on cultural myths which, in their turn, originate from a tendency to give priority to national characteristics. Olie (1990: 206–15) stressed the difficulties following mergers and acquisitions due to cultural incompatabilities. Such a problem will become increasingly common in the future.

In order to understand the leadership process and to make recruitment, mergers and acquisitions more efficient, attention must be paid to these differences. Companies exist in an increasingly international environment and therefore need more knowledge and understanding of cultural differences. Only then will it be possible for a company to retain its national characteristics and at the same enable future executives to understand and adjust to the values of other nations. This accentuated internationalization and the significance of attitudes, values and demands make it interesting to form some conception of the differences in other countries and cultures views on leadership.

This study aimed at answering the following questions:

- Do different countries and cultures vary in the characteristics (both personal and social) they consider to be important for an executive?
- What qualities and behaviours are specified in Swedish, Danish, Norwegian, French, German, British, Italian and Spanish advertisements seeking executives?
- Are the similarities between the Scandinavian countries so pronounced that one can talk about Scandinavian management in general?
- Are the similarities between the European countries so pronounced that one can talk about European management in general?

Method and selection

One way of learning about attitudes, values and demands on leadership is to study and analyse advertisements for executives. An analysis of this nature provides a preliminary idea of the characteristics required in industry and commerce. The characteristics and behaviours specified in advertisements can be assumed, at least partially, to reflect the spontaneous leadership theories held by a company. The advantage of such a study is, among other things, that (a) the data collected is unobtrusive (that is, it does not interfere with the behaviour studied) and (b) that it is easy to obtain comparative data over a period of time and from different sources. In other words, it is relatively easy to obtain culturally comparable data. A study of advertisements can be expected to give an idea of the characteristics and behaviours which are considered important for an executive in the country in question. A brief discussion of how advertisements reflect what is thought important for a leader is in place here. Executives formulate qualities desirable for successful leadership and the advertisements probably express some sort of ideal picture. A Swedish investigation regarding executives' demands on leadership characteristics and behaviour showed, however, relatively good agreement with the requirements expressed in advertisements for executives (Tollgerdt-Andersson 1989; 1995).

Thus, the aim of studying advertisements for executives in British, Danish, French, German, Italian, Norwegian, Spanish and Swedish publications, was to form a picture of possible differences between cultures regarding attitudes, values and demands on leadership. The advertisements were selected on random dates. The Danish, German and Swedish advertisements were collected during 1988. The British, French and Norwegian advertisements were collected in 1992 and the Italian and Spanish advertisements were collected in 1993. The changed economic situation may have had some effect, but a limited comparison with current advertisements in the countries studied in 1988 and 1992 suggests that this is not the case. Two different coders analysed the advertisements and they were unified to 100%. The choice of the countries included in the study can be explained as follows.

Denmark, Norway and Sweden were chosen in order to see if the Scandinavian countries had anything in common in their views on leadership; the Scandinavian countries, together with Britain, France, Germany, Italy and Spain were chosen as representatives for Europe. The objective of this, was to see if there were any common attitudes and values in their views on leadership which could be labelled 'European management'. Of course, this is ony a small sample of European countries, emphasizing the Mediterranean countries and the countries in Northern Europe. In a future study, I plan to analyse advertisements from a larger sample of European countries.

Results

First of all, advertisements for executives were studied in Swedish newspapers and journals. Executive, in this case, is defined as an employee who is responsible for a number of other employees. A total of 225 advertisements from *Sydsvenska Dagbladet*, *Headhunter* and *Dagens Industri* were analysed. Swedish advertisements largely emphasized personal and social qualities. As many as 85% of them mentioned such qualities. Many different characteristics and behaviours were required. In all, 38 different characteristics (or their synonyms) were mentioned. In the Danish newspapers *Politiken* and *Berlingske Tidene* a total of 175 advertisements were studied. Danish advertisements also stressed personal and social qualities. 80% of them stressed some type of personal or social quality. A large number of characteristics and behaviours recur (30). A number of Norwegian advertisements were analysed for comparison. 80% of the advertisements for executives in *Aftonposten* expressed a demand for some kind of personal or social quality. In all, 22 qualities were mentioned in the 173 advertisements studied.

Advertisements in a further five European countries, namely Great Britain, France, Germany (at that time, West Germany), Italy and Spain were analysed. Over 190 advertisements for executives published in the German newspaper *Suddeutsche Zeitung* were studied. Personal or social qualities were mentioned in 66% of the German advertisements. In all, 30 different characteristics (or their synonyms) were mentioned. Advertisements for executives in *The Sunday Times* were also subjected to an analysis. Around 64% of the 163 advertisements scrutinized demanded some form of personal or social ability. In all 25 qualities were mentioned in the British advertisements. French advertisements for executives were studied in *Le Figaro* and *Le Nouvel Observateur*. In all 164 advertisements were analysed. Some form of personal or social ability were required in 54% of them. Over 28 different qualities or their synonyms recurred. Also, 132 advertisements in the Italian newspaper *Corriere della Sera* were analysed. Personal or social qualities were mentioned in 53% of the advertisements. In all, 17 different characteristics (or their synonyms) were mentioned. Finally, a total of 182 Spanish advertisements in *El Pais* were analysed – 52% of the Spanish advertisements stressed some type of personal or social quality. In all, 28 different qualities were mentioned. In Table 10.1, leadership qualities are compared by country. The presence of each quality within the total number of advertisements is expressed in percentage terms.

Regarding Table 10.1, a little clarification is in order. For some countries, for example Spain, the total percentages are more than 100% and for others, for example France, the total percentages are below 100%. The reason is that in Spain a lot of different behaviours and qualities are mentioned in one single advertisement, whereas in France only a couple of qualities are demanded (if personal or social qualities are demanded at all). When the qualities are subdivided into categories such as demographic, social personal or business, there is a clear dominance of qualities reflecting personal or social abilities. For example, only one demographic quality, *age*, is found and also only very few business qualities, such as *business orientation, aim and result orientation* and *customer orientation*.

Generally, there seem to be great differences between the European countries regarding their leadership requirements. Different characteristics are stressed in the various countries. There are also differences concerning how frequently various characteristics are demanded in each country. Some kind of personal or social quality is mentioned much more often in the Scandinavian countries than in the other European countries. In the Scandinavian advertisements, you often see many qualities mentioned in a single advertisement. This can be seen in other European countries too, but it is much more rare. Generally, the characteristics mentioned in a single advertisement do not exceed three and fairly often, especially in Mediterranean countries (in 46–48% of the advertisements) no personal or social characteristics are mentioned at all.

Table 10.1 Qualities most demanded in advertisements for executives

Quality	COUNTRY Sweden 225	Denmark 175	Norway 173	Germany 190	Great Britain 163	France 164	Italy 132	Spain 182
Ability to co-operate (interpersonal ability)	25	43	32	16	7	9	32	18
Independence	22	22	25	9			16	4
Leadership ability	22		16	17	10		22	16
Ability to take initiatives	22	12	16				10	8
Aim and result orientation	19	10	42		5			2
Ability to motivate and inspire others	16	11				9	26	20
Business orientation	12							8
Age	10	25		13		12	46	34
Extrovert personality/contact ability	10	8	12	11				
Creativity	9	10	9	9	5			4
Customer ability	9							2
Analytic ability		10					10	8
Ability to communicate		12	15		23			
High level of energy/drive			12		8			20
Enthusiasm and involvement			14	14				
Organization skills				7		6	12	12
Team builder						5		
Self-motivated					10			
Flexibility					10			2
Precision						7		
Dynamic personality						6		6
Responsibility								10

N.B. The qualities most demanded in Swedish, Danish, Norwegian, German, British, French, Italian and Spanish advertisements for executives, are expressed in percentage terms. N = total number of advertisements analysed in each country. Each entry represents the percentage of the total advertisements requesting by each quality.

Discussion and conclusions

The results show that there are clear cultural differences regarding what is required of a good leader. Even though there are common denominators as regards the qualities required in European advertisements, it is difficult to discern any pronounced or recurring pattern in these countries. It is possible that differences between Anglo-Saxon, Germanic and Romanic cultures are mirrored in these different views on leadership. The Scandinavian countries, however, differ in this respect from other European countries. They seem to have a certain common pattern regarding desirable leadership qualities. Italy and Spain also seem to have a common pattern concerning desirable leadership characteristics.

As regards personal and social abilities, Germany and Great Britain appear to have roughly the same requirements. In these countries, personal and social qualities are mentioned in 64–68% of the advertisements. In the Mediterranean countries, on the other hand, personal abilities appear to be in less demand. Only 52 to 54% of the advertisements express such requirements. This is hard to explain. Perhaps greater emphasis is placed on formal education and references in France, Italy and Spain, or is it simply that personal and social abilities are taken into account first in connection with the employment interview? In Spain and Italy, however, the required qualities seem to be more similar to the Scandinavian ones, than the most commonly required French characteristics. It is interesting to note that a photograph of the applicant was required in 45% of French advertisements. Furthermore, in 28% of the cases, a handwritten letter was required, which is not surprising, as a common selection method in France is graphology (Shackelton and Newell 1991), suggesting that personality is, after all, of some interest. Age is very often specified in the Italian and the Spanish advertisements, and very often an almost exact age is required.

Even in this respect, Scandinavia differs from other countries. Sweden, Denmark and Norway place considerably greater demands on personal and social abilities. Between 80 and 85% of the advertisements for executives mention this type of quality. Figure 10.1 shows that Scandinavian advertisements placed greater emphasis on personal and social abilities than the other European countries. This is hard to explain. Naturally some kind of personal and social capability is required in all cultures. Maybe formal education is regarded as more important in the non-Scandinavian countries and personal and social qualities are first considered when candidates have been selected for an interview.

To summarize, there are pronounced differences between the European countries regarding what is required of a competent leader. The similarity between the Scandinavian countries is the most pronounced and, to some extent, one can talk about 'Scandinavian leadership'. The cultural and

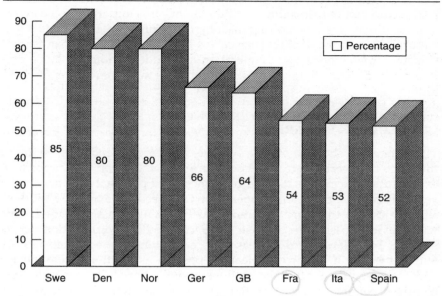

Figure 10.1 Distribution of the different countries' requirements regarding personal and social abilities of executives (expressed in terms of percentage)

historical development of the Scandinavian countries is also very similar.
The same applies to company development. Trade Unions, the law of co-
determination and similar democratic processes have played an important role in Scandinavia, which may have led to the emphasis placed on
personal and social ability regarding leadership. Future development
with an increased demand for democracy within companies, may lead
to similar demands being made in other quarters.

Another interesting question is whether emphasis is placed on acquiring that which is felt to be lacking, or on that which is considered
important and given priority in working life. Do executives in Scandinavia need to be more socially and personally oriented than, for example,
executives in the Mediterranean countries? Comparison with other
research (Hofstede 1980; 1984) seems to suggest that the overall structural organization in Sweden, Norway and Denmark gives top priority to
interpersonal relations, democracy and consensus in decision making,
whereas leadership in France is more centralized and top-managed.
However, even in the United Kingdom, a lot of importance seems to be
placed on interpersonal relations, even though they are seldom explicitly
mentioned in job advertisements. Consequently, the cultural differences
seen in job advertisements are difficult to interpret. A current interview
study (to be published in 1996) confirms the above mentioned differences.

In face of future co-operation within the EC, it is important to be aware of these differences when trying to strengthen European. It is possible that cultural differences manifest themselves even in areas other than leadership within a company. If co-operation and understanding is to be productive and flourish in a 'new Europe' one must be aware of these differences.

CONCLUDING REMARKS

The differences should not, however, be over-emphasized as there are at the same time certain areas of common interest. All countries appear to expect future executives to have good social and personal qualities. In the years to come, European co-operation will need to make the most of similarities and to regard differences as enriching and stimulating. This will provide possibilities of instigating competitive co-operation across national boundaries and increase the conditions for economic power within the EC. If tomorrow's leaders possess international competence and understanding of other cultures it will, hopefully, result in the increased competitive co-operation which is essential if European commerce and industry is to compete with, for example, the USA and Asia.

REFERENCES

Ayal, E.B. (1988) *Determinants of entrepreneurship in LCD with special reference to Northern Thailand.* Paper presented at the 13th IAREP Collogiqum, Leuven, Beligium, Fall, 1988.

Cherns, A. (1982) Culture and values: The reciprocal influence between applied social science in its cultural and historical context, *The Theory and Practice of Organizational Psychology* (eds N. Nicholson and T.D. Wall) Academic Press, London.

Finkelstein, S. and Hambrick, D.C. (1990) Top-management team tenure and organizational outcomes: The moderating role of managerial discretion. *Administrative Science Quarterly,* **35**, pp. 484–503.

Hambrick, D.C. and Mason, P. (1984) Upper echelons: The organization as a reflection of its top managers. *Academy of Management Review.* **9**, pp. 193–208.

Heller, F. (ed) (1992) *Decisionmaking and Leadership*, Cambridge University Press, Cambridge.

Hofstede, G. (1980) Motivation, leadership and organization: Do American theories apply abroad? *Organizational Dynamics,* **75**, pp. 42–63.

Hofstede, G. (1984) *Culture's consequences*, Sage, London.

Hollander, E. and Offerman, L. (1990) Power and leadership in organizations: Relationship in transition. *American Psychologist,* **45**, pp. 179–89.

House, R., Spangler, W. and Woycke, J. (1991) Personality and charisma in the US presidency. A psychological theory of leader effectiveness. *Administrative Science Quarterly*, **136**, pp. 364–96.

Jacob, T.O. and Jaques, E. (1987) Leadership in complex systems. in *Human productivity enhancement* (ed J. Zeidner), Praeger, New York, pp. 7–65.

Kotter, J. (1982) *The General Managers*, Free Press, New York.

Kotter, J. (1988) *The Leadership Factor*, Free Press, New York.

Kouzes, J.M. and Posner, B.Z. (1987) *The Leadership Challenge: How to Get Extraordinary Things Done in Organizations*, Jossey-Bass, San Francisco.

Lorbiecki, A. (1993) Unfolding European management development. *Management Education and Development*, **24**, pp. 2–4.

Lord, R.G., DeVader, C.L. and Allinger, G.M. (1986) A meta-analysis of the relation between personality traits and leadership perceptions: An application of validity generalization procedures. *Journal of Applied Psychology*, **71**, pp. 402–9.

Meindel, J.R., Ehrlich, S.B. and Dukerich, J.M. (1985) The romance of leadership. *Administrative Science Quarterly*, **30**, pp. 78–102.

Naulleau, G. and Harper, J. (1993) A comparison of British and French management cultures: Some implications for management development practices in each country. *Management Education and Development*, **24**, pp. 14–25.

Niehoff, B.P., Enz, C.A. and Grover, R.A. (1990) The impact of top-management actions on employee attitudes and perceptions. *Group and Organization Studies*, **15**, pp. 337–52.

Nunez, G. (1990) Managing the foreign service employee. *SAM Advanced Management Journal*, Summer, 1990, pp. 25–9.

Olie, R. (1990) Culture and integration problems in international mergers and acquisitions. *European Management Journal*, **8**, pp. 206–15.

Payer, L. (1989) *Medicine and culture*, Penguin, London.

Pearce, J.A. II and Zahra, S.A. (1991) The relative power of CEOs boards of directors: Association with corporate performance. *Strategic Management Journal*. **12**, pp. 135–53.

Shackleton, V. and Newell, S. (1991) *Journal of Occupational Psychology*. **64**, pp. 23–36.

Skapinker, M. (1989) American CEOs take a parochial view of competition, *Financial Times*, **16**.

Smith, J.E., Carson, K.P. and Alexander, R.A. (1984) Leadership: It can make a difference. *Academy of Management Journal*, **27**, 165–76.

Taylor, C., and Frank, F. (1988) Assessment centers in Japan. *Training and Development Journal*. **27**, pp. 54–7.

Tollgerdt-Andersson, I. (1989) *Ledarskapsteorier, företagsklimat och bedömningsmetoder*, Ekonomiska Forskningsinstitutet, Stockholm.

Tollgerdt-Andersson, I. (1990) *Framgång eller motgång? En utmanande analys av svenskt ledarskap*, Liber, Malmö.

Tollgerdt-Andersson, I. (1992) *Attitudes, values and demands on leadership – a cultural comparison.* Paper presented at Workshop on managing in different cultures. EIASM. Cerby-Pontoise, 23–24, November 1992.

Tollgerdt-Andersson, I. (1995) *Chef i Landsting – ledarskap i politiskt styrda organisationer,* Landstingsförbundet, Stockholm.

Chapter 11

Sensitivity to societal culture in managerial decision-making: An Anglo-Brazilian Comparison

Carlos Alberto Arruda and David J Hickson

INTRODUCTION

Although calls for more, and more carefully thought out, cross-societal cross-culture research continue to be justified, during the last quarter of a century work of this nature has expanded apace. It has progressed from a stage when there was a mere handful of publications to survey, to a stage where sophisticated syntheses and appraisals become not only possible but necessary. Those by Boyacigiller and Adler (1991), Triandis (1982–3), Lachman, Nedd and Hinings (1994), Redding (1994) and Smith (1992) all testify to this, in themselves and in the substantial lists of references they encompass.

The reasons are both practical and theoretical. The advent of the jet engine made travel easy and, for those in richer lands, affordable. Hence more Westerners could study other Westerners and more Westerners could study non-Westerners, the latter a virtual one-way flow due not only to the ability to pay the air fare but perhaps also to less affinity by some non-Westerners with Western research methods and thought ways. A second practical stimulus was the economic rise of Japan and subsequently of other nations of the Asian Pacific rim, which drew to itself the attention of Westerners generally and Americans especially.

Theoretically, some conceptual commonality was needed which, even though disputed – as it properly should be – offered a point of departure for research. Here the vital impetus was given by the work of a single Dutch individual, Hofstede (1980; 1991). Until he brought into organizational analysis four sociologically derived concepts of 'work-related values' there was no widely recognized conceptual means of comparison across societies. Like them or not like them, these concepts – power distance, individualism-collectivism, uncertainty-avoidance, masculinity-femininity (and a fifth added later, 'confucian dynamism' (Hofstede and Bond, 1988) or long-term-short-term), showed how necessary it is to have concepts of culture pertinent to this field of research that run across societies. Others have tried to follow Hofstede's lead (e.g. Trompenaars, 1993 – see Chapter 17 in this book).

The point has been reached where it is even becoming possible to attempt to portray world-wide the cultural linkages with management and organization. 'World-wide' is the term used by Hickson and Pugh (1995) for their series of succinct portrayals of the approaches to management which typify the Anglos, the Latins, the Northern Europeans, the East-Central Europeans, the Asians, the Arabs and developing countries generally. Though sometimes the evidence is thin and the portrayals precarious, such an attempt exemplifies the current rapid widening of perspective to encompass the many 'mindscapes of management' (Maruyama, 1994).

It is an enthralling perspective, partly because it reveals so many conceptual puzzles. It shows how the cultures of societies enter unevenly into features of management and organization. Management and organization-relevant characteristics of societal cultures make more of an impression in some directions in some societies, in other directions in other societies. This is well illustrated by Tayeb:

> Take three collectivist nations – Japan, India and Iran, for example. These societies are characterized by, among others, a strong sense of the group and the community. A typical Japanese, Indian or Iranian person is very loyal to his or her own group or team and places the interest of the group before his or her own interests. On the face of it, one would expect to see this characteristic – collectivism – carried over into their work organizations in the form of, for instance, hard work and a high degree of commitment, dedication and emotional attachment to the company. However, a close examination of societal cultures, employees' attitudes and values and the management structure of work organizations in these countries (Tayeb, 1979; 1988; 1990) reveals that it is only in Japan where the collectivism of Japanese culture has been carried over into its companies. The Iranians and Indians as employees are as detached from their work organizations and have as individualistic a relationship with their work places as any individualistic nation. There are, of course, several cultural and non-cultural reasons for this, but the reasons will reveal themselves only through a careful and detailed study of these nations and their organizations.
>
> *Tayeb (1994: 38)*

The puzzle is, into which features of management and organization do societal cultures enter most? In other words, how uneven is organizational culture-sensitivity? This is a question put in a different way by Redding (1994: 341) when he asks the seventh of seven questions about 'cross-cultural OB': 'Which aspects of organizing and managing may be said to be universal and which are most affected by culture (that is, if there is such a construct as managing which can be disembedded at all)?'

CASES IN POINT: BRAZIL AND ENGLAND

This puzzle was brought out by a comparison of top management decision making in Brazil and England. Decision making at this level involves a number of individuals, sometimes just a few, sometimes many and the weighing of the interests involved, which again may be few or many (across 150 British cases reported by Hickson *et al.* (1986) the number of interests ranged from two to twenty, a mean of almost seven). It is a socio-political process, of a kind which a priori would be thought to be highly susceptible to the influence of societal culture.

It was decided to compare such processes among Brazilian and English managers because of the sharp contrast between a Latin New-World culture and an Anglo Old-World culture. The lead given by Tayeb (1987; 1988; 1994) was followed as far as possible. Cross-national research had been criticized both for failing to separate clearly the characteristics of a culture from those of management and organization that they were supposed to explain and, even more, for retrospective explanation – that is, for finding differences between organizations in different societies and attributing them to 'cultural effects' with no direct evidence for that (for example, Child, 1981). In response, Tayeb (1987; 1988) gave a remarkable demonstration of how societal cultures could be defined and operationalized separately from and before studying organization structural and behavioural features, and only then interrelating the two.

To operationalize cultures, she used published sociological research results, histories and literatures together with an original questionnaire administered personally by her to other respondents outside the work situation. Our time and funding did not permit the latter, but prior to defining and operationalizing the variables of decision making on which managements in Brazil and England were to be compared, portrayals of each culture were independently composed from sociological, historical and literary sources (for example, for Brazil: Azevedo 1963; Da Matta 1983; Faoro 1975; Hollanda 1969; Marshall 1966. For England: Commager 1974; Gorer 1955; Lytton 1833; Orwell 1947; Priestley 1973; Tayeb 1988; Terry 1979). In addition, unstructured interviews, which concluded with the completion of questionnaire scales largely taken from Terry (1979), were conducted with six Brazilian (English speaking) managers working in England and six English (Portuguese speaking) managers who had worked in Brazil and/or with Brazilian managers. These interviews explored the experience each had of the other and their views of the other, as a small but separate verification. The results accorded closely, indeed perfectly, with the cultural portrayals that had been built up (Oliveira, 1992).

Management is society and it is culture, of course. The one is part of the other. But they can be separated analytically for explanatory purposes and this is what is done here.

Throughout this research and this chapter we again follow (Tayeb (1987; 1988) in referring specifically to England and the English, not to Britain and the British. All published research deals only with the English, not with the Scottish, Welsh or Irish nations within the United Kingdom and we make no presumptions concerning them.

In brief, the composite cultural portrayals of the Brazilians and the English depicted them as follows:

The Brazilians

The culture of the Brazilians is influenced by a rural plantation past and by recent urbanization and industrialization. This society, which in 1940 found 60% of its population in rural areas, now finds 76% of it in urban centres with several cities of over one million inhabitants each. So its culture is made up of a blend of rural traits, colonial in origin, with urban values. For most sociologists and anthropologists (Azevedo 1963; Da Matta 1983; Faoro 1975; Hollanda 1969) two of the most representative features are legacies from long ago rural Brazil: a strong respect for authority, from the old patriarchal family structure and personalism from a highly collectivist rural society. Respect for authority is, quite possibly, the most traditional trait. Brazilian history is rife with examples: the long incumbency of a Portuguese as the first Brazilian ruler, the great number of military coups, two long periods of authoritarian rule and, in all matters, the importance of the paternalistic family in the make-up of society.

Personalism, which means relating to other people by means of personal knowledge of them rather than in terms of impersonal rights and duties, is accompanied by other characteristics such as informality and cordiality. Thus extensive networks of people who know each other involve almost all Brazilians (Da Matta 1983). These networks limit the privacy and outcomes of individuals and shape their personal development. This emphasis on direct informal relationships has as an attractive consequence the cordiality which is one of the most positive features of these people, in the opinion of both Brazilians and of foreigners visiting the country (Hollanda 1969; Marshall 1966).

Other less traditional, but not less significant, characteristics are immediacy and peacefulness. Brazilian immediacy has been observed by several authors (Amado and Brasil 1991; Faoro 1975; Hollanda 1969; Marshall 1966) who, whilst perceiving Brazil as the country of the future, find

Brazilians mainly concerned with the here and now. Things are needed now and ought to be done now. This is the most criticized feature of this culture since it tends to overcome consideration of future consequences. It may be an escape from uncertainty. It comes together with a propensity for the multification of rules and decrees which, according to Hofstede (1980), create a façade of apparent certainty.

Brazil is seen as a peaceful society, non-aggressive and non-assertive. There is an aversion to violent situations and a strong belief in the efficacy of mediating interventions, of personal negotiations, of the quest for a common solution which will benefit all.

The interviews with Brazilian and English executives reinforced this profile. They saw Brazilians as characterized by a personalized emotional involvement with work and, at the same time, flexibility. Brazilian executives tended to perceive themselves as open to argument and discussion through having a strong respect for all in positions of authority. However, English executives discussing Brazilians, perceived them as capable of taking risks to the extent of daring, but inefficient in transforming decisions into action.

Table 11.1 summarizes this picture in terms which are relative to the English, as in the English portrayal relative to the Brazilian. It uses the expressions 'power distance' and 'uncertainty avoidance' as they are used by Hofstede (1980; 1991).

The English

Historically, being English meant being at the apex of an empire on which it was said the sun never set. And many of the English, secure on their island, still think in this manner. England was the country where the Industrial Revolution began, where capitalism has its deepest roots and

Table 11.1: Brazilian culture profile (in relative terms)

Broad traits	Some associated characteristics
High power distance	Political authoritarianism, autocracies
	Need for strong leadership
Medium uncertainty avoidance	Need for formalized rules
Immediacy	Risk-taking capacity
Personalism	Strong interpersonal networks
	Informality and cordiality
Peacefulness	Low assertiveness

where tradition plays an important role. It is the land of time honoured unwritten law, where class differences are still carefully preserved. Visually, it is the land of ancient ceremony, historic buildings, gardens and parks. It is a land where leisure and life beyond work are important in the lives of every citizen.

English society has been studied over and over by many authors from different angles. Social investigators (Gorer 1955; Terry 1979; Tayeb 1988) as well as novelists and travellers (Commager 1974; Lytton 1983; Priestley 1973; Orwell 1947; Santayana 1922) have written numerous books about this society and its people. In a few words, being English means being a member of a society where due respect for authority is never misunderstood as submission; where the future is not controlled by written laws and rules but by caution, by the belief that changes are a part of a natural and continuous, not abrupt, process. Where relatively reserved behaviour and individual autonomy, together with a law-abiding honesty, and personal development and liberalism are taken as the basic rules of life. But also where the ego can prevail over the social and aggressive assertiveness is a component of daily life.

These aspects are not exclusively English, but this is a particular combination which can be summed up, in Hofstedian terms, as low power distance, low uncertainty avoidance and high individualism associated with personal assertiveness and conservatism under the rule of law. When interviewed, the Brazilian and English executives agreed with these characteristics. Both said that English managers and executives are much too inflexible. Brazilians emphasized their conservative and cautious ways, their slowness in decisions, the lack of emotivity in their business relationships and their arrogance. English executives added that English society is still too tied to traditional class structures with low mobility at the highest levels.

Table 11.2 sums up these characteristics.

Table 11.2: English culture profile (in relative terms)

Broad traits	Some associated characteristics
Low power distance in a finely layered society	Political liberalism Deference in accepting authority
Low uncertainty avoidance	Low formalization (fewer written rules)
Conservatism	Less risk-taking capacity Gradualism
Individualism	Reserved behaviour Less emotional involvement in the work organization
Assertiveness	Greater personal competitiveness

SAMPLE AND DATA COLLECTION

Equipped in advance with these cultural portrayals, of which the above are just a summary of salient aspects, the research then moved on to the empirical comparison of managerial decision making to investigate how far it might accord with them and be held to be explained by them.

In both countries, the chief executives of organizations selected from business directories and/or business association lists were approached by letter and by phone, beginning with those most easily accessible geographically. Co-operation was far harder to obtain in England than in Brazil. In England mangements are now besieged by researchers and students, whereas they are still a relative curiosity in Brazil, much as the second author recalls they were in England in the 1960s. In a neat demonstration of Brazilian immediacy and the English longer (gradualist) conception of time, when phoned for an appointment two or three weeks ahead Brazilians often laughed and asked to be contacted a few days beforehand, whereas the English routinely fixed dates many weeks or even months in advance.

The English sample, listed in Table 11.3, was built up first and it was hoped to match the Brazilians as closely as possible to it. This ideally required matching of both organizations and decisions, that is, finding similar organizations in which similar decisions had recently been or were being taken. That ideal was a very stringent requirement and was achieved in only three pairs of organizations, two universities, two textile firms and two newspapers (these are examined later in this chapter). One obstacle was that the range of business organizations is less varied in Brazil than in England so there were not many to choose from to effect matching. But irrespective of that, the chances of happening upon a similar decision in a similar organization were low.

The Brazilian sample is listed in Table 11.4. In all there are 20 Brazilian cases and 20 English, a total of 40. The decisions to be studied were chosen during the preliminary interview or conversation with the Chief Executive or other senior director, choosing those that were major in relation to the organization and recent enough or current so that memory would be fresh. There is no alternative to relying on memory if more than perhaps one case is to be studied, for the observation of the entirety of even a single decision making process is impossible and this cannot even be attempted on larger numbers. In this kind of research, memories of the main happenings are surprisingly clear and mutually corroborating, for as Cray *et al.* (1988: 23) found from the experience of 150 cases in 30 organizations, 'the difference between shorter recall in concurrent cases and the longer recall taped in interviews is that the story becomes less cluttered and relatively simpler, not that it changes'.

Tables 11.3 and 11.4 show that the 20 English cases of decisions occurred

Table 11.3: English sample of organizations and decisions

| | | Organizations' Main Characteristics | | |
Code	Decision	Activity	Size (Employees)	Ownership	Number of informants
E1	Rationalization of expenditure	Retailing	3,000	Co-operative	3
E2	Introduction of franchises	Dairy Company	5,500	Private	1
E3	Rationalization and reorganization	Food Manufacturer	2,500	Private	2
E4	Re-equipment	Textile	2,000	Private	2
E5	Diversification	Textile	1,500	Private	1
E6	New presses	Daily Newspapers *	1,200	Private	2
E7	Computerization	Daily Newspapers *	1,200	Private	2
E8	Rationalization of expenditures	University *	430	Public	5
E9	Disposal of division	Construction	3,250	Private	1
E10	Reorganization	Chemical *	1,740	Private	3
E11	Budget	University *	430	Public	2
E12	Merger	Chemical *	1,740	Private	3
E13	Acquisition in The Netherlands	Games Manufacturer	4,200	Private	1
E14	New divisions in the USA	Road Transporter	1,600	Private	2
E15	New service	Finance	3,450	Building Society	2
E16	Acquisition of competitors	Construction	1,300	Private	1
E17	Closure of division	Textile	4,800	Private	1
E18	Re-equipment	Textile	900	Private	1
E19	Budget	University	1,050	Public	2
E20	Move the company's headquarters	Retailing	3,500	Co-operative	1

* Organizations with two decisions studied

Table 11.4: Brazilian sample of organizations and decisions

Code	Decision	Activity	Size (Employees)	Ownership	Number of informants
B1	Modify existing structure	Retailing*	1700	Private	2
B2	New branch in Brasilia	Retailing*	1700	Private	2
B3	New presses	Daily Newspapers	1110	Private	2
B4	Merger	Transporter	1650	Private	2
B5	Modify and rationalize structure	Steel Industry *	13400	Public	4
B6	Divisionalization/professionalization	Retailing	2100	Private	3
B7	Computerization	Daily Newspapers	900	Private	3
B8	Budget	University *	2880	Public	1
B9	Increase in the number of staff	University *	2880	Public	2
B10	New division	Retailing *	1700	Private	1
B11	Closure of division	Retailing *	1700	Private	1
B12	Divisionalization	Construction	24300	Private	1
B13	New furnace technology	Steel Industry	1300	Private	1
B14	Introduction of information technology	University	4600	Public	1
B15	Merger	Construction	2200	Private	2
B16	New line of products	Steel Industry *	13400	Public	2
B17	Re-equipment	Textile	1800	Private	1
B18	New image	Banking	2700	Private	1
B19	Takeover bid	Textile	4600	Private	1
B20	Takeover a Portuguese firm	Construction	21900	Private	2

* Organizations with two decisions studied

in 17 organizations (one each in 14 organizations, two each in 3 organizations), the 20 Brazilian decisions in 16 organizations (one each in 12 organizations, two each in 4 organizations). Though there is no claim to exact matching, the organizations overall are not unlike in their broad diversity. The English include 13 manufacturing, 7 service, the Brazilians respectively 10 and 10. The English include 17 privately owned, 3 governmental, the Brazilians respectively 15 and 5. At first sight there is a sharp disparity in mean size, the English 2,264 employees and the Brazilians 5,426 and this does seem to represent a difference in economies, the older British economy having more middle-sized firms, whereas in Brazil there is a greater gap between small businesses and newer large corporations superimposed, so to speak, by recent industrialization. However, if three exceptionally large units are removed from the Brazilian calculation – the nationalized steel business (13,400) and two huge construction firms – sustained partly by lucrative state contracts (24,300 and 2,1900) – then the remaining organizations average out on a par with the English at 2,220 employees.

The tables show that there were one, two or three informants per case (and four in one of the Brazilian cases). There is no question that more would have been desirable, had they been available and had time and funding been available. The practical issue is how great the marginal addition to data would have been. These are informants, giving information about when a decision was reached (the authorized go-ahead for implementation), the kinds of information used, the main interests involved and so on, not respondents talking about details of who had said what or about their own feelings (though they may do so) or psychological processes. This study confirmed again the experience of Hickson *et al.* (1986), reported also by Cray *et al.* (1988), that a second or third informant added remarkably little to what a single centrally involved informant could recount. In any case, employees below the top echelon, even those immediately below, know little of what took place in the making of major decisions, so the number of useful informants is a handful at most. (Data collection took place in 1990 and 1991.)

THE MEANS OF COMPARISON

More than a decade of basic research in England, known as the Bradford Studies since it was (and continues still to be) based at Bradford Management Centre, provided the conceptual and operational means for the research reported here. This is the second cross-national extension of this work, the first having been in Sweden (Axelsson *et al.*, 1991). There is no known previous Brazilian/English study because variables of decision making which could be used for comparison were not available and no data collection experience on relatively large numbers of cases had accumulated, until the publications by Hickson *et al.* (1986) and Cray *et al.* (1988; 1991).

Interviews followed what these precursors had done by being a mixture of narrative case histories, open questions and rating scales (here 5 point scales), so numeral (rating) answers could be understood in the context of case knowledge. Oliveira (1992) contains full results, forty case histories, the interview schedule in English and in Portuguese.

The schedule was designed and tested first in English, guided by that used by Hickson *et al.* (1986). It was then translated into Portuguese by another Brazilian but in co-operation with the Brazilian author of this chapter, Arruda de Oliveira, then independently translated back by a Portuguese speaking Englishman and finally minor discrepancies of meaning were reconciled by all three together.

The salient variables are defined in Table 11.5. They are taken from those devised by Hickson *et al.* (1986), in some instances with improved definitions, except for Meandering Meetings, Meetings Completion, Informal Interaction Off Job, Interpersonal Facilitation and Organizational Innovativeness. These were added to extend the coverage of managerial decision making appropriate to the Brazilian setting. Since the variables used by Hickson *et al.* (1986) had been formulated in the English setting, it was recognized that they would include neither all the characteristics of interest in Brazil nor, therefore, all those pertinent to the comparison. The additional variables were defined so as to detect any reflection in decision making of the Brazilian cultural propensities for sociable personal relationships and for taking risks. Working within a single society, Hickson *et al.* (1986) had had no thought of covering these aspects. If they had not been included in this study the chances of revealing different culture effects would have been markedly lessened. Conversely, their inclusion added some bias towards detecting such effects.

CULTURE-LINKED CONTRASTS

Before any fieldwork had commenced, the two culture portrayals were used to predict what the Brazilian and English positions would be on every variable of decision making, assuming every variable to be highly, and to a similar degree, culture-sensitive. In a few words, predictions from the more leader-seeking, at times authoritarian, cordial, immediatist, optimistically risk-taking, Brazilian culture were that managerial decision making processes would be comparatively centralized, even autocratic, interpersonally interactive, fast and receptive to novel proposals. Whereas predictions from the deferential yet participative, personally reserved, gradualist, cautious English culture were that decision making would be comparatively less centralized, impersonal, slow and wary of innovation.

Table 11.5: Definitions of variables

Influence in favour, influence ratings of those who are favourable to the decision, from (1) a little to (5) a very great deal.
Number of active interests, the number of individuals, or groups (e.g. departments, committees, other organizations) who have influence on the process, not including any participant who although involved had not actively influenced the course of the decision.
Information diversity, a count of the variety of sources of information used (e.g. plans, internal documents, personal knowledge).
Meandering meetings, how far meetings meandered before becoming decisive, from never (1) to very often (5).
Meetings' completion, how far meetings finished the agenda, from never (1) to very often (5).
Overall informal interaction, how much discussion and toing and froing took place, in addition to pre-arranged meetings, from little (1) to a very great deal (5).
Informal interaction in breaks, how far people continued chatting about the decision during breaks in the working day, from never (1) to very often (5).
Informal interaction off the job, how far people continued chatting about the decision after normal working hours, from never (1) to very often (5).
Interpersonal facilitation, how far the right people knowing each other personally beforehand helped in coming to a decision, from not at all (1) to a great deal (5).
Negotiation scope, how much negotiation and compromise there was during the process, from little (1) to a very great deal (5).
Duration, the length of time from the first identifiable action which began movement towards a decision, to the moment when implementation was authorized or, in some cases, when the implementation began.
Perceived pace, how rushed was the decision, from not at all (1) to a great deal (5).
Organizational innovativeness, the extent to which decisions, in general, in the organization are novel, from not at all (1) to a great deal (5).

The main results are given in Tables 11.6 and 11.7. It must be stressed that in these tables and in the text, all results are relative. That is, indications of magnitude, of more or of less, are of Brazilian managements by reference to the English, of the English by reference to the Brazilian.

Table 11.6 contains those variables in which the strongest differences

Table 11.6: Culture-linked contrasts in decision making

	BRAZIL*	ENGLAND*	One Way: F	Sig.
	Hierarchical (smooth) slope	Participative (layered) slope		
Authority				
Influence in favour:			–	–
Active interests permitted:	5.5 (2.5)	6.8 (2.1)	2.9	087
Information diversity admitted:	3.0 (1.6)	4.6 (1.5)	11.3	001
Interpersonal Interaction				
Meandering meetings:	4.4 (0.9)	3.2 (1.1)	11.8	002
Meetings completion:	3.6 (1.1)	4.2 (0.5)	3.6	067
Informal interaction off job:	3.7 (1.7)	2.7 (1.6)	4.9	034
Interpersonal facilitation:	3.8 (1.7)	2.7 (1.6)	4.0	052
Temporal				
Duration (months):	8.2 (9.3)	12.2 (11.0)	1.5	ns.
Innovation				
Organizational innovativeness	3.9 (1.4)	2.9 (1.1)	5.1	030

* Mean scores, standard deviations in parentheses

Table 11.7: Common managerialism

In making major decisions, both Brazilian managements and English managements:
Confine the process, to the top élite.
Squeeze out opposition.
Interact and negotiate informally among themselves, on the job, about the matter on hand.
At least prepared to handle internal reorganization decisions.

were found between the two societies. The impact of their cultures is plain to see.

First, there is a marked difference in how authority is used. Forty 'control graphs' were drawn from the influence ratings given to those actively involved,- excluding those opposed, following Tannenbaum (1968). All are reproduced in Oliveira (1992), together with their grouping in terms of angle and smoothness of slope. At the extremes, there were six Brazilian cases of steep, unbroken hierarchical slope, that is, dominant chief executive influence unrivalled by any other. There were no such English cases. But there were nine English cases of a 'double-zed' type, that is, a layered slope with successive Z shapes in which each layer or step represents influence by others, lesser influence but nevertheless strong influence. There were fewer Brazilian examples of this, namely five. Overall, Brazilian cases inclined towards the more hierarchical slope, English cases towards the more layered slope.

Figure 11.1 shows contrasting examples. Brazilian Case 2 is a typically opportunistic fast president-only decision (president's influence 5) to launch a retail chain cross-country out of its accustomed regional market into the capital Brasilia. Only the corporation's bank manager (influence 3) and a consultant acquaintance of the president (1) figured at all. Whereas the English decision, by coincidence also numbered Case 2, involved a series of others. It switched retail doorstep distribution from employees to a franchise form of operation, involving the managing director (president), operations director and production director, all of whom had an equal say (all influence 4), the sales director (3), the marketing director, with his deputy and staff, the finance director with his deputy and staff (all 2), and holding company's chairman and a colleague director (1). During interviews, many Brazilian managers remarked that this was 'the President's decision', whereas the English cases did not identify a single pre-eminent personage.

The two cases in Figure 11.1 also illustrate vividly the difference in the

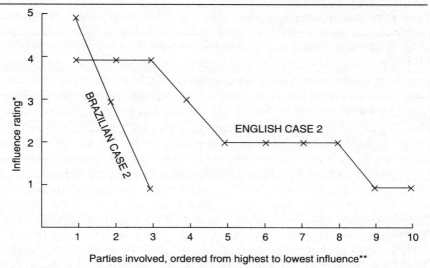

Parties involved, ordered from highest to lowest influence**

*   from 1 = little to 5 = a very great deal

**   informants were allowed to name whomever they perceived as being
        involved, individuals, departments, other organizations, etc.

Figure 11.1 Patterns of influence among the élites

number of active interests drawn in that appears in Table 11.6. The short
sharp Brazilian slope encompasses only three, whereas the way in which
authority is used in the English cases involves more – and more diverse –
in this instance ten. The diversity extends, also, to the diversity of sources
of information used. The less authority-focused, more involving, English
processes draw on more sources.

The greater Brazilian readiness to exploit personal relationships and
face to face contacts, in a cordial manner, compared to which English
social inhibitions produce an aloof façade, shows plainly in the variables
grouped in Table 11.6 under Interpersonal Interaction. In Brazilian decision making, meetings are more inclined to meander on to other subjects,
including personal matters, whereas the English more often stick to the
point. In consequence, whereas the English are likely to complete the
agenda, the Brazilians are more likely to leave matters unfinished and,
one of the most distinctive differences, to talk things over after work or in
sociable situations at weekends, such as barbecues. To the English, sully-
ing the social scene by 'talking shop' is, as another English expression has
it, 'not done'. At the end of the working day, Brazilian executives could be
found chatting over coffee in designated lounge corners: not so the
English, who went home with a bulging briefcase or worked on at a
solitary desk. Not surprisingly, the English more impersonal style pays

less attention to knowing the right people (interpersonal facilitation), whereas the well-known 'jeitinho brasileiro', the Brazilian little way, uses contacts to find a way around.

The difficulty of interpreting statistical signficance arises with duration, the time taken to reach a decision (counting from the first identifiable action which set off the overt process, for example, discussions leading to placing the matter on an agenda, a presidential phone call, the preparation of a report). The spread of times taken by both Brazilian and English cases is wide. Either can take a long time or be quick. The difference between them is not numerically significant. Yet five Brazilian decisions were accomplished in only a month, under the impulse of presidential direction, as in the example in Figure 11.1, whilst no English decision was that fast. Table 11.6 shows an English mean of 12.2 months, which is extraordinarily close to the 12.4 and 12.5 obtained at different times from different samples by Hickson *et al.* (1986) and Mallory (1987), as also is the distribution (a finding which tends to validate the methods used). By comparison, the Brazilian mean is less, just over eight months, as would be expected. So Hickson *et al.*'s (1986) presumption that strategic decisions most often take around a year would seem to have been culture-bound. As is Eisenhardt's (1989) finding of fast decision making, which must be accelerated by the American cultural setting as well as by its occurring in small electronic firms.

Did Brazilians feel stampeded, rushed off their feet? Did the English feel impatient? Not at all. If anything, the inclination was the other way around. Few Brazilians suggested that they felt hurried along, whereas many English managers felt there should have been more time to consider information, with less pressure from competitiors, customers or shareholders. Hence an intriguing contrast. Where the Brazilians and the English differed in this respect, the immediatists felt their shorter time had been enough, the gradualists felt their longer time had rushed them!

Finally, in Table 11.6, the English saw themselves as running organizations less receptive to novel decisions. The Brazilians more often saw theirs as innovations. Other interview data implies that Brazilian managers see risk in a lack of information rather than in innovation itself and are willing to accept that risk and welcome an innovative disposition in their organizations. The English however, whilst they may well innovate no less than Brazilians when they have to, do so more as a necessity and are less inclined to regard innovativeness as attractive in itself.

The contrasts in Table 11.6 therefore bear out predictions of culture effects. Here is societal culture at work within work. In these respects, managerial decision making is culture-sensitive. Brazilian élites are relatively authority-centred, personal and sociable, wanting to get a move on and open to innovation. Not so the English. Their élites are relatively receptive to wider influences, impersonal with a clear separation of work and play, patiently slow-moving, cautious about innovating.

Common managerialism

Table 11.7 shows the opposite to Table 11.6. It presents those ingredients of managerial decision making in which there are no noticeable differences between the way the Brazilians go about it and the way the English do. In these managerial ingredients they are, more or less, the same.

In organizations in both societies, the major decisions are taken above the heads of those below. Mostly they are unaware of what is going on, certainly of exactly what is being discussed among the élite and of how that discussion, if there is much discussion, is going. This means that those fully in the know are a topmost group of just a few, maybe up to a dozen or so, but hardly more. Analysis of what happened in the Brazilian and English cases to those who did get to know and did not like what they heard, shows that they were in all instances effectively squeezed out. These were occasional middle managers, technical or financial staff, unions and shareholders. Their unfavourable views were of little effect, their influence minimal. In two Brazilian and three English cases where one of the élite (a director) disagreed, the consequences for him and usually his department were adverse. Either the individual subsequently lost his job or his future prospects deteriorated.

For example, in Brazilian Case 1, the Commercial Director opposed a decision to reorganize the management structure, following a proposal by American consultants to decentralize retail operations. During two difficult years the atmosphere in the executive suite worsened, until the Commercial Director realized he had to go. This he did, at an emotional meeting. He was succeeded by one of the President's sons. It may be wondered how this proposal stemming from American values may have been carried out in so Brazilian an organization.

In English Case 3, opposition to a decision to drastically rationalize the traditional varieties produced by a biscuit (cookie) manufacturer led to a diminution of the responsibilities of the Sales Director and his department. Loyal to longstanding customer retailers who had always had custom-designed lines, they resisted the change, but lost out and lost position.

In the organizations in both societies, the most immediate effect of such opposition was usually an increase in discussion and negotiation, as might be expected.

In any case, informal interaction and negotiation, in the sense of talks in the corridors or, more likely, the offices of power, was the norm for both Brazilian and English managers, over and above anything that took place in arranged meetings of committees or task groups. This is task-oriented talking with not, for the English, the degree of sociability woven in by the Brazilians.

Table 11.7 indicates that the inherent complexity of whatever is being decided also transcends societies. Both in Brazil and in England, decisions over internal reorganizations or external mergers and takeovers were experienced as the most complex, that is in essence most unusual, radical and serious. Decisions about new products or services and especially on budgets or personnel questions, were less so. In these latter decisions, managers (irrespective of whether they were Brazilian or English) appeared to know what they were about, whereas with reorganizations, either internal or external, they faced the indefinable. These were decisions the dimensions of which were not quantifiable, nor the consequences calculable.

Indeed, these unknowable matters could have strange effects. In some respects they seemed even to reverse the usual culture-imbued contrasts. Faced with such an issue, Brazilians seemed to become more cautious, using more information and taking longer over the decision, English style. Conversely, the English case histories contained more instances of off-the-job getting together and inconclusive meetings on-the-job, as if they coped by adding some interaction Brazilian style.

Here then is the kernel of a common managerialism in the handling of major decisions which is little, if at all, sensitive to differing societal cultures. It cuts across them, the way of the world managerially speaking, which Brazilians and English share equally. It is the mutually most readily recognizable content of what transpires. Each would take for granted, and be right to take for granted, that this kind of decision making by the other would be an élite process within the highest two echelons, reaching beyond or below only for information inputs, brushing doubters aside, continually alive in talks around the office desk in addition to any committee work (brief and limited though this may sometimes be in a Brazilian hierarchy), groping with the unfathomable when the issue is changing the organization itself. In these respects, it would be a process just like their own.

TESTING THE RESULTS

It will be recalled that these results are from samples that are not exactly matched. This defect can be partly overcome by making comparisons of decisions in organizations of as near as possible equivalent sizes, purposes and ownership.

First, two sub-samples in the same size bands were compared: eight decisions each in Brazilian and English organizations from 1,050 to 1,800 employees, plus five Brazilian and six English decisions in organizations from 2,000 to 3,500. Second, decisions were compared in service organizations (ten Brazilian, seven English) and in manufacturing organizations (ten Brazilian, thirteen English). This included some degree of simultaneous control for size, services in both countries being smaller and manufacturers larger. Third, private owner-managed firms were compared (thirteen and seven respectively) and government owned undertakings (five and three).

The outcomes were overwhelmingly and reassuringly the same as on the full samples. There were two variations, most probably showing common organizational effects.

In the largest organizations, especially manufacturers, the number of interests involved in the Brazilian cases reached English levels and this, together with the greater numbers of senior colleagues, placed more restraints upon the president as impersonalism began to intrude.

In the public sector universities, English informal interaction and decison times were close to the Brazilian. These speedy English decisions, around six months in duration, supported the finding by Hickson *et al.* (1986) within their British sample that university decision making is not unduly slow, as often averred, something which they attributed to smooth flow-through committee systems. Decision making in universities, as in other public services, has been found to be more concerned with process than with resources, relative to manufacturers (Rodrigues and Hickson, 1995).

These tighter tests compare kinds of organization, but still do not compare like with like in decisions. For this, the three matching pairs mentioned earlier were used. These were two regional newspapers, the managements of both of which had decided to re-equip with new computer-controlled presses, two textile manufacturers where it had been decided to expand and modernize production capacity and the corporate budget and business plan decisions of the universities (cases B3 and E6, B17 and E18, B8 and E19 in Tables 11.3 and 11.4).

Comparison of these cases feature by feature, combining numerically expressed variables and narrative case histories, was both the most stringent and most exhaustively detailed test. It too accorded with the results given so far in this chapter. In summary, the Brazilians were again seen to have taken more risks in more of a crisis atmosphere, interacting in a smaller clique around the president, failing to finish within meetings and continuing outside working hours, off the job. Once more the English appeared more cautiously defensive, but kept matters within working hours despite involving more participants. Both had in common the same holding of the interactive process within the bounds of the top echelons alone.

There was one exception to the accordance with the results from the full samples. The chairman of the English textile firm took things into his own hands and pushed the decision through quickly, in a manner that could be described as Brazilian-style. For some time the production and marketing directors had been pressing for new equipment, anxious about requests from their main customers for improved quality to equal that obtainable from competitor suppliers. Once capital became available, the chairman short-circuited the proper procedure laid down for an investment decision which required double scrutiny, from a steering committee and from an implementation committee both specially constituted. He himself acted alone in the capacity of 'steering committee' to approve the detailed proposal drawn up by the implementation committee, and ensured its rapid rubber stamping by the main board. In such ways do organizational imperatives for survival, faced in common by managements everywhere, override what may be the more accustomed approach.

CONCLUSIONS

How far can this study be construed not only to have posed the puzzle 'into which features of management and organization do societal cultures enter most', but to have fashioned a part of the solution?

Certainly, managements in a variety of organizations in Brazil and in England have been shown to differ sharply relative to one another in how they take major, indeed strategic, decisions. These differences have been attributed to differences in societal cultures, the more confidently because those cultures were portrayed prior to collecting data on decision making and predictions made of what differences they would make to it so that cultural explanations could not be put down to ex post facto wishful thinking. These cultures themselves originate in Latinesque Portuguese colonization of a New World still expansive and spacious and in the Anglo-Saxon takeover a thousand years earlier of an island where even then Old World traditions were taking shape.

So, in making decisions the Brazilians weave patterns of effusive inter-action around dominating authority figures, ever hopeful but unwilling to wait long for a future that in an unsettled continent may not come. The English move coolly and cautiously, respecting but not over-needful of an authoritative lead, in time which for them stretches from a long settled past into an equally long future so that, as they say, patience is a virtue. Of course, these are stereotypical summaries. Not every Brazilian manager, not every English manager, is like this in all things all the time. There is widespread variation and these are, in effect, statements of differing central tendencies.

They are central tendencies which envelope but do not suppress a common managerialism that belongs to both. A managerialism at the top, moving decisions through an élite coterie who talk them over again and again inside meetings and out. What else is to be expected? Only the chief executive sees an organization whole, whole as far as the view downwards can scan and only his (there was no her in this study, anyway) nearest colleagues can see enough from their more partial perspectives, to talk with him and each other about matters so weighty. Others have neither the authority nor the outlook at that level to be able to take part in the same way. Once a pyramidal purposive organization has been set up, this is its effect on decision making whatever the society and whatever the politico-economic system.

Which then has the greater consequences, cultural difference or common managerialism? On the face of it, Table 11.6, which concerns the former, has more variables than Table 11.7 which concerns the latter. But counting variables must be nonsense. They and their effects cannot be added and weighed. Yet taken together, these tables and their elaboration in the text, could be interpreted to mean that those aspects of management which are interpersonal (that is, the use made of authority over others and of personal relationships with them) and philosophical (that is, the view taken of time and of change) are the most susceptible to cultural variation. How each deals with and responds to their fellow humankind and conceives of the temporal situation of humankind, are at the heart of societal culture. Fundamentally they define the nature and progression of life. Small wonder, then, that they imbue managerial behaviour and distinguish by it the organizations of one society from those of another. Ultimately, the decision making that is at the core of management is itself 'social representation' (Laroche, 1995).

Whereas the more formal structural features of organization design, in those aspects which are everywhere much the same, engender the same structure-linked responses everywhere. They give rise to internally interactive élite processes. It may be some part of the solution to the puzzle as to which managerial and organizational features are most and least societal culture-sensitive. It is, however, derived from a Brazilian–English comparison only, of decision making processes only.

REFERENCES

Amado, G. and Brasil, H.V. (1991) Organizational behaviors and cultural context: the Brazilian 'jeitinho'. *International Studies of Management and Organization*, **21**, 3, pp. 38–61.

Axelsson, R., Cray, D., Mallory, G.R. and Wilson, D.C. (1991) Decision style in British and Swedish organizations. *British Journal of Management*, **2**, pp. 67–79.

Azevedo, T. (1963) *Social Change in Brazil*, University of Florida Press.

Boyacigiller, N. and Adler, N.J. (1991) The parochial dinosaur: organizational science in a global context. *Academy of Management Review*, **16**, 2, pp. 262–90.

Child, J. (1981) Culture, Contingency and Capitalism in the Cross-

National Study of Organizations, in *Research in Organizational Behavior* (eds L.L. Cummings and B.M. Staw) JAI Press, pp. 303–56.

Commager, H. (1974) English Traits One Hundred Years Later, in *Britain Through American Eyes* (ed H. Commager) Blackwell, Oxford.

Cray, D., Mallory, G.R., Butler, R.J., Hickson, D.J. and Wilson, D.C. (1988) Sporadic, fluid and constricted processes: three types of strategic decision-making in organizations. *Journal of Management Studies*, **25**, 1, pp. 13–40.

Da Matta, R. (1983) *Carnavales, Malandras y Héroes*, Zahar.

Eisenhardt, K. (1989) Making decisions in high-velocity environments. *Academy of Management Journal*, **32**, 3, pp. 543–76.

Faoro, R. (1975) *Os Donos do Power*, Globo.

Gorer, G. (1955) *Exploring the English Character*, Crosset Press.

Hickson, D.J., Butler, R.J., Cray, D., Mallory, G.R. and Wilson, D.C. (1986) *Top Decisions: Strategic Decision Making in Organizations*, Jossey-Bass.

Hickson, D.J. and Pugh, D.S. (1995) *Management Worldwide: the Impact of Societal Culture on Organizations Around the Globe*, Penguin.

Hofstede, G. (1980) Culture's Consequences: International Differences in Work-Related Values, Sage (summarized in D.S. Pugh and D.J. Hickson *Writers on Organizations*, 4th edition, Penguin, 1989).

Hofstede, G. (1991) *Cultures and Organizations: Software of the Mind*, McGraw-Hill.

Hofstede, G. and Bond, M.H. (1988) The Confucius Connection. *Organizational Dynamics*, **16**, 4, pp. 4–21.

Hollanda, S.B. (1969) *Raíces del Brasil*, José Olympio.

Lachman, R., Nedd, A. and Hinings, R. (1994) Analysing cross-national management and organizations: a theoretical framework. *Management Science*, **40**, 1, pp. 40–55.

Laroche, H. (1995) From decision to action in organizations: decision-making as a social representation. *Organization Science*, **6**, 1, pp. 62–75.

Lytton, Edward (1833) *England and the English*, Berkley.

Mallory, G.R. (1987) The Speed of Strategic Decision-Making. PhD thesis, University of Bradford.

Marshall, A. (1966) *Brazil*, Thames and Hudson, London.

Maruyama, M. (1994) *Mindscapes in Management: the use of Individual Differences in Multi-cultural Management*, Dartmouth.

Oliveira, C.A.A. (1992) Societal Culture and Managerial Decision Making: The Brazilians and the English. PhD thesis, University of Bradford.

Orwell, G. (1947) *The English People*, Collins.

Priestley, J.B. (1973) *The English*, Heinemann.

Redding, S.G. (1994) Comparative management theory: jungle, zoo or fossil bed? *Organization Studies* **15**, 3, pp. 323–59.

Santayana, G. (1922) *Soliloquies in England and Later Soliloquies*, Constable.

Smith, P.B. (1992) Organizational behaviour and national cultures. *British Journal of Management*, **3**, pp. 39–51.

Tannenbaum, A.S. (1968) *Control in Organizations*, McGraw-Hill.

Tayeb, M. (1979) Cultural Determinants of Organizational Response to Envionmental Demands: an Empirical Study in Iran. M Litt. Thesis, Oxford.

Tayeb, M. (1987) Contingency and culture: a study of matched English and Indian manufacturing firms. *Organization Studies*, **8**, 3, pp. 241–61.

Tayeb, M. (1988) *Organizations and National Culture: A Comparative Analysis*, Sage.

Tayeb, M. (1990) Japanese management style, in *Organisational Behaviour*, Pitman, London.

Tayeb, M. (1994) Organizations and national culture: methodology considered. *Organization Studies*, **15**, 3, pp. 429–46.

Terry, P.T. (1979) An Investigation of Some Cultural Determinants of English Organization Behaviour. PhD thesis, University of Bath.

Triandis, H.C. (1982/83) Dimensions of cultural variation as parameters of organizational theories. *International Studies of Management and Organization*, Winter, pp. 139–69.

Trompenaars, F. (1993) *Riding the Waves of Culture: Understanding Cultural Diversity in Business*, Economist Books.

Chapter 12

A comparison of British and German managerial roles, perceptions and behaviour

Rosemary Stewart, Jean-Louis Barsoux, Alfred Kieser, Hans-Dieter Ganter and Peter Walgenbach

INTRODUCTION

In our Anglo-German study we set out to:

1 Contribute to the understanding of managerial behaviour by improved conceptualization and methodology and by paying more attention to the context within which the managers work.
2 Learn more about the behaviour of German managers which has been little studied.
3 Explore the functions of middle management and ask whether they are similar to top management.
4 Compare the jobs, perceptions and behaviour of German and British middle managers.

This chapter will focus on the fourth aim, as that is the one that is most relevant to this volume. A book reporting the research has also been published (Stewart *et al.* 1994). In Britain, the research was funded by the Anglo-German Foundation; in Germany, by the Deutsche Forschungs-gemeinschaft and the Centre for European Economic Research, Mannheim.

METHODS

Case studies were chosen as the most suitable method for the complexity of the research. It is, therefore, a qualitative study. In our selection of companies and jobs to study, we sought for comparability across the two countries and for variety of jobs and industries within the limitations of research time. The aim was to study middle managers in pairs of compar-able companies in Britain and Germany. The main selection criteria for the companies were that they should be:

– in different industries
– of comparable size
– the industries should be about the same size in the national economy
– not foreign-owned.

Our choice was limited by the need to find firms willing to co-operate in both countries. Within this constraint, the firms selected were in brewing, as a representative of manufacturing using process production; construction, a different example of manufacturing using unit production and life insurance, as a representative of the service sector using a form of mass production. Ten middle management jobs were studied in each company, making 60 in total. The jobs selected were in technical/production, commercial and administrative/finance, so as to provide a variety of functions. The aim was to study comparable jobs in each pair of companies after studying the organization charts of the companies or, where they did not exist in one of the German companies, developing one.

For purposes of data-collection, we relied on the following:

Library search	– information on industries and companies studied
Initial interview	– company organization and relevant policies
Pre-interview questionnaire	– factual information on jobs being studied and jobholder's qualifications and career
Semi-structured interviews with the sixty managers	– about their job and their perceptions of it
Semi-structured interviews with each manager's boss	– boss's demands and expectations; performance measures and amount of freedom
Non-participant observation 2–3 days, solo and joint 27 managers.	– cross-check on interviews, provide tangible evidence, offer unexpected insights.

We decided to use joint observation to offset the cultural bias that would be inherent from using only an observer of the same nationality.

Full team meetings were held at intervals in alternate countries to plan and review research. More frequent meetings were held between the field researchers – the joint observation also gave them time to review and compare observations. Research tools were jointly devised. The questionnaires were first written in English, then translated into German by the German team, back into English by an independent translator and reviewed with the British team. The main questionnaire to the middle managers was piloted in both countries and modified. We agreed relevant prompts to be used with particular questions. Different chapters were written by British or German members of the group then agreed with the other team, with final editing by the British team.

We then set out to probe the following:

– perceptions of tasks, responsibilities and priorities
– feelings about the job and nature of difficulties

- work pattern
- contacts, networks and relationships
- what they expect of others and what they think others expect of them
- understanding of management
- what they see as effective or ineffective management

We often could not find, as planned, paired jobs to study in the British and German companies because they were organized differently. German managers were much more reluctant to be observed, possibly because (a) they were not used to being observed or (b) they did not expect to learn anything. Both problems contributed to understanding the differences between managers and their jobs in the two countries.

Stewart's (1982; 1991) model of demands, constraints and choices was used for the comparison of jobs and of the managers' perceptions of them. The role episode model of Katz and Kahn (1966) was used for its focus on role sending and Kotter's (1982) agenda and networks as ways of conceptualizing the managers' activities. In seeking to understand the context within which the managers worked and to explain the differences that we found, we drew on other concepts but the discussion of these does not form part of this chapter.

HOW THE PAIRED COMPANIES DIFFERED

In organization the German companies were flatter, with fewer employees in relation to output and more integrated departments (see Lawrence 1980; Lane 1989). The difference in staff numbers may be partly explained by differences in the organization. Another possible explanation is that they may have been partly due to the relative economic situation: in Britain the staff numbers had not yet fallen to reflect the slump and in West Germany (where we were studying) had not yet risen to catch up with the boom from the integration of East Germany.

We found more organizational routines constraining the middle managers in the German companies, as well as more change taking place in British companies, especially minor modifications to the organization and the quality initiatives. The above were the general differences but there were also specific differences, e.g. life assurance in Britain is more competitive, has more types of policies and the German company was more automated.

In German insurance, we found grouping by customer rather than by different aspects of customer service in the British company; in German brewing production and maintainance were integrated, which were separate in the British company. A common boss judged the performance of potentially conflicting managers on the way they worked together in German companies and in construction, the same pair of technical and commercial managers for different projects were retained. The British managers had to spend more time in liasion meetings and there was an independent quality function. The individual objective setting in Britain could also hinder cooperation.

DIFFERENCES IN THE BACKGROUND OF BRITISH AND GERMAN MANAGERS

The main difference in our sample was that 24 of the 30 German managers had completed a technical or commercial apprenticeship, whereas 16 of the British were members of professional institutions. Eberwein and Tholen (1990) found that 55% of the German senior executives they studied had completed a technical or commercial apprenticeship. For Britain, the figure for the number with professional membership is disproportionately high, reflecting the strong professional tradition in the three industries. The German bosses of the middle managers had more educational qualifications than the British – as shown in wider studies (see Sorge and Warner, 1986 for example). Formal qualifications seemed less important in the British companies as we found examples of managers being appointed who did not have the qualifications required in the job specification.

Both British and German managers had been with their companies for many years, 17 of the British and 18 of the German for more than 20 years. This similarity makes the differences shown in Table 12.1 even more striking: the German middle managers stayed much longer in the same job. Wheatley's (1992) study shows that the frequent job moves of the 30 British managers is a British practice – a practice which reflects a belief that staying long in the same job can be stultifying. Job movement, including lateral movement, is also easier in Britain because jobs are less tied to qualifications.

Table 12.1: Length of time middle managers had held their current position

	British managers	*German managers*
Less than 2 years	13	3
2 to 4 years	12	7
5 to 9 years	4	8
10 to 19 years	1	6
20 or more years	0	6
	30	30

COMPARISON OF THE DEMANDS, CONSTRAINTS AND CHOICES OF THE GERMAN AND BRITISH MANAGERS' JOBS

Both British and German managers saw two common demands: to run their department smoothly and to create a good working climate. The British had demands that arose from having their own departmental budget – the German middle managers did not have their own budgets. The British had to spend more time securing co-operation as their organizations were less integrated and less stable.

The dominant constraint for both was the economic environment – at the time there was a recession in the UK, so the financial constraints were greater. At that time there was no recession in Germany, where a major constraint was felt to be excessive workloads. German managers were more constrained by organizational routines and formal systems (but saw these as preferable to personal checking by their boss). However, the British complained more of organizational constraints, perhaps because they were expected to exercise more initiative than the German managers and so were more likely to run into organizational constraints. German managers felt constrained by the shortage of staff and, surprisingly, complained more about their staff being inadequately qualified.

The British had more choice to shape their own job as expectations of what they would do were more negotiable: 'a job is what you make it'. The British, unlike the German managers, had regular meetings with their boss to discuss objectives. The likely explanation is that the German managers had been in their jobs for a long time, working within well-established routines so they needed a less institutionalized communication of expectations and objectives than in Britain. In the British companies the jobs and the jobholders changed much more often so this flux and uncertainty made it more important for the boss and subordinate to have regular meetings to redefine job responsibilities and agree objectives. The British had more freedom in when they worked, which could mean starting late, spending more time at lunch but also working late. The Germans worked hard for set hours.

The British and Germans differed in their choice of priorities. One of the German choices was which technical tasks they did themselves. The British would expect to develop their subordinates to do the technical work. Both British and Germans had some choice in the frequency and number of contacts with subordinates.

DIFFERENCES IN SOME ACTIVITIES

The time that the managers spent in meetings varied considerably between the industry and the functions as well as between the two countries. The number and duration of meetings seems to be explained by the factors influencing the need for personal co-ordination:

- the type of product
- the type of job
- the organizational structure

But there also seemed to be national differences: British meetings lasted longer, possible explanations are that the:

- British are less time and task conscious
- British more interested in exchange of information

The British use meetings to assist co-ordination whereas the Germans rely more on structure and routines.

Telephone calls, informal exchanges, enquiries or requests took most of the managers' time in both countries. The Germans had many more per day, an average of 52 compared with 33 for the British, but they took less time in total. The German contacts with subordinates tended to be short technical queries. On average the Germans spent more time alone, an average of 36.5% of their time compared with 19.9% for the British.

For the German managers, facts and rational arguments were seen to be the means of persuasion. The British laid more emphasis on 'selling' and persuasion and the need to understand the individual to be persuaded. The British managers were more given to networking: developing a wide range of contacts who could be useful.

Both British and German middle managers spent a lot of time checking the work of their subordinates. The Germans tended to have a specific and technical approach to checking, personally checking on a subordinate's output and would check the subordinate's technical knowledge in conversation. The British, except in the construction industry, tended to check on the progress of the people rather than on the work itself by asking frequent, short, open-ended questions; they also relied more on checking by personal observation.

UNDERSTANDING OF MANAGEMENT

We asked the managers what were their major responsibilities. The British and German managers differed in whether they:

- emphasized technical or managerial responsibilities
- went into detail about them

as shown in Tables 12.2a and 12.2b.

The British managers were very conscious of a hierarchical division between managerial and technical work. They talked of their role as a manager. They seemed keen to distance themselves from technical invol-

Table 12.2a: Identification of technical responsibilities

Identification of job-(technical) responsibilities	German middle managers	British middle related managers
No identification	2	11
General identification	8	18
Identification/description of specific aspects	20	1

Table 12.2b: Identification of managerial responsibilities

Identification of managerial responsibilities	German middle managers	British middle managers
No identification	15	6
General identification	11	18
Identification/description of specific aspects	4	6

vement. Management through expert knowledge seemed to be the main way in which the German middle managers understood management. The Germans spoke as if they viewed technical duties and managerial responsibilities as inseparable. The differences in careers and in specific qualifications for the job could help to explain why the Germans attached so much more importance than the British to technical work.

We asked the managers what were their personal guidelines for managing. The British answers were far richer and lengthier. They seemed ready to philosophize about management; the main themes were: fairness, listening, communication, honesty, integrity and an ability to understand others and to put oneself in their position. All their answers revolved round relationships and the way the manager was perceived. There was never any hint that management was technically challenging. At times, the German emphasis on getting things done seemed, to British eyes, like brusqueness: requests were much more direct and there was no informal preamble on the phone; similarly, a task might be completed before acknowledging another's presence. Almost all the German managers rejected the role of supervisor. They saw themselves as colleagues who supervise. Some forewent managerial privileges, for example, clocking in. The Germans relied upon their technical expertise as the main basis for their role as a supervising colleague.

The British managers were readier to believe that they could learn from others. More broadly, this is reflected in a greater participation in management programmes and in improving managerial competence. In Germany until recently there has been less writing, thinking and talking about management. This background may help to explain why the German managers had a more specific understanding of management.

ATTITUDES TO UNCERTAINTY

Hofstede (1980), who has done the major study of cross-cultural differences, suggested that one of these is 'uncertainty avoidance' – see Chapter 9 in this book. On a scale from 0 (high tolerance) to 100 (low tolerance), British managers scored 35 to Germans (FR) 65.

We noted various examples of this difference:

- German managers' reluctance to be observed
- Differences in organization, and in the importance attached to structure
- Differences in career patterns
- German concern for punctuality
- British focus on quick and practical solutions 'thinking on your feet'. 'back of the envelope calculations'
- interpersonal formality in the German workplace

All three British companies had some organizational changes during our research there (about a month). Changes in personnel were used as opportunities to make changes to jobs and responsibilities. There was a willingness to make changes to accommodate the strengths and weaknesses of the person available and to create development opportunities. The three German companies were stable and there was a concern to preserve the 'integrity of the structure'.

HARMONIOUS CO-OPERATION VS INDIVIDUAL ACHIEVEMENT

Another of Hofstede's (1980) categories is individualism compared with collectivism. He found that the Germans were more collectivist than the British. The German managers in our research stressed the value of co-operation, mutual support, team spirit and avoidance of conflict. This, together with their greater task orientation meant that personalities needed less consideration than in the British companies. The British took the individual as their focus in replies to questions about job satisfaction, expectations of bosses and of subordinates and job priorities. They stressed self-fulfilment, being seen to do a good job and the opportunity to do things their way.

WORK AND PRIVATE LIFE

The German managers worked hard with little of the socialization that often exists in British office life. They arrived on time and left on time. For the British managers observed, there was more overlap between work and leisure – shopping, visits to the dentist, banking, lunch at the pub, personal phone calls were all witnessed. So the British managers' work was less sustained but they were also likely to work late, take work home and even drop into the office or factory at the weekend – even though they, unlike some of the Germans, did not describe work as 'fun'.

DISCUSSION

The findings support the view that societal norms, to do with uncertainty, individualism, view of management and so on, affect the way that managers go about their jobs. But these cultural differences account for only some of the differences of managerial behaviour. This paper has only referred briefly to some of the other contributory factors, such as education, careers, economic circumstances, organizational structure and type of technology.

The study confirmed the findings of several writers (see Lawrence 1980; Sorge and Warner 1986; Lane 1989) on Anglo/German comparisons, that German management is more concerned with the structure and British with the process. German and British middle managers have a different understanding of management and so manage in different ways. The German managers occupied a post, whereas the British managers had more of a view of expectations being negotiable. They saw the job in more individual terms as in part what they could make of it. The differences in structure found in earlier studies still exist; hence the impossibility of finding matched jobs in the same functions.

The findings suggest that managerial careers are markedly different in Britain and Germany. The wide differences in the amount of time that the British and German middle managers spent in the same job and the lack of lateral mobility is related to the perception of management and career development. It is a difference that would be worth exploring in a wider matched sample.

The German firms studied had greater structural stability. This may partly reflect more stable financial markets where growth by acquisition, with its effects on structure, is not so common. It may also reflect greater care in the initial development of structure, together with more standardized qualifications, so that there is no need to adapt the structure to the people.

It is interesting how contrary the relative structural stability of the German firms studied is to the Anglo-American writings about the need for fluid organizations. One conclusion from the research is the managerial imperialism of Anglo-American writings about management and especially about managerial work and behaviour. The research process is itself culture-bound as the view of management influences what questions are asked and what is observed.

The cultural bias is very difficult for Anglo-American researchers and those influenced by them to avoid, given that nearly all our constructs and theories for understanding and categorizing management come from the Anglo-American countries. Joint research, including joint observation, is a way to try to offset this mind-set.

The study of these German middle managers suggests that the following common Anglo-American views may need reappraisal:

- Change is productively stimulating; hence new people can turn around a situation; moving jobs is often developmental; changing the organization is a major ingredient of a change programme.
- Networking and persuasion are essential aspects of management. Networking exists in German management but seems to be more important in Britain (and America), both to get tangential information and for self-promotion.
- No evidence in five of the six companies studied that the role of middle management was vanishing
- Management does not have to be seen from an individualistic perspective with its assumptions about motivation and rewards.

A potential lesson for British managers (and American) is to ask whether their emphasis on 'managing' is overdone? Perhaps more involvement in, and more knowledge of, operations would make for greater effectiveness.

REFERENCES

Eberwein, W. and Tholen, J. (1990) *Managermentalitat-Industrielle Unternehmensleitung als Berufunder Politik*, Frankfurter Allgemeine Zeitung, Frankfurt.

Hofstede, G. (1980) *Culture's Consequences: International Differences in Work Related Values*, Sage, Beverly Hills CA and London.

Katz, D. and Kahn, R.L. (1966) *The Social Psychology of Organizations*, Wiley, New York.

Kotter, J. (1982) *The General Managers*, Free Press, New York.

Lane, C. (1989) *Management and Labour in Europe – The Industrial Enterprise in Germany, Britain and France*, E. Elgar, Aldershot.

Lawrence, P. (1980) *Managers and Management in West Germany*, Croom Helm, London.

Sorge, A. and Warner, M. (1986) *Comparative Factory Organisation*, Gower, Aldershot.

Stewart, R. (1982) *Choices for the Managers*, Prentice-Hall, Englewood Cliffs, N.J.

Stewart, R. (1991) *Managing Today and Tomorrow*, Macmillan, London.

Stewart, R. *et al.* (1994) *Managing in Britain and Germany*, London, Macmillan.

Wheatley, M. (1992) *The Future of Middle Management*, British Institute of Management, p. 10.

Chapter 13

Management development: contradictions and dilemmas arising from in-depth study of British and Czech managers

Richard Thorpe and Karel Pavlica

INTRODUCTION

It is understandable that one of the focuses of attention in the economic transition of the Czech Republic should be management education and management development. From the perspective of those who wish to speed the Republic's transformation, this problem requires the application of knowledge and understandings gained from Western management theory practice and ideas. For others, however, doubts have been cast on the value of using Western management approaches in the area of management education and development. Rosemary Stewart comments that 'management literature has usually discussed management as if it was a single activity that required uniform abilities and a common knowledge'. (Stewart, 1988:107).

For many organizations problems have arisen from attempts to directly apply some of these singularly Western management approaches and the practice of having foreign 'experts' fly in to teach Czech managers 'what they need to learn' has raised more questions than it has solved.

Studying 249 managment students in the USA, Powell and Butterfield found that students made distinctions favourable to their managers when compared to managers from another culture. Perhaps more significantly, they saw that good managers were predominantly male and white (Powell and Butterfield, 1979).

Andre Laurent (1983) confirms suspicions about cultural influence and individuals' preconceptions about management behaviour. Laurent believed that individual managers hold their own set of beliefs about good and bad management behaviour that are moulded from their own national cultures.

> Every manager has his own management theory, his own set of representations and preferences that in some way guide his potential behaviour in organizations; and it is critical for managers, management researchers and educators to identify and understand these implicit theories of management better.
>
> (*Laurent 1983:76*).

Which means also understanding fully the cultural context in which these ideas were formed.

Following empirical research over a two-year period with groups of upper-middle-level managers from a variety of Western countries, he concluded that when comparative phenomenological approaches are used to study managers and organizations the findings cast serious doubt on the universality of management and organizational knowledge and practice. He suggests that:

> . . . it may very well be that the management process in these Western countries is as much culture bound as their cooking, and that international management has to avoid the trap of international cuisine. National cultures may still offer some genuine recipes.
>
> (*Laurent 1983:95*).

These experiences can be directly linked to two developing areas of cross-cultural literature. The first area covers the findings of sociologists and psychologists who have focusd on the cultural aspects of management (Hofstede 1994; Mead 1994; Randlesome 1993). These writers demonstrate that each society creates its own preferred way of defining and practising management. Their contribution stresses the importance that needs to be placed on management practitioners being encouraged to understand and be sensitive to the social and cultural aspects of the society in which they work.

The second area covers findings from a different perspective with views (Gergen 1992; Shotter 1993) which stress the social and rhetorical nature of management knowledge and practice and suggest attention should focus away from theory choice and application and more towards how knowledge is constructed through language and conversation within organizational contexts. It is within this second context that the study we report here is located. Our aim is to gain insights into cultural understanding from managers about management and their management practice in two countries, the Czech Republic and Great Britain. We argue that through the adoption of a discourse analysis methodology it is possible to identify the concepts they use and the perceptions they hold. Comparison of these between the two cultures can identify a number of interesting and different aspects of management which might lead to new approaches being used in management education development and change in both countries.

At the level of methodology we demonstrate how discourse analysis can be helpful as an illuminative tool to provide understanding and explanation from both qualitative and quantitative data. The study is based on comparisons between Czech and British management cultures as articulated by executive MBA students and graduates from both countries. The rationale for the choice of this particular sample is a result of the close links that exist between the University of Economics, Prague and PIBS (Prague International Business School) and the Manchester Metropolitan University.

METHODOLOGY RESEARCH DESIGN AND METHODS OF ANALYSIS AND INTERPRETATION

Accepting and building on social constructionists' views of management and management research, our preferred approach was to analyse the discourses managers used in accounts and discussions about their work and their identity. Our interest lay in both their espoused theories – what and how they explained what they thought and did as well as, as far as we could tell, what they actually did.

Amongst social constructionists the views of Gergen (1992) and Shotter (1993), have been influential. According to Gergen, a strength of an organization and its management lies in its ability to construct the world through spontaneous and responsive interaction with those outside the organization. Managers are seen as 'repairers' able to maintain or build 'routine flows of actions' or make sense of chaos. This, it is argued, is more important than only stressing internal cohesion and power relationships. 'Power', to Gergen, is not possessed by individuals, but derived through a co-ordinated system of negotiated relationships according to agreed norms within a particular social system. Exclusion from this process of those outside the organization and/or marginalized voices inside the organization will lead to an organization's isolation and eventual demise.

This general vision of Gergen's corresponds closely with Shotter's idea of a manager as a practical author. Organizational settings are constructed through joint action and the manager is an author in this. Within this view Shotter sees a manager's success as depending not on researching and applying 'true' theory, but rather by providing appropriate explanations of chaotic impressions. Of importance is whether a manager can act 'from outside' – a theory application or 'from within' – a theory construction. Acting 'inside' – being able to master a variety of 'sense making' discourses of organizational life – is seen by Shotter as an essential managerial skill, quite different from learning or applying the appropriate theory of the day, whether it be derived from 'rigorous research' or from experience that is, 'knowing from within', in contrast, is constituted through interaction and is negotiated. So attention needs to be focused on actual conversations.

If management is viewed as being socially constructed and rhetorical in nature, an analysis of the discourses through which managers interact and converse becomes important and the insights that different disciplines can reveal from the discourses add a further dimension to any study. Turning to the concept of discourse and how it might be analysed, the field is very broad, with a great number of writers, all with different views and interpretations. As a consequence we must stress that the perspective we are taking is in the English sociology and psychology tradition elaborated by writers such as Wetherell and Potter (1988) and Parker (1992). This body of literature is focused on a criticism of the traditional positivistic view that language and knowledge are linked to 'objectively' known facts or phenomena and suggest that a more fruitful way is to focus on discourses. These they take to be devices through which people construct the world in which they live and argue for their practical and/or moral positions.

Within this definition two aspects are important. The first is the identification of interpretive repertoires – discourses; the second, the recognition of their social function.

Our congnitive abilities are not inherent but are based in action – meaning comes from the moment.

Within the framework of our research design, we have found of particular importance the idea that speech and thought have a particular dilemmatic and argumentative character. Seen in this way we can show how discourses are often built around contradictory themes which provide the possibility of argument and discussion (Billig 1988 and 1991). Thus any speech or utterance can be understood as argumentative on two levels, – the first when it is formulated as an explicit argument against counter-position and the second at an implicit level, where it can even contradict itself because the same discourse can be used and interpreted within different contexts.

In a similar vein, Shotter (1993) argues that what individuals have in common with other members of a group is not so much a set of shared beliefs as traditionally assumed, but rather a set of shared 'ethnomethods' – ways of making sense. These 'methods' are not single-theme and one can adopt different argumentative positions when using them.

In the context of the ideas presented above it is possible to claim that the conceptualization of management and managing cannot readily be seen as the application of theory but rather as a socially dilemmatic, a contingent and contradictory process that is informed by and realized through the application of a number of different discourses.

The general objectives of this study then can be stated as the identification of those discourses which inform the ways in which management and management development is conceptualized in the Czech Republic and Britain. Through such a process we will be able to identify and understand the cultural dilemmas 'inherent' in the ways managers interpret and practice their profession. These insights can help to develop more appropriate educational and teaching programmes.

To do this, three techniques of data collection were used. Written accounts by managers, repertory grid technique and Hofstede's value survey module, a quantitative survey type questionnaire.

Written accounts from questionnaires

First, we employed a qualitative questionnaire. This method involved asking British and Czech managers to answer a series of fairly open questions. These questions were focused on the managers' own perceptions of their career, a description of their everyday professional activities and a request for them to describe a critical incident, relating to a particular managerial problem. The objective was to give managers the opportunity to articulate their own perceptions of the work they do and its relationship to their life and career. Discourse analysis was focused on identifying the themes and rhetorical patterns that emerged from the utterances of the managers.

Repertory grid

Second, repertory grid technique was used in conjunction with in-depth interviews in order to gain rather different insights. Although this technique was originally designed as a device to understand an individuals' mental constructs, taking a social constructionist perspective a discourse analysis approach applied here also allows us to claim that the constructs will help us understand how managers conceptualize their world by giving us concrete dimensions for the discourses through which managers argue for their practical and moral positions.

The use of repertory grids to enrich the accounts managers give of their work represents an interesting methodology. Rather than use grids in their pure form, they were used in conjunction with discourse analysis in a less conventional way. Normally an in-depth interview is used as a vehicle to elicit constructs for a grid which is then analysed and is the focus of the results. In this study the emphasis was the reverse, in so far that it was the completing of the grid that was the vehicle for revealing and enriching the discourse and it was from this narrative we drew our analysis – very much in the same way as we had done in the written accounts.

So the social constructionist view taken enabled us to see the contextual and active nature of the constructs elicited during the interviews and shifted the attention to the analysis of the discourse in the accounts and arguments used by respondents.

Of no less importance was that this approach also enabled the themes and patterns that emerged to be compared with others as one would naturally do with a grounded theory approach.

The five elements we used were:-

- myself as I am;
- myself as I would like to be;
- characteristics of a successful manager;
- characteristics of a less successful manager;
- characteristics of someone who was not a manager.

Hofstede's VSM

The third research technique was the use of Hofstede's international VSM'94 questionnaire. This research instrument offers a quantitative methodology which some may argue is rather out of keeping with our other methods and approaches to research. However, we believe that careful discourse analysis of the possible cultural meanings of the responses on individual questions can bring valuable insights to research within a cross-cultural context. These were as follows:

1 The identification of the similarities and differences between the ways Czech and British management conceptualize their identity.
2 The ways in which qualitative and quantitative data can be linked and the compatibility of the two different methodological approaches within one research design. This particular use of the VSM was discussed and agreed with Geert Hofstede.

The sample

All our data information was drawn from Czech and British managers. All were managers in their countries completing their MBA part-time. Although the managers interviewed could not be strictly matched in a traditional sense by age, experience, profession and so on, they were comparable in so far as they were all being taught a very similar MBA curriculum and as a consequence all had a similar formal knowledge of management theory. They were also actual managers holding down responsible senior positions in their organizations and in many ways the organizations in which they worked and the stage of their career that they were at were very similar.

MAIN FINDINGS – DISCOURSES OF HOW MANAGERS CONCEPTUALIZE THEIR JOBS AND IDENTITY AS A MANAGER

Qualitative questionnaires

Qualitative unstructured questionnaires were distrubuted between March and November 1994. We collected 49 Czech and 59 English written accounts covering a number of aspects of managerial work. The information gained provided us with a variety of understandings of management.

Discourses about the description of careers

In explaining the nature of their managerial careers, managers from both groups used three different kinds of discourses. First, we identified a discourse 'ethnotheory' which explained their career development as one of natural evolution, i.e. **'My move into management has come as a result of my gradually attaining seniority etc.'**

This kind of discourse has as its foundation an assumption of some kind of 'natural' process underlying career progress and growth. As such its users are able, for example, to present themselves to an organization as loyal employees. In this context it is not surprising that Czech managers used this sort of discourse more often than their British colleagues. During the communist past it was culturally sensible and moral to talk of individual careers in terms of rewards coming logically from such things as merit or as a result of increases in experience rather than suggesting it was a self-centred pursuit.

A second discourse used to explain career was one we labelled as chance or default theory, i.e. **'Fortunately there was a reorganization; I became a manager totally by chance'**.

This discourse appeared equally frequently in both samples. The presentation of a career through this discourse enables managers to show themselves as 'the children of fortune'. This explanation works as a warranting voice for a person's higher managerial authority and increased material status – after all, nobody can be blamed for having good luck.

The third discourse detected was related to individual will and personal choice -**'I decided not to continue to work on the shop floor . . . I sought supervisory experience'**.

This discourse enabled managers to be perceived as stong, assertive and independent individuals – an important part of the aura of being a manager. Interestingly, we found discourses of this kind appearing frequently in both groups.

Although these discourses indicate the different moral positions of their users they were not used mutually exclusively in the accounts we analysed. Those that occurred most commonly were the discourses of 'chance' and 'personal decision'.

It should be said that references to the 'natural process' discourse did not necessarily exclude a manager's wish to be perceived as a decisive and ambitious individual. This became clear when our respondents described their future plans and strategies. In both groups the most frequent strategy was the explicit wish to advance to a senior post – an issue to be discussed later when we deal with management dilemmas and contradictions.

Discourses related to the effects of management work on home and family life constructs

Here Czech and British managers adopted very different perspectives in their descriptions of the consequences of their work and role, highlighting important contextual and cultural differences.

A dominant theme of the Czech accounts was their appreciation of a new found status – material and social. Within this context, Czech managers tended to use a discourse of individual fulfilment and self-actualization, of contacts and interactions with important and interesting people, of high self-confidence or high living standards and explain these as compensations for their increasing absence from home.

Similarly, when Czech managers wrote about what they liked and disliked about their jobs, the most commonly mentioned discourse was their appreciation of the variety of work they had and the relative independence and freedom their job and role provided. On the other hand they were critical about some of the social aspects of their work and role – they frequently used discourses that blamed poor employee attitudes to work and were critical of 'incompetent' top-management and the failure of many to embrace the enterprise culture.

British managers, on the other hand, conceptualized their accounts of their experience of managerial life around a dominant theme of criticism of the negative effects that being a manager had on their lives – see also Chapter 12 in this book. They talked of working for long hours, of the stress felt at work, of having no social life and few friends except for contacts through work. In addition, these discourses were accompanied by accounts of work disrupting family life and leading to marital breakdown.

Criticism also dominated the British descriptions of what aspect of managerial work they preferred. The most common complaints were about being overloaded with administration and conflicts with insensitive senior managers. On the other hand a relatively strong voice was one of enjoyment emanating from staff interaction and the variety of their work.

The comparison we draw does not mean that Czech managers were not critical about certain aspects and consequences of their jobs and that British managers were totally critical, rather it points to the cultural preferences of certain discourses in relation to management work and the presentation of their role and identity.

Summary

With respect to the findings presented above, we came to the conclusion that Czech managers tended to see themselves as taking on the role of missionaries who have to change people (usually their subordinates) and their attitudes in order to overcome old structures (more often than not in spite of rather than with the help of top management) in order to introduce 'new' Western styles of life and practice. British managers, on the other hand, tend to conceptualize themselves as critical practitioners who are aware of the consequences of being a manager in today's society – having to work long hours, continually facing conflicts with family life. Unlike in the Czech Republic, management is not a new phenomenon in Britain and the problems there are not one of establishing the legitimacy of the role, but adapting the role to ever changing circumstances. In Britain, a recurrent discourse was one of 'new' managerialism particularly within the public sector - one that stressed the need to introduce changes.

Discourses that account for moral positions in problem or conflict situations

By analysisng the discourses that related specifically to descriptions of problem situations at work, we came to the conclusion that although our respondents labelled these situations with reference to technical terms such as 'improvements in technology', they actually wrote about different kinds of social conflict – most common were conflicts with senior management and with staff. This occurred in both groups of managers, Czech and British.

With respect to the argumentative nature of the managers' rhetorics and thinking, we considered it 'natural' that within their descriptions of conflict situations our managers attempted to slant them in such a way that they declared their own moral positions. Again, this analysis was made by attempting to understand the different discourses. Although managers from both samples wrote about generally similar kinds of conflict situations they used different discourses which betrayed their own practical moral positions.

Czech managers, for example, conceptualized senior managers in terms of both their practical and theoretical incompetency and out-of-date frames of reference and styles of thinking, their conservatism and their inflexibility. Here we could detect the influence of the official Czech political discourse the struggle against 'old structures'.

British managers, on the other hand, when criticizing senior management used discourses related to poor managerial skills, of their isolation from practice and of overly bureaucratic practice. These are also political in their nature but derive directly from managerial practice and are not 'borrowed' from some abstract concepts.

Czech managers conceptualized their staff through discourses that characterized employees as passive and resistant to changing their attitudes to work, habits and routines. This is seen as the legacy of communism and as such works as a warranting voice for actions which might otherwise be perceived as anti-social and insensitive.

British managers, in their descriptions of conflicts with staff, used discourses related to the need to discipline disobedient subordinates and of re-educating employees through new knowledge and skills. This is also a warranting voice for the power and status of managers but, as in the case of their criticism of senior management, these voices are directly derived from existing management theory and practice.

Apart from these general political rhetorics which show our managers' moral positions, our managers also explained their reactions to these problems. For example, accouting for a lack of motivation through a discourse of their lack of power when faced with an inflexible and strange organization; accounting for their assertiveness through a discourse of decisions being based on a knowledge of employees' negative views; accounting for the source of conflicts through a discourse of the poor reading of a situation by the other party; accounting for a right to exclude another party from discussion through a discourse of them not having all the facts and being less able to understand the complexity of a problem.

All these rhetorics were extremely varied and, as a consequence, difficult to place into themes within or between our samples. The most important finding however concerns the fact that it was possible to trace the moral dimension in our managers and this we feel is important.

Developing this further, unlike the traditional view of the rational manager, our analysis identifies managers as being inherently both objective and biased, individualistic and collectivistic, dependent and independent. What they appear to need to do is to present themselves and their actions though the discourses they use as intelligible and logical in any given situation. Within the Czech cultural context it is possible to build a general strategy for this upon the predominant uses of the metapolitical discourse of the old communist regime which prevented managers acting on their own initiative. In the British cultural context, what strategies there were are built around existing management and policy issues of organizational power relationships and the need for continual development and change.

Findings from the repertory-grids

In order to gain rather different and deeper insights into our managers' understandings, 20 rep-grid interviews were conducted with Czech and

20 with British managers between March 1994 and April 1995. The following text presents some of the main findings from this stage part of our research.

Discourses which show how managers distinguish between managers and non-managers

One of the most interesting findings of our analysis of the discourses from the repertory grid interviews relates to ways in which Czech and British managers see themselves as different from those not occupying managerial positions.

Czech managers, when asked, offered definitions of management in the following ways: Discourses describing the variety of skills and competencies managers are required to have, for example, '*a manager is an amalgam of lots of things – he should understand the way problems relate, he should be able to offer vision, he should have sense for inter-personal relationships.*' Discourses describing their responsibility for people, for example, '*a manager is a man with responsibility for his firm and the people in it*'. Discourses describing the pre-ordination of managers to manage, for example, '*you must be born as a manager and all your development, at school for example, directs you towards a managerial post*', and discourses describing management as a preserve of the male sex, for example, '*in terms of his private life, I would say that he has got a better chance to get a first rate female.*'

These discourses imply that Czech managers see themselves as multi-skilled individuals who are pre-ordained to lead and as strong male individuals. These views correspond well with discourses relating to those in non-management functions.

The most common view among Czech managers was the idea of a non-manager as a technician, for example, '*a non-manager can be a very capable person – for example technicians become absorbed by problems, can solve them but can't lead a team.*' Another discourse relating to those who aren't managers was built upon the rhetorics of passive staff with an inherent resistance to change, for example, '*a non-manager is self-satisfied and not interested in further development. He finishes his working day and then he is free whereas my working day includes even the night – I still think when I sleep.*'

This idea of non-managers as passive or lazy links to findings reported earlier where Czech managers complained about staff in general. There they were used as devices to legitimize a manager's power and status. In a similar way, the discourse of a non-manager as a technician enables managers to argue for their position of top in the pecking order whereas by contrast a technician is somebody who can't interact and communicate because he only has a narrow view of the world and limited professional areas of interest. Technicians are portrayed as 'absent minded' and impractical people and as a consequence must be led.

In comparison to the Czech managers' preference for these individualistic discourses, the British respondents used discourses of an interactive and social nature. For example, *'one fundamental aspect of management is the importance of relationships – relationships not only with non-managers, but also with clients and this is important when understanding the culture and potitics of an organization.'* Another different aspect with British managers was the use of the discourse of change and development, for example, *'successful managers need to be aware of change. They must allow freedom so development can continue to take place.'*

Even though there were these differences it was still possible to detect notions of individualism in the views of the British managers. Communication skills, staff development and so on are seen as tools with which to manipulate within the context of complex social reality and can be seen in the way in which our British respondents described non-managers.

Similarly as in Czech interviews, non-managers were conceptualized as people with less initiative, for example, *'non-managers are happy not to take responsibility.'*

They also used discourses relating to socially constructed notions of divisions of labour, of job roles, for example, *'they are responsible for doing their job and I am responsible for people. If you take Maslow, for example, a non-manager is very often an individual who has achieved his basic needs and has made a conscious decision not to move into management'*. Although non-managers are seen as having less initiative and responsibility, British managers saw them as having developmental potential. Discourses of problems in distinguishing conceptually between managers and people who were not managers were also used within this group, for example, *'I wouldn't say there is anybody who doesn't manage in some way. Everybody in some respect is a manager, everybody interacts with people.'*

Also, these discourses offer managers warrants for their claim for leadership. However, although British concepts of the management/non-management relationship are still individualistic, this individualism is not as abstract as in the Czech case as it recognizes the importance of social and interactive aspects of management. The Czech managers however see themselves as superior beings who give sense and direction to all social and managerial life; British managers understand themselves as individuals who are able to manage others in a way that fulfils their ambitions.

Findings from the VSM 94 and their link to qualitative data

Our VSM 94 data was collected between November 1994 and May 1995. The following samples were obtained:

From the Czech Republic – 97 (8 females, 89 males) the average age being 37. Their job positions were 55 middle managers, 34 senior managers, 8 individual professionals.

From Great Britain – 108 (31 females, 77 males), the average age being 37. Their job positions were 51 middle managers, 43 senior managers, 14 individual professionals.

What we have included below are some of the most interesting and important findings from this analysis and how these quantitative findings can be related to our previous research conducted using qualitative methods.

Formal VSM 94 Index Values

The first stage of the VSM 94 analysis was to calculate the VSM values using Hofstede's recommended formulas – see Chapter 9 in this book. Doing this we obtained the following results:

Table 13.1: The VSM values

Index	CR	GB
PDI	47	15
IDV	50	101
MAS	90	5
UAI	49	4
LOT	27	47

(PDI = power distance index; IDV = individuality index, MAS – masculinity index, UAI = uncertainty avoidance index and LOT = long-term orientation index).

According to these results, the cultures of the Czech Republic and Great Britain are quite different on each of the VSM 94 dimensions. From this it follows that managers' approach to management will also be different. If we follow Hofstede's index definitions (see Hofstede 1991) we can deduce that within Czech society power inequalities are perceived as being more acceptable than in Britain. British managers are more individualistic than Czech; Czechs have a strong masculine orientation making them more prone to seek material rewards and are more assertive. From a time perspective, Czech managers appear to be more concerned with structure and order and wish to avoid ambiguity. They are also less concerned with the future and value those things less that might offer rewards in the future. In order to go beyond this rather superficial analysis it is necessary to examine in more detail the cultural meaning of our VSM 94 data.

Those VSM 94 questions answered in the greatest variety of ways

Within our general qualitative framework we managed to identify those questions which were answered in the greatest variety of ways. These, we feel, point to those areas of greatest contradiction in the way managers conceptualize their practice or see their role. It is these areas we feel might be the most open to negotiation and development.

To identify which questions these were, we used as criteria those questions that had a standard deviation bigger than 1 and a mean score of between 2.5 and 3, 5, (the VSM 94 uses a 5 point scale).

In the Czech sample, five questions were identified as answered in a dilemmatic way. They concerned the trust people placed in others, the need to have precise answers to subordinates questions, whether organizational rules can be broken, the importance placed on variety in the job and the degree of competition among employees. Two of these we felt deserved closer attention.

First, the importance given to the question of variety in the job seems to be in direct contradiction to our qualitative findings. According to these, Czech managers appreciated greater variety at work. Two issues must be noted here. First, within the general ideological and theoretical orientation of the Czechs to an appropriate management model, for many of our respondents job variety was seen as either unimportant or irrelevant. Second, the Czechs described their actual jobs within the discourse of material reward and appreciation of social status within which the opportunity of works variety was linked to individual ambition and satisfaction at work.

Second, the ambiguity shown around competition between employees was common in both samples. In the Czech case, this could be explained as a consequence of the confusion between two ideological concepts. The communists' view of loyalty to the party line and the competition associated with the capitalist market economy. In the case of the British, other issues must be taken into account; in particular, the ambiguous nature of the term competition. It can imply achievement, motivation and the aggressive struggle between employees. This absence of a full definition of the notion of competition in traditional management literature is, we feel, part of the problem.

As well as ambiguity with regard to competition, British managers were also ambiguous about matrix structures where individuals may have one or more bosses and where individuals take personal responsibility for failure. This can be detected in the findings from our qualitative data. The British appear to have a practical concern for certainty, but feel unable to argue against the implementation of new, less formal, structures.

VSM 94 distinctive cultural stereotypes

Here, we focused on the identification of those questions which were answered in the most distinctive and consistent manner. From a socio-logical point of view, it was possible to relate the findings to the influence of one or more cultural stereotypes which were of a fairly constant nature.

These most distinctive areas of management were identified by the means of two criteria: one was where the value of a particular mean score was equal to or higher than 1,281 (the 90 percentile), the other was through the exclusion of cases which had already been identified as contradictory.

In the Czech sample, five questions were identified as having been responded to in a relatively distinctive way. These were, the importance ascribed to personal stability; the low respect for tradition; the high frequency with which subordinates were afraid to disagree with super-iors; the view that individuals are responsible for their personal failures; and the high importance ascribed to working and co-operating with others.

The first four cases could be easily linked to our qualitative data findings, for example, the discourse of the managers' appreciation of the material status and well-being management brought; the denial of their communist past; complaints about other staff; and their general sense of individualism. The Czechs' strong agreement of the importance of working with others who co-operate well can be seen as a contra-diction.

However, if we remember the Czech managers' manipulative view of the staff, for example through the rhetorics of the passivity of non-man-agers, their laziness and their need to be managed, as well as the stress placed on material possessions, we can assume that co-operation is seen in an instrumental way to achieve success rather than as a virtue *per se*.

Among British responses there were four areas of management that were identified as distinctive. These were: the importance ascribed to good relationships with superiors; the high importance placed on variety at work; the low respect for tradition and a certain amount of tolerance with organization rule breaking.

Two facts are interesting here. First, there are links between these results and the British orientation to practical and social aspects of management, for example, those discourses that are related to the importance of inter-actions; complaints about too much administrative work; and those that focus on change and development.

Second, unlike their Czech counterparts, they appear to wish to solve the frequent conflicts with superiors through improved relationships. This does not mean that the Czechs are unconcerned about conflict, rather that their criticism of superiors stems from an ideological and political position, i.e. one of anti-communism to destroy and remove 'old structures', rather than not to improve relationships.

If we now compare Czech and British management cultures we can perhaps say that the views of Czech management are stongly influenced by the stereotypes of individualism, likening managers to heroes, that they have a manipulative view of their current reality which is egocentric, short-term and unsubtle. British managers also appear to be influenced by stereotypes and these appear to relate to the need to influence social change and for individuals to have the right to development themselves. Why it is that we see these British concepts as stereotypes will be explained later.

VSM 94 significant differences in Czech and British responses.

The last stage of our VSM 94 data analysis focused on the identification of questions in which there were significant differences between Czech and British responses. These differences have been explained using our findings from our qualitative data, the implications of this explained for both the indexes and the understanding of cultural differences.

According to a t-test (where tv3.291 – 0.01 level of significancy) there exist some nine areas where there is a significant difference between our samples. These areas are as follows:

Power Distance Index CR = 47 GB = 15
Three of four items included in the calculation of this index were identified as significantly different. British managers saw good relationships with their direct superior as more important than did the Czechs (this has already been discussed); similarly, to be consulted about decisions made by superiors was seen by British managers to be of more importance than by the Czechs; and Czech managers tended to see less problems with having two bosses than the British.

Managers in both groups offered similar views of the vulnerability of subordinates.

This comparison can be explained by the hierarchical nature of Czech organizations where there is relatively poor communication between the different levels of management. There is also a high concern for power and this corresponds with our qualitative data. Behind the British responses is a strong stress on the quality of the interaction with colleagues and on communication and understanding within the organization.

Individualism CR = 50 GB = 101
Two of the items included in this index offered significant differences. The first was that Czech managers see time spent with their family and for their personal life as less important than British managers. Second, as has

already been discussed, Czech managers are contradictory about the importance variety in the job should have – this is in stark contrast to the British.

These results also support our qualitative data findings, that Czech managers were more concerned with the introduction of management practice than with the implications this might have for individuals at work and home.

Similarities in our sample existed to the extent that both groups placed importance on good working conditions and on security in employment. These views are related to Hofstede's original interpretation of collectivism as opposed to individualism. This issue will be discussed later.

Masculinity CR = 90 GB = 5

It is on this index that we have found the highest differences between our samples. However, it is only one question that represents this significant cultural difference. That is, the Czechs' strong association with an individual's responsibility for personal failure, the British were more ambiguous about this.

There were, however, a number of similarities identified. One was the importance of working with co-operative individuals; the importance placed on the opportunity for advancement in the job; and the importance of being able to trust others. However, these results should be linked to our previous findings relating to the Czechs' manipulative instrumental view of co-operation, the Czechs' ambiguity about trusting people and their egocentric view of careers. On the other hand, the British saw the importance of social change and development.

Uncertainty CR = 49 GB = 4

There were two questions included in this index that we identified as significantly different. The first was that British managers stongly disagreed with the statement that organization rules should not be broken, in contrast to the Czechs who gave more ambiguous answers, similarly the Czech managers were ambiguous about the need to have precise answers to subordinates' questions whereas British managers thought this was not necessary.

The British managers' more pragmatic orientation in relation to social change and development in contrast to the rather abstract theoretical concerns of the Czechs (in their use of appropriate management models) should be taken into account as an explanation here. Similarities did appear to exist in their views of stress at work - managers from both groups felt only occasionally stressed at work.

Another interesting finding in this section relates to the fact that in the Czech cases the UAI index was created from three questions, all answered ambiguously which has the effect of making them less reliable than the other indexes.

Long-term Orientation CR = 27 GB = 47

In this index there was only one question in four included in the calculation of this index which we identified as a question which produced differences in our samples. According to the Czech responses, Czech managers are much more concerned with personal stability (already discussed as being a distinctive aspect of Czech maanagement) than their British colleagues.

Low importance appeared to be attached by both Czech and British managers to views relating to thrift, persistence and their respect for tradition. The concept of thrift is all that has attracted attention here.

The moderate importance ascribed to thrift in both countries implies, according to Hofstede, a rather short-term orientation. In the case of the Czechs it could be said that the concept of thrift might be an opposite to the current orientation which is for immediate profits or 'get rich quick' culture. In the British culture, with their orientation on change, we should perhaps think about the semantical distinction between thrift (saving money) and investment for future developments which might necessitate spending money for the long-term.

CONCLUSIONS

This research enables us to formulate several practical and theoretical conclusions.

First, as we have illustrated, management development is not just a matter of the correct application of appropriate theories or models. Rather, it is a complex process within which management practice is socially constructed through different discourses. The implications are that to follow simple solutions in management development policy would be at best inappropriate and at worst, potentially harmful. It is necessary to understand management in context of the history and the culture.

We illustrate this by showing that although our MBA respondents were taught on similar curricula they produced quite different cultural understandings of management. Views of universal theories of management are therefore a forlorn hope. Learning, as is confirmed in learning theory research, is a social activity within which individuals need, when learning, new concepts to understand the views and ideas of others in the context of their cultures and to resolve the dilemmas this brings through debate, discussion and negotiation.

Successful and efficient management development policy must be based on the understanding of the managerial dilemmas as they emerge from management theory and practice. Instead of preparing managers for certainty by teaching techniques of problem solving and decision making, they should perhaps be encouraged to recognize the complexity in which they exist and teach them to understand their practice through their ability to master and use a variety of different discourses.

Further, we have demonstrated that we need to accept both the level of the current development of managers in a particular culture as well as the dimensions on which management is viewed as a distinctive area of practice in that culture. If this is not done, management development policy will not be recognized as appropriate or can even be seen as irrelevant.

On a methodological level, we have illustrated how a combination of qualitative and quantitative data analysed from the perspective of a discourse analysis framework offers an interesting insight into management.

Finally, we believe that we have illustrated the importance of our qualitative data to illuminate the VMS 94 results. Doing this has led us to question some of the original Hofstede definitions and propose alternatives. The introduction of VSM 94 offered a new but also unifying perspective to our thoughts on management culture in the Czech Republic and Britain and showed the merit of linking qualitative and quantitative data in a single scheme – an approach we can commend to other researchers.

REFERENCES

Billig, M. (1988) *Ideological Dilemmas*, Sage, London
Billig, M. (1991) *Ideology and Opinions*, Sage, London.
Gergen, K.J. (1992) Organisation Theory in the Post-modern Era, in *Rethinking Organisations* (eds M. Reed and M. Hughes) Sage, London, pp. 20–42.
Hofstede, G. (1991) *Cultures and Organisations: Software of the Mind*, McGraw-Hill, London.
Hofstede, G. (1994) Management scientists are human. *Management Science*, **40**, pp. 4-13.
Laurent, A. (1983) The cultural diversity of Western conceptions of management. *International Studies of Management and Organisation*, **13**, pp. 75–96.
Mead, R. (1994) *International Management*, Blackwell, Oxford.
Parker, I. (1992) *Discourse Dynamics*, Routledge, London.
Powell, G.N. and Butterfield, D.A. (1979) 'The good manager, masculine or androgynous'. *The Academy of Management Journal*, **22**, pp. 395–423.
Randlesome R. *et al.* (1993) *Business Cultures in Europe*, Butterworth-Heinemann, London pp. 203–263.

Shotter, J. (1993) *Conversational Realities.* Sage, London.
Shotter, J. (1993) Bakhtin and Vygotski, internationalisation as a boundary phenomenon. *New Ideas in Psychology,* **11**, pp. 61–75.
Stewart, R. (1988) *Managers and their Jobs, A Study of the Similarities and Differences in the Way Managers Spend their Time,* Macmillan, Basingstoke.
Wetherell, M. and Potter, J. (1988) Discourse Analysis and the Identification of Interpretive Repertoires, in *Analysing Everyday Explanations* (ed C. Antaki) Sage, London, pp. 20–34.

FURTHER READING

Bell, C.R. (1988) Theory – appropriate analysis of repertory grid data. *International Journal of Personal Construct Psychology,* **1**, pp. 101–18.
Blackler, F. (1993) Knowledge and the theory of organisations. *Journal of Management Studies.* **30**, pp. 863–84.
Burgoyne, J.G. (1994) Managing by learning. *Management Learning,* **25**, pp. 35–55.
Burkitt, I. (1991) *Social Selves,* Sage, London.
Burman, E. and Parker, I. (1993) *Discourse Analytic Research,* Routledge, London.
Easterby-Smith, M., Thorpe, R. and Lowe, A. (1991) *Management Research,* Sage, London.
Finkielkraut, A. (1993) *Destrukce mysleni,* Atlantis, Praha.
Fromm, M. (1993) What students really learn: students personal construction of learning items. *International Journal of Personal Construct Psychology,* **6**, pp. 195–208.
Goodrich, R.A. (1993) Deconstructing constructs: pitfalls in personal construct theory. *Educational Philosophy and Theory,* **23**, pp. 71–82.
Grey, C. and Mitev, N. (1995) Management education: a polemic. *Management Learning,* **26**, pp. 73–90.
Hassard, J. (1994) Post-modern organisational analysis: toward a conceptual framework. *Journal of Management Studies,* **31**, pp. 303–24.
Holman, D. and Pavlica, K. (1994) *Rethinking Experiential Learning in Management Education: The Contribution of Activity Theory.* Paper in British Academy of Management 1994 Conference Proceeding, Lancaster University; The Management School, pp. 185.
Kubes, M. and Benkovic, P. (1994) Realities, Paradoxes and Perspectives of HRM in Eastern Europe. The Case of Czechoslovakia, in *Human Resource Management in Europe* (ed P. Kirkbride) Routledge, London, pp. 100–120.
Laurent, A. (1981) Matrix organisations and Latin cultures. *Studies of Management and Organisation.* **10**, pp. 101–114.
Leontiev, A.N. (1978) *Activity, Consciousness and Personality,* Prentice Hall, Englewood Cliffs, N.J. Prentice Hall.

Michael, M. (1994) Discourse and uncertainty. Post–modern variations. *Theory & Psychology.* **4**, pp. 383–404.

Roper, M. (1994) *Masculinity and the British Organisation Man Since 1945*, Oxford University Press, Oxford.

Shanon, B. (1993) *The Representational and Presentational. An Essay on Cognition and the Study of the Mind*, Harvester Wheatsheaf, London.

Taylor, D. (1990) Making the most of your matrices. *International Journal of Personal Construct Psychology*, **3**, pp. 105–19.

Vygotski, L.S. (1991) The Genesis of Higher Mental Functions. The Concept of Activity in *Soviet Psychology* (ed J.V. Wertsch), Sharpe, Armonk, N.Y., pp. 144–85.

Wertsch, J.V. (1991) *Voices of the Mind*, Harvester Wheatsheaf, London.

Chapter 14

Managing in Asia: cross-cultural dimensions

Rosalie L. Tung

INTRODUCTION

The economic transformation that has taken place in East and South-east Asia in the past several decades has been remarkable. Four of the six richest 'emerging' countries tracked by the *Economist* come from this region: Singapore, Hong Kong, Taiwan and South Korea (*Economist*, May 20–26, 1995). These countries, along with Japan, have all been influenced by the teachings of Confucius and hence are commonly referred to as Confucian or neo-Confucian societies. Some attributes shared by Confucian societies are hard work, thrift, perseverance, hierarchical ordering of relationships and scholarship (Hofstede and Bond, 1988). While the teachings of Confucius are central to these societies, it is erroneous to ignore the influence of other philosophical approaches, such as Taoism, the legalist school, and the writings of military strategists. The influence of these latter schools of thought on management strategies and practices has been significant.

To avoid duplication with other contributions (see Chapters 15 and 16 in this book) which focus specifically on Japan, this piece seeks to examine the mind-set which underlies East Asian business principles and practices. Thus, while on the surface organizational structure and management systems in East Asia may resemble those in the west, as they develop both technologically and economically, fundamental differences continue to exist in how they behave in interpersonal relationships and in the manner in which they approach competition and co-operation and, indeed, in the formulation of business strategies. Fujisawa, co-founder of Honda Motor Corporation, once remarked that 'Japanese and American management are 95% the same and differ in all important respects'. This observation captures the underlying differences which separate the East Asian mind-set from that in the west (see also Chapter 17).

Specifically, this chapter will identify: (1) the themes which guide the East Asian approach to business; (2) the role of *guanxi* (connections) and its relationship to business performance; and (3) the concept of face and how it affects organizational functioning and behaviour. This does not imply that East Asians can be construed as one homogeneous group. Diversity across countries and within countries is recognized, and, where relevant, will be identified and discussed (see Tung 1996).

THEMES GUIDING THE EAST ASIAN APPROACH TO BUSINESS

Through an analysis of four classical works widely disseminated and read by business practitioners in East Asia, Tung (1994) identified twelve principles which guide the East Asian approach to business co-operation and competition, and to the formulation, reformulation, and implementation of business strategies. These four classical works are:

The Art of War (or *Bingfa*) purportedly written by a Chinese military strategist who lived about 2,500 years ago, Sun Tzu (spelled Sun Zi under the *pinyin* version currently used in China). This book is considered as a 'bible' or handbook for business people in East Asia. It has also been widely read in the west. Napoleon reportedly used the principles of *Bingfa* to conquer Europe.

The Book of Five Rings which was purportedly written by Miyamoto Musashi, a Japanese samurai in the late sixteenth and early seventeenth century. When it was published in English by Bantam Books in 1982, it bore the subtitle, *The Real Art of Japanese Management* and was quickly dubbed as Japan's response to Harvard's MBA.

The Three Kingdoms was written by Lo Kuan-chung, a fourteenth century Chinese novelist. In *Sanyo's Road to Success*, Kaoru Iue, former president of Sanyo Electric Corporation of Japan, noted that his company gives each executive a lined note-pad and a copy of *The Three Kingdoms* when the executive is promoted to senior management. The lined note-pad is designed to help the executives to practice legible writing to avoid making costly mistakes that stem from illegible handwriting. *The Three Kingdoms* is designed to help the executives understand which defensive and offensive strategies apply in various situations.

The Thirty-six Stratagems is based on the principles in *The Book of Changes* (or *I Ching*, which contains the basic tenets of Taoism) and on the military strategies presented in twenty-four volumes of Chinese history and literary classics, including *The Three Kingdoms*.

Together, these four classical works reveal twelve themes or principles which underlie strategic management thought in East Asia. These are:

The importance of strategies

To Sun Tzu, the highest form of victory is attained through strategy (Hu 1996). He wrote: 'To subdue the enemy without fighting (i.e., to use strategy) is the supreme excellence'. From the East Asian perspective, there are preferred methods for any type of confrontation, business or otherwise. These methods, in descending order of preference, are:

- to devise a brilliant strategy to deal a swift and fatal blow to one's adversary;
- to resort to diplomacy (negotiations, mutual discussions, use of intermediaries) to resolve a confrontation;
- to engage in non-diplomatic means to resolve a confrontation, i.e. open warfare and, in a business context, expensive and protracted litigation;
- to attack a fortified city.

Because of the emphasis on strategy, East Asians tend to play mind games – they ferret out the hidden message in any type of communication (written, verbal or silent) and develop a strategy to counteract the perceived message (Chu 1988). 'Mind games' are considered as manifestations of intellect. This penchant to engage in mind games may have contributed to the stereotyping of East Asians as 'inscrutable Orientals', or as the conniving Dr Fu Manchu.

Transforming an adversary's strength into weakness

According to the Taoist principle of *yin* and *yang*, all events occur in cyclical patterns. Thus, strengths can be converted to weaknesses and vice-versa. *Bingfa* and several of the stratagems in *The Thirty-six Stratagems* called for exhausting the opponent with false alarms to drain the enemy before the start of the real battle. Similarly, one's weakness can be transformed into a strength. This principle is clearly illustrated by the post-war industrial development in Japan. From the destruction and ruins of World War II, the Japanese imported foreign know-how to enable it to leapfrog decades of technological development and, thus, establish a modern industrial base from which it could compete with the United States and the rest of the industrialized world. Furthermore, the Taoist belief that everything occurs in cyclical patterns warns against complacency about one's strengths/assets and helps avoid despair over one's limitations/liabilities. This has contributed to the East Asian tendency to emphasize frugality and be modest about one's achievements and good fortunes.

Deception as a means to a strategic advantage

Westerners consider deception as immoral because of the influence of Judaism-Christianity. In East Asia, where there is no indigenous religion akin to Judaism and Christianity, deception is considered as a neutral concept which should be engaged in if it led to a greater good. From the East Asian perspective, 'the greater good' embraces the well-being of the nation-state, the clan (the geographic region from which a person's ancestors came), the extended family, the nuclear family, the corporation (employer) and the self. Their order of importance, however, varies among East Asian countries. In Japan, for example, the nation-state is considered paramount. In China, Hong Kong and Taiwan (Greater China, in short), the family is usually considered more important. The East Asian view of deception points to an important difference in norms and standards used across countries. What is moral or immoral in one country may not be considered as such in another. This points to the need to avoid using one's own mind-set when trying to predict how members of another culture will act and when assessing the morality of such actions.

Understanding contradictions

Under the *yin/yang* principle, contradictions and opposites are inherent in all matters. Moreover, there is a unity of opposites. As Lao Tzu, generally considered as the spiritual leader of Taoism, wrote: 'There is one universal principle and the one becomes the many'. Since all matters have positive and negative attributes associated with them, the key to success is to accentuate the positive and minimize the negative. Consider, for instance, the difference between an oak tree and a blade of grass. The oak tree is strong and mighty. No one can trample on it when it stands. A blade of grass, on the other hand, is small and fragile. It can be stomped on and crushed. But this picture changes during a storm. The tree may collapse under the wind's force, while the blade of grass yields to the gusts and stands firm.

Compromise

Compromise is often considered necessary to achieving a specific goal. To attain a bigger outcome, one must often sacrifice smaller gains or use a bait. Thus, gift-giving, lavish entertainment and bribery are common practices in East Asian societies. Compromise, however, requires an ongoing relationship (whether co-operative or competitive); otherwise, the parties have nothing to trade off. This accounts in part, at least, for the East Asian's emphasis on developing ongoing relationships.

Striving for total victory

While East Asian philosophy emphasizes compromise, it also stresses the need to strive for total victory. In other words, a temporary victory should not lull people to complacency; otherwise, they will lose sight of their ultimate objective. Besides avoiding complacency, this principle stresses the need for people to think about the long-term consequences of their actions. They must project their opponent's next move, to intercept that move.

Taking advantage of an adversary's misfortune

Since East Asians believe that fortunes and misfortunes occur in cyclical patterns, they try to make the most of current situations. Consequently, if an adversary is down, they seize that opportunity to eliminate the adversary. While this may appear unethical from the Westen perspective, it is important to bear in mind that East Asians are a pragmatic people. The Chinese emphasize pragmatism even more than their counterparts in Japan and Korea. This partly explains why religion and politics do not play significant roles in the daily lives of the average person from Greater China. This pragmatism on the part of the Chinese also leads to another major difference between the Chinese and the Japanese, namely the course of action to pursue where defeat is both certain and imminent. The Chinese option is to escape, while the Japanese would choose suicide. The Japanese are taught that facing death is courageous, while the Chinese subscribe to Sun Tzu's admonition that 'bravery without strategy is folly'. Some people attribute this difference between the Japanese and Chinese to the size of their respective countries and to the supply of natural resources in each. Japan's limited land mass and few natural resources led its people to believe that death is preferred, since there is no escape. The Chinese, on the other hand, who have an extensive land mass and vast natural resources, believe it is always possible to escape and regain strength (Chu 1988).

Flexibility

Since East Asian philosophy draws its inspiration from nature, it is used in many analogies. Sun Tzu, for instance, invoked nature when he preached the importance of flexibility to accommodate changing conditions and fortunes – 'just as water ceaselessly changes its flow, there are no constant methods of directing military operations'. This emphasis on flexibility accounts, in part, for the East Asian perspective of written legal contracts as organic documents that can be altered as circumstances change.

Gathering intelligence and information

Both Sun Tzu and Miyamoto Musashi strongly emphasized the importance of gathering information and intelligence about the opponent. Such information can be obtained through a variety of sources: spies, entering into alliances with local nationals and employing local nationals. Gathering intelligence also includes spreading erroneous information to contaminate and frustrate the opponent's strategies. In addition to obtaining technical information, knowledge also includes intelligence about key players. It takes a long time to accurately assess human nature, however. So East Asians devote significant effort to find out the true intentions of business counterparts. Such intentions can be unravelled only through time. This explains, in part, the slow pace of East Asian business.

Grasping the interdependent relationship of situations

The inherent duality and contradictions (*yin/yang*) in all matters may not always be obvious, particularly from a western perspective. Moreover, spiral and non-linear logic are common in East Asia. Consequently, to fully understand the interdependent relationship of occurrences, one has to take a holistic approach and adopt a long-term perspective in analysing events/situations.

Patience

There are several reasons why the East Asian pace is slower. One is the focus on the long-term implications of actions. A second reason is the importance attached to the development and nurturing of human relationships. A third reason is the belief that everything occurs cyclically. If East Asians lose their fortunes and the moment is inopportune, they will wait patiently until the situation reverses. The importance of patience differs across countries, however. Koreans, for instance, generally make quicker decisions than their Chinese and Japanese counterparts. This is possible in the Korean context because many of the businesses are still run by the owner/founder of the company and his family. This belief that events are cyclical in nature does not imply that East Asians subscribe to fatalism in the pessimistic sense of the word. The Buddhist concept of *karma*, translated into Chinese as *baoying*, implies that one's future state is influenced by the good or bad actions that one has performed in a previous existence. In other words, East Asians subscribe to a merit and demerit system which will be balanced in the longer term. Thus, it is desirable to do good and accumulate virtue so as to enhance the probability of a better future existence. This again reinforces the notion that one should not be complacent about one's good fortune nor abuse the privileges associated with it, but rather be modest about one's achievements.

Avoiding strong emotions

Confucius preached moderation. Similarly, Sun Tzu warned that a military commander should never fly into a rage. These admonishments are at the root of the East Asian aversion to harbour or display strong emotions, since they may ruin carefully conceived plans. There are differences across countries, however. In comparison with the Japanese and Chinese, the Koreans are emotional. Common occurrences in Korean business offices include chest-beating, desk-pounding and shouting matches (Tung 1991).

GUANXI

Guanxi has been identified as a key building block of Confucian societies (King, 1991). *Guanxi* (*kankei* in Japanese and *kwankye* in Korea) is often translated as 'relationship' or 'connection'. *Guanxi* is analogous to networking and nepotism in the west. Similar to networking, a relationship (*guanxi*) can be established between two hitherto independent (i.e. unconnected) individuals to permit a mutually beneficial flow of social transactions. In practice, however, *guanxi* often resembles nepotism where someone in authority makes decisions on the basis of family ties or connections rather than objective indices (Yeung and Tung 1995).

In a survey of 2,000 Chinese from Shanghai and its surrounding rural community, 92% of the respondents confirmed that *guanxi* played a significant role in their daily lives. Furthermore, the younger generation tended to place greater emphasis on *guanxi* (Chu and Ju 1993). In fact, utilitarian *guanxi* has become more widespread in the recent past. 'Utilitarian *guanxi*' refers to using connections to advance one's personal goals and interests (King 1991). Ralston, Gustafson, Terpstra and Holt (1995:11) compared the value system of Chinese managers prior to and after June 4, 1989 (Tiananmen incident). They found that in post June 4 society, there was a marked increase in the score on the Machiavellianism dimension. The latter is a 'measure of the degree to which a person places self-interest above the interest of the group . . . self-interest may be individual or extended family set against those beyond the intimacy of family relationships'.

Most business practitioners who have experience in doing business with East Asians will readily agree that in order to succeed in these countries 'who you know is more important than what you know'. In other words, having connections with the appropriate individuals and authorities is often more crucial than having the right product and/or price.

What accounts for the significance of *guanxi* in Confucian and neo-Confucian societies? The answer lies in Confucianism. Confucius preached that each individual occupies a place in a hierarchical ordering of social relationships, with its commensurate obligations and benefits. In this way, peace and harmony can be attained and maintained. The focus of such social relationships was primarily on the family (ruler-subject, father-son, older brother-younger brother, husband-wife, friend-friend).

Even the two relationships which appear to fall outside the family can be viewed within a familial context. The ruler constitutes a father figure for his subjects and close friends become part of the family circle. This strong emphasis on the family generates a marked distinction between members of the in-group and out-group. Lin Yutang (1935:180), a noted Chinese sociologist, once wrote: 'The family, with its friends, became a walled castle, with the greatest communistic co-operation and mutual help within, but coldly indifferent toward, and fortified against, the world without. In the end, as it worked out, the family became a walled castle ouside which everything is legitimate loot'. Thus, while interaction within the 'walled castle' is characterized by trust and communal sharing, the attitude toward those outside the 'walled castle' is one of suspicion and cold indifference. Chu and Ju (1993) found that 84.5% of the 2,000 respondents would not trust outsiders until they had the opportunity to know them better. Furthermore, 71.7% of the respondents indicated their preference for using *guanxi* connections, over normal bureaucratic channels, to solve day-to-day problems and to advance personal interests. This in-versus out-group distinction explains why it is so difficult for outsiders to accomplish anything in Confucian societies. To succeed, an insider has to establish *guanxi* with the appropriate individuals.

In an exploratory study (Yeung and Tung 1995) of the relationship between *guanxi* and financial performance among 19 Hong Kong, American, Canadian, German and Swiss firms with business operations in China, *guanxi* was the only item among eleven factors which was consistently identified as a key success factor (mean = 0.83) to long-term business success in China. In that study, financial performance was defined as the rate of growth of annual net income or pretax profits between 1991–1994.The other ten factors which can affect success were: choosing the right business location; choosing the right entry strategy; competitive prices; complementarity of goals; familiarity with Chinese negotiation style; flexibility in business operations; long-term commitment to the China market; management control; product differentiation/quality; understanding of China's policy. The respondents attributed the significance of *guanxi* to the ambiguity of Chinese legislation. Despite the Chinese government's efforts to enact legislation pertaining to business activities, the legal infrastructure remains underdeveloped. Where laws are vague, they are subject to the interpretation of those in authority positions (see Warner 1995). Furthermore, under Confucianism, governance by ethics (*li zhi*) has been preferred over governance by law (*fa zhi*). Thus, institutional law is downplayed. This accounts for the general distate for law and litigation in Confucian societies, including Japan and Korea, where the legal infrastructure is more highly developed. In Confucian societies, the locus of influence is thus shifted to those in positions of authority (*ren zhi*). This accounts for the significance of *guanxi* 'since an individual, rather than institutional authority, defines what is acceptable and permissible in a given context at a particular time' (Yeung and Tung 1995:6).

While *guanxi* is crucial to successful market entry in to China, it is a necessary but insufficient condition to ensure the continued success of the operation in China. Yeung and Tung (1995:12) found that 'the significance of *guanxi* alone in ensuring continued success decreased over the life of the venture. In other words, once the operation is established, to sustain continued success, other conditions have to be met. Of these conditions, technical competence is most important. Technical competence refers to the supply of appropriate products of high quality, the adoption of suitable business strategies, and the possession of in-depth knowledge of the market'. This finding parallels Tung's (1989) research on the relation between 'knowledge of cultural differences' and success in US-Chinese business negotiations. She found that 'knowledge of cultural differences' was a necessary but insufficient condition for success. In other words, while knowledge of cultural differences will not always guarantee business success, in its absence (i.e. ignorance of Chinese culture, including the role of *guanxi*), the negotiations or business dealings are almost doomed to failure.

Yeung and Tung (1995) also found that, in general, small and medium-sized companies placed heavier emphasis on *guanxi* than larger companies. Since the latter can contribute to the economic development of a city or region, Chinese government officials are eager to court their investment. Hence, the Chinese partner may actually take the initiative in establishing the relationship.

The Chinese emphasis on family merits further attention . In Japan and Korea, the dominant organizational forms are the *keiretsu* and *chaebol*, respectively. Keiretsus consist of horizontally-linked large firms in a diverse range of industries. Chaebols, on the other hand, are diverse businesses and firms which are closely controlled by a central holding company. In Hong Kong, Taiwan and Singapore, the leading organizational form is family-run business. The latter are usually small-to medium-sized companies. Redding (1990) has characterized this as Chinese capitalism and Tu (1991) has dubbed it as '*guanxi* capitalism'. Because of the in- versus out-group distinction, it is usually difficult for Chinese enterprises to attract outside managerial talent. Some have asserted that, in time, Chinese organizational forms should evolve to parallel those of their western counterparts. Redding (1990), however, argued that this evolution to western models may not occur because family-run businesses appear to best fit the ethos of the Chinese with its traditional emphasis on the family unit. Family-run enterprises allow insiders to exercise the maximum control over one's fortune and destiny. Redding noted that if the Chinese had wanted to, they had plenty of opportunity to develop along western models a long time ago.

FACE

Face is another key building block of Confucian societies. While face is important in any culture, it is more significant in Confucian countries where it operates at a higher level of sensitivity. In East Asia, 'face' constitutes more than esteem or self-respect, the connotation usually associated with that construct in the west. In Confucian societies, there is a popular saying that 'Face is like the bark to a tree; without it, the tree dies. Similarly, a person cannot function without face'. Once people lose their face, they have brought shame to themselves and their family and, thus, become social outcasts.

There are two dimensions to 'face': *lian* and *mianzi*. *Lian* refers to the moral character (decency, integrity) and is more ascribed than achieved. *Lian* functions as a 'social sanction against immorality' and acts as a strong psychological deterrent ('pull' factor) against immoral behaviour. At the same time, it serves as a powerful motivator ('push' factor) to comply with established moral standards (Liu 1992:9). In that way, *lian* is more akin to the western concept of guilt and functions as a moral conscience. If people wish to preserve their *lian*, they will be honest in their dealings with others and honour their obligations and commitments. In Confucian societies, to accuse a person of having no *lian* is 'about the most severe condemnation that can be made of a person' (Hu 1946:52) *Mianzi*, on the other hand, refers to one's status and/or reputation that have been acquired through one's own efforts. It is more achieved than ascribed. Thus, *mianzi* serves as a 'strong psychological push' to attain greater successes and, in the process, attain even more reputation and status in society. There is really no 'social stigma' associated with a person who has no *mianzi*. It merely means that the person has failed to attain success (Redding and Ng 1982:205).

While separate, the two dimensions of face are closely related – 'long-standing *lian* is reinforced by repeated practice of *mianzi*. Once *lian* is lost, *mianzi* will be hard to maintain' (Liu 1992:9). As Hu (1946:63) noted: 'Once the community has acknowledged that a person is honest in his dealings and lives up to his obligations,he has credit far beyond his perhaps very modest possessions'. The concepts of *lian* and *mianzi* have several important implications for business practices. These include: the emphasis on trust; the penchant toward long-term orientation; the possession of a 'shame' culture. Each of these is discussed briefly. Since *lian* connotes honour and integrity, the concept of trust is built into the construct of 'face'. Furthermore, this trust can only be established through time. These dual concepts account for the East Asian emphasis on trust and relationships over legal contracts and again points to the need to adopt a long-term perspective.

Another important implication of 'face' is the notion of shame. The west operates primarily as a guilt culture. Under the influence of Judaism and Christianity, people feel guilty if their behaviour violates certain pre-scribed norms because of the internalized conviction of sin. Confucian societies, on the other hand, operate as a 'shame' culture. Face is 'exter-nally mediated' – in isolation, 'face' cannot be gained nor lost. Rather, it operates in relation to others (Redding and Ng 1982:207). In other words, 'face can never be felt without others feeling it. Hence face work in business dealings involves all parties, and the exchange of face granting is embedded in tangible things such as formalities and etiquettes' (Liu 1993:10). Because of the greater importance assigned to giving and main-taining 'face' in Confucian societies, face-giving and face-saving have developed into an elaborate art form. This is referred to as 'face work'. In addition, face is contextual, i.e. it depends upon situational factors. For example, the executive of a medium-sized company is not offended when he is relegated to the back row in an event sponsored by a larger company. However, if the host were a smaller concern than his own, such an action will be considered as an affront on his status. In addition, face is reciprocal – it is something to be given as well as received. In light of the importance of face and face–saving in Confucian societies and the fact that they are externally mediated, direct confrontation is to be avoided. Direct confron-tation does not allow another person to back out gracefully from a situation without losing face. By making an East Asian partner lose face, there is nothing to gain and everything to lose. This accounts for the East Asian partners' reluctance to say 'no' to requests and their indirectnesss in communication.

To save face, interpreters are often used in cross-national business negotiations. This allows a negotiator to change position by shifting the blame to interpreters for inaccurately translating messages. Since inter-preters usually occupy a lower status in the organizational hierarchy, they are often obliged to save the face of their superiors by assuming respon-sibility for errors. In this capacity, interpreters can act as 'face-keepers' (Liu, 1993:12). Since face is contextual and an interpreter usually occupies a lower organizational position, he/she does not lose too much face in accepting the blame.

DISCUSSION AND CONCLUSIONS

This chapter has identified and discussed the salient characteristics which underlie the East Asian approach to competition, co–operation, and strategic formulation and implementation. Many of these characteristics have been deeply ingrained in the mind-set of people from this region for thousands of years. This does not mean that culture does not change nor evolve over time. After all, 'culture is an evolving set of shared beliefs, values, attitudes and logical processes which provide cognitive maps for people within a given societal group to perceive, think, reason, act, react and interact. This definition implies that culture is not static; rather, it evolves over time' (Tung, 1995:491). While changes take place, they evolve slowly, and, in some cases, may revert back to its original form, that is, the more things change, the more they remain the same. A knowledgeable Chinese once remarked: 'After thirty years of communist rule, the Chinese (in the People's Republic of China) have converted Confucius into a socialist. With almost twenty years of reform and opening up to the outside world, this socialist is changing back to Confucius again but this time wearing a Christian Dior suit'. Similarly, in the case of Singapore, economic modernization and development have not led to a renunciation of Confucianism. Instead, in the recent decade, there has been a revival of interest in the study of Confucius' writings and precepts in the island-state.

REFERENCES

Chu, C.N. (1988) *The Chinese Mind Game*, AMC Publishing, Oregon.

Chu, G.C. and Ju, Y. (1993) *The Great Wall in Ruins*, State University of New York Press.

Hofstede, G. and Bond, M.H. (1988) The Confucius connection: From cultural roots to economic growth. *Organizational Dynamics*, Spring, pp. 5–21.

Hu, H.C. (1946) The Chinese concepts of face. *American Anthropologist*, pp. 45–64.

Hu, Y.S. (1996) Sun Tzu, in *International Encyclopaedia of Business and Management*, (ed. M. Warner), Routledge, London, 6 volumes.

King, A. (1991) *Guanxi* and network building: A sociological interpretation. *Daedalus*, **10**, pp. 63–82.

Lin, Y.T. (1935) *My Country and My people*, Reynal and Hitchcock, New York.

Liu, S. (1993) Family, face, and fate in *guanxi* capitalist societies: Their business implications for North American firms. M.B.A. project under the supervision of Prof. R.L. Tung, Simon Fraser University, Canada.

Musashi, M. (1982) *The Book of the Five Rings*, Bantam Books.

Ralston, D.A., Gustafson, D.J., Terpstra, R.H., and Holt, D.A. (1995) Pre-post Tiananmen Square: Changing values of Chinese managers. *Asia Pacific Journal of Management*, **12**, pp. 1–20.

Redding, S.G. and Ng, M. (1982) The role of 'face' in the organizational perceptions of Chinese managers. *Organization Studies*, **3**, pp. 201–19.

Redding, S.G. (1990) *The Spirit of Chinese Capitalism*, Walter de Gruyter, New York.

Tu, W.M. (1991) Cultural China: The periphery as the center. *Daedalus*, Spring pp. 1–29.

Tung, R.L. (1989) A longitudinal study of United States-China business negotiations. *China Business Review*, 1, pp. 57–71.

Tung, R.L. (1991) Handshakes across the sea: Cross-cultural negotiating for business success, *Organizational Dynamics*, 14, pp. 30–40.

Tung, R.L. (1994) Strategic management thought in East Asia. *Organizational Dynamics*, Spring, pp. 55–65.

Tung, R.L. (1995) International organizational behaviour, in *Virtual OB* (ed F. Luthans) Primis Database, McGraw–Hill, New York.

Tung, R.L. (1996) Business strategies: East Asian, in *International Encyclopaedia of Business and Management*, (ed. M. Warner), Routledge, London, 6 volumes.

Warner, M. (1995), *The Management of Human Resouces in Chinese Industry*, Macmillan, London.

Yeung, I.Y.M. and Tung, R.L. (1995) Who you know is more important than what you know: *Guanxi* (connections) and business success in Confucian societies. Working paper.

Chapter 15

Work-values in Japan: Work and work motivation in a comparative setting

Anders Törnvall

INTRODUCTION

There is now a growing co-operation between Japanese and European auto-mobile manufacturers and producers. This also means a need for knowledge and understanding of their different attitudes to work. These attitudes and their roots in tradition and culture have often been neglected in spite of their importance.

This chapter is written on the basis of research in the automotive industry. The first two studies were made at Toyota in Japan. Comparative studies were also carried out at Volvo and SAAB in Sweden and at GM in the US. The aim was to study work motivation and work ethics in a comparative setting. I chose the automotive industry for the following reasons:

1 It is a truly multinational industry which means that automobile companies sell their products all over the world.
2 All of them co-operate more and more using the same parts and sometimes the same engines because it is too expensive to develop new engines by themselves.
3 Another reason is that in such automobile companies almost the same categories of workers and managers can be found, which makes it easier to make a scientific comparison.

In this study we were particularly looking for the different basic philosophies, cultural values and social patterns and their relationship to the attitudes towards work and work motivation among a sampled group of employees.

WORK MOTIVATION

Motivation in individuals is a complicated characteristic to measure or account for (see MOW 1987). It is also difficult to find an accurate definition. However, in this discussion we adopt a broad statement which looks at 'the most important determinant of the difference between what a person can do and what her or she will do' (Amabile 1983: 357). In the case of motivation among Asians, these stereotypes are increasingly common. But scholars agree that among explanations for high motivation, cultural approaches are important (Yao 1985). Conclusions such as 'folk theory of success' (Ogbu 1987) and the concept of 'need to achieve' (De Vos 1983) are said to be more predominant in Asia, particularly in Japan.

Behind these statements, most researchers are united in the idea of the importance of Confucianism – see Chapter 14 in this book – as a principal source of dynamism contained within a rich culture and history. They agree on such variables as self-denial, frugality, patience, fortitude, self-discipline and dedication, learning and interest in applied sciences and mathematics. When it comes to group orientation, there are variables such as acceptance of authority, seniority, consciousness and dutifulness (Rozman 1991). The cultural arguments in Japanese studies are that the success of Japan's industry is due to high motivation, culturally specific phenomena impossible to duplicate in any other country (Tsukuda 1984).

In a comparison between Japanese and American experience, three aspects of considerable differences are noted. The first is the historical and cultural tendency toward centralization in Japan. A second major sociocultural difference relates to varying sex roles with respect to higher education. In Japan, females concentrate on Junior College Education whereas in America they compete with males students in higher education (see Cummings 1984).

A third, even more difficult and important to analyse, is the concept of self. However, Fetters et al. (1983) suggested that a high percentage of high school seniors agreed with three statements on self-esteem: I am a person of worth; I am satisfied with myself at times; I think I am no good. Kobayashi (1984) found that Japanese, contrary to American, education was closely related to business. Professional and vocational training directed towards the production process was very common. The large business enterprises prefer to recruit students from faculties of law, economics, management and engineering because there motivation is supposed to be strong, due to the cultural learning that takes place in Japan. This produces high work motivation at all levels.

In a large comparative survey about employee work attitudes and management practice in the US and Japan, Lincoln and Kallenberg (1990) found that the high commitment to work among Japanese workers is strongly linked to discipline and high motivation in the work place. However, researchers seldom try to go behind this to find the ultimate reason. They are satisfied by the common explanation that Japanese efficiency is due to effective organization or good management style etc. It is not enough, though, for understanding the deep Japanese motivation for work ethics in production management and professionalism. The basic philosophy must be taken into consideration in this process.

WORK IN A PHILOSOPHICAL PERSPECTIVE

Ishida Baizan (1966) is considered to be the founder of modern Japanese work ethics. He developed a reward system in his company for employees and their families, which encouraged loyalty towards the owner and thus a patriarchal system was supported. These conditions were further developed in competition between companies.

Shosan Suzuki (1979) was the creator of a sort of Zen theology for businessmen and workers, out of which a Japanese model for social ethics grew. In this view Buddha is the true essence of the world and Buddha's nature was the ideal nature. The daily work was one way which led to the right attitude to work, thus fulfilling Buddhaship. Shosan placed the worker in the Buddhist ascetism tradition: the harder and the more difficult one's work the more purifying it is for one's next life. A person who does not accomplish anything cannot achieve ascetism and is useless to society: 'Work is a part of the cosmic order and one should adjust to it trying to achieve Buddhaship'. Baizan can also be regarded as some kind of founder of pragmatism as he easily combined Buddhist work ethics and Confucianism. He believed in a syncretistic religion which developed into a popular ethic, which in turn created a central concept of harmony, 'Wa'. But Baizan also used in his work motivation the concept of honskin which means 'from the inner heart', a kind of self-esteem applied on a physical, spiritual and psychological level. But self-esteem demanded central traits of character like honesty – honesty towards oneself and those you believe in. This honskin is needed because no external power can control you, only yourself, The assignment you are given or have taken upon you in life is determined by the honskins you have. Thus the profession of the warrior was determined by a hereditary disposition. Baizan developed a theory or principle for all people which motivated their position in society. Everybody and everybody's work was needed and linked together.

In Japan, 'family' traditionally does not mean a 'nuclear' family in the Western tradition but more a 'tribal' family with people related to each other and built on 'blood relation'. To belong to a blood related family created the strongest motivation for work for your family. Other forms of families were built on territorial community. Most important here is the samurai family but this form was weaker because it was related to conquest and could be lost. But according to Hiedeyoshi (1536–1598) the main point was to develop a work function. This resembles the original structure of the American society – a piece of land and a special function in society. Then the motivation appears very strongly. The sense of community fits well into the special group community which has always existed in Japan and has its roots in the agrarian working tradition in the rice fields. The working community, based on professional community, is the backbone of Japanese work ethics. Those who work part-time or temporarily, and therefore are not part of the community, are obliged to work on a contract basis and will not obtain full rights. Therefore, people strive at full community through hard work and to be as closely linked to the company as possible.

Hajime (1967) describes some major characteristics in the Japanese way of thinking affecting directly or indirectly the motivation for work. First, the acceptance of actuality. That means an apprehension of the absolute in the phenomenal world. 'This worldliness acceptance of natural human qualities, spirit of tolerance, cultural stratification'. The second feature he underlines is the tendency to emphasize a particular solar nexus. This is to say, an emphasis on human relations which are more important than the individual but also an absolute view of limited social organizations and a reverence for family morality. The third feature is, in short, the non-rational tendency. This can be divided into several parts like non-logical tendencies, a weakness in ability to think in terms of logical consequences but instead a use of intuition and emotional ability, a fondness for simple, symbolic representations and weakness in knowledge of objective processes.

From this framework, several question areas found in a pre-study emerged, in the analysis of the attitudes among both students and managers these are:

- Experience of work in general
- Attitudes to work
- Motivation for work
- Work ethics
- Company's philosophy on work
- Personal philosophy on work

From these areas the individual questions were put in the in-depth interview and in the construction of the ranking list. The ranking list focused on finding the reasons for motivation covering the following items: economic, social, personal, traditional, idealistic reasons and so on.

THE METHODOLOGY OF THE STUDY

In this section we will first discuss the connection between basic philosophy and work ethics. Then we will analyse a pre-study among students and teachers at Japanese senior high schools. The main study was made at five companies: Fuji-Kiku Ltd., a spare parts company related to the automotive industry in Japan, in Hamamatsu, Japan; Toyota Motor

Corporation, Nagoya in Japan; Volvo Truck in Gothenburg; SAAB Automobile in Trollhätten, Sweden and GM in Saginaw, Michigan in the US. The methods used were in-depth interviews, questionnaires, and ranking lists.

The methodology was developed from the design. Interviewees were selected by drawing lots. After this, they were given exactly the same written and oral information about the goals and procedure of the study by the researcher. The interviews were made one by one, followed up by ranking the list of items. The analysis of the outcome was made as follows: all information given was put together in the main areas and topics that came out of the answers. For instance, information about the relationship between education and motivation was put under the subject of education.

After this, the result of the statistically calculated ranking list was added to those subjects in order to get a complete picture. The different topics and clusters of information can be found in the following pages (for instance in the Toyota case). The content of the subject was ranked according to how frequently they appeared in the data. After this, a careful analysis of the information was made, resulting in the statements presented in this chapter. The last part was an overall comparative analysis made in order to find some common aspects useful for a 'synergy approach'. This conclusion was not made on a ranking level but more from the researcher's idea of what was important.

After doing comparative research in Japan, in Europe and in the USA, I would, however, like to point out some experiences from ten years' of struggling with the problems of finding a common definition, particularly when it comes to concepts like philosophy, personality and human values.

The definitions of the same conceptions can be very different and difficult to conceptualize because they rest on different understandings of reality and non-reality. For example, in Japanese thinking the concept of ultimate truth, so important in western religions and ideologies, does not exist. The concept of humanity can also be very different. In order to handle this problem we need two things. First, a knowledge of Japanese values and philosophy. Second, the source of deep knowledge of ourselves and our traditional thinking.

WORK MOTIVATION AND WORK ETHICS IN SCHOOL EDUCATION

We now turn to how work motivation is developed in the Japanese school system, thus affecting working life outside school. Due to limited space, data has been chosen from just a few questions in a wider study to show these attitudes.

First, we focus on students, who study work ethics, then teachers, theoretically and practically involved in the education process. The students

Table 15.1 Motivation for doing schoolwork properly

Question 6 I do my schoolwork properly in order to:				
Alternatives	Ranking	1	2	3
get a good job after school		153	148	19
get a good position in society and a good salary		39	135	146
be able to work for my ideals, like helping other people and friends		118	53	149

were selected at random from senior high schools in Tokyo and in Sapporo. By studying school and education we also got an idea about how a Japanese institution transfers morals and work ethics to students.

The overwhelming majority of the students work in schools in order to get a good job after finishing school (see Table 15.1). This is shown by the first and the second ranking. Next to that is the third alternative; work for ideals. And in third place, they wish to get a good position in society. It is quite natural that the majority want good jobs. Japanese students know better than many other pupils how important this is. They have been told from their childhood the importance of work and of doing one's duty. This is repeated in school and in advertisements and of course in the company (*Kaisha*). The competition is very hard, too. Every company and institution has tests, interviews and test-jobs in order to get the best staff. Thousands of preparatory schools (*Juku*) help the applicants to get into the right company.

It is also quite natural to work for your ideals such as helping other people. Some students certainly have other ideals which can make them hesitant. But there is no reason to believe that Japanese students do not have these, as do many other students in the world. There is also a certain tiredness on focusing on materialism and striving for 'new products' all the time. The last alternative does not differ very much from the first; however, it is necessary to find out the attitude to the position. Rising standards in the country encourage new fortunes and an almost euphoristic feeling of being able to buy everything now. There is also an awareness of the difference in salaries throughout the unions and the students also realize that they have to take account of the paycheck and not just work for the benefit of the company and the group.

This particular research-study shows the following main results:

1 Work should develop a person as much as possible. The goal is a perfect professional.
2 This development could mainly occur not only through science, particularly computer science and high technology, but also through aesthetics.

3 The development must be linked to the group, because in group relations there is always an exchange of ideas, also important for a person's identity.
4 The student is willing to sustain hardship, even physical, to reach his professional goal.
5 To achieve and generate knowledge for your personal development is urgent. Therefore, the older generation must be respected because of their professional experience.
6 To develop yourself means to develop the company or the environment in which you operate, as well as your country.
7 Behind the forces shaping your attitude to life and work lie traditional concepts, more or less hidden. Spirituality, philosophy and the striving for security and comfort in working life are key values here.

A summary of these conclusions relevant for managing across cultures shows us how important ideals, philosophies and principles are in order to understand the Japanese approach to work and work motivation. Also personal and group involvement mean a lot (c.f. Sano 1995).

WORK MOTIVATION AND WORK ETHIC IN THE AUTOMOBILE INDUSTRY

We now focus on two types of industry we studied in Japan. The first one is a company which delivers parts and spare parts to the Japanese automobile industry, Fuji-Kiku Co. Ltd. The second is the biggest car manufacturer in Japan and number two in the world, Toyota Motor Corporation in Nagoya (Cases 1 and 2). Then we have made the same study at Volvo Automobile (Volvo Truck) in Gothenburg and SAAB Automobile in Trollhätten, Sweden, as well as at GM in Saginaw, Michigan in the US, in order to compare a Japanese industry with Western industries in the same field (Cases 3–5).

Our analysis throughout the whole study will be divided into the following six different areas appearing in the interviews and questionnaires. These criteria will be used in all cases in order to find out how motivation is built up during a person's lifetime.

– Personal, individual aspects
– Family and social aspects
– Educational aspects
– Company aspects
– Society aspects

Case 1 – Fuji-Kiku Co Ltd, Japan

We use the outcome from the study at Fuji-Kiku to show that the results are relevant in small and middle-sized companies. Here, three answers from the respondents illustrate well the personal reasons for motivation at this company:

'Satisfaction is the progress for oneself to fulfil the duty and to feel self-fulfilment'

'It is the responsibility given to me and the faith shown in me as a professional worker'

'I get satisfaction by being able to accomplish a task for my company'

Two words regularly coming up in the study are accomplishing and developing. Accomplishing means fulfilment and self-fulfilment to the utmost ability even if it sometimes can be 'in absurdum'. Developing means, in this context, professional development but also developing character.

Case 2 – Toyota Motor Corporation Ltd, Japan

The guiding principles for Toyota set out in 1993 have many versions. One sentence repeated many times in several documents states that production should be 'for people, for society, for the Earth'. This thinking is developed in seven points:

1 Be a world-wide company
2 Serve the greater good of people everywhere by devoting careful attention to safety and to the environment.
3 Assert leadership in technology and in customer satisfaction.
4 Become a contributing member of the community in every way.
5 Foster a corporate culture that honours individuality while promoting teamwork.
6 Pursue continuing growth through efficient global management.
7 Build lasting relationships with business partners around the world.

We found that personal aspects named by the respondents concentrated on *inner and outer approval*. Inner motivation was described by the respondent with words such as these, ranked according to frequency:

1 Confidence
2 Faithfulness
3 Trust
4 Pride

Outer approval was described with key words such as

1 Promotion
2 Higher salary
3 Good product

In order to reach this motivation the respondents ranked three tasks:

1 To discipline yourself
2 To control yourself
3 To solve problems

From Toyota, we can summarize the tasks of the company as follows:

> The company should give the workers pride.
> The company should give the employees a human value, because work in Japan very much decides a person's worth, not only inside, but outside the company, in the family and in the community.

Case 3 – Volvo Automobile AB, Sweden

The Volvo case shows the strong impact of the father as a model for the work, particularly for the son. There were two obvious ways of doing that: first, to tell the children about their duty to work, doing their best and so on. One quotation: 'Remember, my son, that you should always do your best in all professions'. The next was to take the profession very seriously, always go to work, taking on all kinds of responsibility. The schools, indirectly, through their very practically oriented curricula give a realistic view of work. The company should also motivate by keeping up the best quality in the production. The group should create the best work environment and partnership within the team and towards the management.

Society should show their appreciation of the skill and workmanship the employees developed in Volvo, the flagship of Swedish industry. Some respondents underlined the fact that the city of Gothenburg is very dependent on Volvo for their financial survival. There is a so called 'Volvo spirit' revealed in the following response in the interview:

> 'A Volvo employee always does his/her best, aiming to build the best car in the world'.

In the goals and guidelines of 1995, called the Volvo Philosophy, Human Resource Development is emphasized rather strongly. This philosophy is affected by Japanese Management Philosophy. For example, one goal is continuous improvement, in Japanese called *Kaizen*, creating common values among employees and a communication structure inside and outside the company. The striving for human quality and competence in the teams are said to be important. When it comes to a 'Volvo identity' communication with the market and international customers should be open, structured and built on facts both in 'success and failure'. Basic values should be founded on trustfulness, respect for human beings and their environment. The employee of Volvo should above all care about its customers.

Case 4 – SAAB Automobile AB, Sweden

SAAB Automobile is the second automobile manufacturer in Sweden next to Volvo. It grew out of aircraft production, both medium-sized civil aircraft, and fighters for the Swedish airforce and for export like the airliners. The company has gone through a rationalization after years of heavy deficits. The last few years have shown an improvement, with recent success with two new models. This could be the result of implementing the TQM philosophy in a Japanese version. The new basic philosophy is stated in the following vision: SAAB should be like a 'team for which development, production and sales of exclusive, high-class Swedish automobiles give inspiration to pride and engagement'. It also says that knowledge and devotion are important for personal involvement in production.

The programme has a different approach from the Volvo philosophy. SAAB underlines that all activity of the personnel should more directly support production. The request for developing new ideas and improving production is important, and also to solve problems by asking five 'why' questions when something goes wrong. One interesting aspect here is the request for patience with the customers and above all discipline and trust in all relations within the company and with customers.

When it comes to personal aspects of work the SAAB employees put forward security – to have a job and not being laid off. Behind this is the confidence in the company not to let them go. Also important was the possibility to develop their skill and participation in the manufacturing process. This security is necessary for the task of supporting the family, not losing their integrity by being just a social welfare client. There are a lot of expectations, particularly in the in-house education and in-service training. This should not just enrich the skill but also the intellect, in fact the whole personality, leading ultimately to a higher position in the company. The company's role was, in their opinion, to take more responsibility for education and also to put the customer more in focus according to the TQM philosophy with the support of Japanese experts in the factory. As the city of Trollhätten, where SAAB Automobile is located, depends very much on SAAB, the city should concentrate on a kind of social contract with the company creating security and respect.

Case 5 – General Motors, USA

General Motors, in co-operation with their trade union the United Auto Workers (UAW) focus on the individual 'and hope to meet the challenge of the future by developing its people'.

The GM philosophy (1995 version) also focuses directly on the 'human being', so a conclusion could be that intercultural communication must concentrate more than ever on anthropocentric dimensions and humanistic aspects in managing.

A very conclusive finding of the study gave us first of all a personal view on the motivation of workers according to very American virtues: to develop your personality, to increase the confidence in yourself, to take on challenges, to be creative and 'getting the job done' as soon as possible.

From the family, to be responsible for everything and stand up for convictions. In education, even in the in-service training, freedom of choice was underlined as much as possible. The difference between Japanese workers and American workers could even be seen through their outfits. Where the Toyota workers wore uniforms, all GM workers were dressed in a very personal style.

CONCLUDING REMARKS

As can be seen in this chapter, we have used a Japanese approach to cross-cultural activity. This is partly due to the fact that American management philosophy should be counter-balanced in a multicultural strategy. Theoretical and practical thinking could be stimulated by a Japanese or even a wider Asian approach, not just an Asian answer to American problems in their management models.

The movements can be seen in Figure 15.1: It is not a question of changing models totally – rather a movement leading to a 'more balance

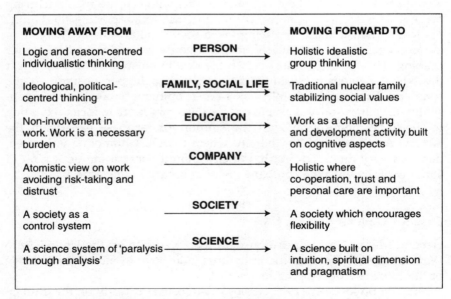

Figure 15.1 Movement towards a more 'balance in synergy' strategy

in synergy' strategy. We think that in Western countries, a movement from the Western concept of thinking and managing towards an Asian one is needed. Of course, this is only a start but it can serve as a platform for future discussions about managing across cultures.

REFERENCES

Amabile, T. (1983) The social psychology of creativity. A componential conceptualization. *Journal of Personality and Social Psychology*, **45**, pp. 357–76.

Baizan, I. (1966) *Seiri Mondo*, Tokyo.

Cummings, W. (1984) *Japanese Images of American Education*. Paper presented at the East-West Center Conference on Learning from Each Other, Honolulu.

De Vos, G.A. (1983) Achievement motivation and intra family attitudes to Korean immigrants. *Journal of Psychoanalytic Anthropology* **6**, pp. 25–71.

Fetters, W.B., *et al.* (1983) *Schooling Experience in Japan and the US*. A Cross National Comparison of High School Students, Educational Research Orientation, Montreal.

Hajime, N. (1967) Basic features of the legal, political and economic thought of Japan, in *The Japanese Mind*, (ed C. Moore) University of Hawaii, Hawaii.

Kobayashi, V.N. (1984) Tradition, modernization and education. The case of Japan. *Journal of Ethnic Studies*. **12**, pp. 95–118.

Lincoln, J.R. and Kallenberg, A.L. (1990) Culture, control and commitment. *A Study of Work Organization and Work Attitudes in the United States and Japan*, New York.

MOW International Research Team (1987) *The Meaning of Working*, London.

Ogbu, J.U. (1987) Variability of minority school performance. A problem in search of an explanation. *Anthropology and Education Quarterly*, **6**, pp. 25–71.

Rozman, G. (ed) (1991) *The East Asian Region. Confucian Heritage and its Modern Adaptation, Princeton University Press*, Princeton, N.J.

Sano Yoko (1995) *Human Resource Management in Japan*, Tokyo.

Shosan Suzuki (1979) *Roankye*, Tokyo.

Tsukuda, M. (1984) *A Factual Overview of Education in Japan and in the United States*. Paper presented at East-West Center Conference, Learning from Each Other, Honolulu.

Yao, E.L. (1985) A comparison of family characteristics of Asian-American and Anglo-American high achievers. *International Journal of Comparative Sociology*, **26**, pp. 198–208.

Chapter 16

Culture, education and industry: managing management studies in Japan

Malcolm Warner

INTRODUCTION

Japan's economic success has unquestionably been built on the contribution of its educational system amongst other major factors. Growth in the economy has in turn financed further social investment in that system. The result is a 'virtuous circle' of mutual reinforcement of forces benefiting the public good. In this sense, Japan may be presented as a 'model' for advanced countries, stressing the value of education and training as a preparation for life-long learning. Not only has Japan's primary and secondary educational system helped create the pre-conditions for a high level of competence in the general population, it has also engendered values appropriate to economic development such as the well-known 'achievement-orientation' central to many theories of modernization. Yet, this has been combined with a special Japanese flavour, summed up in the phrase *wakon yosei*, which may be translated as 'Japanese values, Western know-how' (see Warner 1994).

The transmission of traditional values combined with modern ones lays at the heart of such a process. Japan selectively blended both exogenous and endogenous influences (see Westney 1987) to create a culturally and economically appropriate system:

> Japanese education reflects Japanese social, religious and cultural foundations. Japanese culture has been strongly influenced by Buddhism and Shintoism; Chinese civilization and its writing and literary traditions; Confucianism with its respect for learning, hierarchical relationships, harmonious social and personal relations and morality; and the 200 years of isolation under the Shogun rule when Japan shunned all contact with the Western world and began to broaden its elementary education base. In the nineteenth century, Japan reopened its links with the West and borrowed selectively from both the United States of America and German educational traditions. Following the devastation of the Second World War, Japanese education was reformed on the

American 6-3-3 system, which still persists but in a form modified to suit Japan. After the restoration of full Japanese sovereignty in 1952, successive Japanese governments vested more power in the Monbusho, reintroduced moral education and reverted to appointed school boards rather than the elected ones introduced by the occupying powers.

(HMI 1991: 3)

Whether we put forward *economic* explanations on the one hand, or *cultural* ones on the other to explain Japan's economic success, education still remains pivotal as it can fall into either camp (Sheridan 1993: 179). Educational investment ensured both *quantitative* and *qualitative* aspects of labour supply, for example. The quality of Japanese labour inputs has unquestionably been a major ingredient in its success story to date. The government's contribution was vital in these developments, providing a highly effective infrastructure. 'Collective goods and services' were amply provided for, including education and training. Marshallian externalities were therefore available in abundance. Japanese economic policy to achieve the above based on the appropriate 'consensual support for national aims and economic means of achieving them' (Sheridan 1993: 195).

JAPAN'S EDUCATIONAL EXPANSION

The post-World War II period saw the percentage of those in the age-cohort going into further secondary education rise from 43 % in 1950, to 55 % in 1960, 82% in 1980 and over 96% by 1990. There was also a wave of new universities created by the end of the 1980s (see Stephens 1991: 84). The system ensures 'a very high level of numeracy and literacy throughout the population. It is higher than that of the United States or Western Europe' (1991: 85).

The total spent on education is, however, relatively constrained – less than one-seventh of government expenditure, which comes to about one fifteenth of GNP. All higher education institutions choose their students by 'meritocratic' selection from those who can afford the fees, whether in public or private universities; the latter's fees are subsidized but are still above the level of the public ones. The Confucian cultural inheritance of self-development, added to by the desire to 'achieve' in modern society, makes the system 'tick'.

As Dore and Sako note (1989: 1):

Japan is well known for having what is probably in the younger age-groups the world's best educated (at least most educated) population. The rapid expansion of the system and the, by international standards, very high enrolment levels in secondary and higher education, are clear enough . . . showing change over thirty years in the educational experience of new labour force entrants in manufacturing and finance.

The system may be summed up as follows:

- commitment to education by all levels of Japanese society
- high participation rates in the tertiary education sector
- close working relations between industry and education
- special training-schools producing technicians with skills equivalent to Western degree levels
- impressive completion rates of students in the tertiary sector
- high status conferred on teaching-staff at all levels
- strong commitment to training by Japanese companies which provide in-house training for over 30 million employees
- levy-system by government to fund its own training programmes and to sponsor those of companies.

As a British official report summed-up:

The key aims of Japanese education include the fostering of harmonious relations and the encouragement of hard work and perseverance. Rote learning, repetition and memorization play a significant part in the learning process. There is a strong belief that hard work rather than innate ability is the key to success. Not all Japanese agree with this approach, but the achievements of Japanese children, shown by many favourable international comparisons, are such as to cause the Japanese to be cautious when they are urged to adopt new approaches to the education of their children. However, there is growing concern that Japanese education does not sufficiently encourage creativity and innovation and that, if Japan is to continue to be one of the world's leading economies, it will need to develop the more creative aspects of society. Many believe that to achieve this radical changes will be needed in the approach to learning at all levels. even the more radical thinkers are concerned lest they throw the baby out with the bath water.

(HMI 1991: 3–4)

The conclusions of Dore and Sako (1989: 1–12) on the general school system, however, confirm the view that although Japanese education puts less stress on specific skills, innovation and creativity, it does culturally inculcate a greater attention to detail and discipline than many Western systems. At the final output end, its products are highly trainable. Education therefore has a preparatory role for the future acquisition of skills at work and life-long learning in the enterprise.

Another expert source (Refsing 1992: 116 ff) argues that variables external to education, such as demand and supply of the labour force, do not explain the growth of schools and universities. Most employers do not expect the educational system to be a source of specifically skilled and knowledgeable employees. They look for individual qualities and social skills, which can be built upon by in-house training and the inculcation of the 'company spirit' within the context of the respective company cultures (1992: 118).

The expansion of the educational system may be associated with the decline in jobs for teenagers. It is indeed paradoxical that the Japanese system is characterized by late entry into the labour market as well as early exit (with no encouragement of immigration *pari passu*). Socialization for work in general is certainly one function of the system and perhaps the tight labour supply ensures a bunched, generously sized cohort entering the labour market at a point in time convenient for employers to pick and choose.

Refsing (1992: 122) believes that:

A rapidly expanding educational system will soon create a kind of vicious circle in the sense of producing an upgrading of formal educational requirements for positions which formerly had lower requirements or none at all.

MANAGEMENT STUDIES: HISTORICAL BACKGROUND

The history of management studies broadly defined in Japan dates back to the early part of this century, at least (see Okazaki-Ward 1993: 24 ff). Moves to set up commercial education go back even further in time to the Meiji Restoration of 1868 (see Sugiyama and Nishizawa 1988; Sugiyama 1994).

The founding-father of commercial education in Japan was Mofi Arinori (1847–89) a progressive, liberal reformer of the Japanese Enlightenment (Sugiyama and Nishizawa, 1988: 151). His goal was to develop 'Captains of Industry', based on the American model. Mori was Japan's first Ambassador in Washington, DC (and later the first Minister of Education) and very inspired by US practice in commerce. His efforts to emulate their methods and to transfer their business culture led to the setting-up of the Commercial Training School, as it was initially called in 1884, subsequently transferred to the Ministry of Agriculture and Trade and renamed Tokyo Commercial School. It became the Tokyo Higher Commercial School in 1902 and the first collegiate School of Commerce in Japan, a model soon copied by other such schools in Japan. It was eventually to become the renowned Hitotsubashi University (so-named in 1949) of contemporary importance, with around 5,000 students, concentrated in the commerce, economics, law and social studies faculties, with a research institute and graduate school.

By contrast, Tokyo University, set up along Western lines in 1877, was primarily intended to train bureaucrats for the state-apparatus (see Francks 1992: 33) offering studies in law, liberal arts, medicine and natural sciences, later adding engineering and agriculture. It was subsequently renamed the Imperial University in 1886. In the same period, a wave of private universities were established, such as Chuo, Hosei, Meiji, Shenshu and Waseda and many others. Kyoto Imperial University followed in 1897 but was government-supported like Tokyo.

Such developments occurred at about the same time as many of those in the US (see Locke 1989). For example, the Wharton Business School (1881) was one of the first to be founded and later the Colleges of Commerce in California and Chicago respectively (1898). In Germany too, Leipzig set up its *Handelhochschule* in the same year and Cologne followed (1901); similarly, Birmingham founded its Faculty of Commerce (1902) and, a little later, Harvard inaugurated its Business School (1908). The Japanese had directly taken their template from Belgium, from the *Institut Supérieur de Commerce d'Anvers*, a leading promoter in commercial education in Europe at the time. The London School of Economics (1902) also had a minor influence with its emphasis on commercial curricula.

Very shortly, Kobe Higher Commercial School (1902) opened its doors, and together with Keio, became a supplier of teachers for the field. Tokyo's Higher Commercial School's strength was commercial science, unlike Keio's and Tokyo University's which was political economy *via* respectively the influence of the American academics, Professors Garett Droppers and E.F. Fenollosa respectively (see Sugiyama and Nishizawa 1988: 162; Sugiyama 1994). The overall strategy of the pioneers of commercial education was to train a future business élite but, whereas the German model emphasized general education, with economics as the pivotal subject, the Japanese were keener on specialist training. Adapting Western models was always culturally mediated (see Warner 1994). Fukuda Tokuzo, then studying in Germany, was a leading advocate of university-level education for future business leaders (Sugiyama and Nishizawa 1988: 162).

The noted economist Michio Morishima (cited in Locke 1989: 192) remarks that:

> the first clause of the Imperial University Edict of 1886 . . . states (that) the Imperial University shall have as its purpose instruction in the arts and sciences such as accords with the cardinal principles of the state and research into their deepest mysteries. Japanese higher education did not exist for the sake of the individual; the individual was educated for the state in accordance with the needs of the state.

The German and Austrian influences were strong here with the role of the state exalted, in contrast to the more liberal British and US models

(Checkland 1988: 268). Fukuzawa Yukichi (1835–1901) an early visitor to the West, was the founder of *Keio Gijuku* as it was called. His college became the first Japanese institution to teach western economics before the Meiji Restoration in 1868 (Morris-Suzuki 1989: 48). His credo *Gakumon no Susume* (An Encouragement of Learning) was first published in 1872 and he emphasized the learning of foreign languages as a priority. His philosophy can be summed-up as 'laissez-faire within the nation and imperialist expansion outside' (Checkland 1988: 262).

Against Morishima's view, this leading nineteenth century reformer stressed a more liberal position:

> Fukuzawa's primary aim in education was to instil in each individual student the spirit of freedom and independence which he conceived as the essence of modern civilization. Only those people with such spirit would be able to form a powerful nation capable of standing free and independent among the nations of the modern world.
>
> As for learning, he considered it a tool for attaining this freedom and independence. He therefore emphasized basic and general education for developing reliable and independently minded individuals at first. This specialized education, or university education, he said, was for the selected few who would work to raise the cultural level of the nation and to ensure its freedom and independence in a competitive world.
>
> (*Keio University Catalogue 1991: 9*)

The university in question was to become one of the outstanding private universities in Japan and a bastion of independent opinion vis-a-vis many others. Again, we can see the cross-cultural transfer was not straight-forward.

Locke (1989: 55) concludes that business studies as a subject was a cultural phenomenon in itself. He goes on to argue that:

> The acceptance of business studies in each country depended on the ability of that country's culture to foster and assimilate it. And it also means that the form and the effectiveness of business studies will be, because cultures *vary*, different in each country. Therefore, the historians who can deal with the specificity of this educational evolution can shed light, more light perhaps than scientists who ignore culture, on the relationship between business studies and economic performance.

UNIVERSITIES AND MANAGEMENT STUDIES

It would be a mistake to focus too narrowly when considering the education and training of the cohorts of potential managers whether at senior, middle or lower levels: hence, the emphasis on university-level management studies teaching, especially at undergraduate level, as well as courses in business, commerce and economics here. There are also some graduate level programmes worth including, but these involve far fewer students and faculty. Such dimensions of management studies as well as teaching in other subjects like engineering, technology and so on, lay the foundations for what may be done later in-house (or indeed externally) by Japanese enterprises (see Okazaki-Ward 1993; Sano 1996 for further details). This phenomenon may be more comparable to the German business education system, where the US-style 'Business School' model did not similarly put down deep roots (see Locke 1984). It is therefore misleading to focus on whether Japan has North American style graduate business schools or not (as indeed it would as well for Germany). Likewise, it is equally not useful to merely look at Japan's elite universities, specifically regarding the contribution of Tokyo's Imperial University. Dore and Sako (1989: 13 ff), for instance, point out that Japan is no longer an 'A-type' society with an elite education system, but a 'B-type' with meritocratic selection and lifetime employment.

To be useful, any examination of the topic must specifically look at those universities which have developed business and management studies, adding in the coverage of economics and commerce, as well as branches of industrial engineering which may be relevant. In doing so, we may see a not insubstantial flow of graduates coming out of such institutions and entering the labour market.

This is not, however, to presume that everyone graduating in those areas are aspirants for managerial posts, but neither does it exclude from managerial postulates those studying other subjects, as we know that in Dore and Sako's words (1989: 25):

As between arts stream and science stream . . . there is little difference whether in prestige, or in material prospects. A science graduate from a university which just missed being a top university is more likely to end up on the board of a major manufacturing company – and probably just as likely to get a job as a MITI civil servant – as somebody from the top of the social science tree – a graduate of the law department of Tokyo University.

National universities are biased towards science and engineering candidates, with the best finally going into academic and research careers. Graduates in these subjects from less prestigious universities are less hesitant in going into industry. Graduates of top universities may largely go to top firms (see Okazaki-Ward 1993: 118 ff), but the latter only constitute a relatively limited proportion of all managerial employment.

Whereas some national universities offer management and related studies, principally at undergraduate level (but with some post-graduate provision) most of the wider range of higher education institutions involved in such subjects have introduced them more recently. If the most noteworthy 'Business School' is in an old University (founded in the 19th century) namely Keio, and its move into management studies came about post-World War II, many of the new universities were not even in existence at that time.

In the inter-war years, Japanese management studies had gone through a phase of consolidation as boom led to slump and imperial expansion then engendered recovery. The expansion of both public and private universities led to the creation of new faculties and departments, especially at graduate level. The Great Earthquake of 1923 caused great damage as, for example, in the case of Chuo University where all facilities were destroyed – the campus was then moved to the suburbs in 1926. Some institutions only became full universities in this period, like Sophia University in 1928.

At this time also the development of 'Scientific Management' also led to both the professionalization of management and to the growth of new subject areas and content in the curriculum (see Warner 1994). The Japan Society for the Study of Business Administration was set up in 1926 to promote studies on commerce and management, under the leadership of Professors Hirai Yasutaro, Masuchi Yojiro, Muramoto Fukumatsu, Nakanishi Torao and Ueda Teijiro, with a membership of 342. (It currently has 1,745 members and meets once a year nationally and several times a year regionally.)

'Corporatist' ideas were common amongst economists and management thinkers in the inter-war years and institutionalized in the Cabinet Planning Board in 1937, an organization of economic experts and bureaucrats having significant powers to control a war-time economy (see Morris-Suzuki 1989: 100). The Showa Research Association was a forum to establish the exchange of ideas between economists, government, businessmen and the military. 'Communitarianism' was the middle-of-the-road ideology, avoiding the extremes of free markets and totalitarianism, with several liberal and left-wing academics participating in its activities.

After 1945, American cross-cultural transfer and an increase in its influence over higher education greatly increased with the Allied Occupation. A group of young 'progressive' managers, the *Keizai Doyukai*, called for more systematic management training and development and was seen as a 'Japanese version of American managerial ideology' (Collins 1989: 178). In the 1960s and 1970s, visits to the US and Europe by leading training personnel and executives led to calls for Japanese trainees to be sent to Western management programmes, to set up their own courses adapted to Japanese practice and to establish business schools (Collins 1989: 181). A survey of nearly 700 company presidents carried out by the Tokyo Chamber of Commerce reported that they had limited in-house training for new university recruits and called for the setting-up of graduate business schools (Ballon 1971: 7–8).

Waves of new universities were characteristic of the 1960s and 1970s in most OECD countries. In the same way, Japan's expansion of higher education is relatively recent, the growth of business administration, commerce and economics teaching at undergraduate level is similarly a post-war phenomenon.

UNDERGRADUATE LEVEL MANAGEMENT COURSES

One commentator makes the point that:

> The purpose of a university is to develop a rounded personality while providing the student with a general academic background. They believe that it is not their responsibility but rather that of the employer to offer graduates specialized professional training . . .
>
> (*cited in MacMillan 1984: 132*)

If training programmes within firms are mostly specialized, higher education courses are more generalist. Some noteworthy top managers started out at centres of excellence like Tokyo University and many trained as graduate engineers. Tertiary, like secondary education, has been used as a filter rather than a training-ground (see Dore and Sako 1989: 13–32), but not entirely so. The Japanese system is said to grade human potential through merit-based higher education, so that the 'best' people go to the 'best' firms. The companies value the ability to learn of these graduates and what they can be trained for internally. Locke (1989: 193) points out that Japanese firms put a considerable emphasis on what he calls 'purposive practical education'.

By the early 1980s, about one in six Japanese universities had undergraduate programmes in Business Administration involving those proceeding straight from high-school and therefore without work experience (see Sasaki 1981). In recent years, there has been 'a major expansion of business studies teaching' (Gow 1988: 25), but this was largely restricted to private universities. As Gow points out:

> Graduates in business studies were deemed increasingly attractive by the firms we interviewed in Japan, especially those firms in the service sector and there are indications of further shifts in the direction of vocationally oriented higher education, specially in the private establishments.
>
> (*ibid. 1988: 25*)

Many universities teach management-related subjects at undergraduate level with around half a million students in both public as well as private higher education sectors. A typical curricular framework is given in Table 16.1. While not all of these students (and those from other subject-disciplines) may enter the privileged *sogoshoku* recruitment stream who are destined to be 'graduate trainees' in Western parlance, the others who

Table 16.1 Typical curricula for undergraduate courses in management and related subjects in Japan

---

Business Administration

Department of Business Administration

Business Administration
Labour Management
Science of Business Management
Business Finance
Management Information Systems

Business Administration of Industry
Public Utility Management
Business Statistics
Business Mathematics

Department of Accounting

Bookkeeping
Principles of Accounting
Auditing
Cost Accounting
Management Accounting
Tax Accounting
International Accounting

Department of Commerce

Marketing
Distribution System
Market Management
Securities Market
Securities
Foreign Trade
Financial Institutions
Transportation
International Transportation
Insurance

Economics

Department of Economics

Theoretical Economics
National Economics
Social Economics
Mathematical Economics
History of Economic Doctrines
International Economics
Foreign Trade Policy
Principles of Economic Policy
Industrial Policy
Agricultural Policy
Social Policy
Public Finance

International Finance
Economic Geography
Economic History
Japanese Economy
Economic Affairs in Foreign Countries
Money and Banking
Statistics
Economic Statistics
Econometrics
Comparative Economic Study
Public Economics
Economics of Modern Technology

Source: An Outline of Kobe University, 1991

---

may enter the *ippanshoku* or routine/clerical job category, and mostly women, cannot be disregarded in any analysis of the Japanese labour force. It is, however, worth noting that female students make up less than a quarter of those attending four-year colleges (see Okazaki-Ward 1993: 52).

Of ten selected Japanese universities, a mix of private and state universities was chosen for further analysis, ranging from just over 3,000 students to just over 40,000 in their enrolment (in alphabetic order, Chuo, Hitotsubashi, Keio, Kobe, Kyoto, Shiga, Sophia, Tokyo Institute of Technology, Tsukuba, Waseda). The percentage of commerce, economics and management students ranged from over two-thirds to under one tenth of total undergraduate numbers, taking the most recent statistics. (This number should be matched against one in six nationally overall.) The smallest and relatively new Shiga University had around 3,000 students, with just over half studying economics and management subjects, as did Hitotsubashi with 5,000 undergraduates in all; the largest, the older Waseda University with over 40,000 students, had over a quarter pursuing economics and commerce studies. The numbers enrolled for Masters and Doctoral studies in these fields were uniformly very small.

Looking at just a few of the above set in greater detail (two private, two public) we find the following characteristics.

Chuo University

Founded in 1885 as the English Law School. It was later renamed Chuo (meaning Central) University in 1905, with faculties of Law and Economics, with Commerce added in 1909. It is now one of the best-known private universities in Japan with over 1,500 academic staff, with five faculties, later adding science and engineering and literature, with one campus in the centre of Tokyo and another in the suburbs; it has over 25,000 students, of whom over forty percent are studying for a four-year economics and/or commerce course at undergraduate level, with over 25% of all graduate students taking such Masters courses.

The Faculty of Commerce at Chuo University is divided into three departments: Business Administration; Accounting; Marketing and Trade. It has a four-year programme, with additional foreign language-teaching and an international exchange arrangement with France (with the École Supérieure de Commerce de Paris) and the USA (with Carleton College).

Keio University

A large private higher education institution, which traces its origins back to 1858, now with over 25,000 students at undergraduate level, with over 2,000 graduate students (of which around most, namely two-thirds, are Master's graduates), with the rest registered for doctorates. About four percent of undergraduates gained a four-year degree in economics and a comparable number in business and commerce, making eight percent in all. About five percent of all graduate students are studying for Master's degrees in these areas (data on the MBA programme follows in a later section).

Kobe University

A post-war national state institution, set up in 1949 and now has over 1,150 faculty staff. It incorporated Kobe University of Economics, which in turn absorbed Kobe University (formerly College) of Commerce set up in 1902. A Graduate School was set up in 1953. It now has science and engineering faculties as well as law, literature and medicine. Just under 20% of undergraduates (of the 12,000 or more in the university) are studying four-year economics and/or business administration courses and over 10% of all graduate students are enrolled on such Masters courses.

Tokyo Institute of Technology

For many years has been the leading centre of excellence in higher education of science and engineering. Founded by the government as Tokyo Higher Technical School in 1881, it is a national-level institution of learning, becoming a university in 1929 and now has over 5,000 under-graduates and over 2,500 graduate students. It has over 1,700 faculty staff, of whom just under a third are professors. There are three Faculties: Science, Engineering; and Bioscience/Biotechnology and its Graduate Schools date from 1953. The Institute plays a major part in turning out Japan's leading engineers.

Management Studies are taught at the Tokyo Institute of Technology in the Department of Industrial Engineering and Management. It sets out to familiarize students with the engineering aspects of business administration and to teach techniques to help them make decisions regarding management problems. The programme covers the fundamentals of engineering, economics and management, management science and systems analysis. There are four professors and 18 other faculty staff. The divisions are

- Industrial management
- Industrial engineering
- Management principles
- Production engineering
- Process control

The Department has around twelve percent of all undergraduates on four-year management-related courses and about two percent of all Masters students and Doctoral students.

GRADUATE-LEVEL MANAGEMENT COURSES

Of the 500 or so universities in Japan, about three in five have a graduate school. Some offer Masters programmes only, but many have both Masters and Doctoral courses.

Even closer to the present is the growth of graduate-level courses in these areas, mostly dating from the late 1960s (and not unlike the British experience of setting-up its initial MBA courses but less likely to take root). The Sophia University Master's Programme started in 1967, with Keio University's coming two years later. The Sanno (University) Management School was established in 1978. Tsukuba University put on its two-year Master's programme in 1973, with the International University of Japan launching a similar one in 1988. The Aoyama Gakuin Graduate School also offers a Masters of International Business degree. Altogether there are over 4,000 students on commerce, economics, management courses but this constitutes less than one percent of the total undergraduate numbers in the relevant areas of study. Some leading examples of MBA courses follow.

Keio Business School

As the first full-scale, professional management school of its kind in Japan, when it was set up in 1962, Keio University had entered into a collaborative arrangement with the Harvard Business School. The Graduate School of Business Administration was established in April 1978, with an MBA Programme (launched ten years earlier in 1968) which lasts for two semesters, over a two-year period. The campus, with 20,000 students in all subjects, dates from the late nineteenth century.

Sophia University

Founded by Jesuit Fathers early this century in Tokyo it began a Master's Programme in International Business and Management as far back as 1967 (see Collins 1989: 185). It has over 500 full-time faculty staff (of whom around 120 are foreign) with over 10,000 students over all academic subjects. The Institute of Comparative Culture covers both undergraduate and postgraduate courses, and it is within this centre that a limited number of international management courses are taught, with around 60 graduate students.

Tsukuba University

Built as a new university over twenty years ago, the institution is geared to a 'high-tech' environment in Japan's most innovative 'science city' (initiated in 1967) located in Tsukuba, within easy reach of Tokyo, to the north-east. The Graduate School of Systems Management, set up in 1973, concentrates on internationalization, orientation towards the future and the development of problem solving abilities. It links the 'fusion' areas of Management, Computer Science and Mathematics. In 1991, there were over 8,000 undergraduate students at Tsukuba in all subjects, with over 500 in the College of Socio-Economic Planning. There were just under 300 at Masters level in Management Sciences and Public Policy Studies, of whom about a third were practitioners.

The International University of Japan (IUJ)

Launched the International Management MBA Programme in September 1988 and claims it is the only programme of its kind to be accredited by the Ministry of Education. Its courses, which are taught entirely in English, were developed in collaboration with an American institution, the Amos Tuck School of Business Administration, which originally offered the world's first graduate degree in business at Dartmouth College in New Hampshire, a decidedly Ivy League institution (see Locke 1984). The MBA programme graduated its first class in June 1990, although the university (IUJ) itself was founded early in 1982. Up to fifty MBA candidates a year are admitted, half from Japan and half from overseas.

Even so Japan's extensive overseas investment has encouraged a growing number of the country's most able young managers to learn foreign management and methods at Western business schools. Going to overseas MBA courses provides company employees with a more in-depth knowledge of Western business. However, the overall number of students with MBAs in Japan remains low by international standards.

It is, however, hard to find precise figures on Japanese management students abroad. One source suggests that one percent of potential top executives in top firms are sent on courses in overseas business schools (see Okazaki-Ward 1993: 261, Table 5–12). It is estimated that there are over 3,000 in the US, mostly at high-status business schools such as MIT's Sloan School of Management, where one in eight Master's candidates are from Japan. Against this total, it is said Japan itself only produces around 1,000 MBAs as such a year, apart from other Master's degrees in related fields.

We may conclude that cross-cultural transfer at graduate business schools level has been limited and that those offering MBA degrees are not the rule in Japanese management education, but could perhaps ultimately expand in a similar way to Western Europe, which previously had only a patchy representation of such schools up to the early 1980s. It is still early days as yet, however. The number of Masters courses is relatively low, with even fewer on Doctoral programmes in management and related areas. Japan has frequently been a 'late developer' in many respects (see Warner 1987) but whether there will be more than a modest expansion of such advanced-level courses in the near future remains to be seen. In turn, management programmes offering cross-cultural skills remain limited.

CONCLUDING REMARKS

While academic-level management studies was long considered rather remote from the world of Japanese corporate culture, this has changed in recent years. Formerly, undergraduate courses were seen as merely a cultural spearhead of foreign influences in the form of classroom interpretations of North American management theories and research. Now, more local academic experts and university departments are involved in management training in large enterprises at a practical level (see Okazaki-Ward 1993: 454 ff) as part of the need to 'globalize' their activities and prepare suitable pesonnel to fit into these. Not only external management education provision is in flux, but in-house training and development are also undergoing many changes (see Sano 1996). Japanese Business has its sights on the twenty-first century, and the highly qualified labour force it will need to cope with its new challenges. Whether they will have the appropriate cross-cultural management skills to cope with an increasingly globalized world is, however, debatable.

ACKNOWLEDGEMENTS

I would like to thank the Japan Institute of Labour, Japan Institute of Social Economic Affairs and *Monbusho*, the Japanese Ministry of Education, Science and Culture for their assistance in providing data on higher education in Japan.

REFERENCES

Ballon, R.J. (1971) Top executives and company presidents in Japan: Function and personality. *Bulletin No 27*, Sophia University Socio-Economic Institute, Tokyo.

Checkland, O. (1988) 'Vain' learning and the advent of political economy in Meiji Japan in *Enlightenment and Beyond: Political Economy Comes to Japan*, (eds C. Sugiyama and H. Mitzuta) University of Tokyo Press, Tokyo, pp. 257–71.

Collins, K. (1989) Management Education in Japan, in *Management Education: An International Survey* (ed. W.J. Byrt) Routledge, London, pp. 172–209.

Dore, R. and Sako, M. (1989) *How the Japanese Learn to Work*, Routledge, London.

Francks, P. (1992) *Japanese Economic Development*, Routledge, London.

Gow, I. (1988) Japan, in *Making Managers*, (eds C. Handy *et al.*) Pitman, London, pp. 16–50.

HMI (Her Majesty's Inspectorate) (1991) *Aspects of Upper Secondary and Higher Education in Japan*, Department of Education and Science, HMSO, London.

Ishizaka, K. (1989) *School Education in Japan*, International Society for Education Information, Tokyo.

Keio University (1991) *Keio University Catalogue*, Keio University, Tokyo.

Kobe University (1991) *An Outline of Kobe University, 1990–1991*, Kobe University, Kobe.

Locke, R.R. (1984) *The End of Practical Man*, Cambridge University Press, Cambridge.

Locke, R.R. (1989) *Management and Higher Education Since 1940: The Influence of America and Japan on West Germany, Great Britain and France*, Cambridge University Press, Cambridge.

MacMillan, C. (1984) *The Japanese Industrial System*, De Gruyter, Berlin.

Monbusho (1993a) *Statistical Abstract of Education, Science and Culture*, Monbusho (Ministry of Education, Science and Culture), Tokyo, English edition.

Monbusho (1993b) *Report on Schools' Survey*, Monbusho (Ministry of Education, Science and Culture), Tokyo, Japanese edition.

Morris-Suzuki, T. (1989) *A History of Modern Japanese Economic Thought*, Routledge, London.

Okazaki-Ward, L. (1993) *Management Education and Training in Japan*, Graham and Trotman-Kluwer, London.

Refsing, K. (1992) Japanese educational expansion: Quality or equality, in *Ideology and Practice in Japan* (eds R. Goodman and K. Refsing), Routledge, London, pp. 116–29.

Sano, Y. (1996) Japanese management education, in *International Encyclopedia of Business and Management* (ed M. Warner) Routledge, London, 6 volumes.

Sasaki, N. (1981) *Management and Industrial Structure in Japan*, Pergamon Press, Oxford.

Sheridan, K. (1993) *Governing the Japanese Economy*, Polity Press, Oxford.

Stephens, M. (1991) *Education and the Future of Japan*, Japan Library, London.

Sugiyama, C. (1994) *The Origins of Economic Thought in Modern Japan*, Routledge, London.

Sugiyama, C. and Nishizawa, T. (1988) 'Captain of Industry': Tokyo Commercial School at Hitotsubashi', in *Enlightenment and Beyond:*

Political Economy Comes to Japan (eds C. Sugiyama and H. Mizuta) pp. 151–69.

Warner, M. (1987) Industrialization, management education and training systems: A comparative analysis. *Journal of Management Studies*, **24**: pp. 91–111.

Warner, M. (1994) Japanese culture, Western management: Taylorism and human resources in Japan. *Organization Studies*, **15**: pp. 509–34.

Westney, D.E. (1987) *Imitation and Innovation: The Transfer of Western Organizational Patterns to Meiji Japan*, Harvard University Press, Cambridge, MA.

Chapter 17

A world turned upside down: doing business in Asia

Charles M. Hampden-Turner and Fons Trompenaars

INTRODUCTION

Approaches to values and to moral reasoning differ markedly among nations: (Hofstede 1972; Hall 1976). The view taken here is that while virtually all members of the human race engaged in enterprise face the same problems or dilemmas, their responses to these vary widely (Hampden-Turner 1994).

All human beings have a logical, sense-making view of the world which works for them, after a fashion. In the case of Japan it obviously works *very* well in certain fields, while remaining strange to westerners. In the case of China, it has resulted in 10.4% annual growth rate averaged over a decade. That happens to be faster than any nation has *ever* grown in the history of capitalism. And it is not happening in Taiwan or Hong Kong with relatively small populations. It is happening to 1.2 billion people, with parts of China, Guangdong Province, for example, with a population larger than England and Wales, growing at 25%–30% a year.

In the industrial revolution in Britain and North America, GNP annual growth rarely topped 3%. Around 0.5% to 1.0% was the norm (Dobbs 1951). The rest of the world was not growing at all and the technologies had to be pioneered which the Chinese have only to borrow. Nevertheless, 10% growth per annum for 1.2 billion people is going to change everything. The centre of gravity for world economic development is going to swing decisively eastwards. That a country still officially communist has beaten all capitalist growth records is, to say the least, ironic. Since 1987, Thailand has grown 11.8% and growth rates in Malaysia, Singapore, Korea, Taiwan, Indonesia and Hong Kong are nearly all from 5% to 8% per annum. Although Japan's recent slowing of growth is consistent with the ideas that mature economies slow down, Singapore's 8% forecast for 1995 to 1997 is not.

DILEMMA METHODOLOGY

Our methodology (Trompenaars 1994; Hampden-Turner and Trompenaars 1994) assumes that everyone in the world is alike in certain key respects, but are almost opposite and nearly upside down in others. We are all alike in the fact that we face key dilemmas. All of us have to reconcile communities with individuals, rules with exceptions, wholes with atoms or parts, ideas within us with developments outside us, time passing with timeliness, equality with hierarchy. Conflicts between these elements constitute dilemmas and dilemmas are as old as recorded civilization. We encounter dilemma in The Garden of Eden and on the road to Thebes when Oedipus confronted the riddle of the Sphinx. Those who cannot solve riddles and dilemmas may be destroyed by them. Cultures try to pass on the answers to future generations and where they cannot, they pass on the problem for future generations to ponder, as in Melville (1981). Sphinx would eat you if you could not solve the riddle, much as people who cannot solve dilemmas are destroyed today. But where people of the world differ is in the horn of the dilemma with which they start the work of reconciliation. Some cultures put the individual before the community. They argue, for example, that if each person were taken care of, the good society would follow. Some cultures put the community before the individual. If the community is taken care of, then individuals will find their fulfilment and happiness in this responsibility. So cultures are very different, indeed they are opposite, in the priorities they set. Yet we are all united by the same issues. Somehow, some way individuals must be joined to their community. We seek the same ends; we employ different means.

THE MEANING OF CULTURE

Culture means 'to work upon'. Hence agriculture works upon crops; horticulture works upon plants; aquaculture works upon the water; culture works upon human environments. Cultures say 'the rule comes before the exception' or vice versa. Cultures are not right or wrong, they simply have orientations to issues. They say 'this is the way you set about to solve this problem . . .' Why must they agree on this? Because there would be chaos unless they did so. Everyone must stop at red lights and go on at green ones. If half the population had a different preference, driving would be a lot more hazardous than it is already. Similarly, if half the population was taught to be selfish and half unselfish, the first half would exploit the second half and there would be furious recrimination. You have to 'work upon' your environment in similar ways if civic order is to be maintained; expectations must be shared.

SEVEN CULTURAL BIFURCATIONS

Trompenaars (1994) identified seven important dimensions on which cultures disagree. Faced with an existential question or basic dilemma of being, they go opposite ways. The seven dilemmas are as follows:

Universalism vs. particularism

When no code, rule or law seems to quite cover an exceptional case, should the most relevant rule be imposed, however imperfectly, on that case, or should the case be considered on its unique merits, regardless of the rule? At stake here is the relative salience of *rules* (universal) or *exceptions* (particulars).

Analysed specifics vs. integrated wholes

Are we more effective as managers when we analyse phenomena into *specifics*, i.e. parts, facts, targets, tasks, numbers, units, points, or when we integrate and configure such details into diffuse patterns, relationships and wider contexts? At stake here is the relative salience of *analysed specifics* vs. *integrated wholes*.

Individualism vs. communitarianism

Is it more important to focus upon the enhancement of each individual, his or her rights, motivations, rewards, capacities, attitudes, or should more attention be paid to the advancement of the corporation as a community, which all its members are pledged to serve?

Inner-directed vs. outer-directed orientation

Which are the more important guides to action, our inner-directed judgements, decisions and commitments, or the signals, demands and trends in the outside world to which we must adjust? At stake here is whether virtue and right direction is located *within* us or *outside* us.

Time as sequence vs. time as synchronization

Is it more important to do things fast, in the shortest possible sequence of passing time, or to synchronize all efforts, just-in-time, so that completion is co-ordinated? At stake is *time-as-a-race* vs. *time-as-a-dance*.

Achieved status vs. ascribed

Should the status of employees depend on what they have achieved and how they have performed, or on some other characteristic important to the corporation, i.e. age, seniority, gender, education, potential, strategic role? At stake is *judging by results* vs. *a priori judgements*.

Equality vs. hierarchy

Is it more important that we treat employees as equals so as to elicit from them the best they have to give, or to emphasize the judgement and authority of the hierarchy that is coaching and evaluating them? At stake is the *equality of process* vs. *the authority of judging and sponsoring* the contest itself.

To say that cultures 'differ' on the relative importance of these values is an understatement: often such issues are loaded with ideological fervour. How often have we heard colleagues call for more 'law and order' (universalism) and less indulgence towards suspected wrongdoers (particularism). Some managers demand 'the facts' and 'the bottom line' (analysis) and regard all attempts to put these into context (integration) as mere window dressing. If there are problems in the organization, they look for specific persons or 'troublemakers' to blame (individualism) for a 'rotten apple in the barrel'. In their view, there is nothing wrong with the organization (communitarianism) that cannot be cured by 'kicking asses and taking names'.

Everyone should be a 'self-starter' (inner-directed) and must beware of 'group think' and running with the herd (outer-directed). Employees must realize that 'time is money' and efficiency the key (sequential time). Workers must get on with the job and not talk all the time (synchronize their efforts). For ten years our manager has been 'busting his gut' to succeed in a job he was given (status by achievement) but now some wise guy has 'moved the goal posts' (altered the kinds of work to which status is ascribed). All he ever wanted was 'an even break' (equality) but the people 'up there' (hierarchy) were not interested.

We can see from these examples that values clash, misunderstandings are rife and getting values to harmonize in ways that create wealth is not an easy task. Foreigners are seen as subversive of what we believe in. Let us take these dilemmas one by one.

UNIVERSALISM VS. PARTICULARISM

How can we measure the relative enthusiasm a culture has for making rules (universalism) vs. discovering exceptions (particularism). Our methodology consists of dilemmas. Here is one:

You are riding in a car driven by a close friend. He hits a pedestrian. You know he was going at least 35 miles per hour in an area of the city where the maximum allowed speed is 20 miles per hour. There are no witnesses. His lawyer says that if you testify under oath that he was only driving 20 miles per hour it may save him from serious consequences. What right has your friend to expect you to protect him?

(a) My friend has a definite right as a friend to expect me to testify to the lower figure.
(b) He has some right as a friend to expect me to testify to the lower figure.
(c) He has no right as a friend to expect me to testify to the lower figure.

Here is how the different nations scored:

Table 17.1 Responses to Question 1											
Universalism 'no right'										*. . . Particularism* 'some or definite right'	
CAN	USA	GER	UK	NL	FRA	JP	SIN	THAI	HK	CHI	SK
96	95	90	90	88	68	67	67	63	56	48	26

Why does Canada, and for that matter America, score so consistently high in Universalism? One reason is that they all share a British heritage in which the rule of law looms large, but in addition to this they are all *immigrant nations*, which causes them to score even higher than the UK. Why should immigration matter? Because under immigration *you have to teach new rules to adults*. You cannot rely on nearly everyone having been taught what is right at their mother's knee, and 'mother's knee' is probably the chief source of particularism. You cherish those with whom you have special relationships, wives, children, husbands, relations, friends (Lipset 1974).

There is also a consistent Protestant background to nations high in universalism. The Protestants believed that the written word of God in the newly-translated bible was the universal code all people should live by. Catholics offered you many special relationships with the saints of your choice. Note the sizeable jump from Protestant Netherlands to Catholic France although both countries are contiguous geographically. The Roman Catholic confessional in which your particular relationship with the priest is secret, cannot easily be generalized from. The six Asian countries in Table 17.1 – Japan, Singapore, Hong Kong, China, Thailand

and South Korea – are, on the whole, even more particularistic, The USA and Canada are consistently the more universalistic cultures on earth (Bellah 1985).

Or consider another question:

You are a doctor for an insurance company. You examine a close friend who needs more insurance. You find that he is in pretty good shape, but you are doubtful on one or two minor points which are difficult to diagnose. What right does your friend have to expect you to shade the doubts in his favour?

A   My friend would have a definite right as a friend to expect me to shade the doubts in his favour.
B   He would have some right as a friend to expect me to shade the doubts in his favour.
C   He would have no right as a friend to expect me to shade the doubts in his favour.

Here is how the different nations answered to Choice C:

Table 17.2 Responses to Question 2

CAN	UK	US	FR	NL	GER	JP	SIN	CHI	IDO	HK	SK
79	70	69	62	59	59	54	52	48	48	42	24

Or consider a third dilemma:

You have just come from a secret meeting of the board of directors of a company. You have a close friend who will be ruined unless he can get out of the market before the board's decision becomes known. You happen to be having dinner at the friend's home this evening. What right does your friend have to expect you to tip him off?

A   He has a definite right as a friend to expect me to tip him off.
B   He has some right as a friend to expect me to tip him off.
C   He has no right as a friend to expect me to tip him off.

Here is how the different nations scored on Choice C:

Table 17.3 Responses to Question 3

JP	CAN	US	GER	UK	NL	THAI	FR	CHI	HK	SIN	SK
87	84	83	66	65	62	56	56	53	47	43	31

Consider the implications for a life-insurance industry seeking to expand into SE Asia?

The first implication is that 'the letter of the law', the requirement that the insured and his/her doctor follow universal rules of truthful witness in making out the application form, is not going to stir up much enthusiasm in SE Asia. In reality, 74% of South Koreans would perjure themselves in a court of law to help their best friend; 52% of mainland Chinese would do so; 58% of the managers in Hong Kong, and we are speaking of the *middle class*, would side with their friend, were they a doctor, examining a patient under contract to an insurer. These are not legal-rational cultures. Just as they have difficulties with the idea of 'human rights' as an abstract Western concept, so they have difficulties with putting abstract codes ahead of living people all together.

If a person cannot help his/her best friend, what is law worth? Your friend pleads with you. You put an abstract principle ahead of your friend, and it is not just SE Asia. It is much of Latin Europe. In our sample, we had a French female executive from Air France. She waved her hand – 'What happened to the pedestrian?' she wanted to know. 'The pedestrian died . . .' we said, '. . . does it matter?' 'Of course it matters!' she said. 'If the pedestrian died I would side with my friend! After all, what can I do for the pedestrian now?' And she had a good point. Only universalists laugh; to a particularist, there are particular people to be helped.

Does this mean that essentially SE Asians, not to mention the French, have no morals to speak of? Not at all. Their moral view is simply different. The particular relationship, in these cases friendship, are seen as stronger in their obligations, than are rules. Confucius, for example, said: 'the son must hide the father's crime. The father must lean towards his son's advantage.' It is clear from this passage that particularism is strongly to be preferred for children and is to be given moderate priority by parents in matters involving their children.

In 1980, attempts by the government to insure bicycles in China had to be abandoned in the face of floods of claims, all with police certificates attached. As of last year you could insure yourself against AIDS for three years, for 90 yen, roughly $12 US. In order to make insurance work in most of SE Asia, friends must sell to friends and false information of false claims must be detectable by the friendship network and must be inconsistent with the maintenance of that friendship network. If claims are subtracted from premiums in every friendship network, so that the seller and the claimant, although strongly related, have an opposite balance of interests, then Asian particularisms will balance out as a bargain.

We have to realize that for these cultures, laws are not unimportant, but they originate in friendship. We must therefore design the system so that

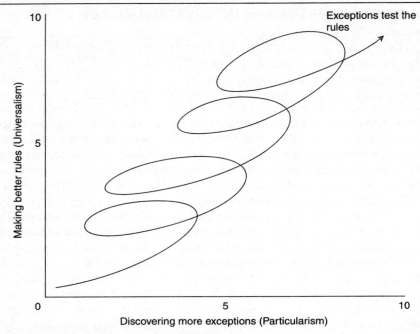

Figure 17.1 Universalism versus particularism

friendship, *not* abstract principle, monitors and controls the process. Do not assume that third parties, like doctors, will be neutral. The doctor must be a friend of the local agent or representatives, or he may sign up people after their cancer has been diagnosed. Readers may feel we are libelling particularist cultures, but this is not so. In our view, rules are breaking down in the West on a massive scale because the particular relationships within the family are breaking down. Law and order must be supported by the networks of friendship and family in a culture. The Chinese concept of *guanxi*, 'bond between people' and the Japanese advocacy of *'wan'* or harmony in relationships are values that underpin morality and will, in most cases, support the law of the land as well. These and 'the spirit of the law' and laws may not survive their absence. Perhaps the clue to understanding Universalism vs. Particularism is to see that they are interdependent views upon the human condition. You can only make better rules if you heed all exceptions. You only appreciate unique exceptions if you are aware of the rules. Each potentially enhances the other so:

The spiral illustrates the concept that people generalize from fortunate experiences during socialization and derive from these particular experiences universal legal and moral principals (see Hampden-Turner 1994).

ANALYSED SPECIFICS VS. INTEGRATED WHOLES

Here the question is what a culture does when faced with a complex phenomenon. Should we immediately analyse it to specific 'points' or atoms, making 'bullet statements', or should we search for the pattern and structure that integrates the whole?

Consider, for example, the definition of 'a good manager':

A Some argue that a good manager is a person who gets the job done. He takes care of the information, people and equipment needed for the execution of the tasks. He leaves his subordinates free to do their part of the job and intervenes only if necessary.

B Others argue that a good manager is a person who gets his group of subordinates working well together. He knows the right answer to most of the questions arising at work. He guides his subordinates continuously and helps them solve various problems, ranging from work-related problems. He is a kind of father.

Question:

Which one of these two descriptions do you think best represents a good manager, A or B?

This question poses a choice between a set of discrete and specific entities, 'gets the job done', 'takes care of people', 'provided information and equipment', 'lets the subordinates do their parts'. All these are specific units or atoms.

The alternative description, however, is irreducible to parts, 'gets subordinates working well together', 'guides subordinates continuously and helps them solve various problems'. Finally a familial metaphor is used. It all speaks of wholeness and integration. Various cultures scored as follows on endorsing A – 'gets on with the job'.

Table 17.4 Responses to Question 4

CAN	FRA	GER	USA	NL	UK	JP	THAI	MAL	CHI	HK	SIN
95	89	87	85	81	78	69	67	63	57	45	38

Here we see that Asian countries Japan, Thailand, Malaysia, China, Hong Kong and Singapore all tend toward the holistic end.

Or consider a second dilemma:

A meeting is called to take a decision about the dismissal of an employee. He has worked 15 years for the company and performed his job in a satisfactory way. For various reasons last year, the results of his work dropped to an unsatisfactory level. There are no reasons to believe that this situation will improve.

The members of the meeting are divided into two parties and come up with the following arguments:

A One part of the group says that the job performance should remain the criterion for the dismissal, regardless of the age of the person and his previous record.

B The other part of the group argued that one cannot disregard the 15 years the employee has been working for the company. One has to take into account the company's responsibility for his life.

Question:

Which one of these two ways of reasoning do you think is usually best in these cases, A or B?

Here we have a choice of narrowing down the discussion to a specific, a single indisputable fact, the employee's work is unsatisfactory, as of now. He is not fulfilling his contract. He is not doing a good job.

Is this the only consideration or must we look at it in context? What about his 15 years with the company, the effect on the morale of other employees, management's responsibility for not supervising him better – does none of this matter? A lot of clarity and precision comes to our thinking, only by excluding several considerations. Here is how the various cultures scored on Choice A:

Table 17.5 Responses to Question 5

CAN	USA	CHI	HK	UK	THAI	JP	GER	NL	FRA	SIN	IND
59	52	48	47	41	38	37	37	36	28	20	13

Here China scores remarkably high. Perhaps the recent legal changes modifying lifetime employment in Warner (1995a and b) give us a clue.

A major element of specific vs. diffuse thinking is the number of mental divisions you make. The Dutch feel they can criticize your work as 'crazy' and this does not insult you. The Italians stormed out of a meeting with Dutch engineers because to call the work of Italian designers crazy is to insult the designers. Their work and their persons are an indivisible whole. Is your boss in charge of your work life only, or is he your boss in all things? Some cultures have a diffuse sense of authority, some a narrow, specific sense of authority.

When, for example, one is invited to speak at a North American

University one can be 'Professor' at the lectern, but Charles in the bar, or worse Chuck or Chuckles at a late night drink, or down at the bowling alley, 'Hey buddy, get outa the way'! In France, Monsieur Le Directeur carries his status with him even in his bathing trunks. In Germany, a wife would be 'Frau Professor' even in the supermarket. Your status spreads around you like ripples in a pond.

We posed the following dilemma to pick up this aspect of specific diffuse:

A boss asks a subordinate to help him paint his house. The subordinate, who did not feel like doing it, discusses the issue with a colleague:

A The colleague argues: 'You don't have to paint if you don't feel like it. He is your boss in the company. Outside the company he has little authority'.

B The subordinate argues: 'Despite the fact that I don't feel like it, I will paint anyway. He is my boss, and you cannot ignore it outside your work either'.

Question:

Which of the two arguments do you think is usually best in these cases, A or B?

The scores were as follows for Choice A:

Table 17.6 Responses to Question 6											
Refuse to paint											
NL	FRA	UK	GER	CAN	JP	HK	MAL	THAI	SIN	IDO	CHI
93	93	93	89	84	83	66	64	60	56	48	28

We see China at the most diffuse end on this issue. Around 72% would paint their boss's house at the weekend even when they didn't want to. We asked several of my Chinese friends why this was. Curiously it has to do with learning which spreads out through diffuse relationships. The maxim is: If a person is your teacher for even one day, he is a lifetime father'. Just as your boss's teaching spreads through your whole life, so must his influence.

Perils of negotiating

Regarding parts or wholes as the starting point occasions massive mis-understandings. When Americans or the British go abroad they tend to 'get to the point'. They say 'Here is my proposition', 'This is the deal', 'Here is my product', 'Let's get down to brass tacks', 'Don't beat about the bush'. We do this to save time and to zero in on 'the target'. After all, there are hundreds of people whom it would be nice to have tea with, but only one or two are likely to do a deal with us. It makes sense therefore to get to know the person *after* we have talked turkey to him or her. That's common sense surely? Here are the two styles:

USA/UK   JAPAN/SE ASIA

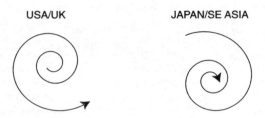

Figure 17.2 Circling round or getting straight to the point

The Anglo-Saxons tend to start in the middle of the spiral on the left and then to circle from specific to more general. The Japanese, Asians generally, but also Southern Europeans and in the American Deep South, there is a tendency to start at the outside of the spiral on the right, talk all around the point for several minutes or even hours and get to the point at the end.

Is this all time-wasting nonsense? Not if you think that the real scarcity is good relationships as opposed to tempting propositions; if you hope that this relationship can last two decades at least; if your biggest night-mare is a relationship that fails five years from now after you have poured your time and money into it. After all, it is easy for A to con B about a profitable deal. It is virtually impossible for A to con B about a broad-ranging discussion that touches on mutual friends and mutual tastes, so the Japanese find that it saves them time and money to simulate, early on, all the variations a durable relationship is likely to encounter. *All cultures are logical.* They simply start from different premises.

Westerners often have difficulty in SE Asia with the idea of contracts. For most of us in the West a contract is what it says, no more, no less. If you don't read the small print the judge will. But in much of SE Asia the general intention of the parties and the fund of goodwill they have for each other is the prime consideration. If circumstances change, they will expect their insurance cover or pension fund to change along with their lives. We are beginning to do this in the West, but these are small departures from the idea of fixity. The Chinese don't have the notion of fixity to begin with. The *Tao*, the *Ying* and *Yang* are eternally ebbing and flowing like the tide – we accommodate each other.

A few years ago the Japanese got into a dispute with Australian sugar exporters. When the world price of sugar fell by $10 the Japanese asked to renegotiate. Was not mutuality the main thing? For the Australians the contract said it all. Get a better lawyer next time! The 'small print' in our contracts is not decisive for most SE Asians. The Chinese way is to get a local wise person to arbitrate, to try and settle disputes amicably and keep the relationship. This can only work if the company's interests are represented at local level. One reason Confucianism is so popular today in China is that Mao tried to suppress it. He failed. The universal communist system with its specific codes could not prevail against the ever shifting tides of personal relationships. As Confucius said: 'If your friend gives you a peach, you give him a plum'. In other words, give him something different, particularly personal, not specified in advance.

An observation of the Japanese is that they do not look at a business relationship as a lot of profitable deals added up. They are often prepared to make seeming losses in the early stages. We say 'seeming' because what is really happening is that you give your partner or customer *more* than was contracted, but your customer must then reciprocate *more* than he was given. He may even go broke if you do not return even more. Many Asian relationships have escalating obligations of this kind. You cannot give away the store, because those you give it to are busy shovelling it back at you. Mutual gratitude and obligations are the cement of these cultures. Once again, Analysing Specifics vs. Integrating Wholes is a reconcilable dilemma, see below. The other side of the world knows the other side of truth.

INDIVIDUALISM VS. COMMUNITARIANISM

Is it more important to focus on the enhancement of each individual, or should more attention be paid to the advancement of groups in which many individuals have membership? 'We believe in the dignity, indeed the sacredness of the individual', wrote Robert Bellah (1984) in *Habits of the Heart*. 'Anything that would violate our right to think for ourselves, judge for ourselves, make our own decisions, live our lives as we see fit, is not only morally wrong, it is sacrilegious'. Americans and Canadians are easily the most individualistic nations on earth, as our research shows. We asked our samples the following question:

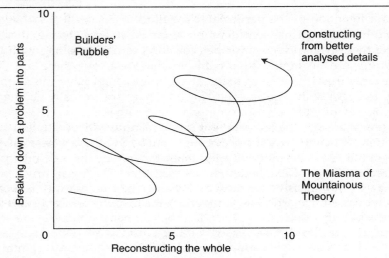

Figure 17.3 Analysing versus synthesizing

In the case one gets promoted, two of the following issues can be emphasized:

A The new group of people with whom one will work.

B The bigger responsibility of the work and the higher income.

Question:

Which one of these two issues would you emphasize more strongly in case of a promotion, A or B?

The answers were as follows for Choice B:

Table 17.7 Responses to Question 7											
Bigger responsibilities and income											
CAN	THAI	UK	USA	NL	FRA	JP	CHI	SIN	HK	MAL	KOR
77	71	69	66	64	61	61	54	50	47	38	32

Clearly Canadians and surprisingly the Thais, go for bigger personal responsibility and personal income. The Chinese, Singaporeans, Hong Kong, Malaysian and Korean managers are all more concerned with the new group of people with whom they will be working. Presumably an independent person would want to find his/her own house and locate his/her own property and would not expect the company or community to provide this. So we asked:

Different people have different opinions about the responsibility a company carries for the housing of its employees:

A   Some people think a company is usually responsible for the housing of its employees. Therefore, a company has to assist an employee in finding a housing facility.

B   Other people think the responsibility for housing should be carried by the employee himself. It is so much to the good if a company helps.

Question:

Do you think the responsibility of a company for housing is best represented by A or B?

The results from our sample of cultures were as follows to Choice B:

Table 17.8 Responses to Question 8												
USA	NL	UK	HK	FR	CAN	GER	MAL	THAI	SIN	JP	IDO	CHI
86	83	83	82	81	77	76	76	76	72	45	26	18

In this case Malaysia, Thailand, Singapore and Hong Kong all side with the West. But 55% of Japanese managers, 74% of Indonesian managers and 82% of Chinese managers expected the company to provide housing. This is a massive responsibility. If you want to fire the employee you must either evict the whole family or have a malcontent on your property. In practice, most employees in Communitarian countries stay put.

We next compared two motives for working:

Two persons were discussing ways in which one could improve the quality of life:

A   One said: it is obvious that if one has as much freedom as possible and the maximum opportunity to develop oneself, the quality of one's life would improve as a result.

B   Another said: if the individual is continuously taking care of his fellow men the quality of life of us all will improve, even if it obstructs individual freedom and individual development.

Question:

Which of the two ways of reasoning do you think is usually best, A or B?

The scores were as follows for Choice A:

Table 17.9 Responses to Question 9												
CAN	US	IDO	NL	HK	UK	CHI	JP	GER	SIN	THAI	SK	FR
79	79	71	69	69	66	64	60	59	50	50	49	48

Here the surprise is how high some nations of SE Asia score. Indonesia is up there with the Netherlands. China is only marginally below the UK with Japan at 60%. We took these results to Chinese colleagues. 'See' we said, 'only the French are still enamoured with dedication to their fellow man'. 'No, you *don't* see', they told us, 'freedom in this context does not mean freedom of the individual but of the *group* to serve the rest of society in the way it chooses. Freedom of the individual from the group hardly exists in China. One person cannot grow rice – it takes at least 12 to 20'. In Japan, for example, the word for individual is 'person-among-others'. You can say 'person-on-their-own' but the expression is one of sadness and regret as you say it – the implication is of an outcast.

North America tends to celebrate 'Man Alone'. Hans Solo of 'Star Wars', Rick the hard-boiled cynical saloon keeper in 'Casablanca'. Such individuals are symbolized by Lone Ranger, Lone Eagles, innovative seagulls, hard-bitten detectives, mountain men, mavericks, lovable bank robbers, pool-sharks, con men, junk bond salesmen, even Colonel Oliver North. TV series' end routinely with the hero riding off alone into the next episode. Extraordinary invention goes into justifying their aloneness, for example, a medical condition in which you turn green and burst out of your shirt.

The point is not that these individuals think of only themselves. Great Britain owes Andrew Carnegie much of its public library system. Individualism properly understood leaves you free to be selfish and selfless. The point is that this is the heroes' choice. Thus, in 'Star Wars' Hans Solo rushes to the rescue of Luke Skywalker and Rick in 'Casablanca' joins the battle against fascism at the cost of his love life.

What distinguishes individualism from communitarianism is not the individual's *motive*, which may be social but where value is seen to accrue. Even in Salem Village, Alcoholics Anonymous or Mothers against Drunk Driving value accrues to the freely associating individual who formed the covenant with others. In Bunyan's *Pilgrims Progress*, Christian literally shakes off his wife and child, shouting 'Salvation, I will have salvation!' He then treks off alone in search of the Celestial City and of his family we hear no more. Once he gets to the city one assumes community will be restored to him. In the meantime and for the whole story, he walks alone amid friends and flatterers. It is a secularly Protestant way of thinking.

One reason for the headlong Chinese growth rates is their savings rate of 37%. This in turn is part of Buddhism. You are likely to be reincarnated at least twice and since no one can remember their previous life, this is the first go round. It follows that you should invest in the environment to

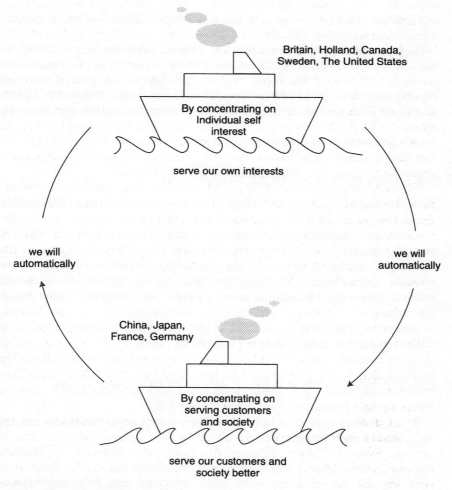

Figure 17.4 Ships that pass in the night

which you will return and the more you invest the higher is the station to which you will return. Chinese levels of investment are far too high to be motivated simply by a personal desire for profit. Money is pouring into China from Hong Kong, Singapore, Taiwan, Malaysia and overseas Chinese populations in towns like Vancouver. These people see their ancient country arising like a Phoenix and they want to be part of its collective expression.

Ever since a Scottish tutor called Adam Smith taught us that an Invisible Hand would turn our selfishness into public service, we have assumed that this is the only way the equation works. SE Asia has turned Adam Smith upside down. These cultures argue in exactly the opposite sequence, from concern for customers and the community will come the self interest of all concerned. We call this 'Ships Which Pass in the Night'. It is illustrated in Figure 17.4.

There is a fair amount of mystification about individualism in the West. We know from psychological research about individuals who refuse to conform (Milgram 1963), refuse to torture a fake assistant in a learning experiment. Refuseniks are *well* socialized, not badly socialized. When you stand alone, all those who ever loved you stand ghost-like by your side.

Let us now turn to our fourth diversion.

INNER-DIRECTED VS. OUTER-DIRECTED

By which moral compass should we steer, by *inner* convictions and beliefs or by the ebb and flow of forces in the *external universe*?

Americans, Britons and Canadians are not just individualists in valuing the individual above the group, they believe that the origins of all important social and physical forces lie within the protean person. It is possible to be thoroughly individualistic, as are the Dutch, and still believe your environment has more powers than you have. The Dutch have learned in their long battle with the sea that huge powers are located in the environment.

We administered the following questions:

A Without the right breaks one cannot be an effective leader.

B Capable people who fail to become leaders have not taken advantage of their opportunities.

Clearly the second option is inner-directed and the first is outer-directed. Here is how cultures scored on Choice B:

Table 17.10 Responses to Question 10												
MAL	US	CAN	SIN	THAI	UK	GER	HK	JP	FR	NL	CHI	IND
82	80	71	70	67	66	52	51	51	50	48	39	36

Note that Malaysia is the most inner-directed of all, although we need to be cautious because most of these results are from one star Motorola plant in Penang. Singaporeans are inner-directed, but Chinese and Indonesians are outer-directed. The scores vary when we vary the questions:

A I have often found what is going to happen will happen.

B Trusting to fate has never turned out as well for me as making a decision to take a definite course of action.

Table 17.11 Responses to Question 11											
CAN	GER	MAL	US	UK	FR	CHI	NL	THAI	HK	JP	SIN
88	83	82	80	73	72	71	68	65	64	49	32

Canadians are especially down on 'trusting to fate'. Singaporeans and Japanese are attracted to this but not the Chinese. One reason we were told is that if you work hard the fates are supposed to respond. You do not trust them, you push them. Small differences in wording make all the difference. Consider:

A Becoming a success is a matter of hard work, luck has little or nothing to do with it.

B Getting a job depends mainly on being in the right place at the right time.

Table 17.12 Responses to Question 12												
MAL	CAN	US	CHI	FR	IND	GER	UK	HK	NL	SIN	THAI	JP
82	72	69	59	57	56	55	50	47	46	44	40	39

The Chinese are decidedly on the side of hard work with luck obliging. But five nations from Hong Kong to Japan feel that being in the right place at the right time is the most important, even the British divide evenly.

A Most people don't realize the extent to which their lives are controlled by accidental happenings.

B There is really no such thing as 'luck'.

Table 17.13 Responses to Question 13												
There is no such thing as 'luck'												
MAL	CAN	FR	US	GER	HK	NL	THAI	UK	SIN	IND	CHI	JP
45	42	39	38	36	31	27	27	25	19	18	14	13

But ask the Chinese to deny the role of luck in their lives and they refuse by a larger percentage, 86%. So what is going on here? Are outer-directed people merely the tellers of hard luck stories? Surely what we are encountering here is a form of moral inferiority, people who decline to take responsibility for their own lives, fail to carry enough insurance and so on.

If that is how it seems then this is because our questionnaires originated in the West and we failed to tap the logic behind outer-directness. In much of SE Asia being stronger or better than your environment is not admired. What is idealized is *wa*, or harmony, that is, being harnessed to your environment. A Japanese axiom states 'Man alone is weak, but harnessed to nature he is strong'. Martial arts like judo and aikido use the strength and momentum of opponents.

Moreover, religions like Shinto or Buddhism are partly nature worship. You should be as serene as the lily pond, fierce as the fire, swift as the wind. Westerners complain when Asians 'follow fast' and catch us up, but that is what outer-directedness is all about. You jump on the back of a new technology invented in the West and domesticate it like a wild horse. You

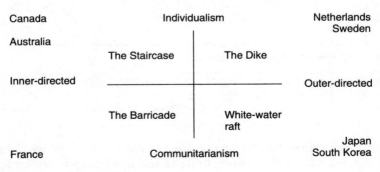

Figure 17.5 Two-way matrix

even get to market sooner with a product for customers because, of course, the outer-directed are more customer orientated.

The Japanese comic book hero is not Superman, but Monkey. The way of Monkey is to spring on the backs of stronger creatures and be borne along in directions he too wishes to travel. There are free rides after all if you understand nature.

If we cross-correlate Individualism-Communitarianism with Inner-direction/Outer-direction we get some interesting combinations. See Figure 17.5.

In Canada, managers see themselves ascending a staircase or career ladder by dint of individual effort. In France the ethos is Communitarian, every worthwhile reform having been achieved by an angry group, but it is also *inner-directed*. Injustices ignite the consciences of organized people. The Netherlands and Sweden show a pattern of outer-directed individualism. Here the little Dutch boy put his finger into the dike to save everyone. Finally the Japanese, Chinese, Koreans, etc. show a pattern of Communitarian outer-directedness. We have caught this with the image of the White Water Raft, something that carries you along but which you adapt to, by hanging in there together. In fact Japanese top managers often refer to themselves as 'white water groups'.

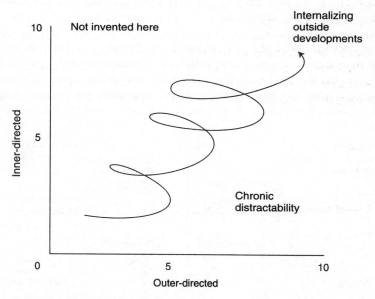

Figure 17.6 Inner versus outer-directed

Once again the ideal is reconciliation. The right direction is both inside us *and* outside us. We have to *internalize outside developments*, so:

Once again we have to avoid the extremes of Not Invented Here and Chronic Distractibility by circling progressively toward synergy.

TIME AS SEQUENTIAL VS. TIME AS SYNCHRONOUS

Should we see time as a *race* in which we must beat an adversary toward a 'finishing post' or is time more like a *dance*, in which steps are timely and elegantly co-ordinated? Edward T. Hall (1976).

The American view of time is time as a race. As the chorus sings in a Broadway musical:

> *When you're racing with the Clock*
> *The second hand doesn't understand*
> *That your back's all ache*
> *And your fingers break*
> *And your constitution isn't made of rock.*

This view of time believes in speeding up the assembly line as products are worked on one by one. The synchronous view does as much as possible in parallel processes and joins these. We measured the managers' conception of time by presenting our respondents with three circles drawn on a half sheet of paper representing past present and future. This is known as a projective test and was designed by Tom Cottle (1968). When we give this test two extreme reactions are possible, see Figure 17.7.

Sequential thinkers put past, present and future in a straight line, time stretched out and synchronous thinkers telescope time. In practice, few managers put the circles inside each other, although nearly one-third of Japanese, Chinese, South Korean and Singaporean managers did. The range is between those who overlap the circles while maintaining direc-

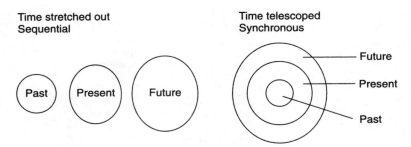

Time stretched out
Sequential

Past   Present   Future

Time telescoped
Synchronous

Future
Present
Past

Figure 17.7 Two models of time

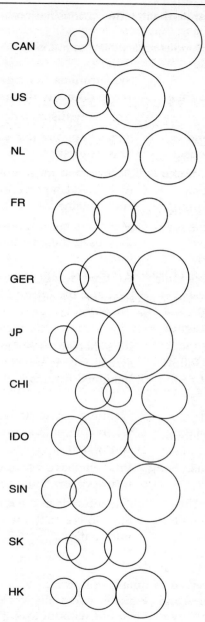

Figure 17.8 A projective test of time-orientation

tion and those who separate them. How various nations score is set out in Figure 17.8.

Sequential and synchronous styles vary as follows:

Sequential Managers	Synchronous Managers
Try to do one thing at a time	Try to do many things simultaneously
Concentrate on the job	Are easily distracted
Regard appointments and time commitments seriously	Regard appointments as modifiable, time as elastic
Accustomed to a series of short-term relationships, quickly broken and quickly reformed	Accustomed to durable relationships with friendships periodically renewed and sustained
Managers are responsible for present performance	Managers are responsible for how they used the past to advance the future
Time is real and objective which means that only the present is really knowable, the past and the future are remote from us	All time is only *ideas* of time. The past and the future are both fused in the present
Rationality is fault-free, provided future events follow immediately on present action like striking billiard balls	Reasonableness is encompassing and synchronizing past events with imagined futures
Planning has to do with forecasting and extrapolating trends.	Planning has to do with scenarios where alternative futures are considered.
Products are regarded as young, mature and dying	Products have genes which pass to future generations.
The future is far away. The discounted present value of a future income stream is usually small.	The future is in the room with us now. Start to create it and discover information.

Various nations conceived of time as follows:

Notice that the Japanese and Germans, two of the world's most successful economies, are highly overlapped but without losing a sense of direction. Our hypothesis is that harmonizing these two senses of time is most effective. Americans are stronger on sequential time than synchronous time, along with most English-speaking economies. For synchronous cultures, time is an old friend who keeps calling your age. He is not a grim reaper hovering near by. Old age is revered. Chinese grandparents play with their grandchildren almost as a cultural ritual.

Buddhist immortality is living through your children, falling like leaves from a tree to fertilize the ground. Life is not over when you die. You are likely not simply to be re-incarnated but watch silently over the welfare of children as an ancestral spirit. In Japanese Buddhism you enter the womb of great-granddaughter to be born again, but always you have watched over her. Products, too, pass on their 'genes', like a strand of DNA is passed on for ever to enrich the generations. Products procreate like families passing on genetic information.

Once again there is a culture of cultures.

ACHIEVEMENT VS. ASCRIPTION OF STATUS

Should all status be *achieved* by what the manager succeeds in accomplishing, or should at least part of it be *ascribed* a priori?

Achievement is close to being the cultural bedrock on which Britain and the USA are founded. It is surely in the interest of any organization that the best employees should rise in their influence and the mediocre or poor should move elsewhere. Employment contracts offer payment in exchange for work. What could be fairer than to pay more for better work and confer recognition and status commensurate with what the organization has received? It partakes of natural justice. Achievement provides feedback on how well the organization and the achiever is

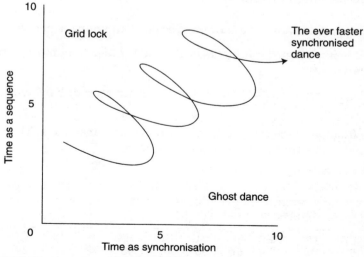

Figure 17.9 Time as sequence and synchronization

faring. By moving resources towards achieving groups you invest in success and amplify ability. Status by achievement is pragmatism applied to progress, rewarding best who or what works best. Achievement is the reality test of human potential . . .

If we have gone over the top in extolling achievement it is only to show how self-evidently right cultural beliefs are to those who hold them.

We asked our samples the following question:

The most important thing in life is to think and act in the ways that best suit the way you really are, even if you don't get things done.

This was rejected in the following proportions:

Table 17.14 Responses to Question 14

US	CAN	UK	GER	SIN	NL	HK	JP	SK	IND	CHI	FR
55	53	47	39	34	33	29	28	28	27	26	26

Of the Chinese 74% endorse being 'the way you are' because this is consistent with Tao. You harmonize with nature. You discover yourself as you discover the environment. The letter 'O' in Japanese means 'the way of'. Hence Bushido – the way of the sword, Shinto – the way of gods. To be 'the way you are' is thus admirable, more so than achieving if this violates your nature.

We asked three more questions about achieved vs. ascribed nature and lumped together the answers:

Older people should be more respected than younger people.

B It is important for a manager that he is older than most of his subordinates.

C Becoming successful and respected is a matter of hard work.

The first two were rejected by pro-achievement managers. The last was accepted. Here are the scores vis-à-vis Choice C:

Table 17.15 Responses to Question 15

US	CAN	UK	GER	FR	NL	SIN	HK	JP	SK	CHI	IDO
63	62	60	58	57	50	44	43	42	37	34	31

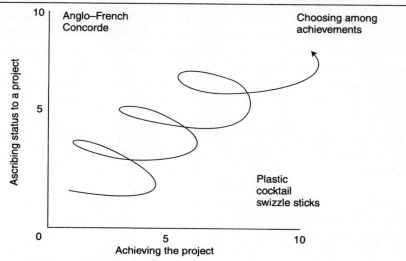

Figure 17.10 Status versus achievement

The mystery to many of us is how SE Asia can develop so fast without putting achievement motivation before anything else. Is the world economy really being changed not by movers and shakers but by people who defer to age and are searching for their own true nature?

What makes ascribed status potentially dynamic are two factors often overlooked. First, if you pay more for older people you have to train them or they simply lumber you with dead wood. Hence investment in human resources is massive in economies like Japan. If you are stuck with people for life you have to develop them. Secondly, status by achievement tends to look backwards towards what you did in the past. Only ascribed status can look to the future, calling something important because you want that project to succeed. Stated differently, to ascribe status to a person, project or technology makes it more likely it will be achieved. It is a self-fulfilling prophecy. For it is surely an advantage to make a product which your culture has long admired, as the British admire theatre, the Japanese miniaturization. In other words, status is first ascribed to particular activities and then they are made to world-class standards. Achieving and ascribing are thus reconcilable. We choose our achievements.

EQUALITY VS. HIERARCHY

Is equality of process more or less important than the hierarchy of judgements that sponsors and judges the contest?

All societies need to encourage participants to give their best. Unless their contributions are weighted *equally* they may be seriously discour-

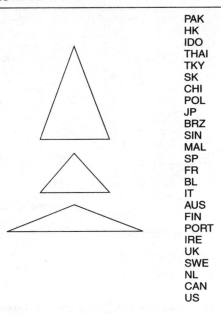

PAK
HK
IDO
THAI
TKY
SK
CHI
POL
JP
BRZ
SIN
MAL
SP
FR
BL
IT
AUS
FIN
PORT
IRE
UK
SWE
NL
CAN
US

Figure 17.11 Flat versus steep hierarchies

aged, yet someone has to choose the contest itself and someone not competing in that contest has to evaluate those taking part. This cannot be achieved without hierarchy.

We showed managers various hierarchical shapes, see Figure 17.11.

How different nations of the world chose flat or steep hierarchies is revealed in the same figure.

What is puzzling about these results is how well some hierarchical nations are doing economically, even in fairly complex fields like electronics. All North American tradition suggests that a steep hierarchy will cripple you. You will not get desperately needed information from the field to the top of the organization, so why isn't Japan crippled? Why doesn't Singapore and South Korea rigidify and grow stupid?

Because the degree of hierarchy is not the only variable, there is also the Analysing-Integrating, our second dimension:

At the top left we have Command Economies: they are hierarchical *and* give specific orders. This fails. It is a disaster. At bottom left Western Pluralism has a lot of ideas jostling each other and contending in a roughly equal market place. At bottom right we have Germany with its highly integrated structural networks of businesses and its decentralized federalism. But most interesting and least familiar is Information Ordering. This is hierarchical but socially intimate and close like a family.

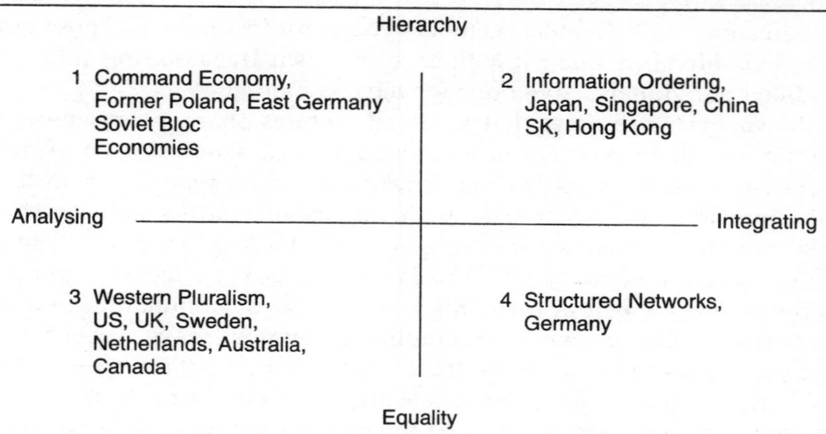

Hierarchy

1 Command Economy,
  Former Poland, East Germany
  Soviet Bloc
  Economies
	2 Information Ordering,
	  Japan, Singapore, China
	  SK, Hong Kong

Analysing ———————————————————————————————————— Integrating

3 Western Pluralism,
  US, UK, Sweden,
  Netherlands, Australia,
  Canada
	4 Structured Networks,
	  Germany

Equality

NB At the top left we have Command Economies; they are hierarchical **and** give specific orders.

Figure 17.12 A four-way model

Because holism is high status, the people at the top have the theories and the concepts and the people lower down the data. These cannot give orders to each other, rather they have to meet and match up their contributions. The Japanese hierarchy *mimics the hierarchical ordering of information itself*, with theories and laws at the top, general propositions in the middle and data at the bottom. All levels need to integrate with each other. This may be the future of all knowledge-intensive organizations. They are in the business of creating knowledge from seas of data.

CONCLUSION

We have seen that China and much of SE Asia is both a mirror-image and an up-ending of traditional Western management culture – see Chapter 14 in this book. Yet these economies are now developing fast, faster in most cases than the West's own 'catch-up' economies.

Our main conclusion is that the values at stake are complementary, an insight contained within Taoist traditions, but less developed in the West where 'the market place of ideas' is adversarial. For example, Universalism (or the rules) are not genuinely opposed to Particularism (or exceptions). Rather the rule *needs* the exception. This is true whether your aim is to improve rules by studying exceptions, or whether you aim to celebrate the unique and the exceptional by transcending the present rules. In either case, each value is definable only in contrast with the other.

This applies to all the bifurcations discussed. A good community requires that its individual members vouch for its qualities. Those extolling individualism must test their enthusiasm by inquiring into what 'fulfilled individuals' have done for the common good.

We suggest, therefore, that what all cultures share, everywhere, are certain key dilemmas. All need to analyse and synthesize, to attribute values and achieve these, to take streams of passing time and co-ordinate these 'just in time'. We are different in our *logical priorities*, in 'what comes first' but these, however shocking and bewildering, are really disputes about 'where a circle starts'. The larger truths are circular. Exceptions improve rules which in turn enhance exceptions. Communities nurture individuals who enhance communities in original ways. Problems are analysed so as to be better synthesized, so that all details can be examined, including qualities of the whole not present in the parts. It causes us anxiety, sometimes suspicion to be thrown in among people who reverse our favourite axioms, but they are describing the other half of key cultural experiences. We have everything to learn from them.

REFERENCES

Bellah, R.N. (1985) *Habits of the Heart*, University of California Press.

Child, J. (1994) *Management in China During the Age of Reform*, Cambridge University Press, Cambridge.

Crutchfield, R. (1955) Conformity and character. *American Psychologist*, **10**.

Cottle, T.J. (1968) The location of experience: a manifest time orientation. *Acta Psychologica*, **28**, pp. 129–49.

Dobbs, C. (1951) *Studies in Capitalism*, Longman, London.

Hall, E.T. (1959) *The Silent Language*, Doubleday, New York.

Hall, E.T. (1976) *Beyond Culture*, Doubleday, New York.

Hampden-Turner, C.M. (1994) *Corporate Culture: Vicious and Virtuous circles*, Piatkus, London.

Hampden-Turner, C.M. and Trompenaars, F. (1994) *The Seven Cultures of Capitalism*, Piatkus, London.

Hofstede, G. (1980) *Culture's Consequence*, Sage, Beverly Hills.

Hofstede, G. (1991) *Cultures and Organisations: Software of the Mind*, McGraw Hill, London.

Lipset, S.M. (1974) *The First New Nation*, Doubleday, New York.

Melville, H. (1981) *Moby Dick*, New American Library, New York.

Melville, H. (1981) *Billy Budd: Foretopman*, New American Library, New York.

Milgram, S.L. (1963) Behavioral study of obedience. *Journal of Abnormal and Social Psychology*, **67**.

Trompenaars, F. (1994) *Riding the Waves of Culture*, Nicholas Brealey, London.

Warner, M. (1995a) Managing China's human resources. *Human Systems Management*, **14**, pp. 239–58.

Warner, M. (1995b) *The Management of Human Resources in Chinese Industry*, Macmillan, London.

Part III

Cross-cultural issues

Chapter 18

In search of the transnational: a study of structural choice in international companies

Ian Turner and Ian Henry

INTRODUCTION

The relationship between a firm's business environment, the strategy which it pursues and the organizational structure it evolves has been a focal question of management research for over 30 years. As is well known, Alfred D. Chandler's (1962) original study documented the link between the increasing complexity of the business environment and the adoption of multi-divisional (or 'm-form') structures in large US firms like Du Pont and General Motors. He showed how the diversity of products and markets caused by a policy of diversification could only be success-fully mastered by separating activities into divisions or business units charged with managing operations, whilst responsibility for strategy and control was retained by the centre. Chandler's proposition that structure followed strategy has since been developed by Caves, (1984) and extended to a range of national and industrial settings (Rumelt 1974).

Chandler's historical approach to the strategy/structure question was also complemented by the work of organizational theorists. Lawrence and Lorsch (1967) developed an influential 'contingency theory of complex organizations' which linked environmental uncertainty with structure. Their main contention was that successful firms adapt the organization of each department or division to the demands of the organizational environment (Miles and Snow 1978).

An important sub-theme of Chandler's work was the international spread of modern enterprises. The growth of multi-national activity and the consequent organizational problem of managing activity in many countries was the focus of some important research in the 1970s (Wilkins 1970). Particularly influential was the work of Stopford and Wells (1972) which showed how organizational structure had evolved over time in multi national enterprises. According to their model the approach favoured by firms initially, when international business was still a com-paratively minor and peripheral activity for a company mainly focused on its domestic market, was the international division. Although located in the home market, the international division was often isolated from the locus of decision making in the mainstream business activities, however. Thus, as the proportion of the firm's overall business done outside its domestic market increased, the organizational solution changed. Creating area divisions, which co-ordinated activities in geographical regions like Europe, North America or the Far East, was one answer. An alternative solution, where a company had become more diversified in product-market terms at the same time as it extended its international presence, was to structure around world-wide product divisions, directed from the home base but with a remit to control activities globally within each business area.

The Stopford and Wells model related structural choice to two para-meters: foreign product diversity and the extent of overseas sales, (see Figure 18.1). It was widely adopted as a prescriptive model of how multinationals should organize, although more recent research by Egelh-off (1989) on European multi-nationals has highlighted the significance of overseas *manufacturing* as a factor inducing firms to adopt area divisions (see Figure 18.2).

The late 1970s and early 1980s saw the rise of two important concepts, whose validity has since been challenged. In 1983 Theodore Levitt's thesis

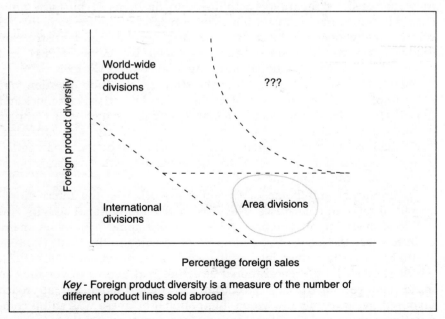

Figure 18.1 The Stopford and Wells model of strategy and structure in international companies

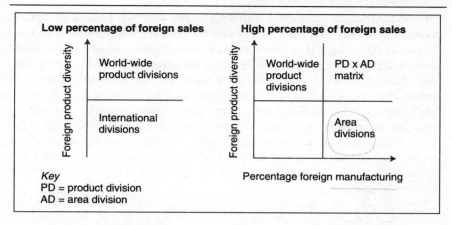

Figure 18.2 Egelhoff's model of strategy and structure in international companies

was that markets and consumer behaviour, influenced by exposure to common experiences, international media and advertising, were becoming more homogeneous the world over. It followed, therefore, that successful companies should pursue strategies for global standardization of goods and services and structure themselves to reap the benefits of economies of scale which standardization opened up (Levitt 1983).

Levitt's proposition was immediately challenged by those who pointed to the significant remaining differences in national markets, the localization pressures from national governments and the declining importance of economies of scale in manufacturing (Doz 1986). Companies could not afford to simply ignore national differences or steam-roller over local sensitivities. Multiple tensions had to be resolved structurally and one obvious solution was to create multi-dimensional matrix organizations (Davis and Lawrence 1974). However, despite some well publicized experimentation in the late 1970s and early 1980s, matrix structures proved to be a dead-end (Bartlett and Ghoshal 1989). Managers for the most part could not cope with multiple reporting lines, conflicts amongst the different organizational dimensions were accentuated rather than mollified and decision making was made more bureaucratic and cumbersome.

TOWARDS THE TRANSNATIONAL MODEL

By the mid-1980s there was an emerging consensus amongst scholars and practitioners that a new type of organizational structure was required to cope with the challenges of a fast-changing and unpredictable international business environment.

Bartlett and Ghoshal (1989) contended that *successful* firms traditionally achieved a fit between what was needed to win in their industry and what the company was good at. Thus in markets like food and detergent, where there were distinct national differences in consumer needs, a company like Unilever decentralized responsibility to national subsidiaries to ensure market responsiveness. When economies of scale and low cost production were critical, however, Japanese consumer electronics companies like Matsushita adopted a centralized global approach and when rapid dissemination of knowledge from subsidiary to subsidiary was the key to success, as in telecommunications, a successful firm like Ericsson with a small home market became skilled at transferring expertise within the group.

Historically, therefore, a successful company was organized along the lines best suited to its environment. The dominant organizational solution in turn formed part of the firm's administrative heritage which was shaped by the culture (e.g. the predominance of family business and personal ties in the UK and Germany), the organization's history (e.g. Philips' evolution as a federation of distinct autonomous national subsidiaries) and the firm's leadership (e.g. the impact of Harold Geneen's tenure at ITT or Lord Hanson at Hanson Plc). As a consequence, most multinationals in the 1980s had one dominant organizational dimension which, despite attempts to reduce its importance, remained the locus of power in the firm: functional (as in Procter and Gamble) world-wide business units (as in Matsushita) or geographical (as in Philips).

Ghoshal and Bartlett's thesis was that, despite their very different starting points, companies in the 1980s and 90s would tend to converge towards a common configuration. This was because in all cases the environment was becoming more complex: thus firms in consumer electronics which had been organized for world-wide efficiency found that the market was dictating greater national responsiveness; detergent companies, meanwhile, found that technological changes and the creation of large integrated markets like Western Europe required a shift from local differentiation to greater central co-ordination, whilst telecommunications companies faced with de-regulation and massive investment requirements had to organize to reap economies of scale. The organizational solution to these problems was to move towards what Ghoshal and Bartlett called the transnational model, '. . . in which increasingly specialized units world-wide were linked into an integrated network of operations that enabled them to achieve their multi-dimensional strategic objectives of efficiency, responsiveness and innovation' (Bartlett and Ghoshal, 1989: 89).

The transnational company would be capable of thinking globally, but acting locally. The organizing principles would be: dispersal of assets and resources to capitalize on local strengths and minimize political risk;

specialization of task to achieve economies of scale when necessary, but also to achieve greater focus of expertise; and interdependence between organizational units to foster information sharing, organizational learning and concerted implementation. In practical terms that meant not managing everything from the centre, but devolving responsibility for particular business areas or technology to the national unit with the greatest expertise ('regional centres of excellence') 'modularization' of products so that products could be locally differentiated by combining standard sets of components, thus retaining economies of scale; and international project teams brought together to work on specific 'off-line' tasks for the organization as a whole.

Ghoshal and Bartlett were not arguing that one standard approach should govern all relationships between units of a multinational company. They recognized that subsidiaries varied in the importance of their markets and the expertise of the local organization. At one extreme some subsidiaries could be capable of taking the lead within the company, as IBM's UK operations now do for its world-wide communications business, for instance; whilst at the other extreme subsidiaries may simply not be capable of anything more than implementing existing group policy.

Ghoshal and Bartlett also fully recognized the organizational obstacles to adopting the transnational model. That is why they emphasized the need to manage the process, starting at the top. Instead of relying exclusively on the traditional mechanisms of co-ordination installed in companies – centralization (in Japan), formalization of controls (in the USA) or socialization of employees (in European firms) – transnationals should build a balanced portfolio of these co-ordinating processes. But the most important way of achieving co-ordination was not through creating structures but by creating a management mentality conducive to collaboration and interdependence. Matrix *management*, not *structures*, was the motto.

Ghoshal and Bartlett's ideas have not been without their critics. Porter's work on the competitive advantage of nations, for instance, runs counter to the idea that successful multinationals could derive their primary source of competitive advantage from anything other than their domestic markets (Porter 1990). This was a theme developed by Hu (1992), who showed that most so-called multinationals in the 1990s continued to be dominated by their home market nationalities in strategic and organizational terms. In addition to these important issues of substance, it is worth pointing out that Ghoshal and Bartlett's work barely mentions the other ways in which organizations were changing in the 1980s: the ubiquitous trend towards 'downsizing' and de-layering of organizations, the devolution of authority down the organization to 'empower' management (Kanter 1989) and the impact of information technology on the 'coming of the new organization' (Drucker 1988). Despite these criticisms the transnational model has become the orthodox view of the 'ideal' organization form to which firms in the 1990s should aspire. Indeed, companies with famous names like Unilever (Maljers 1992), BP (Financial Times 1990), ABB (Business Week 1990), Nestlé (Lorenz 1991), IBM (Lorenz 1990) and Electrolux (Lorenz 1989) have all subsequently been described as actual or potential transnationals by informed observers.

Clearly, the transnational model has been immensely influential in business. Consultants, like Theuerkauf at McKinsey, have also jumped on the bandwagon, in his case operationalising the model into a 3 stage process (Theuerkauf 1991). Theuerkauf makes no bones about the implications of the model:

- Group headquarters (intervening between corporate headquarters and subsidiaries) should be abolished.
- Shared central functions should be reduced and wherever possible placed on a market footing.
- Country managers should be phased out.
- Regional headquarters should assume some of the functions previously exercised at corporate HQ.
- Corporate headquarters should be dispersed.

THE RESEARCH

The research reported here set out to understand how a range of companies, operating internationally, organized and controlled their core activities in different countries, business units and market segments. Companies chosen for study were recognized to be leaders in their fields. They were also well-documented and capable of offering insights into how to organize successfully on an international level. For the most part they operated in mature, technology-intensive industries. A major concern was how a company is able to preserve its original strategic recipe (Johnson and Scholes 1988: 39–43) whilst dispersing its activities and devolving authority outside its home-base. The issues we tried to address were broadly as follows:

- What structural solutions had the companies developed to the problem of managing international business?
- What were the determinants of the structural choice?
- What mechanisms and processes were instituted to manage the structures, in particular what were the reporting lines, communication channels and capital allocation procedures?
- What were the main problems presented by the choice of structure, in particular how did the firm cope with the physical dispersal and separation of core functions?
- What direction was the structure developing towards in the future?

Clearly, however, the answers to these questions have a bearing on the applicability of the transnational model and we shall return to this in our conclusions.

Structural choices in international companies

As one might expect, most of the businesses in the sample adopted a structure based on one organizational dimension alone. In six of the companies the business unit dimension was dominant, but this group included one company – Sun Microsystems – the bulk of whose activities was concentrated in North America. Only in one case – Ford – was the geographical dimension dominant. (It is interesting to note that Ford commenced in 1994 a major reorganization on global lines.) In Unilever the area dimension is dominant, but only outside the developed countries. Nevertheless, most of the business unit dominated firms retained a weaker regional structure either for political reasons, e.g. ICI (pre the 1993 de-merger), or because they wished to present a common face to important clients (IBM, GM). Two companies – Boeing and Ford of Europe – retain the dominant functional structure, although, like Sun, there have been moves – not wholly successful – to shift authority in these firms from functional hierarchies to cross-functional project teams. In other firms, functional hierarchies have been severely reduced (Nestlé) or devolved (GM, Unilever). Only in one – ICI – did the functional dimension appear to be making a comeback at corporate level at the time that the research was done. Our sample also included one company – ABB – whose structure can best be likened to a 'flexible matrix', and one firm – MAN – structured as a holding company with autonomous operating subsidiaries.

As suggested by Bartlett and Ghoshal (1989) and Theuerkauf (1991) structural choices, in particular decisions to centralize or decentralize responsibility for specific business, areas or functions, vary even amongst companies with a pronounced bias towards one particular organizational dimension. The model predicted by Theuerkauf would look like Figure 18.3, with certain corporate functions (e.g. finance, treasury management) centralized; basic research controlled from the centre, but development devolved; manufacturing centralized but sourcing dispersed and marketing and sales located closer to the end-user.

Influencing factors in structural choice

The companies in our sample are not always close to this ideal, however, as Table 18.1 indicates. The dominant business unit structure is eminently appropriate where a company has diverse products or businesses in its portfolio, needs to standardize to maximize its investment in new

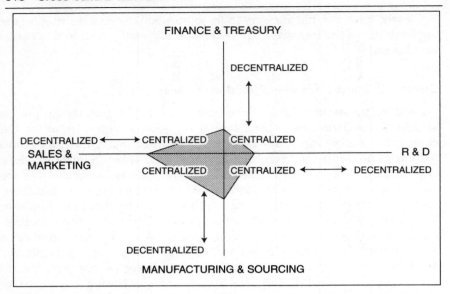

Figure 18.3 Centralization and decentralization of functions in multinational companies (Based on Theuerkauf, 1991)

technology, requires volume to be efficient and has a high percentage of foreign sales in markets which are broadly similar (Stopford and Wells 1972). Dominant functional hierarchies, on the other hand, tend to be adopted in businesses with a single product focus – like car or aeroplane manufacture – and where sales or production are concentrated in the home area. Dominant area units are also associated with a less diverse corporate portfolio, but are often preferred where market differences or political barriers between geographical areas are very distinct. In such a situation an alternative solution is to adopt a matrix form.

This form addresses both the market heterogeneity and the need for economies of scale. Few companies seem capable of operating this form, however. It requires a high tolerance for ambiguity and a natural propensity for consensus: qualities most often associated with Scandinavian companies like ABB or Electrolux. Even in these cases, the matrix structure can place a great strain on the organization leading to employee discomfort and lack of clarity of purpose. Interestingly, in both the companies mentioned, the matrix structure is closely associated with forceful leader figures and doubts have been expressed about its viability after their departure. The remaining organizational solution – the holding company – seems to work best where there is little or no affinity between businesses in the group so that any co-ordination occurs within the

Table 18.1 Determinants of structural choice

	Dominant Business Unit	Dominant Functional Hierarchy	Dominant Area Unit	Flexible Matrix	Holding Company
Diversity of Products & Business (v Synergy)	XXX	O	X	XXX	XXX
Importance of Technology	XXX	XXX	X	XXX	X
Economies of Scale	XX	XX	X	XXX	X
Proportion of Foreign Sales	XXX	O	XXX	XXX	X
Proportion of Foreign Production	XX	O	XXX	XXX	X
Homogeneity of World Markets	XXX	XXX	O	O	X
Sample Companies	Nestlé, Unilever, Sun, GM, ICI, IBM	Boeing, Ford of Europe	Ford, Unilever*	ABB	MAN

* Outside Europe and North America

KEY XXX Strongly Associated
     XX Somewhat Associated
     X   Not associated
     O   Negatively Associated

autonomous group companies. The holding company is a common structure amongst Anglo-Saxon conglomerates like Hanson or BTR (Goold and Campbell 1987), but it is surprising to see it adopted by a strategically oriented European engineering company like MAN. Ultimately, the member companies in such a structure must ask what value the corporate centre is adding.

The transnational: myth or reality?

To what extent have the firms in our research project adopted the organizing principles of the transnational model, as described by Ghoshal and Bartlett? Table 18.2 takes Ghoshal and Bartlett's three organizing principles of dispersal, specialization and interdependence. To this we have added a column on control mechanisms. We should disregard, for this purpose, those companies whose domestic sales are dominant, or whose principal activities are located in the home-base (e.g. Sun, Boeing), as these firms cannot be expected to be subject to the same organizational tensions which were said to necessitate the transnational solution. Of the others, it is striking how many of the world-wide business units in such companies are still directed from the firm's home country. IBM's Communications Division is a good example of the dispersal of responsibility for a line of business to the geographical area which makes the best strategic sense. But this is the only one out of 8 'lines of business' whose HQs are located outside the home country. Ford has made moves in this direction, by devolving responsibility for launch manufacturing of a 'world car' to Europe, but it remains to be seen whether it can successfully combine global co-ordination with regional differentiation by this means. Nestlé and Unilever come closer to the ideal, but even here the intended creation of Nestlé's 'strategic business units' with headquarters in France (mineral water) and the UK (chocolate), owes much to Nestlé's acquisition strategy and still has to fulfil its promise, whilst the continuation of Unilever's dual location of headquarters – with all the cost this entails – seems to owe more to internal balance of power politics than any explicit business logic. ABB probably has gone further down the track on dispersal but not just by following the centres of excellence approach. The firm relies in addition on very small but highly mobile headquarters staff at corporate and business unit level allied to devolution of decision making to country managers. ABB notwithstanding, there are clearly still powerful forces within international companies restraining the dispersal of assets and responsibilities:

- The continued domination of the home market (even where the proportion of foreign sales is high, the home market is very often the largest single market).

Table 18.2 Elements of 'transnationalism' in sample companies

	DISPERSAL OF ASSETS AND RESOURCES	SPECIALIZATION OF TASK	INTERDEPENDENCE OF UNITS	CONTROL OF PLANNING
ABB	Small corporate HQ Permanently mobile business segments based in Zurich	Centralization of key component production	Board members have BU and area responsibility; trust fostered through teams and information exchange	Core functions directed, but not controlled from HQ. Country and BU operations highly autonomous in product development, logistics
BOEING	Main assets and resources concentrated in one area of USA	Centralization of functions	777 project team seen as new model for simultaneous engineering	Highly centralized, reflecting concentration of company location
FORD OF EUROPE	Research and manufacture integrated in Europe. Attempt to integrate world-wide by making Europe responsible for new car	Centralization of design and manufacture on European basis Decentralization of sales and marketing	Co-ordination through committees and new vehicle teams	Centralized finance and planning
GM	GM Europe responsible for development in all non-US business	Components manufacture decentralized vehicle assembly increasingly concentrated	Dual reporting to BU and geographical HQs	Ultimate control resides in US, but European autonomy increasing
IBM	All BU HQs in USA except communications (UK) Regional dispersal in Europe	Separation of manufacturing and development from marketing and sales	Use of teams and IT to collaborate on process	Historic centralization being reduced and delegated to operations

Table 18.2 Continued

	DISPERSAL OF ASSETS AND RESOURCES	SPECIALIZATION OF TASK	INTERDEPENDENCE OF UNITS	CONTROL OF PLANNING
ICI – (pre-1993 de-merger)	BU HQs in UK, dispersal of manufacturing and marketing	Central control and co-ordination of functions Decentralized R and D	Performance and policy committee integrates strategy; directors have BU/ functional/area responsibilities	All highly centralized
MAN	Corporate and BU HQs located in Germany but operating companies dispersed in Europe	Radical decentralization within framework of financial control	Linkages only encouraged at lower levels e.g. via. NPD	Centralized finance and strategy. Decentralized operations and finance responsibility/accountability
NESTLE	Most SBUs based in Switzerland except mineral water and confectionery	Centralization of basic research, decentralization of applied research and manufacture	Directed from the centre	Highly centralized and directed from HQ in all core functions, especially local marketing initiatives, but some financial independence
SUN	All BUs have HQs in USA Certain design and development operations located in France, Japan and Canada	Decentralization to (dominant) BU – except purchasing, which is controlled from the centre > 75% product value bought in	New programme introductions uses simultaneous engineering	BUs decentralized, with P & L responsibility. HQ carries out treasury management
UNILEVER	Product groups located in London or Rotterdam	Centralization of detergent and food manufacture. Centralization of basic research, decentralization of development	Transnational 'network' directors can have dual functions Conflicts between units resolved at product or regional group level	Centralized finance and product planning. Company culture dispersed through rotation of staff across organization

- The hegemony of home country nationals who resist transfer to other locations.
- The political pressures from home country governments not to abandon the home-base (and place the firm outside the state's jurisdiction for tax and other economic benefits).

As one might expect, the process appears to be much more advanced within regions, where in companies like Ford, Unilever, IBM and GM, responsibilities are dispersed to national 'centres of excellence'.

In *task specialization* the firms again exhibited great variations in approach, which reflected their different starting points. In general, the firms were concerned to reduce overheads and bureaucracy by cutting down corporate functions and stripping out layers of management. Thus, decentralization was frequently invoked at MAN, Nestlé, ABB and Sun as a tenet of the organization. On the other hand, two companies (Unilever and ICI pre-1993) were making conscious efforts to re-centralize. In the case of the former, this was to achieve operating economies from rationalization and co-ordination whilst, in ICI's case, the main aim seems to be to control activities more closely. Moreover, in two other firms – Ford of Europe and GM – already centralized organizations were centralizing certain core processes like R and D, product planning and purchasing even further in response to economic and political integration in Europe. However, even in firms where control is being centralized, manufacturing and assembly operations are becoming increasingly dispersed, e.g. Ford has established a seat cover plant in Poland and a lighting plant in the Czech Republic, whilst GM has car assembly in Hungary. Nor do these trends necessarily imply convergence on an approximate common model – these structural decisions remain contingent on the organization, its strategy and environment.

Turning to the principle of *interdependence* between units, clearly all the companies have evolved mechanisms for satisfying the conflicting tendencies in their organizations and encouraging collaboration and consensus. These included:

- Encouraging greater sharing of information (e.g. in ABB).
- Socialization through in-house training (e.g. in Unilever).
- Committees to integrate different organizational perspectives (e.g. at Ford and ICI).
- Specially developed information systems to facilitate dispersal of knowledge (e.g. in ABB and IBM).
- Allocating responsibility to senior executives for business units and geographical areas or functional responsibilities (e.g. in ABB, Unilever and ICI).

In general, there seems to be a trend away from multiple reporting lines, although GM, ABB and ICI are exceptions. This reflects the necessity of streamlining decision making to encourage greater organizational responsiveness. One co-ordinating mechanism which is clearly becoming more prevalent is the use of international project teams. Ghoshal and Bartlett described this in their work as a way of exploiting expertise located in different parts of the organization and as a means of promoting organizational learning. Whilst this is undoubtedly the case, much of the project team activity is clearly linked to new product development. As such it reflects the adoption of 'simultaneous engineering' techniques designed to reduce 'time to market' cycles in a period of increased technological competition (Womack *et al.* 1990).

CONCLUDING REMARKS: IMPLICATIONS AND FUTURE TRENDS

It is clear that for most international companies the transnational model is more of an aspiration than a reality. The trend towards closer economic integration and the rapid transfer of patterns of consumer behaviour across borders coupled with the advantages of economies of scale have induced many companies to organize around world-wide product divisions. This trend was anticipated in the 1970s by Stopford and Wells. However, from the evidence available we would hypothesize that the world-wide product division is becoming the 'standard' model in most situations, with the other three ideal-typical structural solutions increasingly marginalized.

If the product line dimension has been dominant, what of the other key organizational dimensions: the functional hierarchies and the geographical unit? This is where, arguably, organizational diagrams fail to convey the true reality of organizational life. In most, but not all, organizations we looked at, functional hierarchies have lost influence at the expense of business units and/or cross-functional teams. It has recently been suggested that in the 'lean enterprises' of the future functions would make a comeback. But their new role would not be executive (these tasks would be carried out by cross-functional teams). Rather, they would act as repositories of expertise, collators of new thinking and disseminators of skills (Womack and Jones 1994). This is a fascinating prospect and a logical development of the lean production/time-based competition philosophy. However, it is some way from the current organizational reality of the firms we studied. The fact is that, irrespective of organizational charts, functions still dominate in many companies: several of our respondents testified to the pervasive influence of the finance in Ford and Boeing, for instance, or marketing in Unilever.

What, then, about the geographical dimension in organizations? In the late 1980s, Egelhoff hypothesized that a trend towards locating manufacturing activities in separate regions would lead to the adoption of the area division structure (Egelhoff 1989). In fact, this only seems to occur with

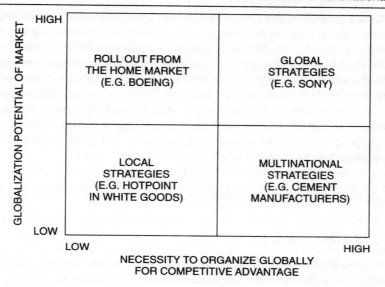

Figure 18.4 Not all companies need be global/transnational to be successful

businesses focused on one core market or technology (e.g. cars). With increased diversity comes separate product divisions who clearly guard their power jealously. Rather than dominant area division structures, we see the evolution of regional structures within business units (Lever Europe in Unilever or GM Europe, for example) coupled with the devolution of authority within the respective business units to a particular national subsidiary for co-ordinating activities across the region (as IBM has done in Europe, for instance). Will the trend towards homogeneity – at least within trading blocs – encourage greater devolution of power from the home-base to the other 'triad regions'? Could the 'ideal typical' international company of the future take a balanced approach which is global, in Ohmae's terms (1990) or transnational (to use Ghoshal and Bartlett's terminology)?

As Yip (1989) and others have observed, this will depend on the inherent global potential of the market as well as the need for companies in the industry to take advantage of the situation by organizing globally for competitive edge (see Figure 18.4). Thus both Boeing and Sony operate in markets which are international and where the advantages from standardizing products on a global basis are decisive. But only Sony needs to structure its business operations in a global way in order to ensure market penetration across the world. Boeing, which has a huge domestic market and substantial scale advantages, can afford to roll out its products from its home market.

At the other end of the globalization spectrum, companies operating in industries where minimum efficient scales are low and national differences in consumer characteristics decisive, can afford to base their competitive strategy on their domestic market as Hotpoint have done in the UK. In the cement industry, by contrast, the cost of transport outweighs any benefits from centralization thus severely restricting the globalization potential of the market, but dominant national and regional players like the Italian cement producer, Ital Cimente, are compelled to sustain their companies' growth by replicating their position in a number of different markets which operate on a relatively autonomous basis.

In summary, not all companies need the degree of cross-national interdependence posited by the transnational model or indeed possess the necessary skills to make it work.

ACKNOWLEDGEMENTS

This chapter has been adapted from an earlier version entitled 'Managing International Organisations: Lessons from the Field', co-authored by Ian Turner and Ian Henry, published in the *European Management Journal*, Volume 12, No. 4, 1994, pp. 417–31, with permission.

REFERENCES

Bartlett, C.A. and Ghoshal, S. (1989) *Managing Across Borders: The Transnational Solution*, Hutchinson Business Books, London, pp. 30–2.

Business Week (1990) The Stateless Corporation, 14 May.

Caves, R.E. (1984) Industrial Organization, Corporate Strategy and Structure. *Competitive Strategic Management*, Prentice-Hall, Inc., Englewood Cliffs, N.J., pp. 134–70.

Chandler, A.D. Jr. (1962) *Strategy and Structure: Chapters in the history of the industrial enterprise*, MIT Press, Cambridge.

Davis, S.M. and Lawrence, P.R. (1974) *Matrix Management*, Addison-Wesley, Reading, MA.

Doz, Y. (1986) *Strategic Management in Multinational Companies*, Pergamon Press, Oxford.

Drucker, P. (1988) The Coming of the New Organisation. *Harvard Business Review*, **66**, January–February.

Egelhoff, W.G. (1989) Strategy and Structure in Multinational companies: A Revision of the Stopford and Wells Model. *Strategic Management Journal*, **9**, January–February.

Financial Times (1990) series of articles on BP, March.

Ghoshal, S. and Nohria, N. (1987) Horses for courses: Organisational Forms for Multinational Corporations. *Sloan Management Review*, Winter 1993, pp. 23–35.

Goold, M. and Campbell, A. (1987) *Strategy and styles*, Basil Blackwell, Oxford.

Hu, Y-S. (1992) Global or Stateless – Corporations are National Firms with International Operations, *California Management Review*, **34**, Winter.

Johnson, G. and Scholes, K. (1988) *Exploring Corporate Strategy*, Prentice Hall, New York.

Kanter, R.M. (1989) *When Giants Learn to Dance*, Simon and Schuster.

Lawrence, P.R. and Lorsch, J.W. (1967) *Organization and Environment*, Harvard Business School.

Levitt, T. (1983) The Globalization of Markets. *Harvard Business Review*, May–June, pp. 92–102.

Lorenz, C. (1989) The birth of a transnational: striving to exploit an elusive balance. *Financial Times*, 19 June.

Lorenz, C. (1990) IBM joins the ranks of transnationals. *Financial Times*, 10 December.

Lorenz, C. (1991) Sharing power around the world. *Financial Times*, 29 November.

Maljers, F.A. (1992) Inside Unilever: The Evolving Transnational. *Harvard Business Review*, September–October, pp. 46–51.

Miles, R. and Snow, C. (1978) *Organisation, Strategy, Structure and Process*, McGraw-Hill, New York.

Ohmae, K. (1990) *The Borderless World: Power and Strategy in the Interlinked Economy*, Collins, London.

Porter, M.E. (1990) *The Comparative Advantage of Nations*, Free Press.

Rumelt, R.P. (1974) Strategy, structure, and economic performance. Division of Research, Graduate School of Business Administration, Harvard University, Boston.

Stopford, J.M. and Wells, L.T. Jr. (1972) *Managing the Multinational Enterprise: Organization of the Firm and Ownership of the Subsidiaries*, Basic Books, New York.

Theuerkauf, I. (1991) Reshaping the global organization. *The McKinsey Quarterly*, **3**, pp. 102–19.

Wilkins, M. (1970) *The Emergence of Multinational Enterprise: American Business Abroad from the Colonial Era to 1914*, Harvard University Press, Cambridge.

Womack, J.P. *et al.* (1990) *The Machine that Changed the World*, Rawson Associates, Collins MacMillan Canada, Maxwell MacMillan International.

Womack, J.P. and Jones, D.T. (1994) From lean production to the lean enterprise. *Harvard Business Review*, March–April, pp. 93–103.

Yip, G.S. (1989) Global Strategy . . . In a World of Nations?. *Sloan Management Review*, Fall, pp. 29–41.

Chapter 19

Executive relocation: personal and organizational tactics

Iain McCormick and Tony Chapman

INTRODUCTION

Moving executives half-way round the world to address global business needs and to help reduce skill and management shortages is now very common. Relocation can offer executives an excellent opportunity for professional development, yet the process is full of potential traps, both on a personal and organizational level. The authors are two expatriates, who while still in the transition process, decided to write about the topic. Both authors moved to Hong Kong, one from New Zealand and the other from the United Kingdom. This article presents examples of adjustment issues which relate to Hong Kong, but the findings are relevant to almost any major relocations. The paper sets out the nature of the transition process, the factors that bring successful adjustment and the steps that organizations can take to help in the effective relocation of expatriates.

Transition has been defined as a discontinuity in a person's life space (Adams, Haynes and Hopson, 1976). Typically, the discontinuity is defined by social consensus. Holmes and Rahe (1967) in their famous social readjustment research demonstrate that there is a remarkable degree of cross-cultural similarity in the social consensus of perceptions of what are important discontinuities.

There is now a wide variety of research and scholarly discussion on transition and executive relocation. The literature has three main areas of focus: descriptive studies; reviews of company tatics to improve relocation success; and papers making suggestions for individuals on how to cope.

The descriptive studies include Austen (1986) who examined the problem of re-entry of executives after overseas service and provided a series of perspectives from experienced expatriates who described their events as they saw them. McClenahen (1987) discusses how personal and corporate parochialism can negatively affect the success of managers overseas and emphasizes that the length of the overseas assignment and the cultural accuracy of the overseas plan is an important determinant of success or failure. McEnery and DesHarnais (1990) described how the failure of the spouse and other family members to adapt to the new environment is a chief contributing factor to expatriate failure. Black and Stephens (1989) documented the influence of the spouse on American expatriates and how this had an impact on the decision to stay or go.

The studies examining company tactics to improve relocation success include the following papers: Befus (1988) who documented the multiple effects of effects of culture shock and proposed a programme of assistance which integrates cross-cultural training methods and psychotherapeutic approaches to help those affected; Blockyn (1989) discussed how three international corporations have worked to overcome the problem of high failure rates for expatriate executives and concluded that the blame can be put on poor selection and orientation; Hogan and Goodson (1990) who stressed the need for integrated selection and cross-cultural and language training for expatriates and their families; Odenwald (1993) set out a comprehensive approach for multinational corporations to develop global training programmes to deal with relocation and cross-cultural management.

The following papers set out advice and assistance to individuals to cope with relocation: Copeland (1987) set out strategies for expatriates to employ to maintain their personal safety and security; Erkut (1986) discussed how and why adolescents react to relocation and gave a list of practical suggestions that parents can use to assist adolescent adjustment; Wederspahn (1988) discussed the separation of spouses due to overseas assignment and outlined the factors affecting separation adjustment and developed a list of coping strategies.

One very fruitful line of research into transition processes is the use of the transition curve to model the individual psychological process experienced by the expatriate executive. This has been used by Adams, Haynes and Hopson (1976) who employed content analysis of over 100 people who attended transition workshops for the purpose of understanding and coping with transitions. The seven stages described by Adams, Haynes and Hopson (1976) were Immobilization; Minimization; Depression; Acceptance of Reality; Testing; Search for Meaning; Internalization. Adams, Haynes and Hopson (1976) reported that very similar results were found by the Menninger Foundation's research on the Peace Corps which also found a seven-step process of changes in self-esteem which individuals typically experienced as they entered and undertook Peace Corps training.

Variations of the curve have been used by Bridges (1985) who identified three major stages, Endings; The Neutral Zone; The New Beginning. Bridges (1985) applies this model to help people adjust to a very wide range of life transitions. Kubler-Ross (1970) in the analysis and explanation of the grief process described five transitional stages: Denial; Anger;

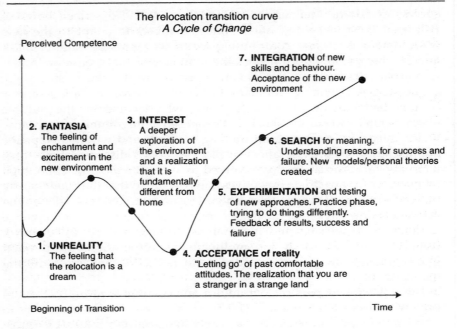

Figure 19.1 The relocation transition curve

Bargaining; Depression; and; Acceptance. Nortier (1995) developed a five-stage change management model which was applied to a variety of situations including expatriate adjustment. The model's five stages were: Initial Equilibrium; Separation; Crisis; Rebirth; and New Equilibrium.

In a study of transferred executives from 26 countries Torbiorn (1982) identified four stages of transition. In the first the individual's behaviour was maladaptive but his or her ideas were not disrupted by the new situation. At the second stage, the person's behaviour was frustrated and their original ideas and beliefs were weakened. The third stage represented the low point with both external behaviour and internal process being imbalanced. In the final state the person developed new more adaptive ideas and behaved accordingly.

Latack (1984) has developed one model of career transitions within organizations. The model views career transitions as a stress-coping model process, influenced by both work and non-work factors. The data support the model, in that individuals experiencing many personal life transitions were more likely to adopt a symptom-focused strategy, as contrasted with a situation-focused strategy, for dealing with job stress during the transition. An important element of Latack's work is a demonstration of the relationships between personal and career transitions.

The present paper integrates the work of Latack (1984) as well as that of Adams, Haynes and Hopson (1976), Nortier (1995) and Torbiorn (1982). It draws on the transition curve of Adams, Haynes and Hopson (1976) but adapts it to the career transition process of executive relocation.

METHODS

Over an eight-month period the two authors interviewed a total of 37 individuals (29 male, mean age 42, and 8 female, mean age 40) who had undergone a major relocation transition. The in-depth interview technique was used as it is enabled the researcher to encompass and probe a wide range of factors, including behavioural patterns. Interviews, moreover, are capable of elucidating emotions, reasoning, affective states and emotional experiences.

The subjects' transitions had involved moving self and often family from the United Kingdom, Australia, New Zealand and the United States to Hong Kong. The individuals were asked to explain in their own words the nature and process of their transition in adjusting to the environment in Hong Kong. The relocated executives worked in a range of public and private sector jobs.

These data were analysed using content analysis and formed the general pattern that has been called the relocation transition curve.

FINDINGS

The relocation transition curve (see Figure 19.1) is designed to present a general picture of the psychological steps that interviewed executives go through in the relocation process. It is not suggested that all individuals go through all steps. But from talking to many relevant individuals all relate to some steps, many see the process as very relevant in understanding what they have been through.

Stage one: unreality

The beginning of the relocation is a very busy time. It often involves selling property, saying farewell to friends, packing, travelling to the new location, living in a hotel, looking for a new home, finding schools for the children, beginning the new job and so on. This stage is therefore characterized by frenzied activity. Typically, this activity is at such a frantic pace that it is not really possible for those involved to psychologically process it. Therefore, the stage is characterized by a dreamlike state and a feeling of unreality. This distancing of the self from the full impact of the reality of the situation is a normal and healthy response to major change. It is a very mild form of shock. As such it enables people to cope by allowing them to take in the major change, one small piece at a time, rather than being overwhelmed by it.

Stage two: fantasia

The second stage involves a fascination with the new environment. Feelings at this time are often running high. For example, Hong Kong is typically seen as a very exotic environment; the markets, the street sweepers with the black cloth rimmed hats, the strange unknown vegetables, the Chinese medicine shops, the sing-song nature of the Cantonese language, the colourful Taoist temples and Buddhist nuns with shaved heads. New migrants in Hong Kong can feel like they are in a wonderful Asian Walt Disney production.

Stage three: interest

The interest stage is typically part of a downwards emotional trend. As the individual interacts with and examines the new environment, he or she realizes that the new place is not a wonderland. For example, the individual discovers Hong Kong is not a British city with a Chinese overlay but a Chinese city where the Europeans are but one minority group. The markets can now seem crowded and dirty, the streets sweltering and smelly, the exotic elements of the local diet can seem repulsive (pigs intestines and chickens feet) and the local language harsh.

Stage four: acceptance

This is the crisis point for many. It is the time when the reality of the situation has to be accepted. The expatriate and his or her family have to realize that this is not home and that they are strangers in a strange land. The relocated executive is forced to let go of many past comforting attitudes about his or her seemingly easy adjustment up to this time.

Typically this is the make or break time. At this stage some executives decide to return home, or their spouses return, or they stay on solely because of the expatriate gratuity element of their contracts but become embittered, racist and cynical. Some individuals never move past this stage but remain stuck psychologically.

Stage five: experimentation

For those who do accept the reality of the relocation and freely acknowledge both the benefits and the drawbacks of their new situation, it is possible to move on. Psychologically this step in the transition process means testing out new approaches. In Hong Kong, this can sometimes involve shifting apartment from a densely crowded area to an outlying island, or giving up on trying to have the same diet as at home, or taking a maid, or changing job. The important point is that in a strange environment the individual is never clear about the best way to deal with foreign situations. As a result he or she cannot make realistic and sensible choices until a range of options is experimented with.

Stage six: search for meaning

As individuals experiment, they find out what makes sense for them in their new environment. For example, purchasing a very expensive club membership, which would be unthinkable at home, provides a place of tranquillity and a social atmosphere. This experience may teach the person that he or she really values a quiet social retreat. This may be something that may have never occurred to the individual until he or she was deprived of it. Alternatively the executive may come to realize the futility of a high paying job that alienates him or her from family life. Having learned this, the family may all return home and the executive accept a lower income and lower promotion prospects in order to maintain a harmonious family life. As executives and their spouses experiment, they learn more and more about what is important and gives meaning to their lives. This enables them to make adjustments and adaptions that are positive and constructive from the individual's perspective.

Stage seven: integration

The final stage in the cycle is integration. That is, the person has come to accept the reality of the relocation, to experiment and identify what he or she likes and dislikes and to understand more about the self and what has value. Typically, the individual feels settled, stable and better able to pursue his or her career with vigour. Integration does not necessarily mean full social and cultural integration into the host country. One Hong Kong expatriate from Canada commented that he thought it impossible for an outsider ever to fully culturally integrate into the Cantonese Hong Kong culture. Stage seven of the relocation cycle means that the person both understands and accepts the reality of the relocation and spends the majority of the psychological effort dealing with work and family issues rather than relocation issues.

This seven-stage relocation transition cycle is an attempt by the authors to map out stages typically encountered by expatriates as they live through the first year or two of adjustment, whether in Hong Kong or elsewhere.

THE KEYS TO COPING

The ability to move through the cycle and adapt to a new environment varies enormously from individual to individual. After talking to many expatriate executives there are five key factors that determine coping levels.

Confidence

Dealing with a new, and at times intimidating, environment requires confidence and sometimes courage. There are many new and strange experiences for which the expatriate has no prior experience to call on as a guide. The first time the person struggles to make a Cantonese-speaking taxi driver understand an English language location or a non-English speaking waiter understand an order, it can be difficult (for both parties). This is especially true if the newcomer's attempts at the native tongue are faltering and causes amusement to the locals. Confidence is essential if the executive is to try new experiences and experiment with lifestyle options. Without the confidence to go through the experimentation step in the transition cycle individuals never find out what they like and dislike in the new unfamiliar environment.

Social support

Relocated executives and their families will cope much better if they rapidly develop a new social support network. In Hong Kong, having a close Chinese companion is extremely useful in understanding the subtle nuances of culture. There are a hundred minor things to find out about such as how much 'lucky money' to give at Chinese New Year and who you should give it to, or why someone says 'yes' when they mean 'no.

It is also very helpful to develop relations with other expatriates who have been through the same process. They can provide both real empathy and ideas worth experimenting with. They will enable the newcomer to discover that he or she is not alone in facing the mountain of frustrations that are so typical in relocation.

High levels of social support are very important at all stages of adjustment. Especially at the low point of acceptance when often the individual's frustration level is high and the sense of loneliness is at a peak.

Lifestyle

Eating a balanced diet, getting regular modest exercise and having some form of daily relaxation is important in any environment, but especially important after relocation. Maintaining a balanced lifestyle can be very difficult for many expatriates. Their diet changes in strange ways, for example, health food conscious expatriates in Hong Kong find to their dismay that it is difficult to buy brown rice. Exercise in a climate with high temperatures and high humidity is very difficult and often forces expatriates into joining sports clubs. This is not a problem if the company has a corporate membership; however, if the person has to pay for the membership themselves it can be punishingly expensive.

Maintaining a balanced lifestyle is important at all stages in the transition. However, at the low point of acceptance it is important to ensure that exercise is regular and that consumption of alcohol is neither excessive nor prolonged.

Welcoming the challenge

Often expatriates are people who have reached some type of career plateau. They have either achieved the goals they set for themselves and want an entirely new challenge or they have found their career path blocked and have decided to take a different route out. For these reasons they often welcome a challenge. However, the huge size of the change needed in relocation can be overwhelming. If expatriates can get through the acceptance stage and start experimenting, typically they discover that change and challenge are important to provide meaning in their lives. When this point is reached, their adjustment process becomes a lot easier.

People who have successfully faced and successfully deal with challenges in the past cope better with relocation.

Being creative

Individuals who are creative can come up with novel and different solutions to problems and typically cope well. Examples of innovative approaches to coping include spouses starting small importing and direct mail businesses to supply goods not readily available in Hong Kong, or taking up local forms of relaxation such as Tai Chi or Buddhist meditation.

A sense of humour

The ability to laugh at oneself or the situation one is in is an important characteristic of those who do well in transfers. Those who use humour effectively take mistakes in their stride and do not take them personally. As a consequence they feel less stress and tension. However, humour must be used with care and disparaging humour is never appropriate.

Marital communication

When couples have good interpersonal communication skills and can effectively deal with problems, the international experience can enhance their relationship. When communication between partners is not open the unique stresses associated with transfer can be very destructive. The quality of marital communication was seen by many respondents as a key to success of the overseas assignment.

WHAT THE ORGANIZATION CAN DO

Organizations can do a great deal to help their employees in relocating. Companies should never probe unnecessarily into their employees private lives, however, when it comes to relocation there are many private issues that greatly affect the success or failure of a move. Therefore organizations should proceed carefully and sensitively in dealing with relocation issues.

Selection criteria

Besides the typical technical, experiential and interpersonal characteristics used to select candidates for overseas posts, it is important for organizations to consider the key factors for coping, discussed above. That is, a high degree of personal confidence; a sound ability to develop new social support networks; an ability to maintain a balanced lifestyle with only modest disruption during a time of turbulence; an enduring desire for a new challenge and a creative approach to problem solving.

Interviewing the whole family

The causes of troublesome relocation are often related to family discontent. The spouse cannot find a suitable job, the children cannot settle at school and so on. Therefore it can be very useful for organizations to interview both the job candidate and his or her spouse. This can be a sensitive matter and families need to be reassured that the organization wishes only to see that the relocation is good for all parties. In the interview the organization can check out that both candidate and spouse wish to move. In addition it can be a good opportunity for the organization to talk through some of the typical chain of reactions experienced by families after relocation.

The preliminary visit

It is very common for the job candidate to have the chance to visit the new location before a decision is made on the move. This is very important. It is equally important that the family (or at least the spouse) also pay a preliminary visit. Although this visit is costly it can help to avoid even more costly relocation failures. It should be considered an investment in the successful relocation.

Social support

Organizations can do a great deal to support their newly relocated executives. This support may mean ensuring that both employee and spouse are invited out to lunch several times by different people during the first week of work. In addition, the executive should be guided as to the most appropriate recreation and sports facilities. Perhaps most importantly the relocated person will need a range of people to talk to and confide in. These should include at least one local, if possible, as well as other expatriates. In some cases, professional independent counselling services can be offered to both executive and spouse, if significant difficulties arise.

Setting realistic performance goals

Relocation can have a profoundly disruptive effect on some individuals' personal life and work performance. Consequently, it is important for organizations to set performance goals that are realistic and modify these if it appears that the relocated executive is having adjustment problems. It is important for organizations to realize that the relocation cycle can take between six and eighteen months to work through. This cycle needs to be considered when setting goals as newly relocated executives typically grossly underestimate the disruptive effect that their move can have on their performance.

International implications for business

Given the growing globalization of business and the current shortage of managers in many countries, organizations have little option but to transfer staff from home countries to overseas posts in order to meet business needs. This trend of relocation of managers seems likely to increase in the future given the rate of business expansion in places such as Asia and Eastern Europe.

The cycle as set out in this paper suggests that a multi-stage process of adjustment is common for relocated executives and their families. This process can take between six and eighteen months. At times newly transferred executives are likely to feel lost, sad and dispirited. This period is not conducive to peak managerial performance. If executives get stuck in an early stage of the readjustment cycle they are likely to remain less than optimally productive for a considerable period. All of this is financially expensive for the organization and emotionally expensive for the executives and their families.

To avoid such costs, organizations are well advised to take great care in selecting staff for relocation and in supporting them as they move through the phases of the relocation transition curve.

CONCLUSIONS

Relocation can be an exciting and energizing experience for many executives. However, it can also impose stresses and strains on the individual and his or her family. This paper sets out one model of adjustment of expatriates coming to a foreign country and suggests the types of characteristics that are important for coping with this type of change. In addition we have made several practical suggestions about what any organization can do to help achieve a higher rate of success in expatriate adjustment.

REFERENCES

Adams, J.D., Hayes, J., and Hopson, B. (1976) *Transition: Understanding and Managing Personal Change*, Martin Robertson, London.

Austen, C. (ed) (1986) *Cross-Cultural Re-entry: A Book of Readings*, Abllene Christian University Press, Abllene, Texas.

Befus, C. (1988) A multilevel treatment approach for culture shock experienced by sojourners. *International Journal of Intercultural Relations*, 12, pp. 381–400.

Black, S. and Stephens, G. (1989) The influence of the spouse on American expatriate adjustment and intent to stay in Pacific rim overseas assignments. *Journal of Management*, 15 pp. 529–44.

Blocklyn, P. (1989) Developing the international executive. *Personnel*, 66, p. 44.

Bridges, W. (1985) *Transitions: Making Sense of Life's Changes*, Addison-Wesley, Reading, MA.

Copeland, L. (1987) Safety and the expatriate: a personal account. *Mobility*, 8, pp. 19–24.

Erkut, S. (1986) Coping with teenagers' resistance to moving. *Mobility*, 7, pp. 39–43.

Holmes, T.H., and Rahe, R.H. (1967) The social readjustment rating scale. *Journal of Psychosomatic Research*, 11, pp. 213–18.

Hogan, G. and Goodson, J. (1990) The key to expatriate success. *Training and Development Journal*, January, pp. 50–2.

Hubbard, G. (1986) How to combat culture shock. *Management Today*, September, pp. 62–5.

Kubler-Ross, E. (1970) *On Death and Dying*, Collier, New York.

Latack, J.C. (1984) Career transitions within organizations: an exploratory study of work, nonwork, and coping strategies. *Organizational Behaviour and Human Performance*, **34**, pp. 296–322.

McClenahen, J.S. (1987) Why U.S. managers fail overseas. *Industry Week*, **235**, pp. 71–4.

McEnery, J. and DesHarnais, G. (1990) Culture shock. *Training and Development Journal*, April, pp. 43–7.

Nortier, F. (1995) A new angle on coping with change: managing transitions. *Journal of Management Development*, **14**, pp. 32–46.

Odenwald, S.B. (1993) *Global Training: How to Design A Program for the Multinational Corporation*, ASTD, Homewood, Ill.

Torbiorn, I. (1982) *Living Abroad: Personal Adjustments and Personnel Policy in Overseas Settings*, John Wiley and Sons, New York.

Wederspahn, G. and A. (1988) Overseas assignment without one's spouse. *Mobility*, **9**, pp. 67–70.

Chapter 20

Entrepreneurs in different environments and cultures, in Britain, Norway and Poland: towards a comparative framework

Krzysztof Obloj and Lars Kolvereid

INTRODUCTION

New business ventures development is one of the most important features of economic performance. Many specific economic and cultural factors that facilitate entrepreneurship have been researched and analysed in depth in Western European countries (Koning and Snijders 1992). However, this is not the case in the post-communist countries of Central and Eastern Europe, where research of this phenomena is mainly anecdotal or parochial. The main aim of this chapter is to explore cultures of entrepreneurs in three selected European countries: Great Britain, Norway and Poland that represent a vast political, economic and cultural diversity of Europe. The diversity of these countries should help to pinpoint most important differences and similarities of situation of European entrepreneurs and therefore can be considered a springboard to build a meaningful framework for quantitative and qualitative comparative research on entrepreneurship in Europe.

The choice of three very different European countries can be easily criticized, as can most choices in comparative studies. The rationale of our choice was obvious and well-documented cultural, political, and economic differences of Great Britain, Norway and Poland. Each of these countries represented at the time of the study (1989–1994) the three largest groups of European countries: European Community (EC) members, EFTA members, and post-communist countries. Hence, we believe that the countries included in the present survey encompass much of the economic and socio-cultural heterogeneity of European countries.

We consider Great Britain as a representative of aggressive, well-developed market economy and a traditional liberal democracy. Great Britain is also a representative of Anglo-Saxon management and entrepreneurship culture (Scheinberg and MacMillan 1988) in which profit is given more generously to the investors than employees. The characteristics that are most significantly present in the English business climate are individualism, deference and acceptance of inequality, self-control and reserve, conservatism, xenophobia, honesty and trust, regard for liberty and class consciousness (Tayeb 1993). In terms of GDP, Great Britain ranks as the fourth economy in the EC (after Germany, France and Italy), and its population (around 57 million) is similar to France and Italy and only slightly less than united Germany. During the 1980s, the British economy was characterized by a vicious circle of a high rate of inflation and unemployment, combined with a low productivity and growth rate (Obloj 1993).

Norway is a representative of the Nordic countries, politically following the social democratic path, with a prosperous and productive economy, in which a state sector plays an important role. Fundamental values of Nordic countries: equality, freedom, democracy, solidarity, security, and practicality, also shape the Norwegian business climate (Gannon 1994). Norway decided not to become a member of the EC in the 1972 and 1994 referendums and opted – consistently with its cultural predominant values – for an outsider role. Norway can be described as a small (population only slightly over 4 million) and rich country (one of the highest GDP per capita in Europe), with a limited but modern industrial base (main role played by oil, metals, forestry and fishery) and corporate portfolio. The unemployment rate has been relatively low by European standards, but rose to an all-time high of 8.9% early in 1993. Since 1987, the Norwegian economy has been in a mild recession.

Finally, Poland has about 39 million inhabitants and represents the largest economy among the post-communist countries of Europe. The country perfectly illustrates all problems of a social transition: political instability, economic recession, cultural change. For many years the best description of business culture was 'social vacuum', a term coined by Nowak (1979) to indicate that between general notion of nation and limited concept of immediate family, Poles did not have an important cultural frame. Hence, lack of developed business culture. In 1989 when Poland abolished communist rule, a drastic austerity program was introduced in order to transform the economy according to liberal market principles (Sachs and Lipton 1990a).

The immediate results of the implementation of so called 'Shock Therapy' received high praise from organizations such as the World Bank and IMF, and Western economists. However, in 1992, the Polish economy became stagnant and the country faced a short but deep recession. In all post-communist countries we observe the decrease of GNP, GDP, industrial production and investment, two-figure inflation and high unemployment persist. The transition from communist regime to democratic, market-regulated system, proved to be much more difficult than it was expected (Gabrisch et al. 1992). The year 1994 witnessed the reverse of many of the negative trends in the economy and showed signs of the economic recovery.

ENTREPRENEURSHIP IN POLAND

Despite the obvious importance of entrepreneurship in post-communist countries, most of the knowledge about entrepreneurs and new business ventures in the post-communist countries is still anecdotal (success or failure stories as reported by the press). Past research projects on Polish entrepreneurs dealt with craftsmen and facers performing in a planned economy and are of no value as a platform to predict or explain similarities and differences between Polish entrepreneurs and entrepreneurs from other countries in Europe.

Small business is not a new phenomenon in Poland. Before the Second World War, and even a few years after, private firms contributed up to 70% of GNP. Only after communists took power in the late 1940s and started the process of nationalization of industry, were strict limitations and closures of private firms operations started (Ploszajski 1992; Connor and Ploszajski 1992). Nevertheless, private entrepreneurs survived – both in the privately held agricultural sector and in the manufacturing and service sectors. The relaxation of regulations in the 1970s speeded up the rate of birth of new firms – about 350,000 firms, employing nearly 600,000 people and contributing 3% of GNP (Arendarski 1992). Since 1988 the number of private firms has grown exponentially and in 1992 the registered number of private firms exceeded 1.5 million, but more than 1.4 million are small in terms of capital, employment and sales.

The tangible and intangible importance of new ventures in Poland is growing. With the collapse of state-owned economy the new business ventures and privatized firms became the leading economic force (Kozminski 1993; Sachs and Lipton 1990b). The total production in the private sector in Poland increased from 17.4% of total industrial output in 1990 to 24.2% in 1991 and reached almost 40% in 1994. The private sector employs more than 50% of the work-force, produces more than 50% of GDP and its share of export increases every year. These figures represent the growing importance of entrepreneurship in Poland and, partly, the contraction of the state-owned sector. There is little doubt that private firms are important change agents in the process of changing norms, values and rules of conduct which is indispensable for market economy to perform correctly (Obloj and Davies 1991).

RESEARCH PROBLEM AND METHODOLOGY

The new ventures can perform their economic and social role successfully if the environment allows them to develop and grow. The major thrust of the economic reform in Poland since 1990 is oriented towards the creation of a market economy. Business environment which is supportive to the new ventures is an important element of this process, but we would expect that it takes time and money to develop the infrastructure required. Since the Polish economic transformation started only a few years ago, under extremely difficult conditions, we would expect that Polish entrepreneurs face an extreme, difficult environment compared to the business environment of new business founders in the developed market economies of Great Britain or Norway.

This proposition was split into two research questions: How do entrepreneurs in the respective countries perceive their business environment? What is the availability of policy and support services?

On the other hand, because of long-lasting differences in political and economic systems, we would expect the reasons leading to new firm formation in Poland and the Polish entrepreneurs' attitudes towards business venturing, to differ from those of Norwegian or British entrepreneurs. In short, we would expect different entrepreneurs' cultures to develop. These expectations are based on three main factors:

- the time lag of cultural, political and economic differences between post-communist country and mature market economies.
- the 'shock therapy' introduced in Poland an extreme form of competitive market economy with 'survival of the fittest' message.
- the new market economy with its high unemployment, poverty and political instability leaves many people with no option but to start business on their own.

Therefore, we expect the financially related attributes and reasons to start up to be predominant in Poland and to find a more diversified perspective in the mature British and Norwegian economies. This second proposition was split into two research questions: What are the reasons leading to new firm formation across countries? What attitudes towards entrepreneurship do the owners of new firms have in each country?

Measures

The research was based on the questionnaire developed by the international group of researchers comprising the so-called Society for Associated Researchers on International Entrepreneurship. The original English version of the questionnaire was used in Great Britain while translated versions were applied in Norway and Poland.

A set of 23 items was included to measure perceptions of the environment at the time of start-up. Respondents were asked to indicate the degree to which they agreed that the statement provided was an accurate description of the environment they faced, using a 5-point scale.

The availability of policy and support services was measured by 19 items. Respondents were asked whether they perceived these services to be available and affordable using a three point scale: 1 = available and affordable; 2 = available but not affordable; 3 = not available. For the purpose of the present analysis, the responses were re-coded into two categories: available and not available.

Reasons leading to start-up were measured by 23 items. The items were selected on the basis of earlier studies by Scheinberg and MacMillan (1988) and Blais, Toulouse and Clement (1990). Respondents were asked to indicate the degree to which each of the items influenced their decision to start the business along a 5-point Likert-type scale.

Attitudes toward entrepreneurship was measured by 21 items selected on the basis of previous cross-cultural research (McGrath *et al.* 1992).

Data collection

The Polish version of the questionnaire was mailed in June–July 1992 to 624 entrepreneurs in all 49 'counties' in Poland and in November 1993 to 450 entrepreneurs. The addresses were randomly taken from new business directories published in 1991 and 1992 as no other sources of addresses was available. After several telephone and direct contacts, 127 questionnaires were returned. In Norway, 1164 questionnaires were mailed out to all entrepreneurs from four (out of nineteen) counties. The addresses were taken from a Bryde's Trade Register (a list of all new ventures) and after one reminder 250 venture initiators answered the questionnaire. In Great Britain, the target sample was abstracted from industrial trade directories and questionnaires were mailed out several times until 744 questionnaires were collected. For the purpose of this study we chose from each data base only those ventures which were established after 1986, thus reducing the number of British cases to 408, Norwegian to 209 and Polish to 77.

Sample

The profiles of the entrepreneurs are important as a background information. First, as shown in Table 20.1, there is a striking similarity concerning the age distribution of entrepreneurs across countries. Entrepreneurs from all three countries are relatively young when they start their first firms (mean age 32–33 years), which indicates that, irrespective of the type of environment or industry, the risk and stress connected with new ventures is a young person's domain. The second similarity is the number of firms started. We would expect that entrepreneurs from Poland should be at a disadvantage as the tradition and conditions for entrepreneurship were limited during the last fifty years. However, in our samples entrepreneurs have similar experiences with, in average, about one former start-up. Third, services is the largest industrial sector among the entrepreneurs in all three countries. The most probable explanation is that

Table 20.1 Profile of the entrepreneurs

	UK	Norway	Poland
Number of respondents			
Total	408	209	77
Male	368	179	70
Female	38 (9.4%)	26 (12.7%)	7 (9.1%)
Industry sector			
Farming, fishing and mining	0	7 (3.3%)	6 (7.8%)
Manufacturing	147 (36%)	25 (12%)	22 (28.6%)
Construction	21 (5.1%)	35 (16.7%)	9 (11.7%)
Services	240 (58.8%)	142 (67.9%)	40 (51.9%)
Location of business			
Rural	101 (24.8%)	114 (54.8%)	5 (6.5%)
Minor city	215 (52.7%)	74 (35.6%)	20 (26%)
Major city	57 (14%)	20 (9.6%)	26 (33.8%)
Capital	35 (8.6%)	0	26 (33.8%)
Highest education level achieved			
Compulsory	127 (31.4%)	34 (16.3%)	4 (5.2%)
High School/Professional	175 (43.2%)	103 (49.3%)	15 (19.5%)
University	58 (14.3%)	56 (26.2%)	45 (58.4%)
Graduate and postgraduate study	45 (11.1%)	16 (7.7%)	13 (16.9%)
Age at first start-up			
age (mean)	33.5	32.4	32.8
age (standard deviation)	9.7	7.8	6.7
Number of previous start-ups			
number of start-ups (mean)	0.70	0.89	1.01
number of start-ups (stan. deviation)	2.6	1.4	1.3

capital, legal, technical barriers of entry and costs of exit are lower than in other sectors.

Two visible differences in our sample deserve attention. While 77.5% of British and 90.4% of Norwegian entrepreneurs in the sample located their firms in a rural area or small cities, this is the case for only 32.5% of the Polish firms. Another notable difference between the samples from the three countries is the education of the entrepreneurs. Polish business founders in our sample have reached a much higher educational level than Norwegian and British entrepreneurs. We believe that the differences in the localization pattern is an artifact resulting from sampling and data collection procedures in the respective countries. We are not sure whether education differences found reflect sampling procedures or actual differences. At least one other study suggests that Polish entrepreneurs tend to have a higher education than new business founders from other countries (Toulouse and Vallee 1993).

Analysis

We proceeded by comparing the data from the three countries by using chi-square tests and one-way analysis of variance. In our earlier paper published in the *International Small Business Journal*, we used a factor analysis trying to minimize a danger that respondents from the different countries may have interpreted the questions differently and the factor structure may differ from country to country. The reader should be aware of this common problem in cross-national research when examining our findings.

The results are presented in the order in which our research questions have been posed: Are there any differences between entrepreneurs in the three countries with regard to: their perceptions of the environment? The availability of policy and support systems? Their reasons to start their business? Their attitudes to entrepreneurship? The items concerning the various concepts are grouped according to our a priori classification.

Perceptions of the environment

To test for differences in the perceptions of the environment we used one-way analysis of variance. Surprisingly, the statistical analysis does not support the common sense general thesis that entrepreneurs in Poland are faced with high scarcity of resources in their business, and a hostile and unstable environment.

Instead, Norway stands out as the country where skilled labour, managerial labour and labour skilled in new technologies are more easily available and the environment is characterized by stability, low hostility and complexity. We can say that it is the Norwegian business environment that is perceived as the most abundant in different resources, rather than the Polish business environment being exceptionally scarce and dominated by shortages.

Availability of policy and support services

To test for differences in the availability of policy and support services, we used simple chi-square tests. The results shown in Table 20.3 indicates that services provided in Poland mostly by the private sector, i.e. legal services, consulting services and accounting services, are evaluated as available, while other policy and support services are virtually non-existent in Poland. Surprisingly, the Polish situation is not unique at all. While cross-country analysis indicates that Great Britain is the country where the largest variety of support services is available as compared to the other countries, entrepreneurs from Norway perceive the relative availability of policy and support services in their countries as very limited. In the case of Norway only plants/offices at reduced costs, loan guarantees and accounting services are considered easily available.

The analysis of the chi-square test indicates an interesting finding. The cross-country comparison across 18 items which constitute policy and support services yields statistically highly significant differences. It means that each of these countries, deliberately or by chance, follow very different routes in their effort to support entrepreneurship.

Reasons leading to start-up

Polish entrepreneurs score significantly differently from their Norwegian and British counterparts on five (of a total of six) status/recognition items (see Table 20.4). It seems that Poles start their business more often than Britons and Norwegians to achieve a higher position in society, to have more influence in the community, to be respected by friends, to increase the status and prestige of the family and through a desire to have high earnings. On all of these items, Norwegian entrepreneurs receive the lowest score, while Britons fall between the two extremes. On the other hand, the British entrepreneurs score higher than entrepreneurs from the two other countries with respect to a desire to achieve something and get recognition for it. While status and money seems more important to the Polish entrepreneurs than to entrepreneurs from the other countries, the British entrepreneurs are more concerned about recognition. For Norwegian entrepreneurs none of these items appear to be an issue.

In fact, the only item on which Norwegians score higher than entrepreneurs from the other two countries, is on one of the innovation/learning items: Norwegian entrepreneurs, more often than entrepreneurs from the other countries, report that they start their business to keep learning.

Table 20.2 Perceptions of the environment across countries

	Great Britain Mean	SD	Norway Mean	SD	Poland Mean	SD	Sig.
LABOUR							
Skilled labour was available	2.6	1.1	2.3	1.1	2.8	1.3	ac
Managerial labour was available	2.6	1.0	2.9	1.1	2.3	1.2	abc
Labour skilled in new technologies was available	2.4	1.0	2.9	1.0	2.5	1.2	ac
Suppliers were available	3.4	1.1	3.9	1.1	3.4	1.2	ac
Machines and equipment were available	3.2	1.2	3.5	1.2	2.8	1.3	abc
CAPITAL							
Capital from financial institutions was available	2.8	1.2	3.6	1.2	2.4	1.3	abc
Capital from other businesses (e.g. suppliers, customers) was available	2.2	1.1	2.8	1.2	2.8	1.4	ac
Capital from other sources (e.g. family and friends) was available	2.6	1.2	2.4	1.1	2.7	1.3	ac
CUSTOMERS							
Customers were already interested in buying the product	3.8	1.0	3.9	1.1	4.0	0.9	
Customers were easily accessible	3.5	1.1	3.8	1.1	3.4	1.2	ac
The customers were mainly local	3.1	1.2	3.4	1.2	2.8	1.3	ac
It was relatively easy to identify a typical customer	3.4	1.3	3.5	1.0	3.3	1.2	

ECONOMY

The local economy was booming	2.8	1.1	3.0	1.0	2.5	1.2	bc
There was a wide range of new incentives to encourage new start-ups	2.7	1.3	2.4	1.0	2.8	1.3	ac
Within my industry there was a wide range of businesses offering similar but not identical products	3.0	1.2	3.1	1.2	3.0	1.2	
There was a wide range of new businesses in the area that I live	2.7	1.1	2.5	1.0	3.0	1.3	ac
There was a wide range of new businesses in my industry	2.6	1.0	2.4	1.0	2.8	1.3	ac

STABILITY

The sales in my industry were relatively stable	2.9	1.0	3.6	1.0	2.9	1.1	ac
The price-cost margin in my industry was relatively stable	3.1	1.0	3.7	0.9	3.1	1.0	ac
The technology used in my industry was relatively stable	3.0	1.0	3.4	1.0	3.2	1.1	a

HOSTILITY

There were a large number of new business failures in the area that I live	2.7	1.0	2.3	0.9	2.4	1.0	ab
There were a large number of new business failures in my industry	2.7	1.0	2.2	0.9	2.4	1.1	a
There was political uncertainty in the country	2.5	0.9	2.3	0.9	3.0	1.4	bc

*a represents a significant difference (p < .05) between UK and Norway; **b** represents a significant deference (p < .05) between UK and Poland; **c** represents a significant difference (p < .05) between Norway and Poland.*

Table 20.3 The availability of policy and support services across countries

	Great Britain Not available	Great Britain Available	Norway Not available	Norway Available	Poland Not available	Poland Available	Chi-square	Sig.
Low cost legal services	240 (227)	148 (161)	124 (113)	69 (80)	20 (44)	56 (32)	36.8	.000
Low cost consulting services	148 (171)	242 (219)	108 (85)	85 (108)	33 (33)	43 (43)	17.0	.000
Courses in new business management	131 (132)	299 (254)	101 (65)	91 (127)	35 (26)	41 (50)	57.0	.000
Market information	178 (197)	207 (188)	103 (97)	87 (93)	52 (39)	24 (37)	13.5	.001
Skills training programs	160 (190)	219 (189)	123 (96)	69 (96)	42 (38)	34 (38)	25.2	.000
Export assistance	191 (222)	159 (128)	135 (117)	49 (67)	59 (46)	14 (27)	29.2	.000
Plants/offices at reduced cost	219 (212)	162 (169)	82 (107)	110 (85)	57 (40)	15 (32)	29.7	.000
Business advisory service	69 (117)	314 (266)	97 (57)	91 (131)	31 (23)	43 (51)	72.1	.000
Tax-free-trade zones/enterprise zones	265 (291)	108 (82)	164 (143)	19 (40)	62 (58)	12 (16)	26.3	.000
Low interest loans	250 (274)	131 (107)	162 (138)	30 (54)	–	–	22.2	.000
Operating subsidies	325 (333)	54 (46)	177 (169)	15 (23)	64 (65)	10 (9)	5.0	.081

							χ²	Sig.
Industry related grants	267 (292)	113 (88)	158 (146)	32 (44)	69 (57)	5 (17)	24.6	.000
Grants to assist in start-ups	208 (250)	173 (131)	149 (124)	40 (65)	66 (49)	8 (25)	53.4	.000
Loan guarantees	271 (257)	102 (116)	111 (132)	80 (60)	58 (51)	16 (32)	15.9	.000
Public venture capital	312 (325)	62 (49)	173 (165)	17 (25)	70 (64)	4 (10)	10.8	.005
Grants to support the development of new products and processes	265 (292)	108 (81)	165 (149)	25 (41)	68 (58)	6 (16)	27.6	.000
Locally-based enterprise support agency	150 (220)	229 (159)	156 (111)	53 (80)	67 (43)	7 (31)	128.8	.000
Low cost accounting services	261 (228)	121 (154)	105 (114)	86 (77)	20 (44)	54 (30)	46.4	.000

The expected value in case of independence among groups is shown in parentheses.

Table 20.4 Reasons leading to new firm formation across countries

	Great Britain Mean	SD	Norway Mean	SD	Poland Mean	SD	Sig.
STATUS/RECOGNITION							
To achieve a higher position for myself in society	2.3	1.2	1.6	0.9	2.7	1.3	abc
To have more influence in my community	1.4	0.8	1.4	0.9	2.3	1.2	bc
To be respected by friends	1.7	1.0	1.2	0.6	2.1	1.1	abc
To achieve something and get recognition for it	2.9	1.3	2.2	1.2	2.6	1.3	abc
To increase the status and prestige of my family	1.9	1.1	1.4	0.7	2.5	1.2	abc
Desire to have high earnings	3.1	1.3	2.7	1.2	3.7	1.0	abc
INNOVATION/LEARNING							
To develop an idea for a product	2.2	1.4	2.7	1.4	3.4	1.3	abc
To be innovative and be in the forefront of technological development	2.3	1.3	2.0	1.2	3.1	1.2	abc
To keep learning	2.9	1.3	3.3	1.1	2.8	1.3	ac
To be challenged by the problems and opportunities of starting and growing a new business	3.1	1.4	2.2	1.2	3.0	1.4	
INDEPENDENCE/FREEDOM							
To have greater flexibility for my personal and family life	3.4	1.3	3.1	1.3	3.5	1.3	ac
To have considerable freedom to adapt my own approach to work	3.7	1.2	3.7	1.1	3.9	1.1	

WELFARE/COMMUNITARIANISM

To contribute to the welfare of my relatives	2.4	1.4	3.0	1.3	3.6	1.0	abc
To contribute to the welfare of people with the same background as me	1.5	0.9	1.6	0.9	2.7	1.3	bc
To contribute to the welfare of the community I live in	1.8	1.0	2.2	1.1	2.4	1.1	ab
To give myself, my spouse and children security	3.4	1.4	3.0	1.3	3.8	1.0	abc

TAXES

As a vehicle to reduce the burden of taxes I face	1.5	1.0	1.6	1.0	1.9	1.2	bc
To have access to indirect benefits such as tax exemptions	1.9	1.1	1.8	1.1	2.0	1.2	

ROLES

I wanted to continue a family tradition	1.3	0.8	1.3	0.8	1.5	1.1	b
To follow the example of a person that I admire	1.4	0.9	1.2	0.6	1.7	1.1	abc

OPPORTUNITY

To take advantage of an opportunity that appeared	3.7	1.2	3.8	1.2	3.5	1.3	
It made sense at that time in my life	3.5	1.3	3.5	1.1	3.5	1.2	

a represents a significant difference ($p < .05$) between UK and Norway; **b** represents a significant deference ($p < .05$) between UK and Poland; **c** represents a significant difference ($p < .05$) between Norway and Poland.

Polish business founders, however, score higher than their British and Norwegian counterparts with regard to the desire to develop an idea for a product and with regard to the need to be innovative and in the forefront of technological development.

With regard to innovation/freedom, Norwegian entrepreneurs score significantly lower than their British and Polish colleagues on the desire to have greater flexibility for their personal and family life. No significant differences between the countries are found on the desire to adapt ones' own approach to work.

Concerning the welfare/communitarianism items, the general tendency is that the Polish entrepreneurs receive the highest score, followed by Norwegian and British entrepreneurs. The exception is the desire to achieve security for self, spouse and children, where the Britons score higher than the Norwegians.

With regard to taxes, the only significant difference found is between Polish entrepreneurs, who appear to have started their business more often to reduce the burden of taxes, than entrepreneurs from the two other countries. This fits into the picture suggested earlier, that Polish entrepreneurs are relatively more concerned about money.

The Polish entrepreneurs report that, more so than entrepreneurs from the other countries, they wanted to follow the example of a person admired. They also score significantly higher than British entrepreneurs on the desire to follow a family tradition.

No significant differences are found between business founders in the three countries with regard to the two opportunity items.

Personal attitudes to entrepreneurship

Norwegian entrepreneurs report change in social status and changes in jobs or residence to be more difficult than entrepreneurs from the two other countries (see Table 20.5). Norwegians also score significantly lower than entrepreneurs from the other countries on the statement indicating that having a lot of money means you come from an influential family. The Polish entrepreneurs, more so than entrepreneurs from Britain and Norway agree that having a lot of money comes from being an expert in your field.

Norwegians score higher than Britons on the item stating that power is giving complete and detailed instructions on the way others should do their work. The British entrepreneurs also score lower than entrepreneurs from the two other countries with respect to the item stating that work is the way through which the respondent develops his or her identity and self-respect.

The Polish entrepreneurs score higher than respondents from the two other countries with respect to the item stating that entrepreneurship

Table 20.5 Personal attitudes to entrepreneurship across countries

	Great Britain Mean	SD	Norway Mean	SD	Poland Mean	SD	Sig.
CHANGE							
Having rights means every citizen is able to influence the decisions of politicians	3.4	1.2	3.4	1.1	3.3	1.3	
Change in social status is possible for everyone	3.9	.9	3.5	1.1	3.9	.9	ac
Change of jobs or residence is highly discouraged and very difficult	2.5	1.0	2.9	1.2	2.3	1.1	ac
MONEY							
Having a lot of money comes from being an expert in your field	2.3	1.0	2.6	1.1	3.2	1.1	bc
Having a lot of money means you come from an influential family	2.1	1.0	1.8	.9	2.3	1.0	ac
WORK							
Time is a limited resource	4.3	.9	4.1	1.0	4.2	1.0	
The private life and time of an employee is a matter of concern for my business	3.5	1.0	3.4	1.2	3.6	.9	a
Power is giving complete and detailed instructions to the way others should do their job	2.3	1.0	2.7	1.2	2.5	1.2	
Work is the means through which I develop my identity and self respect	3.6	1.0	4.1	.8	4.2	.7	ab

Table 20.5 Continued

	Great Britain Mean	SD	Norway Mean	SD	Poland Mean	SD	Sig.
BUSINESS VENTURING							
Being an entrepreneur means being a technical expert	2.0	.8	2.0	.9	2.6	1.0	bc
Entrepreneurs produce existing products in a more efficient way	2.9	1.0	2.8	1.0	3.3	1.0	bc
Being an entrepreneur means not being able to find a job	1.8	.9	1.4	.6	1.8	.9	ac
Starting a business means a risk of not getting your past employment back	3.3	1.1	3.6	1.2	3.3	1.2	a
Starting a business means uncertainty but adds to the excitement of life	4.3	.7	4.1	.9	4.2	.9	a
SUCCESS AND FAILURE							
Failure is associated with losing respect	2.9	1.1	2.6	1.1	2.9	1.1	a
Being successful is associated with making a lot of money	3.3	1.1	2.5	1.0	3.3	1.0	ac
Being successful is associated with being well educated	2.4	1.0	1.7	.6	3.0	1.1	abc

DUTY

I have a duty to uphold the values and reputation of my family	3.5	1.1	3.3	1.3	3.8	.7	bc
I have a duty to give all clients and customers the same treatment	3.8	1.0	3.9	1.1	4.0	.9	

EQUALITY

Equality is everyone's right	3.9	1.1	3.9	1.1	4.0	.9	
Equality is characterized by a stress on rewards based on merit, ability and skill	3.3	1.0	3.9	1.0	4.0	1.0	ab

a represents a significant difference ($p < .05$) between UK and Norway; **b** represents a significant deference ($p < .05$) between UK and Poland; **c** represents a significant difference ($p < .05$) between Norway and Poland.

implies being a technical expert and with respect to entrepreneurs producing existing products in a more efficient way. Norwegians disagree more than other respondents to the item stating that being an entrepreneur means not being able to find a job, but they agree more than Great Britain entrepreneurs that becoming an entrepreneur implies a risk of not getting your past employment back. British entrepreneurs score higher than their Norwegian colleagues on the item stating that being an entrepreneur means uncertainty, but adds to the excitement of life.

In Britain, more so than in Norway, failure is found to be associated with losing respect. Norwegians also disagree more than Poles and Britons that success is associated with making a lot of money. The Polish entrepreneurs agree more to the statement that success is associated with being well-educated, followed by British and Norwegian entrepreneurs.

The Polish business founders score significantly higher on the duty to uphold the values and reputation of the family. With regard to equality, the British entrepreneurs score lower than entrepreneurs from the two other countries with regard to equality being characterized by a stress on rewards based on merit, ability and skill.

CONCLUSIONS

We started our inquiry into environments and cultures of the British, Norwegian and Polish entrepreneurs with two general propositions. The first stated that the Polish entrepreneurs face a less favourable environment than entrepreneurs in developed economies, while the second indicated the dominance of financially related attitudes toward entrepreneurship and reasons for Polish start-ups.

When examining our findings, three trends are apparent. First, the findings indicate that the environmental conditions for starting a new firm are not extreme in Poland, and they are perceived as being more favourable in Norway than in the other two countries. The similarities with regard to the business incubation environment between Poland and Great Britain are more striking than the differences between the two countries. Even though the Polish infrastructure is relatively poorly developed, entrepreneurs in Poland appear to be able to get access to the required resources through alternative means.

Second, the support services are perceived to be better developed in Britain than in the two other countries. Norway stands out only on a few services, such as plants/offices at reduced cost, loan guarantees and accounting services. In Poland, services provided by the public sector in other countries appear to be virtually non-existent, while (private) legal and accounting services appear to be well-developed. These findings only partially support our first proposition that Polish entrepreneurs do not perceive their environment as more hostile, turbulent or scarce than those in Great Britain or Norway, while they agree that the environment lacks necessary policy and support services.

Our third finding relates to those important aspects of entrepreneurial cultures in the three countries that regulate reasons leading to the formation of new firms and personal attitudes to entrepreneurship. In Poland, entrepreneurs start their business mainly to increase their status, to develop a product which often uses a superior technology in order to provide money and a secure future for themselves, their family and their community. We can talk of 'financially-driven' Polish entrepreneurs. Norwegians seem to be more concerned about learning than entrepreneurs from the other countries. Status does not seem to be an issue for Norwegian business founders, but independence and freedom matter. British entrepreneurs appear to be concerned primarily about freedom, recognition and money for themselves and their business rather than their community.

Personal attitudes to entrepreneurship also differ across countries. For Norwegian entrepreneurs, change is perceived as being more difficult to deal with than for entrepreneurs in the two other countries. Becoming an entrepreneur in Norway is not associated with not being able to find a job, but once you have started a business, you risk not being able to return to your previous job. Polish entrepreneurs perceive education to be much more important in Poland than in the two other countries. Having a lot of money comes from being an expert in your field. Polish entrepreneurs relate entrepreneurship primarily to expertise, equality and success. British entrepreneurs are similar to Norwegians with respect to the relatively low emphasis on education, but similar to Poland with respect to money, and the Norwegian reluctance to change.

Let us summarize with a conclusion comparing entrepreneurs operating in an emerging environment in the Polish post-communist economy, with the developed economies of Great Britain and Norway. In spite of the preliminary and pioneering nature of our research comparing entrepreneurs in three very different countries, we can report three generalized trends that shape a culture of Polish entrepreneurs:

- The business environment in Poland is not extremely hostile, turbulent or complex.
- The underdevelopment of a supportive environment is mainly due to the lack of intervention and support of government and will most probably produce 'do-it-yourself' attitude of entrepreneurs.
- Universal values such as freedom, flexibility and new market/product exploration play an important role in shaping Polish entrepreneurs' norms and values, but money became a dominant value of Polish entrepreneurs.

ACKNOWLEDGEMENTS

An earlier version of this paper (using a different statistical approach), titled Entrepreneurship in Emerging Versus Mature Economies: An Exploratory Survey, appeared in the *International Small Business Journal*, Vol. 12, No. 4, 1994, with permission.

REFERENCES

Arendarski, A. (1992) *Polish Private Firms*, Marbis, Warsaw.

Blais, R., Toulouse, J., and Clement, B. (1990) *International Comparisons of Entrepreneurial Motivation Based on Personal Equation, Hierarchical Analysis, and Other Statistical Methods*, Proceedings of the 30th World Conference of Small Business, (eds R. Gomulka and W. Ward) International Council, Washington, DC.

Connor, W.D. and Ploszajski, P. (1992) *The Polish Road From Socialism*, Sharpe Inc, New York.

Gabrish, H. *et al.* (1992) *Depression and Inflation: Threats to Political and Social Stability*, Vienna Institute For Comparative Economic Studies, Vienna.

Gannon, M.J. (1994) *Understanding Global Cultures*, Sage, London.

Koning, de A. and Snijders, J. (1992) Policy on small and medium-sized enterprises in countries of the European community. *International Small Business Journal*, **10**, pp. 25–39.

Kozminski, A.K. (1993) *Catching Up*, SUNY Press, Albany, NY.

McGrath, R.G., MacMillan, I.C., Yang, E., and Tsai, W.M.H. (1992) Does culture endure or is it malleable? Issues for entrepreneurial economic development. *Journal of Business Venturing*, **7**, pp. 441–58.

Nowak, S. (1979) System wartosci spoleczenstwa polskiego (The Value System of the Polish Society), *Studia Socjologiczne*, **4**, pp. 155–73.

Obloj, K. (1993) The European economic community as a core market: diverse cultures and perspectives, in *Organizational Communication and Management: A Global Perspective*, (eds A.K. Kozminski and D. Cushman) SUNY Press, Albany, pp. 105–20.

Obloj, K. and Davis, A. (1991) Innovation without change. *Journal of Management Studies*, **18**, pp. 323–39.

Ploszajski, P. (1992) *Entrepreneurship in Making*, PFIBS, Warsaw.

Sachs, J. and Lipton, D. (1990a) Creating a Market Economy in Eastern Europe: the case of Poland. *Brooking Papers on Economic Activity*, **1**, Brookings Institute, Washington, DC.

Sachs, J. and Lipton, D. (1990b) Privatization in Eastern Europe: the case of Poland. *Brooking Papers on Economic Activity*, **2**, Brookings Institute, Washington, DC.

Scheinberg, S. and MacMillan, I. (1988) An eleven country study of motivations to start a business, in *Frontiers of Entrepreneurship Research* (eds B. Kirchhoff *et al.*) Babson College, Wellesley, MA.

Tayeb, M. (1993) English Culture and Business Organization, in *Management in Western Europe* (ed D. Hickson) Walter de Gruyter, Berlin, pp. 47–64.

Toulouse, J.M. and Vallee, L. (1993) *Entrepreneurship and Integration: The Case of Polish Entrepreneurs in Montreal*. Paper presented at the Third Global Conference on Entrepreneurship Research, Lyon, France, March 8–10.

Chapter 21

Culture, consumer behaviour and global market segmentation

Peter G.P. Walters

INTRODUCTION

The erosion of national boundaries as a barrier to international business has fundamentally altered the competitive climate in many industries in recent years, and the 'globalization' concept has had a powerful impact on business strategy (Porter 1980; Hout *et al.* 1982). Primary forces driving the globalization of markets include greater integration of the world economy, rapid technological change, high R&D costs, advances in communication and transportation, decreased protectionism and an enhanced capability to co-ordinate world wide operations (Terpstra 1987).

These developments imply that global market oportunities and competitive pressures should be the primary strategic focus and that managers need to adopt a world-wide focus unhindered by a domestic market emphasis and prejudices. At the same time, responsiveness to local market needs is often desirable (Doz 1986; Quelch and Hoff 1986). Thus, despite the consensus in favour of a global orientation, there is still disagreement on important issues. These include the extent of international market convergence occurring and the appropriate balance between the conflicting pressures for globally efficient strategies and the need for local market responsiveness.

The epicentre for much of this discussion has been the 'standardization' issue which embraces both of the key questions noted above. In a controversial article, which is the starting point for much of the subsequent debate, Levitt (1983) commented that as old differences in tastes or ways of doing business go . . . common preferences lead to standardization of products. Ohmae (1989) writes in a similar vein that globalization is driven not so much by diversification or competition as by the needs and preferences of customers. Chakravarthy and Perlmutter (1985) argue, along the same lines, that centralization is boosted by the continuing homogenization of product-needs between nations and the marketing systems and their business infrastructures.

The notion of market homogenization and the consequent call for standardization of policies and programmes in overseas markets, sometimes leads to a discussion in which the globalization and standardization constructs are confused. This is unfortunate since there is no determinist linkage between the two concepts. The viability of significant standardization of international business strategy and programmes is often limited, irrespective of the global vision of managers. For example, the feasibility of standardized international marketing policies is frequently constrained by important market differences that cannot be ignored by globally oriented managers (Buzzell 1968; Sorenson and Weichmann 1975; Walters 1986; and Jain 1989).

Despite the sometimes confused discussion, a crucial part of the market convergence debate relates to the impact of the powerful forces promoting interaction on the cultural context and consumer behaviour in global markets. Questions of particular relevance include: To what extent is cultural convergence occurring? Has the age of the uniform global consumer arrived? What are the implications for global market segmentation?

In order to explore these issues, this chapter initially focuses on the convergence issue in regard to the cultural environment and consumer behaviour in overseas markets. The implications of the 'culture-consumer behaviour' nexus for the segmentation of global markets are then evaluated in the light of the preceding discussion.

THE CULTURAL ENVIRONMENT

Definition

Numerous definitions of culture have been offered in the literature – see for example Chapter 2 in this book. They range from complex, anthropological interpretations to popular, non-academic characterizations of the culture construct. Terpstra and David (1985: 47), in an attempt to bridge the gap between scientific and popular descriptions of the concept, have offered the following definition of culture:

> Culture is a learned, shared, compelling, interrelated set of symbols whose meanings provide a set of orientations for members of a society. These orientations, taken together, provide solutions to problems that all societies must solve if they are to remain viable.
>
> (*Terpstra and David 1985: 47*)

Cultural homogeneity therefore implies shared norms, values and perspectives which usually result in patterns of economic, social behaviour that exhibit important common features. Institutional, corporate and political frameworks will also reflect the cultural environment.

Key dimensions

A number of key cultural dimensions have been identified in the literature and these are commonly used when comparing the cultural context in overseas markets. Important cultural variables include religion; language; attitudes to time, change, work, wealth, consumption, the future and achievement; conceptualizations of self and the world; role relationships; and social organization (Samovar and Porter 1976).

Other dimensions of cultural variation have been identified. For example, differences in perceptual differentiation, utilization and evaluation of information, and patterns of action (Triandis 1983); differences concerning the 'language' of time, of space, of material possessions, of friendship patterns and of agreements (Hall 1960); differences in regard to 'power distance', 'uncertainty avoidance', 'individualism-collectivism', and 'masculinity-femininity' (Hofstede 1980).

CULTURE AND CONSUMER BEHAVIOUR IN INTERNATIONAL MARKETS

Models

Mainstream models of buyer behaviour identify culture as a key variable influencing consumer behaviour and Kotler (1991) has commented that cultural factors exert the widest and deepest influence on consumer behaviour. The importance commonly attached to cultural variables is exemplified in mainstream consumer behaviour models such as the Engel, Kollat and Blackwell (EKB) model.

In the EKB model (Engel, Blackwell and Miniard 1993) environmental influences, individual differences and psychological processes are identified as three 'key forces shaping consumer behaviour'. Inspection of the factors identified under these three forces indicates that the majority are variables – such as social class, family, motivation, attitudes, values, lifestyle and learning – which directly or indirectly have a strong cultural dimension. Cultural factors therefore play a key role in the analysis of consumer behaviour.

Little work has been done on models of consumer behaviour with a specific international orientation, and it can be argued that frameworks such as the EKB model have universal validity. However, interesting contrasts emerge when comparing the EKB model with a specifically international framework, such as the pioneering cross-cultural model of buyer behaviour proposed by Sheth and Sethi (1977).

The Sheth and Sethi and EKB models both attach great importance to cultural and social environmental factors as determinants of consumer behaviour. However, Sheth and Sethi place more emphasis on non-cultural variables that are commonly relatively homogeneous within many national markets. Particular significance is given to economic variables such as the stage of economic development, income levels and distribution, technology and the institutional context, particularly in respect of marketing channels and the communication infrastructure.

Other variables, that are not considered in either the EKB or Sheth and Sethi models, may be important in accounting for variance in patterns of behaviour between foreign markets. For example, the legal context and the conditions of product use are likely to have a significant impact on important dimensions of consumer behaviour in many markets.

Most of the factors discussed above are largely outside the control of the firm and thus have to be accepted as exogenous variables. Even when the firm has the possibility of affecting some of these variables, it is necessary to move very cautiously. This is particularly the case if the aim is to intercede to attempt to influence culturally determined patterns of behaviour.

The cultural context in global markets

Many cultural factors vary sharply between overseas markets. Ethno-linguistic variables, such as language and religion, are particularly likely to exhibit strong and continuing divisions in many national and international markets. In some areas, such as Eastern Europe and the former Soviet Union, these differences have increased in significance in recent years. As a result, in the absence of strong central authority, centrifugal forces based upon historic cultural differences are fuelling a process of ethno-linguistic 'Balkanization' of the region. This reflects strong nationalist pressures and rivalry and is evidence of the sharp cultural fissures, often suppressed under authoritarian regimes, that continue to divide peoples in many parts of the world.

In addition to the broad macro forces noted above, there is plentiful empirical data which supports the view that cultural variance is an important fact of life in world markets. For example, Hofstede's (1980) work provides evidence of diversity in over sixty different countries in terms of four basic cultural dimensions – see Chapter 9 in this book. In a similar vein, Ronen and Shenkar's (1985) review of eight studies using attitudinal data to cluster countries also indicates that significant cultural heterogeneity is a fact of life in many international markets.

Although evidence of continuing cultural heterogeneity is incontrovertible, it is also apparent that increased international communication and the erosion of traditional values in many countries is promoting more homogeneity in some key cultural dimensions, most notably lifestyle. Greater convergence in consumer behaviour in international markets cannot therefore be ruled out simply because cultural variance remains strong as measured by traditional ethno-linguistic variables. At the same time it should be noted that an important, but often unarticulated, assumption of proponents of global standardization strategies is that greater cultural homogenization in world markets will necessarily lead to more uniform patterns of consumer behaviour. This mode of thinking reflects the importance generally placed upon culturally based variables as determinants of consumer behaviour.

However, although the cultural context is of great importance, it is only one of a number of variables likely to have an important impact upon consumption behaviour in foreign markets. It follows, therefore, that even if there has been convergence in critical cultural variables affecting consumption, this does not necessarily imply that patterns of consumer behaviour are becoming significantly more homogeneous in the international market-place. Continuing differences in the economic, institutional, legal and other relevant dimensions of the overseas operating environment often result in differences in patterns of consumer behaviour irrespective of the cultural context.

Does this mean that the pursuit of international business strategies and programmes which exhibit significant uniformity in global markets is the wrong path to follow in most circumstances? In order to address this question it is desirable to first assess the evidence regarding consumption behaviour in international markets and then focus on the very important topic of global market segmentation.

Comparative consumer behaviour

Many comparative studies provide evidence of significant diversity in consumer behaviour in overseas markets. Other work identifies relevant common denominators and it is evident that there is no concensus regarding the universality or otherwise of consumer behaviour. The nature of the product-market context and the scope of the study undertaken in terms of the number of foreign markets surveyed are strong influences on research findings. There is also a lack of clarity, in many studies, regarding interpretation of the 'universal' construct.

Evidence of significant differences in consumer behaviour is seen in early work by Green and Langeard (1975), Douglas (1976) and Hoover et al. (1978). Hempel (1974), Anderson and Engledow (1977) and Thorelli and Becker (1980) highlight cross-cultural similarities in consumer behaviour; Urban (1977) identifies differences and similarities in behaviour. Much of the early research is limited in scope and over half of the studies noted above are confined to just two developed countries.

More recent work is characterized by a higher propensity to identify significant differences in patterns of consumer behaviour. This is probably due, in part, to a trend to compare behaviour in much larger groups of countries. Research indicating dissimilarities includes studies by Green *et al.* (1983), Tan and Ngui (1985), Zaichkowsky and Sood (1989), Tansuhaj *et al.* (1991), Yavas *et al.* (1992) and Feick *et al.* (1993). Onkvisit and Shaw (1990), after evaluating six studies on consumer response to advertisements in different countries, note that the evidence points to a lack of consumer similarities, which are overshadowed by market variations and consumer differences.

However, significant evidence of uniformity has also been presented. Farley and Sexton (1982) find many cross-country similarities in their study of consumer behaviour in developing markets; Lee and Green (1991) conclude that the Fishbein model can be used to explain consumption intentions formation in a Confucian culture; and Dawar and Parker (1994) report few differences in the use of quality signals across cultures. Farley and Lehman (1994), after reviewing four buyer behaviour studies, conclude that elasticities computed for a range of endogenous variables do no vary much over countries.

In the light of the literature it can be concluded that non-cultural dimensions of the consumers' contextual situation, which frequently vary significantly, often have a major impact upon behaviour. This implies that modelling consumer behaviour in international markets requires attention to contextual variables that are not highlighted in models focussed on behaviour in a domestic market setting.

It should also be noted that evidence of diversity is not incompatible with the existence of underlying patterns of similarity in consumer behaviour that allow for uniformity of global policy in important areas. Diversity is not unique to the international market-place and although the national character construct is often used to stereotype markets (Clark 1990), patterns of consumer behaviour vary within countries as a result of cultural and other differences.

In the United States, for example, although there are certain basic values of an 'apple pie, flag, baseball' nature that many Americans have traditionally shared, significant divisions based upon cultural factors are also evident. This is due to the relatively high numbers of immigrants living in the United States; cultural traditions passed on from one generation of immigrants to succeeding generations; the existence of significant groups that have not felt themselves to be part of the 'mainstream'; and greater resistance to the 'melting-pot' influences that have played a major role in the traditional assimilation process in the United States.

Many national markets are even more heterogeneous than the United States and economic, regional and other factors, as well as ethno-linguistic variables, play an important role in differentiating patterns of intra-national consumer behaviour. Despite such diversity, the business strategies and programmes of most firms exhibit a pattern of a high degree of uniformity within national boundaries. Market diversity and standardization of important dimensions of business policy are therefore not necessarily incompatible.

As has been noted, there is also strong evidence that some product specific consumer behaviours may not be very sensitive to cultural and other differences. Dawar and Parker (1994) have, for example, investigated consumers' use of brand name, price, physical appearance and retailer as signals of product quality in a multicultural sample. Three levels of universality were evaluated, the *existence* of specific consumer behaviours; the *relative order* of importance of behaviours acrross cultures; and the *absolute* level of behaviour across cultures. The findings indicate that for the purchase of consumer electronics products, the four signals evaluated were found to be universal in regard to all three of the levels of universality investigated.

GLOBAL MARKET SEGMENTATION

In the light of the preceding discussion it is apparent that the objective of delineating significant groups of consumers who, irrespective of their geographic location, exhibit important uniform characteristics in regard to their consumption behaviour and product needs is not an easy task. However, market segmentation skills can be very helpful in allowing for the identification of significant patterns of uniformity in the forest of diversity that, in regard to the cultural context and other important environmental characteristics, still divides many global markets. The segmentation construct offers a powerful tool for penetrating and evaluating global markets. Segmentation allows for underlying similarities to be identified. When international market segments can be delineated, the door is then opened for greater standardization of critical elements of global business operations.

However, cultural similarity does not necessarily imply convergence of consumer behaviour and an emphasis on culturally based segmentation variables, in isolation from other important factors, may lead to erroneous conclusions regarding standardization opportunities. On the other hand, even when the cultural context is diverse, underlying patterns of uniformity in consumption behaviour may allow for standardization of important dimensions of overseas business and marketing operations.

Bases for segmenting international markets

Three desirable characteristics of useful market segments have been identified – measurability, accessibility, and substance (Kotler 1991). Identifying segmentation criteria that allow for the delineation of global market segments that meet these requirements is often a problem. This means that many international market segments will be 'fuzzier' than those firms are used to working with at home.

Several approaches to segmenting international markets have been suggested in the literature. Kale and Sudharshan (1987) suggest two basic aproaches. The first involves delineating segments within target markets and then accumulating them 'across the qualified countries based on similarity'. An alternative method is to 'directly aggregate individuals in all the qualified countries into segments'. Both these approaches offer significant advantages over cruder methodologies where segmentation involves the identification of 'country clusters', with nations being the basic unit of analysis.

Frank, Massy and Wind (1972) have developed a classification scheme for international market segmentation which provides a solid foundation for discussing culturally derived segmentation criteria. In their framework, segmentation is undertaken by distinguishing between 'countries' and 'decision makers' and then using either general or situation specific measures to identify an international demand segment. Segmentation criteria of a culturally derived nature may be used in the case of both countries and decision makers and their potential utility will now be reviewed.

Country clusters

In the light of the earlier discussion on the diversity of many national markets – in terms of the cultural context and other variables – segmentation using country characteristics measures will often be of limited utility. In some cases, where countries are relatively homogeneous and share important common characteristics, it may make sense to segment on a country basis and there is a significant track record of work following this approach (Rostow 1960; Sethi 1971; Goodnow and Hansz 1972; Day et al. 1988).

Although many of the country based taxonomies arrived at are based upon measures of economic development, work has also been done using cultural variables. Perhaps the best known work is that of Hofstede (1980). In a classic study, he uses four underlying cultural dimensions that he has developed – power distance, individualism, uncertainty avoidance and masculinity – to cluster countries – as seen in Chapter 9. He delineates seven clusters, but even his comprehensive work did not include many countries, most notably in Africa and the Middle East.

Ronen and Shenkar (1985) have reviewed eight studies which used attitudinal data to cluster countries and found consistencies in the groupings delineated. Drawing upon these similarities and their own analysis – which highlights the importance of geography, language and religion as factors underlying country clusters – they present a classification scheme of nine groups.

Despite the high quality of some of the research undertaken, the utility of country based segmentation schemes in distinquishing patterns of consumer behaviour in global markets is debatable. In a recent study, for example, Helsen *et al.* (1993) evaluated two country segmentation approaches. One utilized traditional criteria relating to economic, political and cultural factors; the other was based on diffusion patterns. Neither approach proved to be of great use. There was little evidence of stability in diffusion based country segments over time with respect to new product introductions and the traditional country segmentation taxonomy 'provided little guidance as to the success of specific new product introductions'.

When country clustering is utilized in more sophisticated approaches to international segmentation, it is only the first step in a hierarchical process. In both the Kale and Sudarshan (1987) and Kreutzer (1988) international market segmentation methodologies, for example, country segmentation is an initial step to distinguish target markets from all other markets. This is then followed by the delineation of segments within countries and their aggregation across national boundaries. It should also be noted that cultural variables are only one among a broad group of factors suggested as screening criteria in the country clustering processes proposed.

Decision-maker characteristics

Consumer characteristics, either of a general or situation specific nature, offer more promise as segmentation criteria. In the case of culturaly derived segmentation criteria, objective ethno-linguistic measures such as language and race may be useful but are often too broad in their impact. Inferred measures are more likely to delineate cross-national segments exhibiting homogeneous consumption behaviours. Examples of general measures include 'lifestyle' and 'information seekers'; situation specific attitudes and perceptions are also potentially very useful segmentation criteria.

Lifestyle, which is often singled out as a powerful international segmentation measure, is based primarily on inferred criteria concerning consumer interests and perceptions and their 'way of living' in regard to work and leisure habits. Critical dimensions of lifestyle thus include activities, interests and opinions; objective criteria, normally of a demographic nature, may also be used to help define life style segments.

Despite the attractions of lifestyle segmentation, caution is necessary when using this approach. Douglas and Urban (1977) found important similarities in the underlying components of the lifestyle of women in the

USA, France and UK. However, the importance of lifestyle uniformity varied and significant diversity in consumption behaviour within international lifestyle segments was a key finding in the study. Research by Eshghi and Sheth (1985) also warns against the danger of equating lifestyle and consumption behaviour. It was found that although lifestyle has an impact upon behaviour, local cultural and other situational variables played the predominant role in determining patterns of consumption in four countries studied.

Behavioural segmentation also offers interesting possibilites. As an example, consider a 'cross-cultural elite of affluent and information sensitive consumers' that exhibits strong similarity in respect of information acquisition and other important aspects of consumer behaviour which has been identified (Anderson and Engledow 1977). This general cross-national segment of 'information seekers' is primarily composed of upper income, cosmopolitan opinion leaders and is thus of great interest to marketers. Although a distinct minority group in national markets, they form a large and attractive international demand segment which is likely to respond in a relatively uniform fashion to marketing policies for most products. However, Thorelli (1991) has noted that local competition, marketing infrastructure and national laws constrain opportunities to exploit this global demand segment in a uniform fashion.

At the situation specific level, opportunities to delineate patterns of behavioural uniformity globally may also arise. 'Gift giving', an aspect of consumer behaviour that is strongly influenced by cultural factors, provides an interesting example. Although there is strong evidence of major cultural differences between gift giving behaviours in Oriental and Western cultures (Green and Alden 1988), important commonalities have been identified that cross diverse cultural contexts. In one study, two important cross-cultural segments were identified, 'self respect givers' and 'relationship givers' (Beatty et al. 1991). These underlying similarities indicate that values and behaviours may be open to cross-cultural analysis which can lead to the identification of meaningful cross-national demand segments, despite significant cultural diversity.

Another example concerns 'energy conservation' where a four country study found significant national differences in attitudes and consumption behaviour (Verhage et al. 1989). Nevertheless, it was possible to identify three cross-national segments of demand which, due to similarity in respect of attitudes and behaviour, could be targeted with uniform global strategies.

Despite the potential utility of decision maker features as segmentation variables, it is apparent that there is strong potential for significant variance in patterns of consumer behaviour within lifestyle and behaviourally derived global consumer segments. International similarity in lifestyle and behaviour may not, therefore, translate into uniform patterns of consumption behaviour in international markets. Other situation specific variables, such as the product in question and contextual features of the local market, have to be considered. In addition, it can be noted that cross-national demand segments exhibiting strong patterns of uniformity may be limited in size and attractiveness.

CONCLUSIONS

Drawing upon the analysis developed in this paper several conclusions can be presented in the context of the questions identified earlier. Other key points arising from the analysis are also reviewed.

The initial question concerned the degree of convergence occurring between national markets. Although it is evident that significant homogenizing forces are at work and that certain market differences are becoming less significant in many parts of the world, the jury is still out concerning the impact of these developments upon the cultural environment. In respect of important ethno-linguistic variables, the evidence indicates that powerful, culturally based divisions continue to fracture many global markets. This is most evident in respect of language and religion, but is also apparent in the case of other important cultural dimensions.

Despite the focus on the cultural homogenization issue, many other factors, such as the economic and institutional context, also have an important impact on consumer behaviour. In so far as these important contextual features of overseas operating environment continue to vary, forces favouring cultural standardization may not have major implications for consumer behaviour in foreign markets. Consequently, even if the cultural context overseas is tending to become more homogeneous, this does not necessarily result in the emergence of consumers with uniform needs and patterns of consumption behaviour.

The research evidence on comparative consumption behaviour is contradictory and often suffers from a failure to rigorously investigate the universality construct. Ideally, there should be a tripartite focus in terms of not only the degree to which the particular behaviour exists in overseas markets, but also the relative order of importance of the behaviour and its absolute level in global markets (Dawar and Parker 1994).

Evaluation of the literature shows that there is a significant body of evidence indicating that there are often differences in patterns of overseas consumer behaviour and the notion of the 'standard' consumer seems to be a chimera in many global product markets. This reflects diversity between overseas market contexts in terms of important economic and institutional variables and continuing cultural variance. At the same time, there is also evidence of underlying similarities which can sometimes be exploited on a global basis. In these cases, segmentation skills are critical in delineating viable transnational demand segments.

The forces driving consumer behaviour and the complex nature of the culture-consumer behaviour nexus are not always adequately captured in models of consumer behaviour. Commonly, too much reliance is placed upon models, with a single country focus, that understate the significance, in global markets, of variables that are relatively homogeneous in many national markets. As a result, important contextual factors such as the nature of the market infrastructure, economic variables and the legal context tend to be either ignored or downplayed in the analysis of consumer behaviour in overseas markets.

Scepticism concerning the significance of greater cultural uniformity as a force for the homogenization of consumer behaviour does not detract from the desirability of seeking to segment global markets. Research indicates that there are frequently real possibilities to identify international consumer segments that exhibit important similarities in regard to consumer behaviour and demand characteristics. These cross-national demand segments may often not be truly global because of other differences that fracture the world market-place. However, a non-universal market segment may still be attractive.

The utility and relevance of country characteristics as an approach to global market segmentation are clearly limited when viewed from a cultural perspective. The essential problem is that political and cultural boundaries frequently do not coincide. Thus many countries are characterized by a level of ethno-linguistic diversity which invalidates the utility of the country as a segmentation unit. Of course, this is not invariably the case and some nations are quite homogeneous with respect to broad cultural characteristics. Despite this, in most product-market contexts, the notion of country clusters is flawed if the goal is to delineate transnational demand segments that exhibit common cultural and consumer behaviour characteristics. As a result, country segmentation is normally most useful as the first step in a multi-stage segmentation process.

Decision maker characteristrics are likely to be of most utility in delineating global market segments which exhibit significant international uniformity in terms of cultural and consumption behaviour characteristics. Although objective demographic and social indicators may be useful in predicting behaviour, they often group together subjects with widely differing consumption behaviours. Subjective, inferred measures relating to lifestyle and behaviour are likely to be more useful.

Lifestyle segmentation has obvious attractions. However, the interaction between lifestyle and other dimensions of the overseas operating context has important implications for consumption behaviour. For example, the nature of the retail system and the legal context may modify consumption behaviour within a lifestyle segment from one market to another. Behavioural segmentation focuses even more directly upon patterns of consumption behaviour and, as such, is potentially the most valuable approach to delineating homogeneous cross-national consumer groups.

Finally, it is important to reiterate that the culture-consumer behaviour nexus is complex and the degree of similarity of broad cultural factors is often not of crucial importance in regard to overseas consumer behaviour and the segmentation of global markets. This is primarily because of the importance of non-cultural factors with regard to many dimensions of consumer behaviour in foreign markets. As a consequence, cultural homogeneity may not be a prerequisite for a viable global market segment in many product markets. Conversely, a culturally homogeneous global market segment may be of limited interest because consumption behaviour is dependent upon many other factors that are not captured in the culture construct.

REFERENCES

Anderson, R. and Engledow, J. (1977) A factor analytic comparison of US and German information seekers. *Journal of Consumer Research*, **3**, pp. 185–96.

Beatty, S.E., Kahle, L. and Homer, P. (1991) Personal values and gift-giving behaviours: a study across cultures. *Journal of Business Research*, **22**, pp. 149–57.

Buzzell, R., (1968) Can you standardize multinational marketing? *Harvard Business Review*, **46** pp. 102–13.

Chakravarthy, B. and Perlmutter, H.V. (1985) Strategic planning for a global business. *Columbia Journal of World Business*, **20**, pp. 3–10.

Clark, T.L. (1990) International marketing and national character: a review and proposal for an integrative theory. *Journal of Marketing*, **54**, pp. 66–79.

Dawar, N. and Parker, P. (1994) Marketing universals: consumers' use of brand name, price, physical appearance and retailer reputation as signals of product quality. *Journal of Marketing*, **58**, pp. 81–95.

Day, E., Fox, R. and Huszagh, S. (1988) Segmenting the global market for industrial goods: issues and implications. *International Marketing Review*, **5**, pp. 14–27.

Douglas, S.P. (1976) Cross-national comparisons and consumer stereotypes: a case study of working wives and non-working wives in the US and France. *Journal of Consumer Research*, **2**, pp. 12–20.

Douglas, S.P. and Urban, C., (1977) Life-style analysis to profile women in international markets. *Journal of Marketing*, **41**, pp. 46–54.

Doz, Y. (1986) *Strategic Management in Multinational Corporations*, Pergamon Press, Oxford, p 16.

Engel, J., Blackwell, R. and Miniard, P. (1993) *Consumer Behaviour*, 7th edn, Dryden Press, Fort Worth, TX, pp. 33–40.

Eshghi, A. and Sheth, J.N. (1995) The globalization of consumption patterns: an empirical investigation, in *Global Perspectives in Marketing* (ed E. Kaynak), Praeger, New York, pp. 133–48.

Farley, J.U. and Sexton, D.E. (1982) A process model of the family planning decision. *TIMS Studies in Management Science*, **18**, pp. 209–39.

Farley, J.U. and Lehmann, D.R. (1994) Cross-national laws and differences in market response. *Management Science*, **40**, pp. 111–22.

Feick, L.A. Higie, R.A. and Price, L.L. (1993) Consumer search and decision problems in a transitional economy: Hungary, 1989-92. *Marketing Science Institute*, Report 93–113 (August), pp. 1–55.

Frank, R.E. Massy, W. and Wind, Y. (1992) *Market Segmentation*, Prentice Hall, Englewood Cliffs, NJ, p. 103.

Goodnow, J. and Hansz, J. (1972) Environmental determinants of overseas market entry strategy. *Journal of International Business Studies*, **3**, pp. 33–50.

Green, R. and Alden, D. (1988) Functional equivalence in cross-cultural consumer behaviour: gift giving in Japan and the US. *Psychological Marketing*, **5**, pp. 155–68.

Green, R. and Langeard, E. (1975) A cross-national comparison of consumer habits and innovator characteristics. *Journal of Marketing*, **39**, pp. 34–41.

Green, R., Leonardi, J.P. Chandon, J.L. Cunningham, I., Verhage, B. and Strozzieri, A. (1983) Societal development and family purchasing roles: a cross national study. *Journal of Consumer Research*, **9** pp. 436–42.

Hall, E.T. (1960) The silent language in overseas business. *Harvard Business Review*, **38**, pp. 87–96.

Helsen, K., Jedidi, K., and DeSarbo, W.S. (1993) A new approach to country segmentation utilizing multinational diffusion patterns. *Journal of Marketing*, **57**, pp. 60–71.

Hempel, D.J. (1974) Family buying decisions: a cross cultural perspective. *Journal of Marketing Research*, **11**, pp. 295–302.

Hofstede, G. (1980) *Culture's Consequences: International Differences in Work Related Values*, Sage, Beverly Hills.

Hoover, R.J., Green, R.T. and Saegert, J. (1978) A cross-national study of perceived risk, *Journal of Marketing*, **42**, pp. 102–8.

Hout, T., Porter, M.E. and Rudden, E. (1982) How global companies win out. *Harvard Business Review*, **60**, pp. 98–108.

Jain, S.C. (1989) Standardization of international marketing strategy: some research hypotheses. *Journal of Marketing*, **53**, pp. 70–9.

Kale, S.H. and Sudharshan, D. (1987) A strategic approach to international segmentation. *International Marketing Review*, **4**, pp. 60–70.

Kotler, P. (1991) *Marketing Management*, 7th edn, Prentice Hall, Englewood Cliffs, NJ, p. 165.

Kreutzer, R. (1988) Marketing-mix standardization: an integrated approach in global marketing. *European Journal of Marketing*, **22**, pp. 19–30.

Lee, C. and Green, R. (1991) Cross-cultural examination of the Fishbein behavioral intentions model. *Journal of International Business Studies*, **22**, pp. 289–305.

Levitt, T. (1983) The globalization of markets. *Harvard Business Review*, **61**, pp. 92–102.

Ohmae, K. (1989) Managing in a borderless world. *Harvard Business Review*, **61**, pp. 152–61.

Onkvisit, S. and Shaw, J.J. (1990) Global advertising: revolution or myopia?. *Journal of International Consumer Marketing*, **3**, pp. 77–112.

Porter, M.E. (1980) *Competitive Strategy*, Free Press, New York.

Quelch, J.A. and Hoff, E.J. (1986) Customizing global marketing. *Harvard Business Review*, **64**, pp. 59–68.

Ronen, S., and Shenkar, O. (1985) Clustering countries on attitudinal dimensions: a review and synthesis. *Academy of Management Review*, **10**, pp. 435–54.

Rostow, W.W. (1960) *The Stages of Economic Growth*, Cambridge University Press, Cambridge, MA.

Samovar, L. and Porter R. (1976) *Intercultural Communication: A Reader*, Wadsworth Publishing, Belmont, CA. pp. 4–24.

Sethi, S. (1971) Comparative cluster analysis for world markets. *Journal of Marketing Research*, **8**, pp. 348–54.

Sheth, J. and Sethi, S. (1977) A theory of cross-cultural buyer behaviour. *Consumer and Industrial Buyer Behaviour*, (eds A. Woodside *et al.*), Elsevier, New York, pp. 369–86.

Sorensen, R. and Wiechmann, V.E. (1975) How multinationals view market standardization, *Harvard Business Review*, **53**.

Tan, C.T. and Ngui, C. (1985) Ethnic differences in reactions to children's advertising. *International Marketing Review*, **2**, pp. 31–7.

Tansuhaj, P., Gentry, J.W. John, J. Manzer, L. and Cho, B. (1991) A cross-national examination of innovation resistance. *International Marketing Review*, **8**, 1991, pp. 7–20.

Terpstra, V. and David, K. (1985) *The Cultural Environment of International Business*, South-Western Publishing, Cincinnati, OH, p. 5.

Terpstra, V. (1987) The evolution of international marketing. *International Marketing Review*, **4**, pp. 47–59. Vol. 4.

Thorelli, H.B. (1990) The information seekers: multinational strategy target, in *International Marketing Strategy* (eds H.B. Thorelli and S.T. Cavusgil), Pergamon Press, Oxford, pp. 341–51.

Thorelli, H.B. and Becker, H. The information seekers: multinational strategy target. *California Management Review.* **22**, pp. 46–52.

Triandis, H., (1983) Dimensions of cultural variation as parameters of organizational theories. *International Studies of Management as Parameters of Organizational Theories and Organization,* **12**, pp. 139–69.

Urban, C., A cross national comparison of consumer media use patterns. *Columbia Journal of World Business,* **12**, pp. 53–64.

Verhage, B.J., Dahringer, L.D. and Cundiff, E.W. Will a global marketing strategy work? An energy conservation perspective. *Journal of the Academy of Marketing Science,* **17**, pp. 129–36.

Walters, P. (1986) International marketing policy: A discussion of the standardization construct and its relevance for corporate policy. *Journal of International Business Studies,* **17**, pp. 55–69.

Yavas, V., Verhage, B. and Green, R. (1992) Global consumer segmentation versus local market orientation: Empirical findings. *Management International Review,* **32**, pp. 265–72.

Zaichkowsky, J.L. and Sood, J.H. (1989) A global look at consumer involvement and use of products. *International Marketing Review,* **6**, pp. 20–34.

Chapter 22

Cross-cultural factors in competitive advantage at home and abroad

Yao-Su Hu and Malcolm Warner

INTRODUCTION

In cross-cultural management, a generally accepted idea appears to be that 'what works' in one specific culture may not work in another. It is also presumed that culture varies from one place or institution to another (Redding 1994) against the imagery proclaimed by the globalization paradigm of a 'borderless' world dominated by 'stateless' corporations (see Hu 1992; 1996). Such sensitivity to the importance of context and awareness of differences therein is much less in evidence in the strategic management literature, where it is usually assumed that 'an advantage is an advantage is an advantage'. The relativity of competitive advantage should, however, become obvious if we consider a few questions derived from well-known examples.

Why is it that 'blue-chip' corporations that are described as dynamic, competitive and successful at home often fail to achieve as much success when they transplant their operations to another culture abroad? Why is it that the most successful firms abroad are not always the strongest ones at home? Honda, for example, has a market-share at home that is less than one-third that of Toyota and half that of Nissan, yet for years it was ahead of both Toyota and Nissan in the US market. Why are there global firms like Nokia from small countries like Finland? These questions raise the issue of the link between a firm's competitive advantages at home and its advantages abroad. Furthermore, why is it that firms from the Newly Industrialized Economies (NIEs) are successful in their operations in certain foreign countries but not in others? East Asian groups from the Little Dragon economies (Taiwan, Hong Kong, South Korea and Singapore) for example, are to date much more successful in undertaking manufacturing operations in Asia than in the US. To what extent can a firm with a strong position at home utilize its domestic strengths to create a strong competitive position abroad?

In trying to answer these questions and to contribute to a more profound understanding of the international operations of the firm, this contribution to the debate hopes to analyse the relationship between the firms's advantages at home and its advantages abroad and explore the concept of the international transfer and transferability of the firm's advantages. Although these concerns relating to the competitive advantage paradigm have been neglected in both the international business and strategic management literatures (but see Lall 1980) they may readily strike a chord with those who study cross-cultural management, who are perhaps more tuned in to the importance and differences of national and cultural contexts.

The importance of culture as a variable (see Hickson and Pugh 1995) is now becoming increasingly apparent as we move in to a more globalized economy, overstated as the notion of 'globalization' may well be. Nonetheless, international activities of firms, whether we are looking at their policies relating to capital, products, organization structures, strategic management, technology of human resources management (HRM), must more and more take national cultures into account. As a recent work in the field points out:

> Alongside the growing international and intercultural experience of managers themselves, the scholarly effort to describe, analyse and explain organizational behaviour is only gradually coming to pay proper attention to the multitude of influence from societal culture. The worldwide tension between impersonal and personal approaches is just one overreaching consequence of cultural differences that is plain to see. There are many more.
>
> (*Hickson and Pugh 1995: 6*).

Indeed, it is particularly interesting to cite the above observations, coming as they do from the doyens of an approach which has to date concentrated on a stricter 'convergence view'.

THE KEY IMPORTANCE OF ADVANTAGE TRANSFER

At the level of the firm, we would argue that transferable competitive advantages are the main key to any explanation of the firm's ability to engage successfully in international (that is, foreign) operations. In the target foreign country, the foreign firm incurs all the disadvantages of being foreign; in other words, it must confront all the advantages that native players (whether actually or potentially in business as competitors) enjoy from being in their home-territory and environment. It thus needs to command or develop some more-than-compensating advantages in order to operate successfully in the target-economy (see Hymer 1976).

Can the requisite advantages in the target-country be created afresh? The very same reason why the firm needs off-setting advantages also means that it has little advantage when it comes to 'advantage-creation' in the target-country if it were to rely entirely on local resources (which indigenous players can utilize more efffectively) to create such advantages, that is, it has none unless it is able to transfer some (or their ingredients be they 'hardware' or 'software') from outside the country which are not available to indigenous players. This line of reasoning puts advantages and their transfer firmly at the centre of the analysis of the firm's international operations, cross-nationally or cross-culturally.

CONCEPTUALIZING THE FIRM'S ADVANTAGES

In 1960 (in his doctoral work) and predating Michael Porter (1980; 1985) by two decades, the late Stephen Hymer (1976) became the first scholar to draw attention to the concept of the advantages of the firm (as a cause of international operations). Before him, industrial economists such as Bain (1956) had emphasized the advantages which established firms have relative to new firms and potential entrants; these were called barriers to entry. This was mostly discussed in terms of domestic, intra-country competition. Hymer was interested, however, in the advantages possessed by firms of one country relative to firms of another country (when the former undertook operations in the latter's home-turf). After Hymer's seminal work (1976) and work by Kindleberger (1969) and Dunning (1981) the expressions 'monopolistic advantages' and 'ownership-specific advantages' began to pervade the international business literature. (As we shall see, these expressions are misleading; Hymer (1976) simply referred to 'advantages of the firm'.)

Meanwhile, after Porter's first book, the quest for 'competitive advantage' (often understood to mean superior profitability or 'rent') went on to generate a huge literature in the strategic management and related fields. The term 'advantage' is, however, seldom defined, perhaps because (to put it in Popperian terms) the precision of a language depends on the fact that it does not burden its terms with the task of being too precise. Indeed, in science, all the terms we really need must be undefined terms. Nevertheless, it is necessary to adopt a working definition here, if only because the expression 'advantage' which is the conceptual prop of our argument is used with different connotations in different literatures. The firm's advantages and disadvantages may be best defined as its strengths and weaknesses, either relative to the competition in a specific competitive arena or relative to an alternative to the firm itself in a particular context.

To start with, advantage is always relative to something, never absolute. It is not assets and capabilities, however unique and difficult to imitate, that constitute advantages – these stem from assets and capabilities that are superior to those of the relevant competition or alternative, or that are put together and deployed in such a way as to confer a superior competitive position. Which is to say that advantages have to be seen both in a 'holistic' as well as an 'analytic' way. Success may depend on 'flair' in creating new blends of advantages; often it may be an 'art' rather than a 'science' to recombine positive elements which make a firm better placed to succeed in the world market-place. 'Flair' is a rare commodity and is often more than proportionately rewarded. Second, advantages are also relative to the arena or context – what counts as an advantage in one milieu may not count for much in another because the competition may not be the same, the methods of doing business may not be similar or the needs of the customers may not be the same. Third, while the concept of advantages relative to competitors is relatively easy to comprehend, the concept of advantages relative to alternatives refers, for example, to joint ventures (JVs) in which there is no direct competition between the two partners but in which the other side always has the alternative of doing without the JV or of seeking another partner. Fourth, the relevant competition against which advantages are defined refers to both actual and potential competitors; it always refers to indigenous competition and often encompasses competition from other foreign countries. Last, the definition proposed here focuses on the firm's ability to compete rather than the achievement of 'rent' or superior (that is, above-average) profitability; we therefore argue that the sum of the firm's advantages and disadvantages may be termed its overall 'competitiveness'.

How can we best classify such advantages? Writing in 1960 Hymer pointed out that (1976: 41–42), 'There are as many kinds of advantages as there are functions in making and selling a product'. There are several distinct ways of classifying the firm's advantages: for example, according to activities or functions in the firm's value-chain, sources of advantages, types of assets (resources) and skills (capabilities), or order-winning criteria, generic strategies adopted by the firm and so on. In order to further develop the concept of the international transferability of the firm's advantages, however, there are two ways of dividing-up the concept of advantages that may be particularly useful.

The first distinction is between the different levels at which advantages can be identified or defined. Where along the chain of causality is an advantage, as defined, situated? Taking the firm as a whole, at the downstream-level lies the interface between the firm and its customers – at this level advantages, many of which are well-described in the literature, include lower prices, superior products, a superior product range, superior reputation, superior speed or timeliness of delivery, better services provided by the supplier, better financing terms, better relationships (personal and/or institutional) between the buyer and the supplier, and so on. Upstream, at an intermediate level, there may be advantages associated with what the firm is, what it does and what it has, that is, with its superior attributes, activities, assets, skills, internal and external relationships, and so on (always, of course, in a relative sense). At the most upstream level, there may be dynamic advantages such as the superior ability of the firm to continuously learn from internal and external sources, to upgrade its products and processes, to innovate technologically as well as organizationally and to take the long-term view despite cyclical downswings. Today, we refer to such a firm as a 'learning organization' – see Chapter 7 in this book. Because the source of an advantage is itself an advantage, common language makes it difficult to distinguish between different levels of advantages.

It is noteworthy that cultural factors may impinge on all three levels; for example, national and corporate culture affects both quality and speed of service, it affects the way the firm sees itself and does things and it also affects the speed and frequency with which new products, processes and methods are brought to fruition and then to market. In industries characterized by rapid technological progress, it is the upstream, dynamic advantages that will matter most. In stable sectors with slow technological change, the downstream, static advantages will be correspondingly more important. The transfer cannot therefore be discussed without looking at the level at which such advantages may be clearly defined.

ADVANTAGES IN DOMESTIC AND INTERNATIONAL COMPETITION

The second distinction, key to this contribution to the debate, is that between the firm's advantages in domestic competition and that in international competition. The advantages that a firm possesses, relative to firms of its own country, need not be the same as (and may be quite different from) those that it will have relative to firms of another country should it undertake operations there. There are three main reasons for this.

First, if we keep to the principle that advantages are always relative, the advantages that matter will vary between countries and competitive arenas because the players (actual and potential), the customers and the circumstances will be heterogeneous. We cannot assume homogeneity of either management and work-forces (or markets for that matter). Transfers of advantages must take account of their cultural differences as much as their similarities.

Second, we would argue that superiority relative to domestic rivals need not here necessarily mean superiority relative to firms overseas, while lack of superiority relative to domestic competitors does not necessarily signify lack of advantage relative to firms in another country. It may all depend on the level of economic development of the nation and of the industry. For example, a leading firm from a less advanced country may have no technological advantage in a more advanced country; conversely, if a nation has an industry which enjoys world technological leadership, even the followers in that industry will have technological advantages relative to firms based in other countries. To put in formal terms: in the extreme case, all the firms in the home industry may have a technological advantage over all the firms in a less developed country. Similarly, none of the firms in the latter may have any technological advantage over the firms in the more developed country. The analysis becomes more complex (and interesting) when we extend it to three sets of countries and firms at different levels of sophistication (see below). We are, of course, here making the assumption that diffusion of 'best practices' is slower between nations than within them (see Kogut 1991). The failure of many studies to clearly distinguish between domestic and international advantages reflects in part the fact that they examined the international operations of American firms at a time when the US enjoyed clear supremacy in many industries: an advantage in the US automatically entailed an advantage abroad – see Chapter 7. We can no longer be sure that that is now the case.

Last, there are broad-based characteristics and non-proprietary factors of production – arising at the level of the nation, the industry and even the local communities – that bestow on the nation's firms powerful advantages relative to foreign firms in international competition, but these do not constitute 'monopolistic' or 'ownership-specific' advantages in domestic competition between domestic rivals because they are equally available to all the domestic firms. For example, the value of the label 'made in Germany' makes little difference to the domestic competition between German manufacturers but is of great importance in relation to foreign competitors: the label is associated the world over with positive images of quality. Another example refers to differences between countries in the cost of capital and condition of financial support to companies. Although these are general advantages, the firm benefits from them when it competes against foreign rivals and we can say that the firm has (though not in a proprietary, exclusive or monopolistic sense) these advantages relative to foreign firms. These advantages, which have been well-described in Porter's (1990) book, are potent sources of competitive advantages in international competition, largely because they are subject to very big differences between nations – the differences between nations in this respect may be much greater than the differences between firms of the same nationality and their 'firm-specific' advantages. This assumes, however, that indigenous or home companies have superior access to these general factors in their home nation than foreign firms, even when the latter have established local subsidiaries (see Hu 1992; Patel and Pavitt 1991; Patel 1995).

What is interesting here is that many of these general advantages have an important cultural component or can be recast in terms of culture.

Moreover, because culture differs between national communities, its importance in international competition is particularly pronounced, as much as if not more so than other sources of advantage. Whitley's (1992) framework for bringing in the concept of 'business recipes' builds on data from Western Europe and East Asia. It allows us to envisage a typology of organization design clusters, each being comprehensible in terms of cultural, institutional and societal roots of competitive advantage. Such argumentation goes in the face of those who argue for a universal international managerial culture or standard global organizational forms as may be part and parcel of the stereotypical MNC strategy and structure present in much of the literature on the subject. In recent years, there has been a 'sea-change' in the way cross-cultural management scholars have approached the subject. Cultural awareness and sensitivity are now relatively more widespread among such researchers. In a survey of journals, Adler and Bartholomew (1992) found that 70% of all international OB and HRM papers published used the concept of culture (see also Chapter 2 in this volume. Almost all concluded that culture was a key determinant of the variables discussed. The research covered over 28,000 articles in 73 academic and professional journals between 1985 and 1990 (1992: 557). A consensus was emerging that culture was increasingly important as a variable to take into account.

The major strengths of the cross-cultural approach (Tayeb 1994: 429) are: first, cultural values are different in different parts of the world economy and can be seen as such; second, different cultural groups behave differently because of their varying values and attitudes; last, the role of culture is important in shaping work-organizations and the institutional context in which they operate. We therefore must give greater attention to variations in cross-cultural organizational behaviour and particularly how management operates. Both employee (and consumer) behaviour may also be different as a result of the variations in values and attitudes found in one national setting as opposed to another. Such variations may subtly affect 'advantage-transfer' as we shall see.

TRANSFERRING ADVANTAGES ACROSS FRONTIERS

In theory, the transfer of advantages can take place in a number of directions – from the parent company (and the home nation) to the foreign subsidiary, from the subsidiary to the parent, from one subsidiary to another. However, we shall mainly focus on transfer from home nation to foreign countries, for two main reasons.

First, except for the case of 'binational' companies (eg Shell, Unilever, ABB) that have two home-nations, most of the large firms that are described as 'multinational', 'transnational' or 'global' do, in fact, have a geographical centre of gravity and a nationality (Hu 1992). The bulk of the firm's worldwide operations and assets (often more than 60% in the case of US multinationals) are located in the home-nation and the proportion of total R&D (taken as a quantitative indicator of the geographical distribution of the firm's innovative activities) situated in the home-nation is even higher. Studies of US patenting by the world's largest 569 corporations, undertaken at the 'Science Policy Research Policy Unit' (Patel 1995) at the University of Sussex, England, come to even stronger conclusions: in the second half of the 1980s, 89% of these firms' technological activities continued to be performed in their home country, a one percent increase over the previous five-year period. If the major share of the firm's operations, people and innovative effort are located in its home-nation, it stands to reason that the build of its advantages are created or generated in its home-base, where they abide or dwell until transferred or diffused. The transfer of advantages from home-nation to foreign subsidiaries is likely to predominate, quantitatively, over transfers in other directions. This is not to deny that, at the level of individual businesses, segments or products, transfer may originate from a subsidiary that has been given a 'world mandate', but for the corporate group as a whole the home-base is usually situated in the home-nation.

Second, the concept of 'advantage-transfer' is still in its infancy and, at this stage, we can best develop the concept by concentrating on its most important and best understood aspect. Later work can extend to the other directions of transfer. It may be noted here, however, that the concepts of barriers to transferability, developed below are valid whatever the direction of transfer.

It should be noted that the concept of 'advantage transfer' is not necessarily the same as 'technology-transfer' or 'knowledge-transfer' but may often involve these phenomena. Such transfers may take place over both time and space. There may be time lags in the process although these are getting shorter as the pace of change has accelerated. Spatial transfer is also less of an obstacle as technology has helped to bring places closer together with rapid air-transportation. Telecommunications now have also helped to reduce the lags in information transfer in both time and spaces, but in so far as this facility is available to all who are able and willing to invest in it, it does not constitute an advantage in itself. The use of electronic data-transmission, for example, means that invoicing can be done from almost anywhere in the world and airline reservations in the UK could be made for the traveller from a computer-operator in Hong Kong, or the US, but competitors can easily do the same.

It is important to clearly distinguish between the transfer of the source of an advantage and the transfer of the use or exploitation of the advantage. For example, a technological advantage can be utilized in a foreign country even while its source (experience, human capital formation, R&D,

the generation of new technology, etc) remains in the home-nation. The focus here is on use and application.

An international transfer of advantages is defined as the process whereby the firm draws, from its home-base, on some or all of its unique advantages (advantages relative to home competitors) its underlying assets and capabilities, or the general qualities enjoyed by the home-nation and/or industry, and makes use of these things (if necessary in conjunction with 'complimentary assets') to give its operations in a foreign country a competitive edge relative to the competition or alternative. It follows from this definition that non-transferability can occur for two kinds of reasons – the use of an advantage (or a key ingredient thereof) is not mobile internationally or the advantage loses value in the target country. Immobility itself is due to geographical and/or cultural specificity or to the tacit nature of knowledge, while the absence of value may be due to the lack of 'fit' with the environment or to competitors' moves to neutralize the advantage. It is often difficult to know the degree of 'fit' or its absence in advance.

What become advantages for the firm's operations in a foreign country are usually one of three things that are present in the home environment:

1 Unique or 'firm-specific' advantages at home (i.e. advantages relative to domestic competitors at home) – for example, superior products or capabilities or knowledge of the market.
2 'Assets' at home (resources, capabilities, relationships, corporate characteristics) which, while not superior to those of domestic competitors, can turn into advantages relative to local competition in a less advanced country – for example, an American firm might find that a non-distinctive skill such as experience in large-scale production, logistics or marketing, can be an advantage when operating in a country like China where most of these companies have disproportionate advantages in these areas.
3 General attributes and general access to factors of production shared by the industry and/or nation, especially when the industry or country enjoys world-leadership – for example, the German chemical industry or the Japanese consumer electronics industry (or the US computer industry when it was in such a position in the 1960s).

Corporate culture may be an essential dimension of (1) and (2) above while national and perhaps even local community culture may underpin (3).

What should be transferred depends on what would give the firm an edge, given the conditions and circumstances in the target-country (demand and supply conditions, market structure, government policies, ways of doing business and of competition, and so on) while what can be transferred is determined by what advantages, assets and qualities there are at home at the level of the firm, industry or nation (the three levels are often difficult to disentangle). Internationally, the differences between national levels of development, national cultures and national attributes are likely to be more important than the differences between firms based in the same country, so that in international competition the 'national' advantages usually outweigh the 'firm/specific' advantages. These latter advantages may often be due to earlier industrialization, but may be counter-balanced by advantages of 'late development'.

Complementary assets (see Teece 1987) are assets or capabilities that need to be built up or acquired in the target-country in order to fully exploit the firm's advantages in that country. For example, the advantage of having superior products and a superior product range requires – for sustainable success – effective backup in terms of effective after-sales service, technical support, distribution and marketing. This set of factors in turn requires sustained investment in items such as personnel, training, facilities, spare parts and so on. Thus 'wholesale distribution' accounts for 70% of total Japanese direct foreign investment (DFI) in the US (Williamson 1991).

Such developments require not so much the transfer of physical equipment (important though these are) as the transfer of 'service know-how'. Given linguistic problems and immigration barriers, Japanese firms in the US have a limited number of their own nationals there. They therefore have to create a training culture and recruit suitable personnel to service the 'infrastructure' referred to above. The delivery of support-services requires the same TQM which is embodied in the physical goods produced by those firms. Conversely, US firms working in Japan have not always succeeded to anything like the same degree because of their HRM difficulties there (see Ballon 1992).

TRANSFERABILITY, ADVANTAGE AND MODES OF OPERATION

It is well known by students of international business that the transferability of advantages is crucially influenced by the mode of international operations. Thus, an advantage that is transferable in the exporting mode may not be so in the foreign production mode and vice versa. Less well-explored is the idea that intrinsic features in the nature of the advantage affect its transferability. In fact, transferability depends on both the nature of the advantage and the mode of operations, but we shall now concentrate on the former.

The concept of transferability of advantages can best be highlighted by examining non-transferability. Non-transferability happens where the advantage, (the asset, the characteristic or a key ingredient) is not mobile between the home-country and the target-country. There are two main reasons for immobility – geographical and/or cultural specificity and the tacit (non-codifiable) nature of much knowledge, skills, HRM and technology.

Examples of advantages whose use is restricted by geographical and/or cultural specificity include the following:

1 A superior or cheaper work-force is a non-transferable advantage, except for the transfer of key personnel. In the world today, there are ubiquitous government controls on the movement of manual (and even non-manual) workers bewteen nations (except in cases such as Korean workers in the Middle East). The advantages of using relatively cheaper or better qualified human resources can be embodied, however, through local production, in manufactured goods which are then exported, that is, they can indirectly be transferred through exporting.

2 Firms may not able to transfer their domestic strength if it is based mainly on good connections at home (including political connections) which do not travel well across borders.

3 A monopoly position due to government regulations in the home market is an advantage which is transferable, because the limits of the privileged position coincide with the limits of national jurisdiction. However, monopoly positions provide above-average profitability which generates cash-mountains that may then be used to promote foreign expansion.

4 Sometimes success due to 'business acumen' may not be transferable to a foreign country where the cultural and business contexts are different.

5 Possession or control of a superior distribution-network in the home market is an advantage that cannot be shifted abroad, nor does it benefit foreign sales. However, knowing how to establish and manage a distribution network is an advantage that can be transferred to a foreign country (transferability cannot be separated from the level at which the advantage is defined). In the Japanese automotive market, Honda has traditionally trailed behind Toyota and Nissan in terms of marketing muscle and control of the distribution system, but these do not give Toyota and Nissan transferable advantages when it comes to the US market.

6 A firm's reputation is created in a specific market (Kay 1993) and may also be specific to its own specific linguistic and/or cultural contexts. Superior reputation at home may not readily be transferable to other countries (except perhaps to countries characterized by cultural proximity or economic colonization) and reputations often have to be built afresh in foreign countries. If, however, customers at home travel abroad, this helps to transfer the firm's reputation abroad (services such as hotels, credit cards, car rental and so on, are 'experience' goods for which reputation matters more than for 'inspection' goods). In terms of 'experience' goods, Western economies, especially the

English-speaking ones, have a built-in advantage where the 'international' markets are increasingly using English as a *lingua franca*. In hotels, US-owned chains long held a cachet, as in the case of Conrad Hilton Hotels or Marriott; in credit cards, American Express is still a bench-mark company in the market; in car hire, Hertz is still strong and so on. In 'national' markets however, these players may have less share because of brands and advertising geared to local languages. For the international business traveller for example, they none the less still retain an attraction. Where non-Western owned chains try to compete in these markets, they often use English-language advertising or try to create a non-local image. Note, however, that foreigners are usually much more aware of national reputations ('the Swiss, the Germans, the Japanese, the Americans') than of 'firm-specific' reputations, that is, until the foreign firms have established local operations for some time or are 'global brands' such as Coca-Cola. Note also that knowing how to advertise and to promote a corporate image are advantages that are transferable. Western countries have relative advantages in presentation of brand images but Japan, for example, has now caught up in this domain.

7 Relationships with customers or suppliers are advantages that are not transferable abroad unless the customers or suppliers go abroad themselves. Thus, in the 1960s, US banks, consultancies, law and accounting firms followed their major US manufacturing customers over to Europe. Since Japanese automotive manufacturers set up transplant operations in the US and Europe, they have encouraged their suppliers to come as well to help them replicate their 'lean' production system (see Dore 1987). This method is quicker and less costly than trying to educate native firms into becoming Japanese (assuming that it is possible for foreigners to become Japanese). There is also some evidence that 'Japanization' does not necessarily work, anyway.

Advantages based on skills, competences, capabilities, know-how, technology, expertise and so on cannot be reduced entirely to codified knowledge or information (for example, in the form of operating instructions, standard procedures, computer algorithms, predictive models, formulas, or blueprints), while codified knowledge approximates the 'zero transfer-cost' of neo-classical economic theory, tacit knowledge (that is, uncodifiable and person or institution-embodied knowledge) is difficult and costly to transfer because of the following considerations:

1 Tacit knowledge is complex since it involves, by definition, the ability to cope with complexity; moreover it is often context-dependent and if the background is not understood, is difficult to interpret.
2 Tacit knowledge is acquired essentially through experience and

through 'trial and error'. This process may take many years to develop and may involve a great deal of 'human capital';

3 The teaching (and learning) of tacit knowledge – if possible at all – is through demonstration, observation, imitation, practice and feed-back (processes often labelled as apprenticeship and socialization). A small caveat may be entered here: tacit knowledge is becoming increasingly programmable into new technology and, for example, computer-aided production tools may reduce the need for apprenticeship and socialization. Even so, there is evidence that more effective use of CNC machine tools may be possible where the quality of the human resources interfacing with them is high through investment in human capital (see Maurice *et al.* 1980; Sorge and Warner 1987). Apprenticeship and socialization require close personal contacts over a prolonged period of time, which in turn presuppose linguistic/cultural affinity and geographical proximity; it is for these reasons that JVs often send personnel to work in the home-base plants and office, and/or universities and business schools there;

4 Organizational learning and the tacit knowledge that results are often collective in nature (that is, not embodied in a single person) this makes the transfer of tacit knowledge even more problematic.

5 The tacit knowledge that needs to be transferred may not be static, but continuously evolving; a moving target is much more difficult to hit than a fixed one.

6 Although the transfer (foreign posting) of expatriate staff can serve as a substitute for the transfer of tacit knowledge, this is often very costly; and since the tacit knowledge may be collective knowledge, it may require the transfer of such a large number of key individuals from the parent company (not always willing to be sent abroad as is the case in the US) that it would be impractical and unfeasible.

The obstacles to cross-culturally transferring tacit knowledge help explain why dynamic firms are keener to transfer the exploitation of their new technology abroad than to transfer its creation. Thus new products or the capacity to manufacture new products are transferred abroad (through exporting or foreign production) but not the capacity to innovate. What is being transferred are the results of the innovation process, not the innovation process or capability itself. The innovation process also requires dynamic interactions with (and stimulus from) the components of Porter's (1990) 'national diamond' or 'the national system of innovation' (Freeman 1995; Patel and Pavitt 1994); this interaction involves tacit knowledge and, despite the advent of global telecommunications, cannot take place at a distance.

The difficulty of transferring tacit knowledge, especially in industries characterized by rapid technological change, also helps to explain why attempts by foreign firms to acquire American technology by buying 'high-tech' US companies are not always successful. It is one thing to gain access to the codified knowledge, it is another to 'figure out' the tacit knowledge and to integrate that into the collective capabilities of the group. Sony, for example, went to Hollywood to buy 'software' but had little idea how to make successful movies. Moreover, in strategic alliances, the partner whose advantages rest on more codified knowledge may lose out to the partner whose advantages are based on more tacit knowledge, because the latter will learn more easily from the former than vice-versa. Straightforward purchase of firms possessing tacit knowledge and running them at arms-length may be a better option.

According to our definition, the transfer of an advantage fails to take place if the advantage or asset, even though mobile, loses its value in the target-country. This step can occur either because the advantage is no longer relevant in the different context, or because it can easily be neutralized by local competitors. Thus, as we have discussed, management or technology that is superior to that of domestic competitors at home may no longer be so in the context of a more advanced country. Products that are seen as 'better' in the home-market may not offer customer-perceived value in the target-country, either because the price is too high or the degree of sophistication is excessive, particularly true where these have been made for 'market-niches' in the richer country. The value of well-known brand names and trade marks can be neutralized by piracy and imitation. Such infringements of intellectual copyright are present on a massive scale in the Asian market, for example. Technological advantages can be neutralized by the weakness of intellectual property law (or its relative absence) and laxity in enforcing the law. Whether an advantage retains its value depends on the 'fit' or match between conditions in the target-country and the nature of the advantage. Varying the advertising message and adopting the brand-image may be another option here. Doing just this may require tacit knowledge acquired by having worked close to the target-markets – no easy task.

Even where advantages are transferable, their effective cross-cultural transfer may be neither automatic nor easy. Consider the case of Hong Kong hotel groups. Because of geographical location as a regional business and financial centre, Hong Kong has developed a world-class hotel industry. After successfully transplanting operations to the rest of Asia and to Australia, leading Hong Kong hoteliers such as the Peninsula, the Mandarin, the Regent and Park Lane have been establishing operations in Beverly Hills and London, New York and San Francisco, often by purchasing existing hotels. Acquiring and renovating existing hotels, or building new ones, has been relatively straightforward ('only a matter of money'), but it has been more difficult to transfer the quality of service, which is arguably the hotelier's most important competitive advantage. In

Hong Kong, one major ingredient of this quality is a relatively high ratio of employees to rooms, but in the US and Britain labour is much more expensive so that the ratio can simply not be replicated, although the labour cost factor equally affects the competing hotels locally. Therefore, other methods had to be used to transfer the quality of service: rigorous in-house training of staff, recruitment of younger and more enthusiastic staff, higher standards of service than the local norm, larger rooms and more luxurious bathrooms and so on. Discounting to break into the market may also be needed at first. However, transferring top-quality service is not easy, as 'you can't bring Hong Kong to the US'.

This case illustrates that the transfer of an advantage may require adaptation, investment and reconfiguring the ingredients of the advantage. All this requires effort, time and resources.

UNDERSTANDING THE INTERNATIONAL OPERATIONS OF FIRMS

We can now apply the concept of the transferability of the firm's advantages to gain a better understanding of the international operations of firms, particularly MNCs. In particular, we shall consider two questions: the choice between the modes of international operations and why international operations may be successful in one set of foreign countries but not in another.

There are many potential (and economically viable) modes of international operations (including licensing, franchising, joint ventures, acquisitions, international subcontracting, etc). These modes may not be necessarily mutually exclusive and the problem is more one of combining and sequencing them than one of selecting between them. We will try to examine the two most basic forms of international operations, exporting and foreign production vis-à-vis transferability of advantages.

In the exporting mode, all the 'firm-specific' advantages, assets and national/cultural attributes we find are at hand for the firm. In the foreign production mode, only those advantages, assets and factors whose use or exploitation is transferable are available. If vital advantages are transferable with ease, the firm is able to select the foreign production mode; if essential advantages are difficult or expensive to transfer, the firm will be restricted to the exporting mode.

Traditionally, North American manufacturing companies have shown a higher tendency to undertake production overseas than their German and Japanese counterparts, the latter two have tended to rely more on exporting to serve foreign markets, although this is now changing. With innovations in the US, the approach has generally been to reduce the manufacturing process to simple steps; this makes the transfer of production abroad much easier since much of the technology will be in the form of codified knowledge. With German and Japanese industry, continuous incremental progress – *kaizen* as the latter call it – relies on a very skilled work-force and on special ways of working together (lean production, just-in-time and so on); both the skills and the organizational principles involve much tacit knowledge, which is harder to transfer than codified knowledge and skilled production workers and craftsmen are not internationally mobile (in any great numbers). Moreover, these practices are underpinned by cultural values which are deeply embedded and difficult to transfer. There are two basic training strategies that are germane at this juncture. First, the MNC can bring its foreign employees back to base for training, or second, it can take its training out to the foreign country. Sometimes the government of the country where the MNC is based will have a vocational training programme as part of its overseas aid package to the specific country. For example, a decade or so ago, the French, Germans and Japanese each had set up advanced technical training centres in Singapore. Foreign firms, such as German and Japanese firms, however, do create a micro-culture in their foreign plants and select workers locally who will potentially be more likely to fit it.

For companies based in the most advanced countries in the world, an advantage relative to domestic competitors automatically means an advantage relative to firms of other countries; this is not the case however with firms from countries that are lower down the technological ladder. It is therefore instructive to look more closely at the international experience of firms from the four 'Little Dragons' or 'newly industrialized economies' of east Asia: Hong Kong, Taiwan, Singapore and South Korea (see Kumar and McLeod 1981; Lall 1983; Wells 1983).

According to a top Taiwan businessman: 'Most Taiwanese investors who have gone to Europe or the US have failed, while most of those who located in South East Asia have succeeded.' In Singapore the chairman of the Economic Development Board (EDB), Mr Philip Yeo, put it as follows: 'It is hard for Singapore to go into countries like the US and Europe. We will lose our shirts.' Why is there this differential success? And why cannot NIE firms operate successfully in the US, although able to export successfully to the US markets?

In East Asia, Hong Kong has been the prime investor in China (far exceeding Japan, the US or any Western nation) while Taiwan has been the leading investor in Malaysia, Indonesia and even Vietnam. Singapore and South Korea are also active, but the total numbers are smaller. The motives for the direct foreign investment (DFI) are not hard to pin down – to take advantage of lower costs of production, to secure raw material supplies, to supply the local market, to utilize (in the case of textiles) the target nations's export quotas, to exploit perceived profit opportunities and so on. We must therefore ask what transferable advantages do such East Asian firms have.

It should be seen that when we refer to Little Dragon economies, we point to the key Overseas Chinese 'diaspora' which dominates the economies of Hong Kong, Singapore and Taiwan but of couse not South Korea. The Overseas Chinese also have a network of influence throughout South-East Asia, in Burma, Indonesia, Malaysia, Thailand and Vietnam (see Brown 1995). The Chinese family enterprise model is also endemic in these parts of the world (see Redding 1994) with its distinctive organizational structure and 'high-trust' culture among the key members of the enterprise and those they interact with in their organizational environment. Some have juxtaposed the stereotypical Western (or Japanese) MNC with the stereotypical Overseas Chinese firm, to the latter's advantage (see Whitley 1992, for example).

Relative to indigenous firms (existing or potential) the Little Dragon firms often have more production and management experience than indigenous entrepreneurs, stronger financial resources, better connections with the export markets and the like, simply because they are at a more advanced stage of development and industrialization than the South East Asian nations and particularly mainland China. The question then arises: what advantages do these firms have, in these target-countries, relative to the even more advanced multinationals of Japan, US and Western Europe? To start with, the technology used may be simpler, or more easily adapted to local conditions and local inputs; the plants may also be smaller and hence require a lower investment outlay. Second, the costs of sending out expatriate staff is usually much lower for Little Dragon firms than for European or US companies, whose managerial employees' living-expenses are often very high. Last, there is the factor of relative geographical and cultural proximity which makes for better insights into local conditions and, except for South Korean firms as noted earlier, the 'Chinese connection' (with both Overseas Chinese in South East Asia and mainland Chinese in China) gives the Little Dragon firms a clear advantage in operating in the region, an advantage which is denied to the US, European and Japanese MNCs. It should be noted here that this is a major exception to the rule, proposed earlier, that good connections at home are a non-transferable advantage. The cultural affinity of East Asian (and often South-East Asian) firms and the neighbouring markets is a factor to some degree balanced by, for example, the 'feel' European managers may have for adjacent EU markets. Even so, the widely diffused Confucian value pattern in Asia – see Chapter 14 – gives the local East Asian entrepreneurs and managers specific advantages in these markets which are growing at rates faster than in most other parts of the world. Their actual and potential links with China – the Giant Dragon – opens up the vision of immense 'advantage-transfer' with a nation of over a billion and a quarter people.

The position is quite different when it comes to NIE manufacturing operations in the US; for example, the case of Acer, Taiwan's leading computer manufacturer. In trying to reduce its dependence on OEM sales and to build up its market position in the US, Acer acquired, for US$ 6 million in 1987, Counterpoint, a start-up company that built a powerful minicomputer using multiple micro-processors. In 1990, it paid US$ 94 million for Altos Computer Systems Inc, a microcomputer company that had an extensive network of distrubutors. Counterpoint went out of business two years after being puchased and heavy losses at Altos, after the takeover, led in 1991 to the parent company declaring its first loss in 15 years. In Singapore, the drive into Silicon Valley has been led by the government with state-owned Singapore Technology Holdings Corporation forming a joint venture with Sierra Semiconductor Corporation of San Jose to make wafers for integrated circuits and taking a major stake in Momenta Corporation in Mountain View to make pen-based computers. Losses of more than US$ 100 million were recorded in 1992 and Momenta had to quit manufacturing.

It is one thing to be able (and willing) to pay a higher price (than other investors) to acquire a high-tech firm in Silicon Valley, it is another to be able to operate it successfully. Firms from less advanced nations, buying their way into the world's most advanced electronics industry and most competitive electronics markets, may find that they have no advantages in competing in that environment. They were able, however, to export successfully from their home nations to the US, partly because they had access to US technology and to the US market through a number of mechanisms (including the use of US trained Chinese or Koreans), mainly because of lower labour costs (including the costs of employing engineers). As we saw earlier in this chapter, this is not an advantage that is transferable in the foreign production mode; the best that can be done is to make use of home-made parts and components (which embody the lower costs) for foreign assembly, so partially transferred the advantage.

The picture painted above appears, however, to be in the process of changing rapidly. According to data collated at SPRU (Patel and Pavitt 1995) Taiwan and South Korea have both seen substantial increases in their US patenting in the second half of the 1980s, similar to that seen by Japan in the late 1950s. This step puts them way above other developing nations and suggests that technology in South Korea and Taiwan is now attaining world best practice levels in an increasing number of fields. This is more and more the case in computer-technology for example.

IMPLICATIONS FOR MANAGERS

How does a firm then attempt to enhance the transferability of its advantages? To start with, in identifying the advantages to be transferred, it can take a much broader view than merely looking at its 'firm-specific' advantages (unique advantages relative to domestic competitors in the home context). It should also focus as much on non-quantifiable as quantitative data in its strategy planning. It should realize that assets that are not necessarily superior in the home context, general national/ industry characteristics, and cultural differences (at both corporate and national levels) may become important advantages in a foreign country. Advantages may have to be defined relative to alternatives rather than relative to competition – in a joint venture, what advantage does our firm have relative to the other side and relative to other potential partners that he might choose? In foreign-sourcing, what advantage does our firm have relative to the indigenous firm exporting directly?

Second, if a crucial advantage is found to be non-transferable, one should ponder defining the advantage at a different level, for example knowing how to launch and then manage a distribution network rather than owning an existing network, knowing how to create a reputation rather than an ongoing market position and so on. Within culture, one may follow Hofstede (1980; 1989; 1991) in making a basic distinction betwen the values and the practices of the culture – see Chapter 9 earlier. Values are profound and often unconscious, while practices are more superficial and easily recognizable. Practices are therefore more readily transferable abroad, whereas the transfer of values requires the transfer of the people in whom those values are embodied. It also follows from this argument that if the costs of transferring people are excessive, there may be insufficient transfer of values to make the practices work effectively. It is virtually impossible to transfer whole populations, or even the whole work-force from country A to country B. Even at the managerial level to transfer some managers (as HRM departments have often found to their cost) involves great difficulties. Finding expatriates with the 'right' values may be problematic. Even when such expatriate staff are sent out, some foreign nationals may be better adapted to live in the NIC environment than others. Repatriation is expensive and bringing managers and their families home prematurely may be highly dysfunctional (see Tung 1988; Schuler 1996).

Third, if the advantage is non-transferable, the firm should think about whether a different mode of operations (or a different combination of these) would allow transfer. Tacit knowledge may be clearly non-transferable in the licensing mode at arm's length, but may be more transferable to a wholly-owned subsidiary. Exporting the product in which the advantage is embodied may also be a substitute for exporting the capacity to make the goods concerned.

Fourth, transferability may hinge on the choice of target-countries; what has importance in one region or country may not have value in another. However, relative levels of economic development, as well as cultural and geographical specificity, are key influences on transferability.

Fifth, transferability may necessitate sustained investment in complementary assets through training, local personnel and local facilities. For example, JVs in China have invested heavily in these domains, such as in the case of Volkswagen in Shanghai.

And finally, transfer is neither automatic nor easy but may require creative adaptations and effort. Hybrid organizations may be needed so as to blend the best Western and Eastern values and practices to enhance the 'fit' required.

CONCLUDING REMARKS

International transferability of the firm's advantages is a subtle concept (see Hu 1995). At the present stage of its development, it is more a way of asking meaningful questions for future research than of providing answers. We have attempted in this contribution to the debate to raise fundamental questions linking the cross-cultural concepts with economic and strategic ones. These issues are not merely ones of theoretical interest. Transferability is of vital practical concern to businesses with international operations, for (to repeat it) without transferable competitive advantages there can be no successful international operations. We feel the debate cannot advance without building bridges between a number of normally distinct academic fields, such as cross-cultural management, international business, competitive strategy and technological innovation.

To sum up; we have systematically explored in this chapter, we believe, the cross-cultural matrix in which competitive advantage of firms may be placed. The general theoretical points we have raised may be applied to economies involved in 'advantage-transfer' as we have called it, whether they are transferring or having it transferred to them. Examples have particularly been drawn from cases where 'tacit knowledge' has been involved, as opposed to 'codified knowledge' and where transferability involving the former has been more difficult. Where there are obstacles to transfer, we have looked at ways these may be overcome or by-passed, if possible at all. The importance of culture remains a promising avenue for further research with, we believe, great benefits for both theory and practice.

ACKNOWLEDGEMENTS

This chapter incorporates material from an earlier article by Yao-Su Hu that originally appeared in *California Management Review* (Vol 37, No 4: Summer 1995) – copyright 1995 by The Regents of the University of California, reproduced with permission of The Regents.

REFERENCES

Adler, N.J. and Bartholomew, S. (1992) Academic and professional communities of discourse: generating knowledge on transnational HRM. *Journal of International Business Studies*, **23**, pp. 551–70.

Bain, J.S. (1956) *Barriers to New Competition*, Harvard University Press, Cambridge, MA..

Ballon, R.J. (1992) *Foreign Competition in Japan: Human Resource Strategies*, Routledge, London.

Brown, R. (1995) *Chinese Business Enterprise in Asia*, Routledge, London.

Dore, R. (1987) *Taking Japan Seriously*, Athlone, London.

Dunning, J. (1981) *International Production and the Multinational Enterprise*, Allen and Unwin, London.

Freeman, C. (1995) The national system of innovation in historical perspective. *Cambridge Journal of Economics*, **19** pp. 5–24.

Hickson, D.J. and Pugh, D.S. (1995) *Management Worldwide: The Impact of Societal Culture on Organization Around the Globe*, Penguin Books, Harmondsworth.

Hofstede, G. (1980) *Culture's Consequences: International Differences in Work-Related Values*, Sage, Beverly Hills, CA and London.

Hofstede, G. (1989) Organising for cultural diversity. *European Management Journal*, **7**, pp. 390–7.

Hofstede, G. (1991) *Cultures and Organizations*, McGraw Hill, London.

Hu, Y-S. (1992) Global or stateless corporations are national firms with international operations. *California Management Review*, **34**, pp. 107.

Hu, Y-S. (1995) The international transferability of the firm's advantages. *California Management Review*, **37**, pp. 78–88.

Hu, Y-S. (1996) Globalization and corporate nationality, in *International Encyclopaedia of Business and Management* (ed M. Warner) Routledge, London, 6 volumes.

Hymer, S.H. (1976) *The International Operations of National Firms, a study of direct foreign investment*, PhD thesis at MIT submitted in 1960 and later published posthumously, MIT Press, Cambridge, MA.

Kay, J. (1993) *Foundations of Corporate Success*, Oxford University Press, Oxford.

Kindleberger, C.P. (1969) *American Business Abroad*, Yale University Press, New Haven, Conn., pp. 1–36.

Kogut, B. (1991) Country capabilities and the permeability of borders. *Strategic Management Journal*, **12**, pp. 33–47.

Kumar, K. and McLeod, M.G. (eds) (1981) *Multinationals from Developing Countries*, Lexington Books, Lexington, MA.

Lall, S. (1980) *The Multinational Corporation*, Macmillan, London, pp. 3–28.

Lall, S., (ed) (1983) *The New Multinationals*, Wiley, Chichester.

Maurice, M., Sorge, A. and Warner, M. (1980) Societal differences in organizing manufacturing units: a comparison of France, West Germany and Great Britain. *Organization Studies*, **1**, pp. 59–86.

Patel, P. (1995) Localized production of technology for global markets. *Cambridge Journal of Economics*, **19**, pp. 141–53.

Patel, P. and Pavitt, K. (1991) Large firms in the production of the world's technology: an important case of non-globalization. *Journal of International Business Studies*, **22**, pp. 1–2.

Patel, P. and Pavitt, K. (1994) National innovation systems: why they are important, and how they might be measured and compared. *Economics of Innovation and New Technology*, **3**, pp. 77–95.

Porter, M. (1980) *Competitive Strategy*, The Free Press, New York.

Porter, M. (1990) *The Competitive Advantage of Nations*, The Free Press, New York.

Redding, S.G. (1994) Comparative management theory: jungle zoo or fossil bed? *Organization Studies*, **15**, pp. 323–60.

Schuler, R.S. (1996) HRM: Domestic to global, in *International Encyclopaedia of Business and Management*, (ed M. Warner) Routledge, London, 6 volumes.

Sorge, A. and Warner, M. (1987) *Comparative Factory Organization*, Gower, Aldershot.

Tayeb, M. (1994) Organizations and National Culture: Methodology reconsidered. *Organization Studies*, **15**, pp. 429–46.

Teece, D.J. (1987) Profiting from technological innovation in *The Competitive Challenge*, (ed D.J. Teece) Ballinger, Cambridge, MA.

Tung, R. (1988) *The New Expatriates*, Ballinger, Cambridge, MA.

Wells, L. (1983) *Third World Multinationals*, MIT Press.

Whitley, R.D. (1992) *Business System in Asia: from Markets to Societies*, Sage, Beverly Hills, CA and London.

Williamson, P. (1991) Successful strategies for export. *Long Range Planning*, **24**, pp. 57–63.

FURTHER READING

Abegglen, J.C. and Stalk, G.S. (1985) *Kaisha, The Japanese Corporation*, Basic Books, New York.

Patel, P. and Pavitt, K. (1995) Uneven (and divergent) technological accumulation among advanced countries: evidence and a framework of explanation. *Industrial and Corporate Change*, in press.

Index